Excel for Windows 95 Made Easy,
Fifth Edition

About the Author

Martin S. Matthews is the best-selling author of more than 30 computer books, including previous versions of *Excel Made Easy* and *Excel: The Complete Reference*. He has been working with software for over 25 years and is an expert in using spreadsheets, graphic design, and desktop publishing.

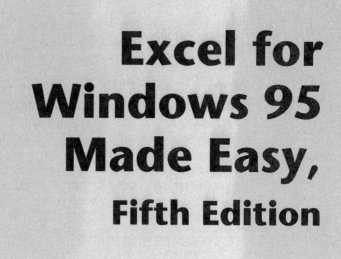

Excel for Windows 95 Made Easy,
Fifth Edition

Martin S. Matthews

Osborne **McGraw-Hill**

Berkeley New York St. Louis San Francisco
Auckland Bogotá Hamburg London Madrid
Mexico City Milan Montreal New Delhi
Panama City Paris São Paulo Singapore
Sydney Tokyo Toronto

Osborne **McGraw-Hill**
2600 Tenth Street
Berkeley, California 94710
U.S.A.

For information on translations or book distributors outside the U.S.A., or to arrange bulk purchase discounts for sales promotions, premiums, or fundraisers, please contact Osborne **McGraw-Hill** at the above address.

Excel for Windows 95 Made Easy, Fifth Edition

 234567890 DOC 998765

ISBN 0-07-882151-7

Publisher Lawrence Levitsky	**Proofreader** Pat Mannion
Acquisitions Editor Joanne Cuthbertson	**Computer Designer** Peter Hancik
Project Editor Claire Splan	**Designer** Roberta Steele
Editorial Assistant Heidi Poulin	**Illustrator** Lance Ravella
Copy Editor Dennis Weaver	**Quality Control Specialist** Joe Scuderi

Contents
at a Glance

1 ▬▬ **The Windows Environment** 1
2 ▬▬ **The Components of Excel** 43
3 ▬▬ **The Excel Environment** 69
4 ▬▬ **Entering and Editing Information** 97
5 ▬▬ **Creating a Spreadsheet** 125
6 ▬▬ **Enhancing a Workbook** 167
7 ▬▬ **Producing Charts** 211
8 ▬▬ **Working with a Database** 259
9 ▬▬ **Linking Workbooks and Using External Files** 309
10 ▬▬ **Dates, Functions, and Macros** 341
11 ▬▬ **Solver and Other Analysis Tools** 387
12 ▬▬ **Using Visual Basic with Excel** 407
13 ▬▬ **Automating a Workbook** 433
14 ▬▬ **Integrating Excel with Office 95** 471

Contents

Acknowledgments . . . . *xv*
Introduction . . . . *xvii*

1 ▬ The Windows Environment **1**
    Introducing Windows 2
    The Windows Screen 4
    Using the Mouse 6
        Mousing Around 7
    Using Windows 10
        Using Scroll Bars 13
        Starting Programs 16
    Using Menus 22
        Using Dialog Boxes 24
    Using the Keyboard 24
        Using the Control Menu 27
    Using the Control Panel and the Explorer 30
        Setting Defaults with the Control Panel 30
        Creating a Folder with the Explorer 34
    Getting Help 38
    Leaving Windows 41

2 ▬ **The Components of Excel** **43**
 Spreadsheets 44
  Spreadsheets and Files 44
  Rows, Columns, and Sheets 45
  Addresses, Cells, and References 46
  Formulas and Functions 49
  Commands 52
  Workbook Windows 59
  Multiple Files and File Linking 60
  Help 62
 Databases 63
  Rows and Records 64
  Columns and Fields 64
  Using Databases 64
 Charts 65

3 ▬ **The Excel Environment** **69**
 Excel's Screen and Menus 70
  The Workbook Window 70
  The Excel Window 72
 Excel's Use of the Keyboard 86
  Direction Keys 87
  Function Keys 91
 Quitting Excel 95

4 ▬ **Entering and Editing Information** **97**
 Typing on a Sheet 98
  Entering Text Versus Numbers 98
  Completing an Entry and Moving to the Next
  Cell 107
  Using AutoComplete 107
 Making Changes 108
  Editing During Entry 109
  Using Undo 109
  Editing After Entry 110
  Using AutoCorrect 111
  Editing with the Mouse 113
 Using Menus 114
 Using Zoom 117
 Using Files 118

Naming Files 119
Saving Files 120
Using Folders 122
Retrieving Files 122
Quitting Excel 123

5   **Creating a Spreadsheet** **125**
Planning a Spreadsheet 126
Placing Labels, Headings, and Titles 128
Setting Up Similar Sheets 128
Entering a Column of Labels 129
Centering a Title 132
Entering a Row of Headings 133
Placing a Border 133
Saving the Workbook 136
Entering Numbers and Formulas 136
Entering a Column of Numbers 137
Building Formulas 138
Copying Formulas 142
Using Assumptions 145
Absolute Addressing 145
Editing Formulas 147
Copying a Column of Formulas 150
Copying 151
Completing the Spreadsheet 152
Producing a Total 152
Calculating a Percentage 154
Copying a Row of Formulas 155
Clearing a Range of Cells 155
Inserting a Row 157
Deleting a Row 158
Inserting and Deleting 159
Making Corrections 160
Customizing Individual Sheets 160
Sheet Summarizing Formulas 162
Saving and Quitting Excel 164

6   **Enhancing a Workbook** **167**
Loading a Workbook 168
Formatting 169

Overall Number Format 170
Formatting Alternatives 172
Setting Overall Column Width 179
Detail Formatting 180
Creating a Percentage Format 181
Adding Currency Formatting 183
Centering and Embolding Headings 184
The Formatting Toolbar 185
AutoFormat 186
Changing the Layout 190
Moving Formulas 190
Deleting a Column 190
Adjusting Individual Column Width 191
Adding Notes to Cells 192
Erasing a Group of Cells 194
Using Undo 195
Printing the Workbook 195
Setting the Parameters 195
Doing the Printing 202
Trial and Error 205
Saving the Workbook 207
Making a Template 207
Changing Titles 207
Copying Values—Paste Special 208
Other Modifications 210
Saving and Quitting 210

7 ▪▪ Producing Charts **211**
How a Chart Is Built 212
Chart Characteristics 213
Chart Tools and Menus 217
The Insert Menu 217
The Chart Toolbar 218
Deciding What to Chart 222
Selecting the Type of Chart 222
Area Charts 223
Bar Charts 224
Column Charts 226
Line Charts 227
Pie Charts 229
Scatter Charts 232

3-D Surface Charts 233
Creating a Line Chart 234
Selecting the Ranges to Plot 235
Creating a New Chart Sheet with the Insert
Menu 235
Saving, Printing, and Closing 239
Using ChartWizard to Create Embedded
Charts 239
Using ChartWizard to Change the Chart 242
Modifying Charts Directly and With Menus 242
Changing Charts with Direct Edits 250
Saving and Printing the Chart 256
Closing a Chart 256
Leaving Excel 257

8 ■ **Working with a Database** **259**
Building a Database 260
Entering Field Names 261
Numbering with a Series 261
Numbering with AutoFill 262
Entering Records 263
Sorting a Database 265
Selecting the Sort Range 265
Identifying a Sort Key 266
Doing the Sort 267
Changing and Re-sorting 268
Selecting Information from a Database 268
Building a Second Database 269
Subtotaling a List 274
Filtering a Database 278
Analyzing Information from a Database 288
Using Database Statistical Functions 288
Creating a Data Table 295
Working with Two-Input Data Tables 296
Creating Pivot Tables 298
Using a Pivot Table 302
Using Lookup Functions 305

9 ■ **Linking Workbooks and Using External Files** **309**
Linking Workbooks 310

Creating Multiple Workbooks 310
Copying Across Workbooks 312
Creating Linking Formulas 317
Saving Multiple Workbooks 321
Combining Files 322
Adding External Ranges 322
Linking External Ranges 326
Saving a Workbook as a Text File 329
Importing ASCII Text Files 333
Opening Tab and Comma Delimited Text
Files 334
Opening Nondelimited Text Files 337

10 ■ **Dates, Functions, and Macros** **341**
Using Dates and Times 342
Dates and Excel 342
Times and Excel 343
Formatting Dates and Times 344
Date and Time Functions 345
Entering and Generating Dates and Times 348
Date and Time Arithmetic 355
Functions 356
Using Functions 356
Additional Functions 360
Macros 364
Excel 4 Macro Basics 365
Creating Additional Macros 372
Entering Macros 379
Function Macros 382

11 ■ **Solver and Other Analysis Tools** **387**
Preparing for Analysis 388
Goal Seek 390
Scenario Manager 392
Creating Scenarios 392
Viewing Existing Scenarios 394
Modifying a Scenario 395
Creating a Summary of Your Scenarios 395
Creating Other Reports 396
Solver 398

Setting Up Solver 399

Constraining Variables 402

Saving a Model 404

12 ▦ Using Visual Basic with Excel 407

Date/Time Stamp in Visual Basic 408

Excel Help and Examples 410

Objects in Visual Basic for Excel 411

The Properties of Objects 412

The Methods of Objects 412

Visual Basic Module Sheets 413

Visual Basic Procedures 415

Calling Procedures 416

Using Variables 417

Declaring Variables 417

Declaring Data Types 418

Using Constants 419

Scope of Variables and Constants 420

Entering and Editing Visual Basic Code 420

Using Comments in Your Code 421

Using Control Structures (Decision Making) 421

If. . .Then. . .Else 421

Select Case 422

Do. . .Loop 423

For. . .Next 424

For Each. . .Next 424

Exit 425

Constructing Expressions 425

Operators 426

Debugging Your Code 427

Setting Breakpoints 427

Using the Debug Window 429

Stepping Through Your Code 431

Setting Options for Visual Basic 431

13 ▦ Automating a Workbook 433

Planning an Application 434

What the Application Will Do 435

How the Application Will Be Laid Out 435

Building the Order Sheet 436

Building Screens   436
Preparing the Orders Database   440
Preparing the Products List   442
Building the Macros   443
Preparing and Controlling the Order Sheet   444
Building the Data Entry Tools   450
Using Data Form for Editing   460
Printing, Saving, and Quitting   462
Building and Using a Menu   465
Automatically Setting Up the Workbook   466
Testing and Correcting the Macros   468
Working Through the Application   468
Future Enhancements   470

14 Integrating Excel with Office 95 . . . .   **471**
Defining OLE and the Office 95 Suite   473
Linking vs. Embedding   473
Compound Documents   475
Office 95 Applications   475
Using OLE   476
Using the Paste Special Dialog Box   477
Dragging and Dropping to Share Data   488

Index **493**

Acknowledgments

A number of people have worked very hard on this book. Among these are:

John Cronan, author and technical writer, who did a large part of the revision for Excel 7 and did it in a very compressed time frame.

Bob Kermish, free-lance technical editor, who materially improved the technical accuracy of the book and did so with much humor.

Martin Matthews
July 1995

Introduction

Microsoft Excel, has become one of the most capable and easy-to-use of all software products. In Version 7 for Windows 95, Excel has added a very powerful, multithreaded, 32-bit engine to improve its speed and performance. With this engine driving its three-dimensional spreadsheets, many helpful Wizards, tools, and toolbars, as well as comprehensive data handling, charting, and macro-building capabilities, Excel 7 provides substantially enhanced ease of use together with greatly improved functionality. *Excel for Windows 95 Made Easy* brings you the full capability of Excel 7 in an easy-to-use, hands-on approach that shows you how to make the most of this power.

About This Book

Excel for Windows 95 Made Easy supplements Microsoft's own documentation by continuing where that documentation leaves off. Whereas the Microsoft documentation presents you with short and simple explanations, *Excel for Windows 95 Made Easy* provides more substantial examples designed not only to get you started, but also to guide you in building your skills so that you can perform more advanced tasks—all with clear, step-by-step instructions.

How This Book Is Organized

Excel for Windows 95 Made Easy was written the way most people learn Excel. The book starts by reviewing the basic concepts. It then uses a learn-by-doing method to demonstrate the major features of the product. Next, the book provides examples and clear explanations of many advanced features.

Introducing Windows and Excel

The book begins by introducing Windows and Excel and providing the basic concepts needed to use them. Chapter 1 explains the features and functions of Windows and the mouse that are needed to use Excel. Included are all parts of the screen, windowing, menus, the mouse buttons and moves, and using the keyboard.

Chapter 2 describes each of the three components of Excel—spreadsheets, databases, and charts, with particular attention to spreadsheets. It quickly introduces rows, columns, sheets, and workbooks as well as cells, references, ranges, formulas, functions, commands, and macros. Also introduced are shortcut menus, tools, toolbars, and Wizards.

Chapter 3 looks at how Excel uses the Windows graphical environment and the mouse to build and maintain spreadsheets. Each of the menus is described, as are the keystrokes and mouse moves necessary to utilize them. This chapter introduces the Standard and Formatting toolbars and all of their tools, and tells you how to display the other 11 toolbars.

Chapter 4 focuses on how to create and modify a workbook, including using the menus, mouse, and keyboard to enter, edit, and align text and numbers. Excel's shortcut menus and Zoom feature are demonstrated in this chapter as are saving a workbook and leaving Excel.

This first part of the book provides the foundation for the rest of the book. This section is slower paced due to the importance of building a firm foundation. If you are a new user of Excel, the first four chapters are vital to your success. If you have some experience with Excel, you need them to a lesser extent. At the very least, you should skim these chapters to assure that you have an understanding of the terms and concepts.

The Fundamentals of Excel

Next, the book covers the fundamentals of Excel—creating and manipulating spreadsheets, producing charts, and using a database.

Chapters 5 and 6 are companions. Chapter 5 shows you how to create a three-dimensional spreadsheet. Included are planning, placing text and headings, entering numbers and formulas, copying formulas, inserting and deleting rows—all on multiple sheets—as well as summing across several sheets. The spelling checker, centering text across columns, and using drag and drop to copy formulas are all demonstrated. In Chapter 6 you format, change, and print the workbook. Included are loading the workbook, formatting numbers and headings, moving, deleting, erasing, and setting the parameters for and printing the workbook. You also learn about the AutoFormat and note capabilities of Excel.

Chapter 7 looks at producing charts, including three-dimensional charts. It describes the chart types and includes selecting the type of chart, determining the workbook ranges to plot, adding legends and titles, viewing, and printing. Both the ChartWizard and manual chart creation methods are used.

In Chapter 8 you learn how to build and use databases. The chapter includes sorting a database and selecting and analyzing information from a database. In analyzing information, you are shown how, almost automatically, you can add subtotals and totals to a database as well as how the PivotTable Wizard is used to build a pivot table that summarizes the database and then allows you to interactively manipulate that summary. The chapter also demonstrates how statistical functions and data tables are used.

These chapters should be read by all levels of users. For new users it provides the experience with which you can create your own spreadsheets, charts, and databases. For intermediate and advanced users, Chapters 5 through 8 provide a refresher course that also offers considerable insight into Excel.

Advanced Uses of Excel

The last six chapters discuss the advanced features of Excel. The pace of presentation quickens here; the focus is almost entirely on advanced topics, with little or no time spent on building the spreadsheets used to demonstrate the topics. You are still encouraged, though, to continue to follow along on your computer.

Chapter 9 describes linking spreadsheets and using external files. Included are setting up links and transferring information among spreadsheets as well as combining spreadsheets, exporting and importing text files, dividing or parsing a text file, and saving related documents in a workbook.

Chapter 10 looks at dates and times, functions, and macros. Under dates and times, you look at entering, formatting, and handling them as well as the functions that relate to them. The section on functions ties together the work already done on functions in previous chapters. It provides a general discussion on using them as well as discussion and examples of the types of functions not previously examined. The macro section looks at macro functions in general, discusses how they are built, used, and debugged using the Excel 4 macro language, and provides a number of examples.

Chapter 11 demonstrates how to use the very powerful analysis tools included in Excel: Goal Seek, the Scenario Manager, and Solver. The tools are used both independently and in various combinations. They provide the means of finding optimal solutions as well as keeping track of solutions as you generate them.

Chapter 12 introduces Visual Basic. It discusses all of the elements of the language and how they are combined to make a program. Included are explanations and examples of procedures, functions, objects, methods, properties, variables, and constants.

Chapter 13 brings together what was presented in Chapter 12 and guides you through all of the steps needed to create an automated spreadsheet using Visual Basic. Included are automatic loading, custom menus, and updating of a database from a custom data entry dialog box, all operated by a set of macro commands. Chapter 13 shows you the full power of Excel.

Chapter 14 looks at how to integrate Excel with the rest of the Office 95 suite. In particular, the chapter describes object linking and embedding (OLE), looking at the differences between linking and embedding and giving examples of how to do both. Then using OLE, the chapter discusses building compound documents in the Office 95 suite.

Rather than reading these last six chapters immediately, new users may want to wait until they have completed several spreadsheets of their own and know they want more out of the capability of the product. Intermediate users probably will want to continue on immediately; it is the next logical step in their Excel education. If you are an advanced user—this is what you've been waiting for!

All readers are encouraged to go through these chapters at some point. The "booster rockets" of Excel are discussed here. Such things as linking spreadsheets, functions, and macros are not as hard to use as you might think, and they significantly increase the power of Excel.

Conventions Used in This Book

Excel for Windows 95 Made Easy uses several conventions designed to make the book easier for you to use. These are as follows:

✦ **Bold type is used for text you are instructed to input from the keyboard.**

✦ Keys on the keyboard are presented in small capitals; for example, ENTER and RIGHT ARROW.

✦ When you are expected to enter a command, you are told to press the key(s). If you enter text or numbers, you are told to type them.

The Windows Environment

1

Excel 7.0 is a Windows 95 application. This means that this version of Excel requires Microsoft Windows 95 for it to run. Windows provides the interface between you and Excel—the way Excel tells you on the screen what it is doing, and the way you tell Excel what to do. This chapter introduces you to some of the essentials of Windows 95. You may never use all of the capabilities and tools available in Windows 95, but when you become acquainted with some of them you will appreciate the potential power of using Excel in the Windows environment.

This chapter is more of a tutorial than the rest of the book. It proceeds more slowly in order to establish a common ground for using this book and Excel. If you are already familiar with Windows 95 and using a mouse, simply scan the chapter to verify that you know the vocabulary used here and the basic operating procedures used in Windows 95.

Introducing Windows

Excel is designed to run "under" Microsoft Windows 95, a true operating system (unlike Windows 3.*x*, which was an extension of the MS-DOS operating system). Windows 95 offers a standard environment for all of the programs that run under it. This environment consists chiefly of a standard screen display, or *visual interface*, that you use in communicating with Windows applications. Once you learn to use Windows 95, you will find that the ways of working with the various Windows applications, including Excel, are very similar.

Windows also provides several ways to transfer information among applications, such as from Excel to Word for Windows or to PageMaker. With one of the ways, the *Clipboard*, you can easily move a portion of an Excel spreadsheet or an Excel chart to a word processing document. A more sophisticated way of transferring information, object linking and embedding or OLE (pronounced O-LAY), allows you to automatically update documents that are comprised of data from other applications. Chapter 14, "Integrating Excel with Office 95," explores using OLE with other Microsoft programs.

Windows allows you to load multiple applications into memory simultaneously and to switch among them with a minimum of effort. You can work with a word processor, a graphics application, and Excel all at the same time. The speed with which you can switch among applications and the number of applications you can have loaded at one time will depend on the amount of memory you have and the speed of your processor.

Finally, Windows provides a set of programs that are handy accessories. How you choose to install Windows 95 and the components that are installed in your computer will determine whether you will have the full complement of these accessories. Table 1-1 lists these accessories and their functions.

Accessory	Function
Backup	A program that backs up folders and files to floppy disks and tape
Calculator	A calculator program for basic and scientific use
CD Player	A set of VCR-like controls for playing audio CDs
Character Map	Tables of characters that comprise the various fonts installed in your computer
Clipboard Viewer	A Windows feature that provides sharing of Clipboard objects by networked computers
Dial-Up Networking	A program that allows remote computers using phone lines to connect to networked computers
Direct Cable Connection	A program that allows two computers to connect with a serial or parallel cable and transfer data
Disk Defragmenter	A program that optimizes file storage on hard disks
DriveSpace	A disk compression program that effectively doubles your disk capacity
Fax Cover Page Editor	A feature of Microsoft Fax to create custom fax cover pages
Fax Viewer	A feature of Microsoft Fax that lets you view faxes in various configurations
Freecell	A solitaire-like card game
Hearts	The traditional card game for networked players
HyperTerminal	A telecommunication program that allows two modem-equipped computers to transfer information
Media Player	A set of VCR-like controls for playing video clips and digital audio
Minesweeper	A game of hide and seek
NetWatcher	A utility that allows you to see who is connected to your computer and control access to your data
NotePad	A text editor for ASCII and other unformatted files
Object Packager	A program that lets you embed or link objects (in the form of an icon) into another document

Windows
Accessories
Table 1-1.

Accessory	Function
Paint	A drawing program
Phone Dialer	A program that lets you use your computer to dial phone numbers from different dialing locations
ScanDisk	A disk repair utility that checks for file and disk problems
Sound Recorder	A program that lets you play, edit, and record sound files when applicable hardware is installed
System Monitor	A graphic representation of your computer's system resource usage
Volume Control	An on-screen sound volume control
WordPad	A word processing program

Windows
Accessories
(continued)
Table 1-1.

Because it operates under Windows, Excel has all these accessories available for the user on demand.

The quickest way to learn about Windows is to start using it. If you have not already done so, turn on your computer and start Windows 95.

The Windows Screen

The basic Windows 95 screen looks similar to the one shown in Figure 1-1. Your screen may look different depending on the options you choose to install and whether you have already customized the appearance of the screen. Figure 1-1 shows the primary components of the Windows 95 screen: the *desktop,* the *Taskbar*, and the *mouse pointer.*

The desktop is the underlying layer of all that appears in Windows 95. Although the desktop has only limited properties associated with itself, it provides the "real estate" on which all other Windows objects appear. Objects on the desktop can be moved, opened, put on standby, or deleted. The common objects on the desktop are: *icons*, which are small graphic representations of Windows 95 features, as well as programs, folders, and files; *windows*, which contain active programs or *folders* that contain files and possibly other folders; and *dialog boxes*, which allow Windows 95 to communicate with you, the user, to exchange information related to a particular task. Figure 1-2 shows a desktop with several objects.

The *Taskbar*, shown at the bottom of Figures 1-1 and 1-2 and following this paragraph, is the primary control and access object on the Windows 95

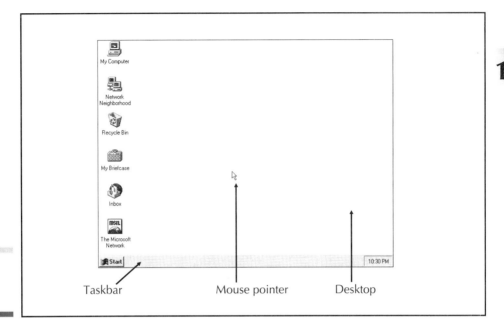

1

Windows 95
screen
Figure 1-1.

Taskbar   Mouse pointer   Desktop

screen. As its name implies, the Taskbar provides a repository for all active
tasks, including programs and open folders. The more tasks that you have
running, the smaller the task names appear on the Taskbar. You can move
the Taskbar from its default location at the bottom of the screen to the top
of the screen or either side by *dragging*, a technique described later in this
chapter. Although the Taskbar performs several functions, you will soon see
it as just another object on your desktop.

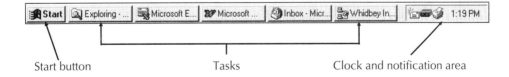

Start button   Tasks   Clock and notification area

The extremes of the Taskbar are devoted to special features you frequently
use. The clock on the right end provides the current time and includes a
notification area where icons are used to tell you such things as the
initiation of printing, the receipt of mail, and the use of a modem. Through
the Start button on the left end of the Taskbar you can access virtually
everything on your computer as well as get help, search for files and folders,

Icons

Window

Dialog
Box

Taskbar

Desktop with
several
Windows 95
objects
Figure 1-2.

change the settings for most functions, and shut down Windows 95. The Start button is your primary control for and gateway into Windows 95.

The final desktop object, and by far the most used, is the mouse pointer. The mouse pointer indicates not only the position where the mouse currently is on the screen; by its shape it also indicates what the current task is. In Figure 1-2, the mouse pointer shape is the default selection arrow used to identify objects.

Using the Mouse

Although Windows allows you to use either the mouse or the keyboard to enter commands, using a mouse will greatly increase the power of Windows for you. Most instructions in this book assume that you'll use a mouse. However, the keyboard does occasionally offer shortcuts, so these shortcuts and some general rules for using the keyboard are also covered later in this chapter.

The mouse is used to move the pointer on the screen. You can *select* an object by moving the mouse until the pointer is on top of it (pointing *on* it) and then pressing the mouse button. Using the mouse in this way allows you to choose, for example, an option on a menu. A mouse can have one, two, or three buttons. Until recently, only the left mouse button had common usage. The left mouse button still is the primary tool for selecting and pointing on objects and is referred to as *the mouse button* in this book.

Windows 95 and Excel also make good use of the right mouse button to display *popup menus,* which are lists of options and properties about the object clicked on. By default, the left button is used for selection, but you can switch the buttons, which you may want to do if you are left-handed. (You'll see how later in this chapter.)

Mousing Around

If you move the mouse across a flat surface such as a table or desk, the mouse pointer (the arrow on the screen) also moves. Practice moving the mouse as follows:

1. Place your hand on the mouse. The button(s) should be under your fingers with the cord leading away from you.
2. Move the mouse now (without pressing the mouse button) and watch the pointer move on the screen.

    If you run out of room while moving the mouse, simply pick it up and place it where there is more room. Try experimenting with this now.
3. Move the mouse to the edge of your work surface, then pick it up and place it in the middle of your work surface, and then move it again.

See how the pointer continues from where the mouse was picked up. When you point on the upper border of the Taskbar, the arrow changes to a double-headed arrow. This tells you that the pointer is on the border. If you press the mouse button here, you can change the size of the Taskbar, as you will see shortly.

This book uses the following standard Windows terminology to describe your actions with the mouse:

Term	Action
Point on	Move the mouse until the tip of the pointer is on top of the item you want
Click	Quickly press and release the mouse button once
Click on	Point on an item and click
Double-click	Press and release the mouse button twice in rapid succession
Drag	Press and hold the mouse button while you move the mouse (to move an object in the work area or to highlight contiguous text that you want to delete, move, or copy)
Right-click	Quickly press and release the *right* mouse button once

Term	Action
Choose	Click on a menu option
Select	Point on an item and click the mouse button (same as "click on")

After the upcoming demonstrations of these terms, this book will assume that you know them. For example, the instruction "Select the File menu and choose the Save option" indicates that you should point on the word "File" in the Menu bar and press and release the mouse button to open the File menu. Then point on the Save option in the File menu and click to choose that option. Practice using the mouse to perform some of the following actions.

1. *Point on* the My Computer icon in the upper left of the screen by moving the mouse (and the corresponding pointer) until the pointer is resting on it.

2. *Select* My Computer by *clicking*—quickly pressing and releasing the mouse button while pointing on the icon. The icon and the title beneath it become *highlighted*: a color mask is placed over them, indicating that they are selected.

3. *Drag* the My Computer icon to the lower-right corner of the desktop. First point on the icon, and then press and hold the mouse button while you move the mouse until the pointer and the icon move to the lower-right corner of the window, as shown in Figure 1-3. As soon as you release the mouse button, the My Computer icon will jump back to the left side (you'll see why in a moment).

4. *Double-click* on the My Computer icon. The My Computer window opens, as shown in Figure 1-4. This window displays the drives (floppy, hard, and CD-ROM) installed in your computer, drives that are networked to your computer, and folders that access your printers and general settings. *Shared* drives, folders, and devices such as printers and modems are set by you to be available to others networked to your computer. They are indicated by a hand holding the particular icon, as the C: icon is in Figure 1-4.

5. *Click* on the My Computer window Close button located in the upper-right corner of the window. The My Computer window closes.

6. *Right-click* anywhere in an open area of the desktop. The desktop popup menu opens as shown here.

| Arrange Icons ▶ |
| Line up Icons |
| Paste |
| Paste Shortcut |
| Undo Copy |
| New ▶ |
| Properties |

My Computer
icon moved to
the lower-right
corner of the
desktop
Figure 1-3.

7. *Point* on the first option in the menu, Arrange Icons. The option will be
   selected and will open the submenu shown next. The right pointing

My Computer
window
Figure 1-4.

triangle next to the option indicates there is a submenu. Note that Auto Arrange has a check mark next to it.

8. *Choose* Auto Arrange by clicking on it. This will remove the check mark.

Auto Arrange automatically moves icons in position, starting in the upper-left corner of the desktop and then working down and to the right. Additionally, the icons are locked in place. The Auto Arrange option is *on* by default (with the check mark next to it), locking in place the icons along the left edge of the screen. When an option is turned on like that, selecting the option removes the check mark next to it, turning it *off*.

It sometimes takes a couple of tries to get the rhythm of double-clicking. A frequent problem is double-clicking too slowly. You will see later in this chapter how to adjust the speed of double-clicking.

Practice moving icons around the desktop. Don't be concerned about not getting them in any order. When you are through, repeat Steps 7 and 8 to turn Auto Arrange back on and align the icons on the left side of the desktop.

Using Windows

A window is an area of the screen that is assigned a specific purpose. Windows containing running programs or applications such as Excel are called *program windows*; windows containing documents used with programs such as an Excel spreadsheet are *document windows*; and windows containing folders with other folders and/or files in them are called *folder windows*. An application window may contain one or more document windows and a document window cannot exist outside of an application window. A folder window simply exists on its own. Both program and folder windows have a *Menu bar*, while a document window does not. All windows have a *Title bar* with the window title in the middle; a *Control menu icon* on the left; and the *Minimize, Maximize/Restore*, and *Close* buttons on the right. In folder windows and some applications such as Excel, you can optionally display a *Toolbar* and a *Status bar*. Table 1-2 explains the use of these and other standard window features. A typical folder window and the location of its

Window Feature	Function
Close button	Closes the window
Control menu icon	Opens the Control menu
File icon	Represents a file
Folder icon	Represents another folder
Horizontal scroll bar	Slides the window contents horizontally
Maximize button	Increases the window size to fill the desktop (application and folder window) or workspace (document window)
Menu bar	Row of menus available in the window (application and folder windows only)
Minimize button	Reduces the window to a task on the Taskbar
Restore button	Same physical button as Maximize; returns a window to its reduced size
Sizing handle	Changes the size of a window in two dimensions
Status bar	Provides information on current tasks and mouse position
Title bar	Displays the application name, folder name and path, and document name, as applicable
Toolbar	Contains buttons that provide shortcuts to commonly used features
Vertical scroll bar	Slides the window contents vertically
Window border	Provides a boundary for a window and allows sizing

A Window's Standard Features
Table 1-2.

standard features are shown in Figure 1-5. Other features that might be in a window are shown in Figure 1-6.

Windows can be quite small, can fill the screen, or can be any size in between. By clicking on the Maximize/Restore button, you can make a window fill the screen. When you maximize a window, the Maximize/Restore button changes appearance. If you then click on the Maximize/Restore button, the window is returned to the size it was just before you clicked the Maximize/Restore button. If you click on the Minimize button, the window shrinks to a task within the Taskbar. By

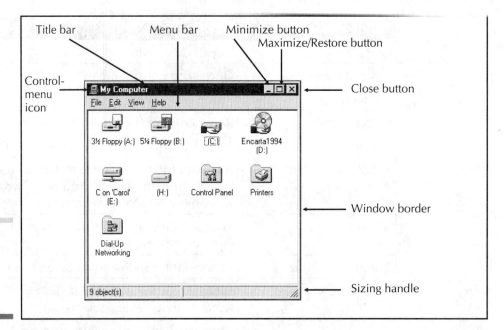

Folder
window and
its standard
features
Figure 1-5.

clicking on that task, you can return it to an open window that is the size it was when you minimized it.

You can make an open window that is not maximized any size by dragging on any border or on any corner, including the sizing handle located in the

Window
and optional
features
Figure 1-6.

bottom-right corner of the window. When you place the mouse pointer on top of a border or corner, the mouse pointer becomes a double-headed arrow. By holding down the mouse button while the pointer is a double-headed arrow and dragging a border or corner, you can change the window size in one dimension (border) or two dimensions (corner). For example, you can enlarge a window upward and to the right by dragging the top-right corner.

Finally, both a program and folder window can be dragged anywhere on the screen. A document window can be dragged only within its program's window. To drag an open window, point on the Title bar of the window (anywhere except on the Control menu icon or the Minimize, Maximize/Restore, or Close button) and drag it where you want.

Practice using some of the window-sizing features by following these instructions:

1. If the My Computer window is not already open on your desktop, double-click on the My Computer icon.

2. Click on the Maximize/Restore button in the upper-right corner of the window. The My Computer window expands to fill the desktop, except for the Taskbar (it can also cover the Taskbar as you will see later in the chapter).

3. Click on the Maximize/Restore button a second time. The window returns to its former size.

4. Point on the sizing handle in the lower right corner of the window. A double-headed arrow appears when the mouse pointer moves over the handle.

5. Drag the lower-right corner toward the bottom right as far as you can.

6. Drag the lower-right corner toward the upper left until the window is about one-quarter of the size it was before you enlarged it, as shown in Figure 1-7.

7. By pointing on the Title bar, drag the window around the screen.

8. Click on the Minimize button. The window closes to a task on the Taskbar.

9. Click on the My Computer task. Notice how the My Computer window opens in the same location it was in when it closed.

Using Scroll Bars

A window on the screen is just that—an opening through which you can see something displayed. If what is displayed is very small, a small window can adequately display it all. If what is displayed is very large, the largest window

Shrunken My
Computer
window
Figure 1-7.

you can create (one that covers the entire screen) may not be large enough
to display it all. In that case, you can horizontally or vertically move, or
scroll, through the contents of the window.

Imagine that you are looking through a microscope at a specimen on a glass
slide. You must move the slide left and right (horizontally) and up and down
(vertically) to see all of the specimen. The *scroll bars* perform the same
function for a window. The scroll bars move the *area being displayed* (not the
window itself) up or down or left or right.

Each of the two scroll bars has three mechanisms for moving the area being
displayed. First, there are four *scroll arrows,* one at each end of each scroll
bar. By clicking on one of the scroll arrows, you can move the display area in
the direction of the arrow by a small increment. Second, there are the two
scroll boxes in the scroll bars. By dragging a scroll box, you can move the
display area by a corresponding proportional amount. Third, there are the
scroll bars themselves. By clicking on the scroll bars (in areas other than the
scroll arrows and scroll boxes), you can move the display area by the height
or width of one window in the direction corresponding to where you clicked.

Open a new window and use the following instructions for practicing with
the scroll bars.

1. Click on the Start button at the left end of the Taskbar to open the *Start
   menu*, point on Settings (fifth option from the bottom), and then click

on the Control Panel option in the submenu that opens. The Control Panel folder window opens, containing several icons. The function of each Control Panel icon is discussed later in this chapter.

2. Drag the sizing handle toward the upper left corner to reduce the size of the window until both vertical and horizontal scroll bars are visible, similar to Figure 1-8. If you can't seem to get both scroll bars to appear, try clicking on the View menu Arrange Icons option and turn off the Auto Arrange option in the submenu.

3. Click on the down scroll arrow at the bottom of the vertical scroll bar on the right of the window. Notice that the display area moved up to display the icons below what was previously shown. Notice also that the scroll box has moved down in the scroll bar.

The position of the scroll box in the scroll bar represents the approximate position of the portion of the file displayed within the total file. When the vertical scroll box is toward the top of its scroll bar, you are looking at the top of the window. Similarly, when the horizontal scroll box is toward the left end of its scroll bar, you are looking at the left edge of the window. When both scroll boxes are in the middle of their scroll bars, you are looking at the middle of the window.

The scroll boxes change length according to the quantity of screen that is hidden. The greater the amount of screen hidden, the shorter the scroll box. Conversely, the lesser the amount of screen hidden, the longer the scroll bar.

4. Click on the right scroll arrow several times until the scroll box is at the far right of the horizontal scroll bar.

Control Panel window reduced so both vertical and horizontal scroll bars are visible

Figure 1-8.

5. Click on the horizontal scroll bar, on the left of the scroll box, until the scroll box is at the far left of the scroll bar. Notice how it takes fewer clicks to move over the length of the scroll bar.

6. Drag the vertical scroll box a small amount toward the middle of the scroll bar. Note how this allows you to move the display area in very precise increments.

7. Click on the Close button.

The three scrolling mechanisms give you three levels of control. Clicking on the scroll bar moves the display area the farthest; dragging the scroll box can move the display area in the smallest and most precise increments; and clicking on the scroll arrows moves the display area a small to intermediate amount.

Now that you used the Start button to open the Control Panel folder, your next step is to use the Start menu to open a program.

Starting Programs

Windows 95 has several different ways to start programs. This includes using My Computer, placing icons on the desktop (called shortcuts), and using the Start menu. In this and other chapters you'll see these various techniques described. This section describes the Start menu, which is the primary and most general-purpose way to start programs.

The Start menu, shown next, comes with seven options. The purpose of each is described in Table 1-3.

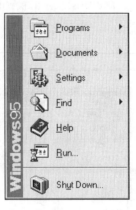

The Start menu Programs option opens a submenu that contains a listing of Windows 95-supplied programs as well as those you have installed in your computer. Figure 1-9 shows a typical Programs submenu. Depending on how

Start Menu Option	Function
Programs	Serves as the gateway to Windows 95 accessories and your own programs
Documents	Provides quick access to the last 15 documents you directly started
Settings	Accesses the Control Panel, Printer, and Taskbar settings
Find	Searches for files and folders on your computer or computers on a network, and information on the Microsoft Network online service
Help	Opens the online Help facility
Run	Allows you to start executable files such as .EXE, .COM, and .BAT files by typing the path or browsing for the filename
Shut Down	Provides options to restart or turn off your computer

Start Menu
Options
Table 1-3.

many applications you have installed, the submenu can grow to fill multiple columns.

There are two types of items listed in the Programs submenu: program

Programs
option
submenu
showing
installed
programs
Figure 1-9.

folders and programs themselves. The Programs submenu (and really part of the Start menu itself) is just another way of displaying the contents of a folder by displaying it in a menu. If you were to look in the Windows directory or folder, you'd see a Start Menu folder, which contains a Programs folder, which contains an Accessories folder, and so on. In the Program submenu, the program folders have a folder icon to the left of their name and a submenu triangle pointing to the right. When you highlight a program folder, a second submenu opens that shows the programs within that folder, as shown in Figure 1-10. The program folders are generally created when you install a new application.

Each individual program in either submenu has an icon associated with it to the left of its name, but no submenu triangle. The program name, when clicked on, provides a *shortcut* to the executable file of that particular program and subsequently opens it.

Windows 95 provides several programs to solve a variety of needs from word processing to games. A majority of the accessories listed in Table 1-1 are grouped together in a folder called Accessories, located at top of the Programs submenu. Each of these accessories is a program that runs under Windows just like Excel. To start a program you simply open the Start menu, point on the Programs option, and then point on the program folders until you reach the program you want to open. Do that now to work with several program windows.

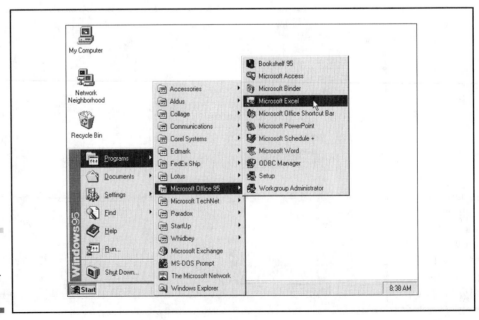

Programs
within a
program folder
Figure 1-10.

1. Minimize or close any windows that might be open on the desktop.

2. Click on the Start button to open the Start menu and then point on the Programs option. Next, point on the Accessories folder in the submenu. Your screen should look similar to Figure 1-11. Your collection of accessories may be larger or smaller, depending on how your computer is configured.

   Notice that the first few items are more folders that categorize accessories, followed by individual accessories. Take a second to point on the folders and see the contents of their submenus.

3. Click on the Paint accessory to open the program, as shown in Figure 1-12. Click on the Maximize/Restore button and the Paint window expands to fill the screen.

4. Click on the Maximize/Restore button again, and the Paint window returns to its original size.

5. Drag the Paint window (by dragging on the Paint window's Title bar anywhere except the buttons or the Control-menu icon) to the right side of the screen.

6. To start another program, click on the Start button, point on the Programs option, point on Accessories, and then click on the Notebook program. The NotePad program starts; its window opens and becomes the *active* window, as shown in Figure 1-13.

Accessories
submenu
Figure 1-11.

Paint accessory
Figure 1-12.

Notice how the NotePad window's Title bar is dark with light letters
while the Paint's Title bar has become lighter with dark letters. This
means that NotePad is now the active program, while Paint is inactive.

NotePad
window open
and active
Figure 1-13.

(There may be some differences between your screen and the screens shown in the figures and illustrations shown in this book because of differences in displays and display adapters and in the options you selected during Windows installation.)

7. Drag the NotePad window until it overlaps but does not completely cover Paint (unless it was that way originally).

8. Click on Paint to activate it. Notice how it now overlaps the NotePad and Paint's Title bar changes color.

9. Click on the NotePad window to reactivate it. Then drag on the sizing handle to reduce the size of the NotePad to about half its original size so both windows can fit side-by-side on the desktop without overlapping.

10. Open a third program by clicking on the Start button, point on Programs, and then click on the Windows Explorer program toward the bottom of the submenu. The Explorer program starts; its window opens and becomes the active window.

    The Explorer is an invaluable Windows 95 feature that allows you to perform many file and disk operations such as copying, moving, formatting, and renaming. It is covered separately later in this chapter.

11. Size the Explorer window so you can see parts of Paint and NotePad, as shown in Figure 1-14.

Explorer
window
Figure 1-14.

12. You now have three programs running in Windows: the Explorer, Paint, and NotePad. Move them around, size them in various ways (notice that you can only size Paint horizontally), and activate first one and then another. Continue this until you are comfortable working with these windows.

    Notice that as you move the mouse among these windows, the mouse pointer changes. In the Paint window, the mouse pointer can be a paint bucket, a pencil, a crosshair, or several other shapes; in the NotePad window the pointer is an I-beam or the familiar arrow; and in the Explorer window the pointer is the arrow or a cross for sizing columns and panes. The pointer is telling you what can be done when it is in the various windows. With the pencil in Paint you can draw, while the crosshairs are for cutting away a part of a drawing. The I-beam is used with text; its skinny shape allows you to insert it between characters. When you click an I-beam you are establishing an *insertion point*, which determines where text you type is placed.

13. Click on the Minimize button of the NotePad, Explorer, and Paint windows. The three become tasks in the Taskbar at the bottom of the screen.

Tasks in the Taskbar are running programs that are just temporarily inactive on the screen. An inactive window and a Taskbar task differ only in the amount of the screen they use.

Manipulating windows and their icons—by selecting, dragging, maximizing, minimizing, sizing, and scrolling—is one of the primary functions of the Windows environment. Practice these techniques until they are second nature. You will use them often.

Another primary function of the Windows environment is the use of menus.

Using Menus

A menu is the primary device you use to give instructions to Windows and its programs. The menus available to you at any given time are shown in the Menu bar. By clicking on a menu name—*selecting* a menu—you open the menu. By clicking on a menu option—*choosing* an option—you make the option perform its function.

Menu options can represent several different functions. Often, when you choose a menu option you are telling the program to carry out a command, such as saving a file or copying something. Other menu options allow you to set parameters or defaults for the items you are working on, such as selecting the size of a page to be printed or the color of an object. Still other menu options are themselves menus—in other words, selecting a menu option opens another menu, the now familiar submenu.

Look at several menus now and get a feel for how they operate.

1

1. Click on the Explorer task to open the program. Click on the Explorer's View menu. It opens as shown here:

2. Click on the Details option to change the way the files and folders are displayed. (This action sets the stage for the discussion in the following paragraph.)

   The Explorer's View menu has ten options. Notice that the Line up Icons option is dimmed, while others are not. Dimmed options are not available in the context in which you are working. For example, since you changed the way the files and folders were displayed from icons to a detailed list, there is no need to have an option to line up the icons because there aren't any. Another example would be if you did not have a selected object in the current window's workspace, you could not move the object in that window; therefore, the Move option would be dimmed. The Options option has an ellipsis (...) after it. When you select such an option, a dialog box opens. A *dialog box* is a place for you to provide further information or answer questions about the option you selected. For example, if you ask to save a file but have not provided the application with a filename, a dialog box opens asking you for the filename.

3. Click on Options in the View menu.

   A dialog box opens that allows you to determine which files are seen and which programs are associated with which files.

4. Click on Cancel to close the dialog box.

5. Click on the View menu again. Then click on Refresh. Your mouse pointer turns into a hourglass while the Explorer updates the window. Since there is no dialog box or submenu associated with this option, when you click on it the action is performed immediately.

6. Click on the File, Edit, Tools, and Help menus in succession to look at each of them.

Notice in the View menu that the Status Bar option has a check mark to the left of it. This means that the status bar is currently active. If you click on the Status Bar option again, the check mark disappears as well as the status bar. The same action holds true for the Toolbar option; click on it to add or remove the check mark, which displays or hides the Toolbar. The group of four options toward the center of the menu determines how the files and folder are displayed. Since they are mutually exclusive (only one of the four options can be active at a time), a dot instead of a check mark is displayed next to the option that is currently active.

Notice also that a menu option may have a series of keystrokes to the right of the option name as in the Edit menu. These are *shortcut keys.* By pressing these keys you can choose the menu option directly without first opening the menu.

Using Dialog Boxes

As you have seen, dialog boxes are a means of providing information about an option you have chosen. Dialog boxes can be simple or very complex, with many different components. Windows uses several types of components to gather different types of information. These components are shown in the dialog boxes displayed in Figures 1-15 and 1-16. These dialog boxes are used for setting up a sheet to be printed and setting properties for Microsoft Fax. The various dialog box components and their uses are shown in Table 1-4.

Dialog boxes provide a very powerful and fast means of communicating with Windows and its applications. It is important that you know the terms described above and are comfortable using dialog boxes.

Using the Keyboard

You can do almost everything (except enter text) with a mouse, but in several instances the keyboard provides a useful shortcut. You have seen how several of the menu options have direct shortcut keys. You can also choose any of the other menu options with a general keyboard procedure. You can open any menu by pressing ALT (you do not have to hold it down) followed by the underlined letter in the menu name. After pressing ALT, you can also use LEFT ARROW and RIGHT ARROW to highlight a menu name, and then DOWN ARROW to open the menu and highlight an option. After a menu is open, you can choose an option by typing the underlined letter in the option name or highlighting the option with the direction keys and pressing

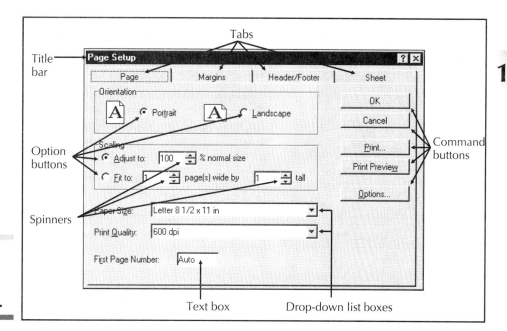

Excel's Page
Setup dialog
box
Figure 1-15.

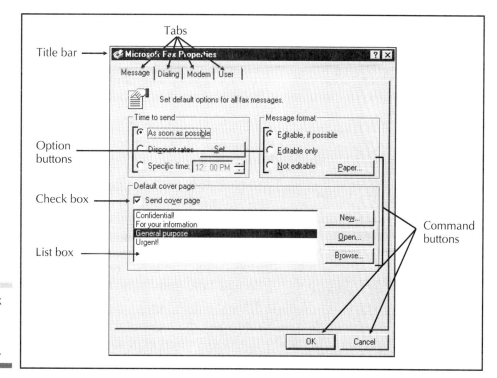

Microsoft Fax
Properties
dialog box
Figure 1-16.

Component	Usage
Check box	To turn options on or off.
Command button	To take immediate action; for example, to close a dialog box, to cancel a command, to open another dialog box, or to expand the current dialog box. Clicking on a command button activates it. OK, the most common command button, is used to complete the dialog box and close it. An ellipsis (...) indicates that a command button opens another dialog box, and two greater-than symbols (>>) indicate that a command button expands the current dialog box.
Drop-down list box	To select (usually) one item from a list in a constrained space. The current selection is shown. Clicking on the arrow to the right opens the drop-down list box. Click on the option desired, possibly using the scroll bar first.
List box	To select (usually) one item from a list. The current selection is highlighted. Click on the option desired, possibly using the scroll bar first.
Option button	To select one item from a set of mutually exclusive options. A selection is changed by clicking on another option.
Slider	To select from continuous values in the form of a horizontal or vertical scale.
Spinner	To continuously increase or decrease a number.
Tabs	To allow you to select between multiple pages in a dialog box.
Text box	To enter text, such as a filename. The mouse pointer turns into an I-beam in a text box. Clicking the mouse in a text box places an insertion point, and any text typed will follow the insertion point. Without clicking an insertion point, any existing text in a selected text box is replaced by anything typed. The DEL key removes existing selected text in a text box.
Title bar	To display the name of the dialog box and provide a means to move it with a mouse.

Dialog Box
Components
Table 1-4.

ENTER. ENTER can also be used to open a menu once you have highlighted the menu name, and the F10 function key can be used in place of ALT to initiate the process. To cancel a menu selection and return to the workspace, press ALT or F10 a second time. To cancel a menu selection but stay in the Menu bar so that another menu selection can be made, press ESC. To return to the workspace, press ESC a second time.

Give the mouse a rest for a moment and access several menu options using the keyboard (the Explorer should still be open on your screen).

1. Press ALT-V to open the Explorer's View menu.
2. Press O to select the Options option. The Options dialog box opens.
3. Press TAB to move among the various fields in the dialog box, and then press ESC to close the dialog box.
4. In general, to move around in a dialog box you first press TAB to move through the major groups of options, normally from left to right and top to bottom, or use SHIFT-TAB to reverse the direction. Alternatively, press and hold ALT while typing the underlined letter in the option or group name to move directly to that option or group. Then use the direction keys to highlight an option within a group, and use SPACEBAR to make the final selection of the option. Finally, press ENTER to complete and close the dialog box.
5. Press F10 to reactivate the Menu bar.
6. Press RIGHT ARROW three times to move to the Tools menu.
7. Press ENTER to open the Tools menu, and then press DOWN ARROW once to highlight the Map Network Drive option.
8. Press ENTER to select the highlighted menu item and open the dialog box.
9. Press TAB four times to place the *focus* on the Cancel command button.
10. Press ENTER to close the dialog box.
11. Press ALT-SPACEBAR to open the Control menu of the Explorer and then press N to minimize it once again to a task on the Taskbar.

Using the Control Menu

The Control menu icon, located in the upper-left corner of most windows, opens the Control menu that allows you to use the keyboard to perform many other of the Windows functions that you have previously learned to perform with the mouse. Use TAB to get to the Explorer on the Taskbar and then open the Explorer's Control menu. No window should be open on your desktop.

1. Press TAB three times. It will circulate among the Start menu, the Taskbar, and one of the icons on the desktop. It only goes in those three

places and always in that order: Start menu, Taskbar, icons. You can tell when the Start menu is selected because it has a dotted black border. Similarly, when an icon is selected, its title will have a dotted black border. You don't see anything when the Taskbar is selected, but if you press a direction key, one of the tasks will be selected. If an icon is selected and you press UP ARROW or DOWN ARROW, the highlight will move to the next icon. Try this until you are certain a task on the Taskbar is selected.

2. When a task is selected, press RIGHT ARROW until the Explorer is selected and then press ENTER to open the Explorer window.

3. Press ALT-SPACEBAR to open the Explorer's Control menu, shown here.

The options available in the Control menu and their functions are shown in Table 1-5.

Now try several of the Control menu options using the keyboard.

1. Press DOWN ARROW to highlight Move and press ENTER to choose it. The pointer becomes a four-headed arrow.

2. Press one or more of the direction keys to move the window in the direction you choose. An outline shows you where you are going.

3. When the outline of the window is where you want it, press ENTER. If you want to cancel the move, press ESC before pressing ENTER.

4. Press ALT-SPACEBAR to reopen the Explorer's Control menu.

Option	Function
Restore	Restores the window to the size it was prior to being minimized or maximized
Move	Allows moving the window with the keyboard
Size	Allows sizing the window with the keyboard
Minimize	Minimizes the window size to a Taskbar task
Maximize	Maximizes the window size, usually to fill the screen
Close	Closes the window

Control Menu
Options
Table 1-5.

5. Press DOWN ARROW twice to highlight Size and press ENTER to choose it. The pointer again becomes a four-headed arrow.

6. Press one arrow key to select one side whose size you want to change, or press two arrow keys simultaneously to select two sides whose sizes you want to change. (Pressing two arrow keys simultaneously is the same as selecting a corner with the mouse.)

7. Press one or two arrows until the window is the size you want it. Then press ENTER. If you want to cancel the sizing, press ESC before pressing ENTER.

8. Press ALT-SPACEBAR to reopen the Explorer's Control menu.

9. Press x to choose Maximize. The Explorer window expands to fill the screen.

10. Press ALT-SPACEBAR to open the Explorer's Control menu and press ENTER to choose Restore. The Explorer window returns to its original size.

11. Press ALT-SPACEBAR again, and press N to choose Minimize. The Explorer window shrinks to a task on the Taskbar.

You use different key combinations to open Control menus for program windows and document windows. Use ALT-SPACEBAR to open an application window Control menu and use ALT-- (hyphen) to open a document window Control menu.

One important Control menu option you have not tried yet is Close. In most windows, Close simply closes the window. At the desktop, with all windows closed or minimized as tasks, using ALT SPACEBAR opens the Control menu for the Taskbar, which you can then move and size like a window. However, Close in the Taskbar's Control menu opens the Shut Down dialog box that you would otherwise get by choosing Shut Down from the Start menu. From the Shut Down dialog box, you can prepare the computer to be turned off, restart Windows, restart the computer at an MS-DOS prompt, or close your programs and have another user log on (as you can see next).

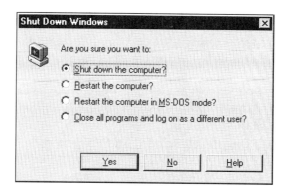

You will close Windows 95 from the Shut Down dialog box later in the chapter. Once the Control menu is open, you can choose Close in the normal ways: by clicking on it, by highlighting it and pressing ENTER, or by pressing C. You can choose Close with the Control menu closed by double-clicking on the Control-menu icon (not available on the Taskbar or Start menu) or by pressing ALT-F4.

The keyboard and the Control menu are important adjuncts to the mouse, but they should be viewed as that and not the other way around. With Windows 95 and Excel, the mouse is by far the most effective and expeditious way to do most things. For that reason, this book usually has instructions for the mouse. Keyboard instructions normally are given only for shortcut keys when you are already typing on the keyboard.

Using the Control Panel and the Explorer

Two of the most used features in Windows 95 are the Control Panel and the Explorer. You were briefly introduced to them earlier in this chapter; however, a more in-depth look into some of their capabilities will provide a better foundation for understanding Windows 95.

Setting Defaults with the Control Panel

The Control Panel is the primary place in Windows where you set the parameters or defaults that tell Windows how you want a number of different functions handled. Open the Control Panel now and look at the options.

Click on the Start button, point on Settings, and click on Control Panel. The Control Panel opens as shown in Figure 1-17. You might need to resize the window so you can see all of the icons. Align the icons, if needed, by selecting the View menu Arrange Icons option to turn on the Auto Arrange option. Your set of icons might be slightly different, depending on how you set up Windows 95 and what hardware you have installed in your computer. Table 1-6 shows the Control Panel icons and the functions each controls.

You can set any of the functions by double-clicking on the appropriate icon and then entering the necessary information in the dialog box that opens. Try that now by setting the double-click rate of the mouse.

1. Double-click on the Mouse icon in the Control Panel. The Mouse Properties dialog box opens with the Button tab displayed as shown in Figure 1-18.

2. If you are left-handed and want to make the right mouse button the primary mouse button, click on the Left-handed option button at the top of the tab.

Control Panel
Figure 1-17.

Icon	Function Set
Accessibility Options	Provides several features for people who have difficulty using the keyboard and mouse, seeing the screen, or hearing the computer's sounds
Add New Hardware	A Wizard that walks you through configuring Windows 95 for new hardware
Add/Remove Programs	Allows you to install new programs, uninstall existing ones, add or remove parts of Windows 95, and create a recovery disk
Date/Time	Allows you to set the computer's internal date and time and to select your time zone
Display	Customizes display properties such as background patterns, screen color and resolution, and whether screen savers are used
Fonts	Provides means to view, add, and remove fonts
Keyboard	Changes the speed, sensitivity, and language of your keyboard

Control Panel
Icons
Table 1-6.

Icon	Function Set
Mail and Fax	Sets properties for the Microsoft Exchange mail and fax facility
Microsoft Mail Postoffice	Allows you to set up and administer a Microsoft Mail postoffice
Modems	Configures new modems and changes properties of one or more existing modems
Mouse	Allows you to change default mouse settings
Multimedia	Customizes various multimedia devices such as CD-ROM audio, sound files, and video
Network	Configures your system to connect with other computers over a network
Passwords	Administers passwords for network and security use
Printers	Allows you to configure your computer to change, add, and remove local or network printers
Regional Settings	Establishes the format for numbers, currency, time, and date based on geographic locations
Sounds	Provides several sound schemes for various computer actions
System	Displays information on your computer configuration and internal settings

Control Panel
Icons
(*continued*)
Table 1-6.

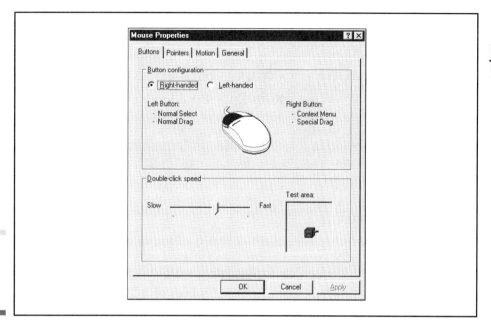

Buttons tab of
the Mouse
control panel
Figure 1-18.

3. Double-click on the jack-in-the-box in the test area to test if you are double-clicking correctly.

4. If the jack-in-the-box does not open and close when you double-click on it, you need to change the speed. Drag the speed slider toward the faster or slower end, whichever is correct for you, and try double-clicking again.

5. Repeat steps 3 and 4 until the double-clicking speed is set correctly.

6. Open the other tabs to see what other sizes and styles are available for the pointer and whether you want to adjust the pointer's speed across the screen or add mouse trails to see the pointer's path (if you are using a laptop computer, mouse trails may help you see the mouse).

7. When you are done with the mouse settings, click OK to close the dialog box and return to the Control Panel window.

8. On your own, look at the other Control Panel functions. You'll find you can do a lot to tailor Windows to your tastes. Unless you want to change something, click on Cancel in each dialog box so you won't change anything inadvertently.

9. When you are done with the Control Panel, double-click on the Control Panel's Control menu icon in the upper-left corner or click on the Close

button in the upper-right corner. This closes the Control Panel and returns you to the desktop and any other open programs.

Creating a Folder with the Explorer

The Explorer, which for Windows 3.*x* users is similar to the File Manager, provides all of the customary file-handling functions such as copying, moving, deleting, and renaming files, as well as some new file and disk manipulation tools. Open the Explorer now and create a new folder named Sheet to store your Excel documents.

If you still have the Explorer as a task, click on it in the Taskbar; otherwise, click on the Start button, choose Programs, and select Windows Explorer in the submenu.

The Explorer is comprised of two panes: in the left pane are the drives and folders for your computer (and any other computer that is networked with your computer), and in the right pane are the folders and files contained in a selected drive or folder. The two panes provide a very powerful way of viewing and working with your folders and their files.

The initial view shows you a hierarchical list of drives and folders in the left pane and icons representing folder contents in the right pane. As you have already seen, you can change the manner in which the right pane displays items by choosing different View menu options. The Large Icons option displays each folder or file as a discrete icon, much like the icons on the desktop. The arrangement for Small Icons and List is very similar: Small Icons lists folders first and files alphabetically from left to right in rows. The List option sorts the folders first and then files alphabetically top to bottom in columns. Details sorts the folders and files alphabetically in one list and creates multiple columns that provide specific data on each file. Figures 1-19 and 1-20 show a typical Explorer's right pane in Large Icons and Details view. In Details view, you can adjust the column width by dragging the vertical separator between column headers, as illustrated next. You can also change how the list is sorted by clicking in the column heading you want it sorted by. Clicking once on a column that has not just been previously sorted sorts in ascending order (smaller to larger numbers, A to Z), clicking a second time sorts in descending order (large to small numbers, Z to A).

Name		Size	Type	Modified
XI01f12.tif		302KB	CorelPHOTO-PAIN...	4/25/95 12:07 AM
XI01f13.tif		302KB	CorelPHOTO-PAIN...	4/25/95 12:11 AM
XI01f14.tif		302KB	CorelPHOTO-PAIN...	4/25/95 12:16 AM

1

Right pane in
Large Icons
view
Figure 1-19.

Right pane in
Details view
Figure 1-20.

Within the left pane, indicators next to the drives and folders show if it contains subfolders or not. If that indicator is a plus sign, subfolders are not displayed. If it's a minus sign, they are displayed, as shown here:

You may open and list the files and subfolders in any folder by clicking on the folder icon. If you were to click on the Excel folder in the left pane (c:\excel or c:\office95\excel, depending on whether you purchased Excel as a standalone product or as part of the Office 95 suite) with Excel 7.0 installed, you would get the right pane display shown in Figures 1-19 and 1-20.

In the right pane you can select or highlight files you want to move, copy, rename, or delete. To move a file, drag its icon from the current folder on the right to a new folder or subfolder in the left pane. To copy a file, press and hold the CTRL key while you drag the file icon. If you drag a file from one drive to another, it's copied by default. If you wish to move, copy, or delete several files at one time and the files are listed sequentially, click on the first filename, and then press and hold SHIFT while you click on the last filename in the sequence. If you want to select several files that are not in sequence, press and hold CTRL while you click on each of the items. To cancel a selected item, press and hold CTRL while you click on the item. To delete, cut, copy, or rename, right-click on the file(s) to open the file's popup menu (shown next) and choose the applicable options. Descriptions of the file popup menu options are provided in Table 1-7.

Alternatively, you can select a file and then select the File and Edit menus to use the same options. An even easier way to rename a file is to click once on

Popup Menu Option	Function
Open	Opens the program that is associated with the file and then opens the file
Quick View	When installed, provides viewing of files without opening their applications first
Send To	Copies the file to a floppy disk drive or sends the file to be faxed (if MS Fax is installed)
Cut	Removes the selected file and places it on the Clipboard
Copy	Retains the original selected file and places a copy of it on the Clipboard
Create Shortcut	Creates a small file that can be moved or copied to another location to open a program. The programs accessed from the Start button use shortcuts
Delete	Removes the file to the Recycle Bin where it can be restored, if activated; otherwise, permanently removes the file
Rename	Allows you to rename a file
Properties	Opens a dialog box that lists properties for the selected file

Explorer Files
Popup Menu
Table 1-7.

a file to select it and then click on it a second time, but be careful not to double-click or the Explorer will try and open the file. After the second click a box forms around the filename and you can type in a new name. Windows 95 breaks the MS-DOS 8.3 barrier for naming files and lets you use up to 255 characters including spaces. However, you cannot use the characters: \ / : * ? " < > | for naming files.

The File menu provides access to several other file functions, which include creating folders. Use that command now to complete creating the Sheet folder to store your Excel spreadsheets.

1. Click on the C: drive icon in the Explorer's left pane to select it.
2. Click on the File menu to open it and point on New. Choose Folder in the submenu that opens.

A new folder is created in your C: drive and appears in the right pane at the end of all the folders and files in the C: drive.

3. Type **Sheet**.

4. Press ENTER to create the folder.

5. When you are done with the Explorer, click on its Close button to close it.

Getting Help

Windows 95 online help is very extensive and context sensitive—it tries to provide specific help about what you are doing. You can get help by several methods. The most available method is to click on the ever present Start button and choose the Help option to open the Windows 95 Help facility, shown in Figure 1-21. The Contents tab of the Help facility contains a hierarchical list of topics on the most common features in Windows 95. It is well worth the time to browse through the topics by double-clicking on them and reviewing any features you are not familiar with.

If you cannot quickly find the definition or explanation you are searching for, click on the Index tab shown in Figure 1-22. By typing in the first few letters of the word or phrase in text box number 1, an increasingly more specific search of the index occurs in the list box numbered 2. When something appears close to your word or phrase, select it by clicking on it and then click on the Display button to open its explanation. Alternatively,

Windows 95
Help facility
contents
Figure 1-21.

you can use the scroll bar to search through the index and you can double-click on an index item to go directly to its description.

The third tab, Find, allows you to create a search list, or database, for any specific words throughout all help topics and descriptions. The first time you try to use Find, you have to create the list. After a short to moderate delay, depending on how specific a search list you chose, the Find tab opens, as in Figure 1-23.

Besides using the Start menu to access Help, you can press F1. If you are in a Windows 95 program or feature, the same Windows 95 Help facility opens as from the Start menu. If you are in a program such as Excel, its own online Help facility opens. Although 16-bit programs, unlike the 32-bit programs specifically designed for Windows 95 (such as Excel 7.0), use a slightly different format for their online help, the basic concept is the same.

In most dialog boxes there is a button next to the Close button with a question mark on it. When you click on this Help button, the mouse pointer is joined by a question mark and allows you to click on any screen element and have a popup box appear with a description of that element. Figure 1-24 shows an example of this context-sensitive help. If you are in a program such as Excel (and most other Windows applications), you can also press SHIFT-F1. The mouse pointer also will become a question mark that you can click on something, a menu option for example, to get specific help about that option.

Windows 95
Help Index tab
Figure 1-22.

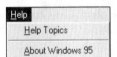

The final and most general-purpose method of getting help is to use the Help menu on most program and all folder windows. You can access the Help menu by either clicking on it or pressing ALT-H. If you are in a Windows 95 window, the Help menu will open as shown next. Other programs will have something similar. The Help Topics option opens

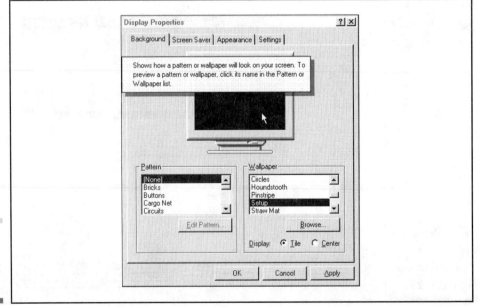

Context-
sensitive help
in a dialog box
Figure 1-24.

the Windows 95 Help facility described previously. The About Windows 95 option opens a dialog box that provides information about your copy of Windows 95, such as the version number, copyright information, licensee, and two interesting systems values: memory available to Windows 95 and percentage of resources used.

Leaving Windows

Windows and many of the applications that run under it, like Excel, use temporary files to store intermediate information as the program is running. If you leave the applications and Windows in the correct manner, not only are these temporary files erased, but you are reminded to save any files you have not saved. The correct manner to leave any window is to click on the Close button, double-click on its Control-menu icon, or choose Exit from its File menu. Simply do any of these actions until you reach the desktop and you will have correctly prepared yourself to leave Windows. To exit Windows and turn off your computer, do the following:

1. Click on the Start button.
2. Click on the Shut Down option.

    Verify that the first option, Shut down the computer?, is selected.
3. Click on the Yes button.

Windows 95 takes a moment to shut itself down and then notifies you when it is safe to turn your computer off. Then, and only then, can you safely turn off your computer.

This chapter has laid a foundation on which you can now begin to add specific knowledge of Excel. Windows 95 is not a simple subject, but it provides a very powerful framework that is fully utilized by Excel. You now have enough knowledge of that framework to use it in Excel, which you will begin doing in Chapter 2.

The Components of Excel

2

This chapter explains the three components of Excel—spreadsheets, databases, and charts—paying particular attention to spreadsheets. It also briefly introduces references, ranges, cells, commands, formulas, functions, and macros.

Excel is considered a spreadsheet program, yet it really has three components that perform three different tasks: the *spreadsheet* component displays and analyzes text and numbers in rows and columns, the *database* component manipulates lists of information, and the *chart* component produces charts.

Each component is really just a different way of looking at and interacting with data that have a common structure based on *rows* and *columns*. This common structure is the spreadsheet. It may contain data from the other components, but underlying the different components is the same row and column structure that contains all of the data. This common data structure makes Excel *integrated*—able to transfer and manipulate data easily among the three components.

Spreadsheets

The easiest way to think of a spreadsheet is to consider an accountant's multicolumn paper spreadsheet—a piece of paper that is divided into rows and columns. Generally, there is a wide column on the left for text labels that describe what is in each row. To the right of the label column are several columns for entering numbers. Paper spreadsheets are used for manually listing sales or expenses, for preparing budgets or financial plans, or for any other similar task.

The spreadsheet component of Excel, shown in Figure 2-1, is an electronic multicolumn spreadsheet that is far more flexible than its paper namesake. Excel provides up to 255 sheets, each containing 256 columns and 16,384 rows. Each column can be between 0 and 255 characters wide, and words and numbers can be intermixed as needed. Excel allows many types of calculations over rows, columns, and sheets; and copying or moving information from one sheet, column, or row to another is easy with Excel.

Spreadsheets and Files

Both the paper spreadsheet and Excel's spreadsheet are a means of analyzing data by organizing it into rows and columns. Excel's spreadsheets, however, are stored on your computer's hard disk in *files* called *workbooks* (*books* for short). Think of a workbook as a file of spreadsheets (*sheets* for short), although it can also contain charts and programming module pages. When you build a workbook, you do so in your computer's *RAM* (random access

2

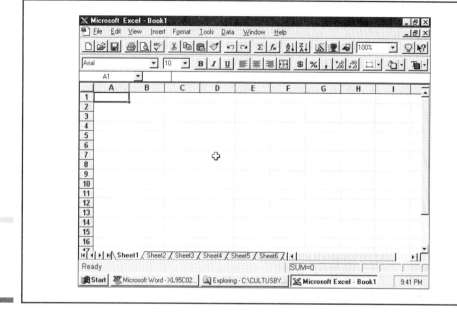

Excel's
spreadsheet
window
Figure 2-1.

memory). When you load another program, or turn off your computer, what is in RAM is lost. You must save your workbook in a file on disk for it to be permanent. A file that has been stored on disk can be read back into Excel, reviewed, altered, and saved again. Also, because a file on disk can be run on another computer running Excel, work can be shared. The only outwardly distinguishing feature of an Excel file is the name you give it. Like a manila file folder, an Excel file is just a collection of information with a name.

Rows, Columns, and Sheets

The row and column structure of a traditional spreadsheet has been expanded in Excel to a three-dimensional structure of rows, columns, and sheets. This structure provides a powerful framework for financial analysis. Consider a company's financial plan or budget, as shown in Figure 2-2. Each row is an account—an element of revenue or expense. Each column is a period of time—months, quarters, or years. Each sheet is a unit of the company—stores, plants, offices, or divisions. Summing across columns you get the total for an account, summing down rows you get the total for a time period, and summing through the sheets you get the total for the company.

The horizontal rows and vertical columns make a two-dimensional grid and the sheets give it a third dimension of depth. The rows are numbered 1 through 16,384, while the 256 possible columns are labeled A through IV (A through Z, then AA through AZ, BA through BZ, and so on through IV).

A company's
financial plan
Figure 2-2.

Sheets start out labeled Sheet1 through Sheet255, but you can rename them
anything you want up to 31 characters. With this grid, you could build a
formula that, for example, adds column C from row 24 through row 32 or
sums Sheet1 through Sheet4, or you can create a graph from the data in row
15 from column AC through column AH.

Addresses, Cells, and References

When information is entered on a sheet, it is stored in a specific location.
You know what that location is by the row and column in which the
information is located. Using Excel's row and column grid, you can give the
information you stored an *address*; for example, column D, row 7. Excel
addresses are written with the column reference first, followed by the row.
Using this convention, you can write the example address as D7. To add a
sheet reference to this, you place the sheet name and an exclamation point
(!) in front of the column and row; for example, Sheet1!D7.

A single address, the intersection of a row and a column on a single sheet, is
called a *cell*. You can think of a sheet as a collection of over four million cells.
These are addressed from A1 for the cell in the upper-left corner to IV16384

2

for the cell in the lower-right corner. Of course, the amount of memory you have in your computer limits the number of these you can use at a time.

Numbers and Text

A cell may contain either numbers or text. Numbers, which include formulas that evaluate to numbers, can be formatted in many ways, including dollars, percentages, dates, or time. Text can include numbers and can be used as titles, row and column labels, and notes on a sheet.

The primary difference between numbers and text is that you can perform arithmetic calculations on numbers but not on text. Think of numbers as arithmetic values and text as everything else. For example, text includes chararacters such as: "Main St," "9 Main St," and "123-45-6789." Excel recognizes the social security number format as well as ZIP + 4 codes as text.

Based on what you type, Excel determines whether your entry is a number or text. If you type only numbers (0 through 9) or these numeric symbols,

$$+ \; - \; (\;) \; . \; , \; : \; \$ \; \% \; / \; E \; e \text{ (in scientific notation)}$$

Excel considers your entry a number. If you enter a date or time value in one of Excel's built-in formats, it is considered a number. Finally, a recognizable formula that results in a number is treated as a number. Everything else is text.

You can enter numbers that range from $-1E-307$ to $9.99999999999999E307$ and format them in several ways. For example, you can enter **3.25**, **3.25%**, **$3.25**, **3 2/5**, **32.5E-1**, or **3,250,325.25**. In other words, you can include commas, dollar signs, fractions, and percent signs in numbers and Excel will interpret them correctly. Methods for entering formulas, which are also numbers, are discussed below, as are procedures for entering, formatting, and aligning text and numbers.

References, Ranges, and Names

A *reference* identifies one or more cells for use in a formula or in an instruction. A reference can be a single cell address like D14; a group of cells identified by multiple cell addresses and a *reference operator*, such as C5:E12; or a name or names that refer to one or more cells, like "Salaries." The reference operators, their names, and their meanings are as follows:

Operator	Name and Meaning
: (colon)	Range, a rectangular group of adjacent cells
, (comma)	Union, the combination of two references
(space)	Intersection, the cells common to two references

Other than an individual cell address, the next most common reference is a *range*. Figure 2-3 shows the four kinds of ranges that can exist on a sheet: a row of cells, a column of cells, a rectangular block of cells, or a single cell. A range cannot be an L-shaped or otherwise nonrectangular arrangement of cells; it must be a complete rectangle. A range can also extend over multiple sheets and can be copied to the desktop for temporary storage of important information as a *scrap*.

Ranges are used in many Excel commands to specify a group of cells you want Excel to work on. To specify a range in a command, you may use the pair of addresses representing the first and last cells in the range (the upper-left and lower-right corners, respectively) separated by a colon, as in B11:G18. You may also highlight the range on the screen or use a name that you have previously given to that particular cell reference. If you want to reference an entire row or column or sequence of rows or columns, you may do so without identifying the second element. For example, to identify all of row 6 you might enter A6:IV6, but you can abbreviate it 6:6. Similarly, if you want to reference all of columns C through E, you can enter C:E.

Unions and intersections are used to describe groups of cells that cannot be described by a range, like those shown in Figure 2-4. *Unions* can describe L-shaped references such as E3:H3,I3:I12 as well as disjoint references like I3:I12,I16. *Intersections* describe the group of cells that are in both of two other references. For example, the intersection C6:C14 B10:E17 produces the

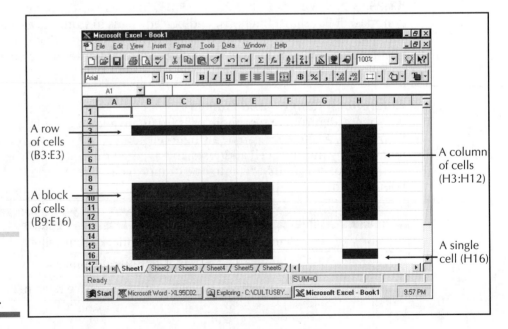

Types of
ranges on a
sheet

Figure 2-3.

range C10:C14. Unions and intersections are referred to using two other references separated by a comma or a space, respectively. Alternatively, you can highlight a union or an intersection by holding down CTRL while you highlight the cells on the screen or you can use a reference name you have previously defined.

A *reference name* is a text string that begins with a letter and can be as long as 255 characters and cannot contain a space. A reference name such as "Salaries" is often used because it is easier to remember and more meaningful than an address reference such as G16:T16. Many of Excel's arithmetic functions use references as arguments and, when a name is substituted for the address, they become very descriptive. For example, to total a group of cells that contain salaries you can use the Excel function =SUM(Salaries) if you have previously defined the name Salaries.

Formulas and Functions

The ability to enter text and numbers is not very useful unless you can do something with them. You need to be able to total columns of numbers, calculate percentages, and perform numerous other mathematical operations. Formulas are the means of doing this. Formulas may operate on

2

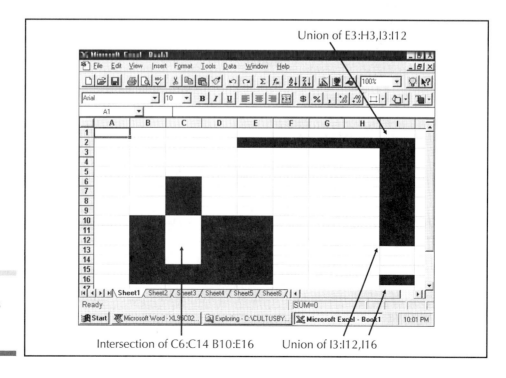

Unions and intersections on a sheet

Figure 2-4.

Union of E3:H3,I3:I12

Intersection of C6:C14 B10:E16   Union of I3:I12,I16

numbers, other formulas, or text. When a formula uses text, it is called a *text formula* and may contain the text operator (&) for *concatenation* (combining two text strings). Formulas that contain the arithmetic operators

$$+ - * / \wedge \%$$

are *numeric formulas*, and formulas that contain the comparison operators

$$< > <= >= <>$$

are *logical formulas* that produce the logical value True or False.

Formulas use standard algebraic notation with nested parentheses, if necessary, and they typically begin with an equal sign (=). You may also enter a formula beginning with a plus sign (+) or a minus sign (–) and Excel will automatically add an equal sign in front of the plus or minus. Formulas may be up to 255 characters long but may not contain spaces, except within a *literal*—a set of letters, numbers, or symbols enclosed in quotation marks. Formulas usually use data in other locations on a sheet by referencing either a cell, a group of cells, or a reference name.

Examples of formulas are shown here.

If the Formula Is	Contents of the Cell Containing the Formula Will Be
=B5	The contents of B5.
=C6–C7	The result of subtracting the contents of C7 from the contents of C6.
=.45*1590	The product of 0.45 times 1590.
=subtotal*tax	The product of the references named Subtotal and Tax.
="Dear "&D5	The combination of the literal string "Dear " with the contents of D5. (Quotation marks define a literal string, character for character.)
=date<=today( )	The logical value True if a reference named Date is less than or equal to a function named TODAY( ) that produces the current date; otherwise, the logical value False.

Order of Calculation

Excel calculates or evaluates a formula in a particular order determined by the *precedence number* of the operators being used and the parentheses placed in the formula. Table 2-1 describes each operator and gives its precedence number. Operators with a lower precedence number are performed earlier in

Operator	Description	Precedence
:	Range of cell	1
(a space)	Intersection of cells	2
,	Union of cells	3
–	Negation	4
%	Percentage (/100)	5
^	Exponentiation	6
*	Multiplication	7
/	Division	7
+	Addition	8
–	Subtraction	8
&	Concatenation	9
=	Equal to	10
<	Less than	10
>	Greater than	10
<=	Less than or equal to	10
>=	Greater than or equal to	10
<>	Not equal to	10

Excel
Operators
Table 2-1.

the calculation. When two operators in a formula have the same precedence number, Excel evaluates them sequentially from left to right.

Parentheses in a formula change the order of calculation. For example, to add two amounts before multiplying them by a third, you cannot use the formula =A1+B1*C1 because the multiplication is performed before the addition, in accordance with the order of calculation. When you put parentheses around the addition operation, the formula becomes =(A1+B1)*C1, and the addition is performed first. Excel performs the calculation within the innermost parentheses first. Parentheses must always be added in pairs and may be nested more than 25 levels deep. Excel has a very handy feature that shows the matching left parenthesis as you enter the right parenthesis. That way you know your parentheses match without having to count them.

Functions

Excel has a number of built-in formulas, called *functions*, that can be used within other formulas or can be used alone. Functions always begin with an equal sign and include calculations of the following types: mathematical, informational, date and time, lookup, logical, database, text, financial, and statistical. A function can be either text or a number, depending on whether it is operating on text or numbers. Table 2-2 lists some examples of functions and their uses.

Functions are discussed throughout this book and are given in-depth treatment in Chapter 10.

Commands

You can give Excel commands in six ways:

♦ Choose an option from a regular menu at the top of the screen.

♦ Choose an option from a popup menu.

♦ Select a tool in a toolbar.

♦ Use the mouse directly on a sheet.

♦ Press particular keys on the keyboard.

♦ Activate a set of commands you have stored in a workbook.

In this book, *command* refers to the first five methods—those implemented directly with the mouse, a toolbar, either type of menu, or with keys on your keyboard. Commands stored in a workbook are called *macros*.

Function	Purpose
=SUM(A4:A7,A9)	Adds A4, A5, A6, A7, and A9
=NOW( )	Produces the current date and time
=PI( )*G3^2	Calculates the area of a circle whose radius is in G3
=PV(C4,F6,B1)	Calculates the present value of a series of equal payments at an interest rate contained in C4, for the number of periods in F6, and with the payment amount contained in B1
=RIGHT(T22,5)	Displays the rightmost five characters of a text string contained in T22

Some Excel
Functions
Table 2-2.

Commands from a Menu

The primary means of giving Excel a command is by choosing an option from a menu presented to you on the screen. When you use menus to choose an option, you sometimes are asked for more information with a dialog box, or you may be presented with a secondary menu. As you saw in Chapter 1, you can begin a menu selection in several ways: by clicking with the mouse on the name of the menu you want to use or by pressing ALT, F10, or / (slash). This book assumes that you usually use the mouse, but you should become familiar with all of the menu selection techniques. For the most part, the instructions in this book state "Select the File menu" or "From the File menu." Whether you use the mouse or the keyboard is up to you.

If you use the keyboard, the ALT, F10, or / keys get you only to the Menu bar; you must still select the menu you want to use (which is one of many good reasons why using the mouse is preferable). Once the Menu bar is activated, there are two methods to select a menu with the keyboard: you can type the underlined letter in the menu name you want or you can use the direction keys to highlight the menu name and then press either DOWN ARROW or ENTER to open the menu.

Once a menu is open, you can choose a menu option in one of three ways: click on the menu option with the mouse, type the underlined letter in the option name, or use the direction keys to highlight the option and press ENTER to choose it. Examples of the three methods follow in which you select the Edit menu and choose the Copy option, as shown in Figure 2-5. The message area on the left side of the Status bar at the bottom of the Excel window displays an explanation of the highlighted menu or menu option. No other change appears on the screen as a result of these steps.

Mouse Method

1. Click on the Edit menu.
2. Click on the Copy option.

Keyboard Method 1

1. Press ALT, F10, or /.
2. Press E (you can use uppercase or lowercase), the underlined letter in Edit.
3. Press C, the underlined letter in Copy.

Keyboard Method 2

1. Press ALT, F10, or /.
2. Press RIGHT ARROW one time (twice if sheet is maximized).
3. Press DOWN ARROW four times.
4. Press ENTER.

Choosing
Copy from the
Edit menu
Figure 2-5.

Because you will be using the menu system extensively as you work with
Excel, menu commands are a primary subject of this book. Chapter 3
introduces each Excel menu.

Commands from the Popup Menu

By using your *right* mouse button, Excel will open a *popup* (also called a
shortcut or context) menu that gives you direct access to the most
commonly used commands for whatever you clicked on. For example,
clicking your right mouse button on the active cell will give you a popup
menu of editing and formatting options, including the Copy option, as
shown here:

Popup menus are also available for manipulating toolbars, rows, columns, and sheets, which are described in Chapter 3, and for editing and formatting charts and databases, which you will read about in Chapters 7 and 8.

Direct Mouse Commands

In addition to its use in choosing commands from menus, the mouse can also be used directly on the sheet. Most importantly, you can use the mouse to highlight a group of cells on which you want to operate—copy, move, or format, for example. You do this by pointing on a cell in one corner of the group of cells, pressing the mouse button, and dragging the mouse (pressing and holding the mouse button while moving the mouse) to the opposite corner. For example, the highlighted range in Figure 2-6 was created by pointing the mouse on C7 and dragging the mouse to E13.

2

If you want to highlight or select a union or an intersection on a sheet, hold down CTRL while dragging across the two or more ranges. For example, if you want to select the L-shaped group of cells shown in Figure 2-7, you would first drag down the column from C4 to C16, then press and hold CTRL while dragging from D12 through H16. This technique can also be used to highlight several ranges on different sheets—just hold down CTRL as you are dragging across each new range and clicking on each new sheet. If you want to highlight the same range on several sheets in a row, click on the first sheet tab, press and hold SHIFT while clicking on the last sheet tab, and then

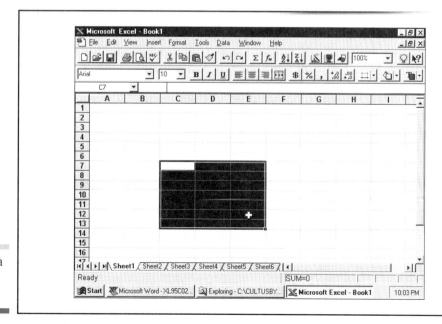

Highlighting a
range
Figure 2-6.

Highlighting
several ranges
or a union

Figure 2-7.

drag across the range on the first sheet (you don't have to keep holding
down SHIFT while you drag across the range).

Other direct mouse commands in Excel include placing an insertion point in
a formula or text string, selecting an entire row or column by clicking on the
row or column headings, widening a column or heightening a row by
dragging on the intersection of two columns or two row headings, and
dividing the window into panes by dragging the horizontal or vertical split
bar. (The parts of the Excel window are discussed in Chapter 3.) Of course,
you can also use the mouse with the scroll bars to change what is being
displayed and to size and move the window, as you learned in Chapter 1.

Commands from a Toolbar

By default, Excel has a pair of *toolbars* as the third and fourth bars on the
screen. These toolbars have a series of buttons that you can simply click on
to accomplish a task that would otherwise take several steps with a menu or
the keyboard. For example, to make a title bold with the toolbar, you select
the title and click on the B button in the Formatting toolbar (two steps).
With the menu, you would select the title, select the Format menu, choose
the Cells option, click on the Font tab, click on Bold as the Font Style, and
then click on OK (six steps).

You can tell what the tools in the toolbars do by pointing on the tool for a
second (don't click); a short description will appear below the tool, like this:

There are many handy tools described in Chapter 3 and other chapters. One of the handiest, located in the top or Standard toolbar, allows you to enter the most used function—the =SUM function—by clicking on the AutoSum tool, as shown in Figure 2-8. Otherwise, you would have to type it on the keyboard or select it from the menu. Additionally, a toolbar is the only means for selecting a drawing tool.

2

There are actually 13 toolbars in Excel 7. Each toolbar contains special tools for various activities. The Standard and Formatting toolbars, shown on the screens in this chapter, are displayed unless you turn them off or replace one or both of them with one or more of the other toolbars. Additional toolbars can be displayed on the screen at the same time and you can customize each toolbar by adding and deleting tools and selecting the order in which the tools appear. Also, you can create a totally new toolbar, which you can name and add tools to of your choosing. Finally, you can position and change the shape and orientation of one or more toolbars. Chapter 3 describes each of the tools in the Standard and Formatting toolbars.

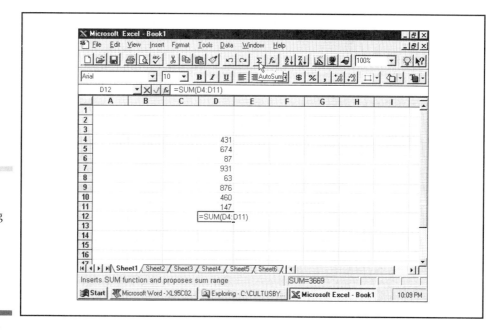

Entering an =SUM formula using the AutoSum tool in the Standard toolbar

Figure 2-8.

Commands from the Keyboard

Most of the keys on the keyboard that are not standard typewriter keys can be used to give Excel commands. Many of the keyboard commands are implemented with the *function keys* F1 through F10 or F12 on the top or left of most keyboards. On the right of most keyboards are the *direction keys*—the keys marked with the four arrows and HOME, END, PG UP, and PG DN. Use these keys to move around the screen, from cell to cell, or through a menu.

Some Excel commands are implemented through the use of two or more keys. Just as the SHIFT key is used with the normal typewriter keyboard to produce alternate characters, the CTRL and ALT keys are used with other keys to produce alternate commands. Chapter 3 describes these keys as well as the function and direction keys in more detail.

Wizards

Wizards provide guidance and in some cases a series of step-by-step procedures to walk you through processes such as the following:

♦ Importing a text file (Text Import Wizard)

♦ Creating and editing a chart (Chart Wizard)

♦ Inserting a function (Function Wizard)

♦ Suggesting easier ways of doing something (Tip Wizard)

♦ Building an interactive table from data on existing sheets or in an external database (PivotTable Wizard)

♦ Asking a question of Excel in plain English (Answer Wizard)

You will learn more about how to use the Tip Wizard in Chapter 3, the Chart Wizard and Answer Wizard in Chapter 7, the PivotTable Wizard in Chapter 8, the Text Import Wizard in Chapter 9, and the Function Wizard in Chapter 10.

Macros

A *macro* is either a set of Visual Basic statements or a set of Excel 4 macro commands that behave like automatic menu, mouse, and keyboard commands when they are executed. Macros, which are stored in a workbook on either Visual Basic module pages or macro sheets, are used to automate or speed up repetitive Excel procedures. You can have Excel record a macro for you by starting the recording, carrying out the steps you want to record, and then stopping the recording. When you are done, you can have Excel execute the macro by pressing two keys, such as CTRL-A. For example, you can format a table (which would take many keystrokes) with a macro.

Almost all commands that you can perform with a menu, the mouse, the toolbar, or the keyboard can be stored in a macro and activated as you choose. In addition, macros, especially Visual Basic procedures, can perform programming functions such as repeating a sequence, testing a condition, or accepting input from the keyboard. With this additional capability you can build custom menus and automate a workbook. Chapter 10 discusses recording and using command macros, Chapter 12 introduces you to Visual Basic, and Chapter 13 demonstrates workbook automation with a set of Visual Basic statements.

2

Workbook Windows

The Excel workbook window, as it appears in Figure 2-8, displays a single portion of one sheet. With the scroll bars or direction keys you can change the rows and columns being displayed, and with the sheet tabs you can change which sheet you are looking at. In every case, however, the view is similar. In addition to this basic view, Excel provides several other views that give you a different look at one or more sheets.

By splitting the window into *panes*, vertically or horizontally or both, you can look at two or four parts of the same sheet at the same time, as shown in Figure 2-9. By doing this, you can scroll each pane separately and look at different parts of the same sheet at the same time. You can also freeze the panes so they move together. To split a window into panes, you can choose Split from the Window menu, or you can drag either the horizontal *split-bar* that is in the upper-right corner of a window or the vertical split-bar that is in the lower-right corner as shown in the following:

Horizontal split-bar

Vertical split-bar

By displaying multiple document windows on the screen simultaneously, you can look at several sections of the same sheet, or you can look at several sheets either from the same workbook or from different workbooks. To display several windows, you can either open several workbooks with the Open option in the File menu or create one or more new windows for an existing workbook with the New Window option in the Window menu. Using the Arrange option in the Window menu, several windows on the screen can be *tiled* (as shown in Figure 2-10), arranged horizontally or vertically, or arranged in a *cascade* (as shown in Figure 2-11).

A single sheet
window split
into four panes
Figure 2-9.

Multiple Files and File Linking

As implied by the last paragraph and as shown in Figure 2-11, Excel allows
you to have more than one workbook open at one time. That means you can

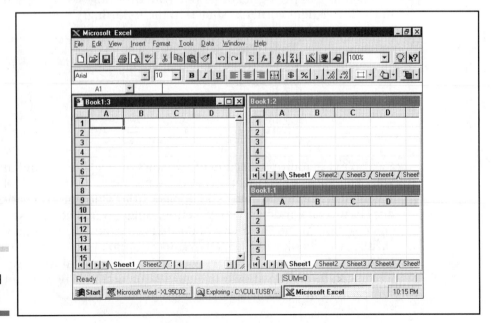

Three
windows tiled
Figure 2-10.

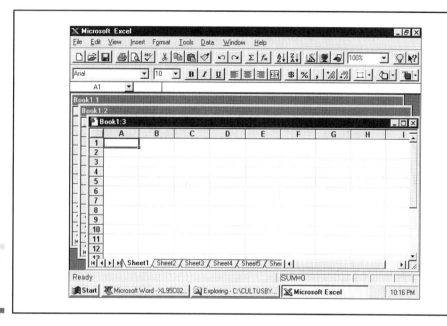

Three-window
cascade
Figure 2-11.

compare, copy, or move information between open sheets. Excel also allows
you to refer in a formula in one workbook file to cells or ranges contained in
a second workbook file. This is called *file linking.* The files may both be open
in memory, or one may be closed on the disk. As a result, you can easily
combine information contained in separate files. A change in one linked file
automatically is reflected in the second file. If the second file is on the disk,
it must be loaded and recalculated before the change is apparent.

To refer to another file in a formula, the formula must contain the filename.
This is accomplished by appending the filename, enclosed in square
brackets, to the front of an address or reference name. For example,
[QTR3BUD.XLS]TOTAL!SALARIES refers to a reference named Salaries on the
Total sheet in a file named QTR3BUD.XLS. If you need to add a path to the
filename because the file is not in the current directory, do so to the left of
the left bracket (outside the brackets), like this:

C:\BUDGET\[QTR3BUD.XLS]TOTAL!SALARIES

Since you can have multiple sheets in a single workbook, you might ask why
one would want to link multiple workbooks. The most common reason is
that you have several people, perhaps in different locations, preparing
different parts of a project that you need to link together. A second reason is
that you may have a model that is so complex that it is easier to handle if it
is in separate files. Another reason is that you may want to look at the same

data in a different way so you link portions of one workbook into another workbook and rearrange it.

Help

As you are learning Excel, and possibly even after you know it fairly well, you may forget how a command works or what the arguments are for a function. To assist you in these instances, Microsoft provides three types of help: context-sensitive help, dialog box help, and a help table of contents. There are, additionally, a quick preview of the product online, a detailed set of examples and demonstrations including a detailed set of *How To* steps that you can leave on your screen after closing Help, and a Tip Wizard to remind you of other ways of performing a task.

Context-sensitive help in Excel is activated either by clicking on the Help tool located on the far right of the toolbar or by pressing SHIFT-F1. The mouse pointer then becomes a question mark which, when clicked on any command or object, will provide information in a help window describing that command or object. For example, if you have a question on the Edit Cut option, click on the Help tool or press SHIFT-F1 to get the question mark, and then click on the Cut option located on the Edit menu. You will get information in a help window describing the Edit Cut option. Additionally, when you get an alert or error message, you can press SHIFT-F1 and get a help window describing the message.

Help is also available by clicking on the Help button in any Excel dialog box. Information on the function of that particular dialog box will appear in a help window. You can accomplish the same thing by pressing SHIFT-F1 while a dialog box is open.

The Help menu on the far right of the Menu bar provides access to Excel's Help facility, as shown here:

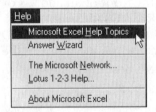

Included on the menu is access to the Answer Wizard that allows you to ask plain English questions, a way for users of the Microsoft Network to easily connect, help for Lotus 1-2-3 users, and the About Microsoft Excel button that opens a dialog box of the same name. Besides showing the customary version number, copyright details, and licensee, there are two buttons that lead to dialog boxes providing information on your computer's internal hardware and setting, and product support from Microsoft.

Some help topics have cross-references, or *jump terms,* leading to other help topics that cover related areas. You can easily identify the jump terms because they are colored green and underlined. If you place the mouse pointer on them, the pointer turns into a grabber hand. To look at a jump term, click on it. If you follow many subjects to their conclusion, you will get a How To window that lists the steps that are needed to perform a given task. Each help window has three command buttons at the top of the window that allow you to go to the Help Topics tab, see a history of your most recently selected help topics, or open an options menu, shown next, that allows you to: add your comments to help topics (Annotate), copy or print the help topic text, change font and color defaults, and choose whether you want the help window to stay on top of other windows.

2

The final way that Excel provides help is with the Tip Wizard, which watches what you are doing and gives you tips on how to do it faster or in different ways. You can turn on the Tip Wizard by clicking on the light bulb on the right end of the Standard toolbar. When you do that, another bar appears on the screen with a tip about the last thing you did. As you work, you will see tips appear that relate to what you are doing.

Databases

The row and column structure of Excel is excellent for storing lists of information. Consider the phone list shown in Figure 2-12. Each entry in the list is called a record and is stored in a single row of the sheet. Each part of an entry—the name, company, or phone number in Figure 2-12—is called a *field* and is stored in a column. You therefore have a natural and common relationship between records and fields in a list and rows and columns in a sheet.

A list of related information organized in a consistent, logical manner is called a *database*. A database must be completely contained on a single sheet, but a single sheet can contain more than one database.

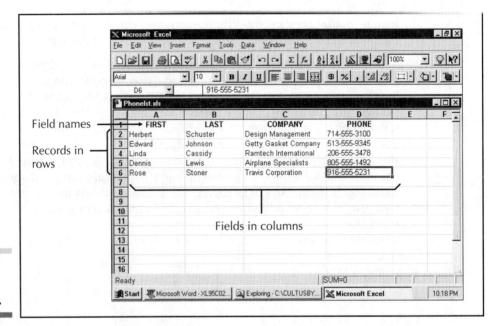

Field names

Records in
rows

Parts of a
database
Figure 2-12.

Rows and Records

Each row of a database, other than the first row, is a record representing a single entry. The first row of a database must contain the names of each field, one per column. These *field names* are used to identify the fields in commands and functions. All rows after the first in a database are data records. They can be blank or contain a divider line (a line across the database), for example, but they are still considered data records. A database can contain a maximum of 16,383 records (one less than the number of rows in a sheet).

Columns and Fields

Each column of a database is a field representing a common data element in all records. For example, the company name in Figure 2-12 is a field. Each field can contain a number, text, or a formula. A database can contain a maximum of 256 fields, one for every column in a sheet, but you cannot have two fields with the same field name in one database.

Using Databases

You can use a database any time you need a list of items. Examples of databases, in addition to the phone list, are stocks in a portfolio with dates and prices, parts of a machine with the part number and supplier, salespeople with their quotas and commissions, and products with their prices and margins.

Within Excel there are specific commands that let you manipulate databases. These commands are called *data commands* because they are all accessed through the Data menu shown here:

2

The options in the Data menu provide for sorting databases, selecting information from them based on filtering criteria, entering data into a database using a form, applying functions to a database such as summing, and rearranging a database in several ways. For example, you can sort the phone list by company, select stocks that are performing below your expectations, find the machine parts from a given supplier, and analyze the change in sales commissions that would result from changes in quotas. Database-related commands and functions are explored in Chapter 8.

Charts

If a picture is worth a thousand words, a chart is worth at least a thousand numbers. A chart allows you to give visual meaning to a set of numbers, to show the differences or similarities between them, and to show the patterns produced. Many people find that they absorb information faster and easier from charts and even that they see things in charts they do not see in the numbers that produce the charts.

An Excel chart is a pictorial representation of one or more groups of cells in a workbook. If you have a reference on a sheet that contains company sales by month, you can produce a line chart that would make it easy to show fluctuations in monthly sales. Given references for expenses and earnings by month, you can produce additional lines on the same chart and determine not only if they are going up or down, but also show how any trends relate to each other. Figure 2-13 shows such a line chart.

A Line chart
showing
financial
performance
Figure 2-13.

The Pie chart in Figure 2-14 shows the proportion each product line
contributes to total company sales by charting a reference containing the
sales by product. Given references containing sales by quarter for each of
four regions, the column chart shown in Figure 2-15 can also be produced.

Pie chart
showing
proportional
contribution
of each
product line
Figure 2-14.

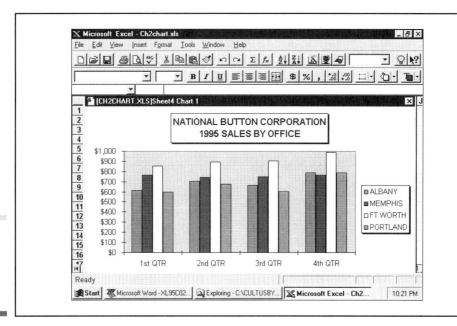

Column chart
showing
quarterly
regional sales
Figure 2-15.

Excel provides eight two-dimensional types of charts: Area, Bar, Column, Line, Pie, Radar, Scatter, and Doughnut; and six three-dimensional types of charts: Area, Bar, Column, Line, Pie, and Surface. There are also several alternatives for each type and several ways to combine two types. As a result you have many ways to chart information on a sheet.

To produce these charts, Excel provides the Chart Wizard to lead you step-by-step through the process, a unique set of menus, and a chart sheet or the option of embedding a chart on a regular sheet. You can select the type of chart you want to produce and identify the references in the workbook that will generate it. You can add titles and annotations, as well as specify the color and fonts to be used. The production of charts is discussed in detail in Chapter 7.

The Excel Environment

3

This chapter and the remainder of the book are written based on the assumption that you will follow along on your computer as you read. This process allows you to see for yourself what a keystroke does and how the screen looks as a result. Most people find that they learn much faster by doing while reading than by reading alone. To use Excel on your computer, you must first install Windows 95 and then Excel.

Excel's Screen and Menus

When you first start Excel, after a brief display of the Microsoft copyright message you'll see a blank sheet on your screen like the one shown in Figure 3-1. This screen contains two windows. On the outer perimeter of the screen is the Excel application window. This contains Excel's menus, the toolbars, the address of the currently active cell, the Formula bar, and the Status bar. Within the Excel window is a single workbook document window. The workbook window is the primary working area in Excel. The Excel application window may contain several document windows, as you saw in Chapter 2. The two primary windows, Excel and workbook, are discussed in the following sections.

The Workbook Window

Initially, Excel opens a single workbook window. As you saw in Chapter 2, you can open additional workbook windows as well, but you generally use only a single workbook window and open other windows only for special purposes.

The workbook window in which you are currently working is called the *active window*. If you have other windows open, they are not active until you click the mouse on them or choose a different window from the Window menu. You can tell which workbook is active because its Title bar and an active cell are highlighted. In Figure 3-2, Book1:3 is the active window.

A workbook window provides the area in which to enter numbers, text, and formulas in order to build what you want. The workbook's inherent structure—its rows, columns, and sheets—allows you to enter and organize your work easily.

Rows, Columns, and Sheets

The blank workbooks in Figures 3-1 and 3-2 show the row, column, and sheet nature of the workbook: the row and column headings are across the top and down the left side and the sheet names are across the bottom. This three-dimensional grid forms individual cells: the intersection of one row

Blank
workbook
screen
Figure 3-1.

and one column on one sheet. A cell is where you enter numbers, text, or a
formula. Only one cell at a time is active and available for entry or editing.

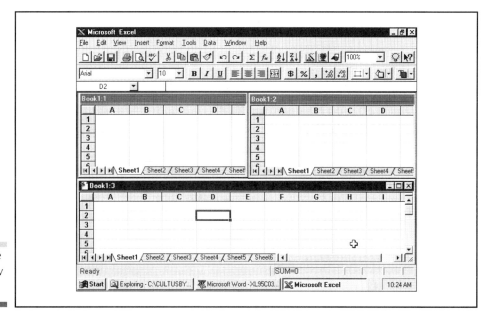

Book1:3 is the
active window
Figure 3-2.

3

You know which cell is active because it has a heavy border around it. In Figure 3-1, cell B3 on sheet 1 is active. This is the cell formed by the intersection of column B and row 3 on Sheet1. Cell D2 on Sheet3 in window Book1:3 is active in Figure 3-2. The address of the active cell can be seen in the upper-left corner of the spreadsheet, just under the toolbar, in the reference area.

You can make a different cell active either by clicking on it with the mouse (moving the mouse pointer to the new cell and pressing the mouse button) or by using the direction keys on the right side of your keyboard to move the active cell border to the new cell.

You can make a different sheet active by clicking on the *sheet tab* at the bottom of the window. Once on a different sheet, you can independently move the active cell where you want it. Often you will work independently on each sheet, but you can make several sheets active at one time and have entries that you make on one sheet appear on all the active sheets, as you will see in Chapters 4 and 5.

By clicking on the scroll bars or dragging the scroll boxes on the right and bottom of the workbook window, or by using the direction keys, you can look at and work on other areas of the active sheet. Compared to Excel's total potential area, the area actually displayed on your screen is quite small—15 or 16 out of 16,384 rows and 9 out of 256 columns (the number of rows and columns depends on your monitor and graphics card). Of course, most applications in Excel also use only a small amount of the total area, but often are larger than what you initially see on the screen.

The Excel Window

The default Excel window contains six bars—five at the top and one at the bottom. The top two bars, the Title bar and the Menu bar, are common to all Windows applications. The other four bars—two toolbars, the Formula bar, and the Status bar—are used by Excel and some other programs. The Title bar is standard throughout Windows applications, with only the name it contains ever changing. The Menu bar, while consistent in layout with other Windows programs, has a unique set of menus.

The Menu Bar

The Excel Menu bar includes eight Excel menus and the standard Windows Control and Help menus. Since you looked at Control and Help in Chapter 1 and Help again in Chapter 2, only the eight Excel menus are reviewed here.

Remember that to open a menu you can click on the menu name with the mouse. Also, you can press ALT, F10, or / to activate the Menu bar and then either type the underlined letter in the menu name or move the highlight to the menu name with the direction keys and press ENTER. With a menu open you can look at another menu, either by clicking on the menu name or by using the direction keys to move to the other menu. If you want to close a menu without choosing an option, press ESC.

File Menu The File menu provides the means of creating new workbooks, opening existing workbooks and other files stored on disk, and closing and saving workbooks or saving all open files. You can view a properties dialog box for the active workbook and determine if you want the workbook shared. The File menu also allows you to set up the page you will print, establish or clear an area of the sheet to print, look at a preview of what you are going to print, and print some or all of a workbook. If you are connected to a network and have a mail system, you can access it through the File menu Send option or add a routing slip to a workbook that distributes it to mailboxes on the network. You can also send files to a Microsoft Exchange folder for inclusion in a mail message. Near the bottom, the File menu provides a list of the last four files you have used. If you want to open one of these files, simply click on the one you want or press its number on the keyboard. Lastly, the File menu provides a way to exit Excel.

3

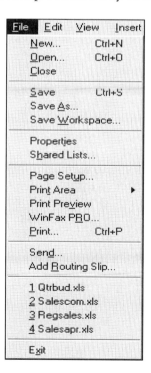

Edit Menu   You use the Edit menu to undo or repeat the last thing you did and to copy, move, clear (delete), or fill the contents of a cell or a group of cells. With this menu you can also delete the cells themselves as well as rows, columns, and sheets. You can move and copy sheets, search and replace cell contents, and go to a named cell or reference. Finally, if you bring objects into Excel, such as graphics or text that you have created in other applications, the Edit menu allows you to display and update the links between the objects and their original applications and to activate the original application from within Excel by selecting the object and choosing the Object option.

View Menu   The View menu is a means for controlling how your screen looks. It allows you to turn on or off the Formula and Status bars, and to select the toolbars you want to display. It provides access to the View Manager add-in program that allows you to save a particular screen setup, including print settings and hidden rows and columns. Also, the View menu allows you to display only the Excel menu and the workbook document window, getting rid of all other bars and giving you the maximum display area for a sheet. Finally, the View menu allows you to change the magnification of the workbook window, from very small cells to very large ones.

Insert Menu   The Insert menu is used to add (insert) cells, rows, columns, sheets, and chart and macro pages to a workbook. You can also insert a page break; add functions through the Function Wizard; create, use, and delete reference names; add notes to cells; and insert pictures, maps, and other objects created outside of Excel.

Format Menu   Through the Format menu you determine how a cell entry looks. If it contains a number, you can format it as dollars or percentages (with or without commas) and set the number of decimal places. Also, formatting for special numbers such as ZIP code, phone, and social security numbers is available. You can align both text and numbers to the left, right, or center in a cell; determine the font and style; place a border around or shade them; and protect a cell from being overwritten. Also, you can determine the size, fit, and hidden status of rows and columns and the name of a sheet and whether it is hidden.

The Format menu's AutoFormat option provides automatic formatting for a selected range. The AutoFormat option provides 16 formatting styles within 7 categories: Simple, Classic, Financial, Accounting, Colorful, List, and 3-D Effects. Each style has an example of how it will look. Autoformatting is discussed further in Chapter 6. With the Format menu, you can define your own style, including number format, font, alignment, type of border and patterns, and the cell protection status. Finally, the Format menu allows you to determine the relative placement of objects on a sheet.

Tools Menu   The Tools menu provides access to the many add-ins that come with Excel. These include:

♦   A spelling checker

♦   An auditing package

♦   Automatic spelling correction of commonly used words

♦   The Goal Seek, Scenarios, and Solver analysis packages

♦   A means of accessing other add-ins

The Tools menu also allows you to turn on or off protection for either a workbook or a single sheet and to record and run macros or assign a macro to a tool. (Macros, you remember, are Excel commands that have been stored in a workbook.) Finally, the Tools menu Options option lets you customize Excel as you wish. Among the settings you can customize are the standard font, the number of sheets in a new workbook, the kind of menus, the type of calculation, whether or not to allow cell drag and drop, and how you want the screen to look.

Drag and drop allows you to copy and move the active cell contents with a mouse, without using a menu. When drag and drop is activated, the lower-right corner of the active cell will contain a small box. Point on the small box with the mouse pointer and the pointer will change like this:

3

As you drag the small box, the contents of the cell are *copied* to adjacent rows or columns, in what is known as a *fill* operation. If you drag the active cell border instead of the small box while drag and drop is activated, you *move* the contents of the active cell to any other cell. Finally, if you press and hold CTRL while dragging the active cell border, you *copy* the contents of the active cell to any other cell.

Data Menu   The Data menu is used to sort a list on a sheet, to select information from a list based on filtering criteria, to enter data into a database using a form, and to apply functions such as summing to a database. Also, for existing lists, you can create a table, consolidate and group data ranges on one or multiple sheets, and interactively transform the layout of data with PivotTables.

Window Menu   The Window menu allows you to open another window for the active workbook, to arrange all open windows so they can be seen on the screen, and to hide or unhide a window. Additionally, you can split a sheet into different size horizontal and vertical panes and freeze a pane so that, for example, column headings remain in place while the rest of the sheet is scrolled. Finally, you can select among open windows.

Dialog Boxes   Menu options with an ellipsis (...) after them require that after choosing the option you enter additional information or choose from additional options. For example, you may have to enter the name of a file to save or choose the type of cell alignment you want. In these situations, a dialog box opens and asks you for more information or to make a further choice. As you saw in Chapter 1, a dialog box employs one or more devices for collecting information. Many of the devices are illustrated in the Options dialog box shown in Figure 3-3. The Options dialog box also shows two devices you may not have seen before: across the top of the dialog box is a

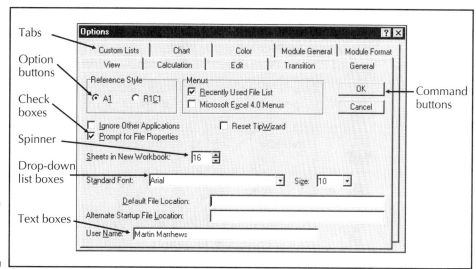

Tabs

Option
buttons

Check
boxes

Spinner

Drop-down
list boxes

Text boxes

Command
buttons

Options
dialog box
Figure 3-3.

3

set of *tabs* that, when you click on them, allow you to select different
options, and in the middle of the dialog box is a *spinner* that allows you to
increase or decrease a number by clicking on either the up or down arrow.

You will have many opportunities in the chapters that follow to become
more familiar with Excel's menus and their related dialog boxes.

Toolbars
The third and fourth bars from the top, just under the Menu bar, are
toolbars. The Standard toolbar is on top and the Formatting toolbar is below,
as shown here:

A toolbar provides a number of tools and buttons to quickly do tasks that would
take several steps with the menus, or could not be done at all. Table 3-1 lists the
tools on the Standard toolbar. Table 3-2 lists the tools on the Formatting
toolbar. A toolbar is used only with a mouse, so if you don't have a mouse, you
can turn off (Hide) the two default toolbars with the View Toolbars option.

There are 13 possible toolbars in Excel 7 when first installed, but you can
add your own. These and their purposes are summarized in Table 3-3.

You can display one, none, or multiple toolbars, as you choose. To select a
toolbar other than one of the two initial ones, choose Toolbars from the
View menu; the Toolbars dialog box will appear. Alternatively, you can open
the Toolbars popup menu by clicking on a toolbar with your right mouse

Standard Toolbar		
Tool	**Description**	**Purpose**
	New Workbook	Creates a new workbook
	Open File	Displays the Open File dialog box
	Save File	Saves the active workbook
	Print	Prints selected sheets from the active workbook
	Print Preview	Displays the Print Preview window, which shows how each page will look when printed
	Spelling	Checks the spelling in documents
	Cut	Removes a selected range or object and places it on the Clipboard
	Copy	Copies a selected range or object and places it to the Clipboard
	Paste	Pastes the contents of the Clipboard to a selected location
	Format Painter	Pastes only the format of a selected range
	Undo	Reverses the last action
	Repeat	Repeats the last action
	AutoSum	Creates a SUM function in the active cell with a reference to the contiguous range of numbers (either in the column above or in the row to the left)
	Function Wizard	Assists you in using functions
	Sort Ascending	Sorts a list from lowest to highest value (A to Z) in the column with the active cell
	Sort Descending	Sorts a list from highest to lowest value (Z to A) in the column with the active cell

Tools on the Standard Toolbar
Table 3-1.

Standard Toolbar		
	ChartWizard	Assists you in creating charts
	Map	Allows you to embed a graphic map and place it anywhere on the sheet
	Drawing	Displays the Drawing toolbar
100%	Zoom Control	Changes the scale so you can see smaller or larger areas of the sheet
	TipWizard	Assists you with tips for using Excel more efficiently
	Help	Changes the mouse pointer to a question mark. Clicking with the question mark on a command or screen area displays context-sensitive help

Tools on the Standard Toolbar (*continued*)
Table 3-1.

Formatting Toolbar		
Tool	**Description**	**Purpose**
Arial	Font	Applies a font to selected cells
10	Size	Selects the size for the selected font
B I U	Bold, Italic, and Underlined	Applies and removes their respective type styles
	Alignment	Applies left, center, and right alignment, respectively, to selected cells
	Center Across Columns	Horizontally centers text in the leftmost cell across selected columns
$	Currency Style	Applies the accounting style to the selected cells
	Percent Style	Applies the default percent style to the selected cells
,	Comma Style	Applies the default comma style to the selected cells

Formatting Toolbar
Table 3-2.

Formatting Toolbar		
Tool	**Description**	**Purpose**
+.0 .00	Increase Decimal	Increases the number of decimal places in the selected cells by one when clicked on
.00 +.0	Decrease Decimal	Decreases the number of decimal places in the selected cells by one when clicked on
	Borders	Applies a border style to the selected cells
	Color	Applies a color to selected cells or objects
	Font Color	Applies a color to the characters in the selected cells

Formatting
Toolbar
(*continued*)
Table 3-2.

Toolbar	Purpose
Auditing	Find errors, track cell relationships, and attach notes to cells
Chart	Create and format charts
Drawing	Create lines, rectangles, ellipses, arcs, and arrows, and add text
Formatting	Format cells, cell contents, and other objects
Forms	Add controls to sheets and charts to allow interaction with user
Full Screen	Expand the document window to take up all of the screen except for the Menu bar
Microsoft	Switch between Excel and other Microsoft programs such as Word
Query and Pivot	Retrieve and analyze both Excel data and external data
Standard	Access the most frequently used commands, like new, open, save, and print
Stop Recording	Stop macro recording
TipWizard	Display tips on current operations
Visual Basic	Insert a new Visual Basic module, create menus, and record and debug macros
Workgroup	Find Excel files, share them within a workgroup, and work with Scenarios

The Default
Toolbars for
Excel 7
Table 3-3.

button. The dialog box lists several of the available toolbars and provides a button to create customized toolbars.

The Customize dialog box provides a list of tool categories and displays the tools that are associated with each category. You can drag individual tools to an existing toolbar to add to it or to almost anywhere on the screen to create a new toolbar. Microsoft Excel provides over 210 predefined tools and 28 that you can define. All of these tools are displayed in the Customize dialog box.

Toolbars can be moved, sized, and arranged to suit your individual needs. They provide a fast and flexible means to make working in Excel as efficient as possible.

The Formula Bar

3

Beneath the toolbars is the Formula bar, which is shown in Figure 3-4. On the left side of the Formula bar is the *reference area,* which contains the address of the currently active cell on the sheet. For example, when the cell address C10 is displayed, this tells you that the currently active cell is in the third column (column C) and the tenth row. If you give cell C10 the name Sales_Qtr1, then Sales_Qtr1 will appear in the reference area while cell C10 is the active cell.

If cell C10 is currently the active cell and you want to name it, you simply click in the reference area and type the name. This is much simpler than using the Name option of the Insert menu. You can also use the reference area to move the active cell to a particular location by typing the cell address in the reference area and pressing ENTER. On the right of the reference area is a drop-down arrow that, when you click on it, opens a list of reference names in the current workbook like this:

Arial		10		**B**	*I*	U
Sales_Qtr1	▼			=SUM(C3:C9)		

		B	C	D
Sales				
Sales_Qtr1				
Sales_Qtr2				
Sales_Qtr3				
Sales_Qtr4				
2			Qtr 1	Qtr 2
3		Seattle	45	86
4		Everett	67	86
5		Kent	3	67
6		Bellevue	5	25
7		Kirkland	62	63
8		Renton	14	56
9		Edmonds	58	92
10		Total	254	475

Current cell reference
Reference name drop-down list
Cancel box
Function Wizard
Insertion point

B2 | ✕ | ✓ | *fx* | =SUM(C3:C9)

Reference area
Enter box
Cell contents
Edit area

Formula bar
Figure 3-4.

By opening the list of names and clicking on a name, you will move the active cell to the cell referenced by the name.

While you are in the process of selecting a range of cells—C3:E4, for example—the reference area tells you the number of rows and columns being selected—2RX3C in the example, for 2 rows by 3 columns. The reference area also has some specialized uses with charts and during several operations. These are discussed later in this book with the related topics.

On the right side of the Formula bar is the *edit area,* where you enter and edit text, numbers, and formulas for the active cell. If you are entering or editing a cell's contents, three boxes appear to the right of the reference area: the Cancel box with an "X" in it, the Enter box with a check mark in it, and the Function Wizard tool. Clicking on the Cancel box cancels any changes you made in the edit area and returns a cell's original contents. The Cancel box is similar to pressing ESC. Clicking on the Enter box is like pressing ENTER. Doing so transfers the edited contents of the edit area to the active cell. The Function Wizard tool is used to place a function in the edit area.

When you begin typing in an empty cell, the letters or numbers that you type go into both the cell itself and the edit area of the Formula bar. In many instances the cell is not wide enough to display all of what you type, but the edit area expands to the maximum 255 characters a cell can hold. After you complete the entry and press ENTER, the edit area still displays the cell's contents. If you move to another cell and then come back, the edit area again displays the cell's contents.

If you want to change or edit the contents of a cell, you do so in the edit area of the Formula bar. First make the cell you want to edit active by clicking on it or by using the direction keys. You then click on the Formula bar or press the F2 function key to activate the edit area. While you are entering or editing a cell's contents, a vertical line appears in the edit area, as shown in Figure 3-4. You'll remember from Chapter 1 that this line is called the insertion point. Characters you type, or a function if you add one, are added to the immediate left of the insertion point. When the mouse pointer is in the edit area, it becomes an I-beam. The I-beam is thin enough to be inserted between characters in the edit area. By placing the I-beam between two characters and clicking, you move the insertion point to where you clicked. You can then insert new characters between existing characters.

While you are making an entry, what you see in the edit area and what you see in the cell are the same. Once you complete a formula entry, the formula is displayed in the edit area, while the cell displays the value resulting from the formula. If the entry is a number or text, it is displayed in both the Formula bar and the cell. Figure 3-4 shows a formula in the edit area.

The Status Bar

3

The Status bar, at the bottom of the Excel window, displays messages on the left and up to five keyboard indicators on the right, as shown here:

Ready		SUM=0		ADD CAPS NUM FIX

Message Area   The message area has several uses that are determined by what you are doing. If you highlight a menu name or a menu option, the message area displays a brief description of the menu or option. If you point on a tool in a toolbar, the message area displays an explanation of what the tool does. When you are using a dialog box or have an alert message on the screen, the message area tells you how to get help. At other times, the message area serves as a mode indicator that tells you what Excel is doing. The most common mode is Ready, meaning that Excel is ready for you to make an entry or use a menu. The other modes are shown with their meanings in the following table:

Mode	Meaning
Calculate	With manual calculation, this indicates that a change has been made to the workbook and it needs to be recalculated.
Circular	A circular reference has been detected where, through whatever route, a cell is referencing itself. One of the cells in the circular path will be identified.
Edit	An entry is being edited in the Formula bar.
Enter	Data is being entered into the active cell.
Filter	A database is being filtered.

Mode	Meaning
Point	You are being asked to highlight a cell or group of cells for use in a formula.
Ready	Excel is ready for a command or entry.
Recording	The macro recorder is recording what you are doing with Excel.

Keyboard Indicators   The keyboard indicators on the right of the Status bar tell you that a certain key has been pressed or that a certain condition exists. The status indicators and their meanings are as follows:

Indicator	Meaning
SUM=	The AutoCalculate feature is providing the sum of selected cells.
ADD	The Add key, SHIFT-F8, has been pressed to make multiple selections.
CAPS	CAPS LOCK has been pressed for uppercase letters.
EXT	The Extend key, F8, has been pressed to extend a selection.
NUM	The NUM LOCK key has been pressed, enabling the numeric keypad to be used for the entry of numbers.
FIX	The Fixed Decimal option has been chosen from Tools Options Edit. This adds a fixed number of decimal places on all numeric entries, similar to an adding machine.

Excel's Use of the Keyboard

Between the mouse and the screen, you can accomplish a lot in Excel. Eventually, though, you will need to use the keyboard, if for no other reason than to enter the text and numbers that represent the body of your work. As you are typing on the keyboard, you may find it easier to also use the keyboard to accomplish other tasks that you could also accomplish with the mouse. Also, there are some keyboard shortcuts that are just plain faster than the alternatives. This section covers how you can use the keyboard for uses other than typing text and numbers.

Most keyboards can be divided into three areas. On the left or along the top is a set of function keys, F1 through F10 or F12. You use these keys to give Excel commands, such as to recalculate the workbook or display a help screen. In the center of all keyboards are the normal typewriter keys, and on the far right of most keyboards is a set of direction keys, either superimposed on or separate from the numerical keypad. The direction keys can move the active cell around the sheet and the highlight bar down a menu. These three regions of the keyboard are discussed in the following sections.

Direction Keys

Eight keys comprise the direction keys: the four arrow keys DOWN ARROW, LEFT ARROW, RIGHT ARROW, and UP ARROW plus HOME, END, PG UP, and PG DN. These keys, either alone or in combination with CTRL and SHIFT on the typewriter keyboard, can move you quickly and easily anywhere on the sheet. Also, the same keys can move you within the menus and dialog boxes and within the Formula bar for cell editing. With mouse capability, the use of the direction keys is not as important as it would otherwise be. Nevertheless it is important to understand how the direction keys can be used.

3

The direction keys have the three-dimensional task of moving the active cell up or down a column, left or right along a row, and back and forth through the sheets. Excel has ways to do this one cell at a time, one screen at a time, to the beginning or end of contiguously occupied cells, or to the first or last cell in the active sheet.

Using Direction Keys in a Workbook

The easiest way to learn about the direction keys is to use them. Try them now. Your computer should be turned on, Excel should be loaded, and you should be looking at the blank workbook screen shown in Figure 3-1, with cell A1 selected as the active cell. If your Scroll Lock light is on, press SCROLL LOCK to turn it off.

Moving One Cell at a Time   The simplest way to move about a single sheet is to go from cell to cell. The four arrow keys perform this task, as shown with the following instructions:

1. Press RIGHT ARROW. The active cell moves one cell to the right, to cell B1.
2. Press DOWN ARROW. The active cell moves down one cell, to cell B2.
3. Press LEFT ARROW. The active cell moves one cell to the left, to cell A2.
4. Press UP ARROW. The active cell moves up one cell, to cell A1—where you started from.

The four arrow keys are the most frequently used of the direction keys. Their function is to move you one cell in any direction, as you saw in the one-cell square you just made.

Moving One Screen at a Time   Moving one cell at a time can be slow if you have very far to go. The next set of direction keys moves you a screen at a time. (Depending on the type of display and display adapter you have and the mode you are running them in, one "screen" may be different than that described here—it may be larger or smaller.) Make a larger square now with these keys.

1. Press PG DN. The active cell and the portion of the sheet shown in the window move down one window-height to the first cell in column A beyond that originally shown—cell A17 (depending on the type of monitor you have and how your screen is set up, you may go to a different row).

2. Press ALT-PG DN (press and hold ALT while pressing PG DN). The active cell and the portion of the sheet shown in the window move to the right one window-width to the first cell in row 17—cell J17 (again, yours may be different).

3. Press PG UP. The active cell and the portion of the sheet shown in the window move up one window-height to cell J1.

4. Press ALT-PG UP (press and hold ALT while pressing PG UP). The active cell and the portion of the workbook shown in the window move to the left one window-width to cell A1.

You have completed another square, one window high and one window wide. PG DN and PG UP are used frequently, but ALT-PG DN and ALT-PG UP are often forgotten.

Moving Around the Periphery of the Active Sheet   The set of keystrokes used to move around the periphery of the active sheet requires that you first enter some information on the sheet to establish what is "active." Simply type the information in one cell using the typewriter keyboard and then press one of the arrow keys to go to the next cell. You can then use a set of direction keys to move around the periphery of the sheet. Try that now.

1. Type **a** and press RIGHT ARROW. The letter "a" is placed in cell A1, and the active cell moves to B1.

2. Do the *combination* of typing **a** and pressing RIGHT ARROW six more times. The final active cell is H1.

3. Type **a** and press DOWN ARROW. The letter "a" is placed in cell H1, and the active cell moves to H2.

4. Do the *combination* of typing **a** and pressing DOWN ARROW nine more times. The final active cell is H11. Your screen should look like Figure 3-5. Now use the direction keys to jump around the information you just entered.

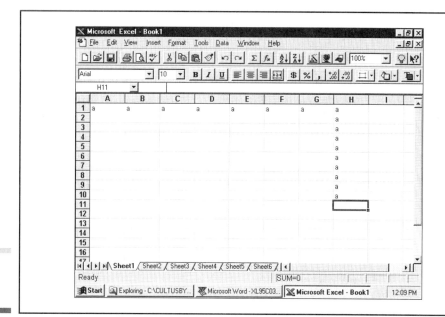

Screen after
entries
Figure 3-5.

5. Press HOME. The active cell jumps to cell A11—the cell on the far left of the current active area.

6. Press UP ARROW, CTRL, and RIGHT ARROW. The active cell jumps to H10—the cell on the far right of the current active area.

7. Press CTRL-UP ARROW. The active cell jumps to cell H1—the cell at the top of the active area.

8. Press CTRL-LEFT ARROW. The active cell jumps to cell A1—the far left again.

9. Press CTRL-RIGHT ARROW. The active cell jumps to cell H1—the far right again.

10. Press CTRL-DOWN ARROW. The active cell jumps to cell H10—the bottom again.

11. Press CTRL-HOME. The active cell jumps to cell A1.

12. Press CTRL-END. The active cell jumps to cell H10.

The CTRL plus direction key combinations are very powerful and extremely useful. You will use them often if you do not have a mouse. You can accomplish the same movement around the periphery of the active area with the END key. Try that next.

1. Press END-UP ARROW. The active cell jumps to cell H1.

2. Press END-LEFT ARROW. The active cell jumps to cell A1.

3. Press END-RIGHT ARROW. The active cell jumps to cell H1.

4. Press END-DOWN ARROW. The active cell jumps to cell H10.

5. Press CTRL-HOME. The active cell jumps to cell A1.

6. Press END-HOME. The active cell jumps to cell H10.

7. Press CTRL-HOME to return to cell A1.

You can see that the functions performed with END and a direction key almost duplicate those performed with CTRL and a direction key. The two exceptions are END-HOME, which has the opposite effect from CTRL-HOME, and END-END, which doesn't exist.

Moving One Sheet at a Time   Excel provides only two keys to move you across sheets. These are CTRL-PG DN and CTRL-PG UP to move you *down* through the stack of sheets (from Sheet1 to Sheet2) and back up again. Try these on your own.

Direction Key Summary

The following table summarizes the direction keys.

Key	Moves the Active Cell
LEFT ARROW or RIGHT ARROW	Right or left one column.
UP ARROW or DOWN ARROW	Up or down one row.
PG UP or PG DN	Up or down one window-height.
ALT-PG DN or ALT-PG UP	Right or left one window-width.
CTRL-UP ARROW or CTRL-DOWN ARROW	Up or down to the first intersection of blank and nonblank cells.
CTRL-RIGHT ARROW or CTRL-LEFT ARROW	Right or left to the first intersection of blank and nonblank cells.
HOME	Left to column A in the row with the active cell.
END	Turns on end mode. When a direction key is next pressed, the active cell moves to the last occupied cell in the direction of the arrow.
CTRL-HOME	Up and/or to the left to cell A1.

Key	Moves the Active Cell
CTRL-END	Down and/or to the right to the lowest and rightmost occupied cell.
END-HOME	Down and/or to the right to the lowest and rightmost occupied cell.
CTRL-PG DN	Down one sheet (from Sheet1 to Sheet2).
CTRL-PG UP	Up one sheet (from Sheet2 to Sheet1).

Function Keys

The function keys F1 through F10 or F12 are located on the top or left of most keyboards. With function keys, you can give Excel special commands using one or several keystrokes (when you press the key itself or in combination with SHIFT, CTRL, or ALT). Many of the commands performed by the function keys are used only in certain circumstances and could not be easily demonstrated here. Try several that can be easily demonstrated now with the instructions that follow. You will use many of the others later in the book. Following the instructions is a table that summarizes each function key.

3

Using Function Keys

The following instructions assume that you are picking up where you left off in the previous section. The active cell is A1, and the sheet is the one in which you entered the "a"s. Excel should be in Ready mode. Also, from your previous work, cell A1 should contain the letter "a." If you do not have an "a" in A1, type it now and press ENTER.

1. Press F1 (Help). A Help window opens with the Help Topics dialog box shown in Figure 3-6. From this window you can select subjects on which to get help.

2. Click on the Help dialog box Close or Cancel button or press ALT-SPACEBAR and then C to return to the sheet. A1 is still the active cell.

3. Press F2 (Edit). The edit area of the Formula bar becomes activated to edit cell A1. Also, an insertion point appears just to the right of the letter "a" in the cell.

4. Press BACKSPACE. The "a" is removed.

5. Type **b** and press ENTER. Excel is returned to Ready mode, and "b" replaces "a" in cell A1.

6. Press ALT-BACKSPACE (Undo). The contents of cell A1 are again "a."

Excel Help
Topics dialog
box
Figure 3-6.

7. Press F5 (Goto). A dialog box appears, asking for the address to jump to.

8. Type **e14** and press ENTER. The active cell jumps to cell E14.

9. Press CTRL-HOME. The active cell returns to cell A1.

10. Press F12 (Save As) or ALT-F2 if you have only ten function keys. The File Save As dialog box opens.

11. Type **ch3** (for Chapter 3) and press ENTER to save the active workbook with the filename CH3.XLS (the .XLS extension is automatically added by Excel).

12. Press ESC to omit adding any summary information in the Properties dialog box.

13. Press SHIFT-F11 (New Sheet) or ALT-SHIFT-F1 if you have only ten function keys. A new sheet appears (probably Sheet17).

Both F2 (Edit) and F5 (Goto) will get increasingly heavy use as you learn Excel. Also useful, although not a function key, is ALT-BACKSPACE (Undo). The Undo command reverses many commands if they were the last thing you did. You can even undo an Undo command. Note that Undo *cannot* undo File commands, such as saving a file on top of another.

Several function keys are shortcut keys for menu options. For example, F3 is the Insert menu's Name option Paste command and F12 is the File menu's Save As option.

Function Key Summary

Table 3-4 provides a summary of the function performed by each function key. The keys are discussed further in later sections of this book dealing with the particular subject to which they apply. For example, F11 (New Chart) is covered in the discussion on charting in Chapter 7.

3

Key	Name	Function
F1	Help	Opens a help window
SHIFT-F1		Displays context-sensitive help
ALT-F1	New	Creates a new chart
ALT-SHIFT-F1		Inserts a new sheet
ALT-CTRL-F1		Creates a new Excel 4 macro sheet
F2	Edit	Activates the Formula bar for editing
SHIFT-F2	Note	Allows entering, editing, or deleting a note that is to be attached to the active cell
CTRL-F2	Info	Displays a window containing information about the active cell
ALT-F2	Save	Opens the File Save As dialog box
ALT-SHIFT-F2		Saves the active document
ALT-CTRL-F2		Opens the File Open dialog box
ALT-CTRL-SHIFT-F2		Opens the File Print dialog box
F3	Name	Opens the Paste Name dialog box
SHIFT-F3		Opens the Function Wizard dialog box
CTRL-F3		Opens the Define Name dialog box
CTRL-SHIFT-F3		Opens the Create Name dialog box
F4	Absolute	While editing, makes a cell address or reference name absolute, mixed, or relative
F4		When not editing, repeats the last action taken
CTRL-F4	Close	Closes the active document window
ALT-F4		Closes the application window (Excel)
F5	Goto	Moves the active cell to the cell address, reference name, or file entered

A Summary of Function Keys and the Functions They Perform

Table 3-4.

Key	Name	Function
SHIFT-F5	Find	Opens the Edit Find dialog box
CTRL-F5	Restore	Restores the size of the active document window
F6	Pane	Moves the active cell clockwise to the next pane
SHIFT-F6		Moves the active cell counterclockwise to the previous pane
CTRL-F6	Window	Moves the active cell to the next document window
CTRL-SHIFT-F6		Moves the active cell to the previous document window
F7		Checks spelling
CTRL-F7	Move	Sets up the active document window to be moved with the direction keys
F8	Extend	Toggles the extension of the current selection
SHIFT-F8	Add	Allows adding a second selection to the current selection
CTRL-F8	Size	Sets up the active document window to be sized with the direction keys
F9	Calculate	Recalculates all open documents
SHIFT-F9		Recalculates the active sheet
CTRL-F9	Minimize	Minimizes the active workbook
F10	Menu	Activates the menu bar
SHIFT-F10		Displays the shortcut menu for the active cell
CTRL-F10	Maximize	Maximizes the active workbook
F11	New	Creates a new chart sheet
SHIFT-F11		Creates a new sheet
CTRL-F11		Creates a new Excel 4 macro sheet
F12	Save	Opens the File Save dialog box
SHIFT-F12		Saves the active document
CTRL-F12	Open	Opens the File Open dialog box
CTRL-SHIFT-F12	Print	Opens the File Print dialog box

A Summary of Function Keys and the Functions They Perform *(continued)*

Table 3-4.

Quitting Excel

You are done with Excel for this chapter. Use the following instructions to leave it:

1. Click on the Close button in the upper-right corner of the Excel program window. (From the keyboard, press ALT-F4.)

2. Click on No (or press N) to not save the file again. You will return to the desktop or any other active program you have running.

3. Click on the Start button and choose Shut Down.

4. If you desire, click on Yes to shut down your computer and turn it off when prompted.

3

Entering and Editing Information

4

In several examples in Chapter 3, you practiced entering and editing information. Entering text and numbers is a simple matter of typing what you want in each cell. You can edit as you type or, after you have completed the entry, you can come back and edit it. These operations are more subtle than they first appear, however, and their considerable power demands further study.

Typing on a Sheet

All information that you type on a sheet is stored in cells. While there are a lot of cells, each cell can hold only 255 characters. The normal practice is to place only a single number or a short text string (usually much smaller than 255 characters) in a cell and to spread most of the information over many cells, using the row and column structure to organize it.

A cell on a sheet can hold either a number or text (which can be both numbers and letters), but not both. You therefore must decide what a cell will contain before you make an entry. If you decide an entry is text, you can then decide if it will be aligned to the left, right, or center in the cell. If an entry is a number, you can determine not only the method of alignment but also the type of format, such as numbers as dollars, percentages, dates, ZIP codes, or phone and social security numbers. You can also determine the font, size, and style of type and whether an entry has a border around it. Finally, when you complete an entry and determine what you want to do next, you can move the active cell in order to accomplish your purpose.

Entering Text Versus Numbers

Whether your entry is considered a number entry (including dates, times, and formulas) or a text entry (letters as well as numbers) depends on the characters you type and the context in which they appear. If your entry contains only numbers or is in combination with these numeric symbols

$$. , ( ) \% \$ E e / :$$

then the entry is a number. If the entry contains anything other than a number or numeric symbol, or the symbols are not in the proper context, the entry is text. For example, if you start an entry with the letter "E," Excel will interpret the entry as text, whereas "1.25E + 2" will be considered a number since the letter "E," in this context, is a numeric scientific notation symbol.

General Alignment

When Excel recognizes that text is being typed, it automatically left-aligns the text in the cell (meaning that it pushes text up against the left side of the cell). When you enter a number, Excel automatically right-aligns it in the cell (pushes it up against the right side). This default alignment—left-aligned text and right-aligned numbers—is called *general alignment.* General alignment also aligns logical values (TRUE or FALSE) and error values (#NUM!, for example) in the center of a cell. With the Format menu's Cells option, or the popup menu Format Cells option, or the Formatting toolbar, you can align text, numbers, and logical or error values to the left, in the center, or to the right, as you choose. You can also change the horizontal or vertical alignment of your cell contents or even change the orientation of how your data is displayed.

Figure 4-1 shows some of the various types of alignment.

Typing Text

Try entering some text now, following these instructions:

1. Load Windows and Excel. A blank workbook should appear on the screen. (If you still have the work you did in Chapter 3 on your screen, click on the workbook's Close button to close the workbook. Then, from the File menu choose New, ensure the Workbook icon is selected, and click on OK to create a new workbook.)

2. As shown in Figure 4-1, you'll want to have the Standard and Formatting toolbars displayed on the screen as well as the Status bar.

   If your screen looks different from Figure 4-1, click on the View menu and make sure that there are check marks beside Formula bar and Status

4

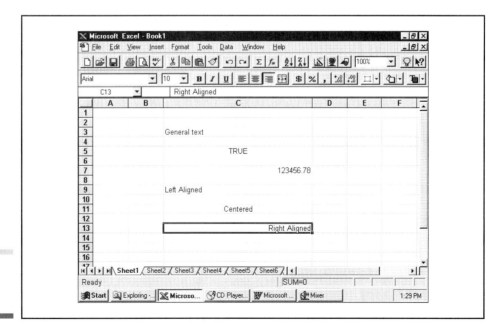

Types of alignment
Figure 4-1.

bar. If not, click on these options to place a check mark beside them. Then choose Toolbars (also on the View menu) to open the dialog box and, if they are not already checked, click on both the Standard and Formatting options to display both of these toolbars. Then click on OK.

3. In cell A1, type **This is some text**. As you type, you will see the letters go into the edit area of the Formula bar as well as into cell A1. If you make a mistake, press BACKSPACE to correct it. The top-left corner of your screen should look like this:

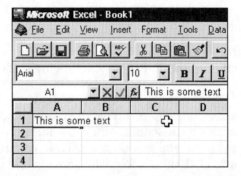

You will notice that the text in A1 spills over into cell B1. Also notice whether the blinking line, which is the insertion point where new text will be entered, is in the cell or the edit area. The default is for it to be in the cell, so that is probably where you'll see it. If not, you will see in the following step how to change the position of the insertion point.

4. Press ENTER or click on the Enter box (the check mark) in the Formula bar. The edit area is deactivated (the insertion point, Cancel box, Enter box, and Function Wizard disappear). Also, the text in A1 adjusts itself so you can see it all, although it does not fit completely in a single cell and seems to occupy cell B1 as well. The active cell remains in A1. (If your pointer moves to A2, you'll see why in the following step, as well as how to change it.)

The choice of whether you type text into the cell or the edit area is set in the Tools menu. You will set that next.

5. Click on the Tools menu, then click on Options near the bottom of the menu, and again on the Edit tab. You will see the dialog box in Figure 4-2.

The first option, Edit Directly in Cell, controls whether your editing changes will be entered into the active cell or into the edit area located in the Formula Bar. The default is to edit directly in the cell and that option should be checked. If it is not, click on it to place a check mark next to the option.

The Edit tab in
the Options
dialog box
Figure 4-2.

4

Another option that you will be using is Move Selection after Enter. This controls whether the active cell moves to the cell below, above, left, or right of the current cell after ENTER is pressed, or whether the active cell remains where it is. The default is to move the active cell to the cell below it. You'll want to turn that option off so that the active cell will stay where it is. (There are other ways to immediately move to another cell with one keystroke, as you will see in a moment, and ENTER is the only way to complete an entry and stay in the cell.) If the Move Selection after Enter option contains a check mark next to it, click on it to remove it.

6. After you have verified that the Edit Directly in Cell option is checked and that the Move Selection after Enter option is not checked, click on OK to return to the sheet.

   You may also have observed that the text in A1 is left-aligned, unless your alignment default has been changed. You did not align it; it is left-aligned because of Excel's general alignment default. Look at the various types of alignment next and see how you can change them.

7. If necessary, move the active cell to A2 by pressing DOWN ARROW on the right side of your keyboard.

8. Type **left** and press RIGHT ARROW. The word "left" is left-aligned in cell A2, and the active cell moves to B2. Notice how you completed the entry and moved to the next cell in one keystroke as promised. Arrow keys are used as movement keys, and are a preferred alternative to ENTER.

9. Type **right** and press ENTER. The word "right" also is left-aligned in B2.

10. To experiment with aligning text, click on Format in the Menu bar and then on the Cells option.

11. Click on the Alignment tab and the Alignment dialog box opens, as shown in Figure 4-3.

12. Click on Right in the Horizontal list and then click on OK to close the dialog box. The word "right" in cell B2 is right-aligned. Press RIGHT ARROW to move to C2.

13. Type **center** and click on the Enter (check mark) box in the edit area. Then click on the Center tool in the toolbar, as shown here:

The word "center" is centered in C2. You can see that both Left align and Right align are also available from the toolbar. Press RIGHT ARROW to move the active cell to D2.

14. Type = and press ENTER. With the mouse pointer in cell D2, click the right mouse button to get the popup menu. Click on Format Cells, then on the Alignment tab and Fill option, and finally OK. The = is repeated to fill D2, less one space. Press RIGHT ARROW.

Type **555-1234** and press RIGHT ARROW. Cell E2 contains a left-aligned text string in the format of a phone number.

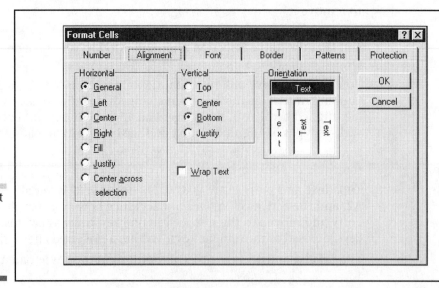

The Alignment tab in the Format Cells dialog box
Figure 4-3.

Type **=555-1234** and press ENTER. The equal sign turns this into a formula, and the cell contains the right-aligned number –679 (the results of 555 minus 1234). From this example, you can see that to make this entry, a number that can be used in calculations, you must tell Excel it is a formula.

Your screen should now look like Figure 4-4. The contents of E2 look different in the edit area and in the cell.

You may have noticed that use of the Format menu, Cells option, and Alignment tab combination to align a cell is cumbersome. The popup menu is only a little better. The alignment tools in the Formatting toolbar are by far the fastest way to change the alignment of one or more cells' contents. You can align the contents of a group of cells by highlighting the group before selecting the alignment from the popup or Format menus, or by clicking on an alignment tool.

Column Width Versus Contents Width

The first entry you typed in the previous exercise, shown in cell A1 in Figure 4-4, is wider than the cell—it hangs over into cell B1. Because there is nothing in B1, the full text from A1 is displayed. If you enter something in B1, the text in A1 would appear truncated, limited by the width of column A. Try that now.

4

Text and numbers on the sheet

Figure 4-4.

1. Press CTRL-HOME and then RIGHT ARROW to move the active cell to B1.

2. Type **new text** and press ENTER. The words "new text" fill B1 and, on the screen, truncate the text from A1. The full original entry is still in A1; you just can't see it all in the cell.

The top portion of your screen should look like the following.

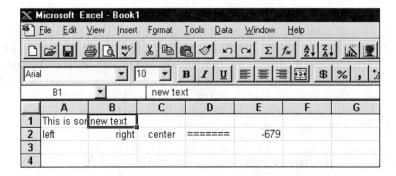

The width of a sheet area is considered in terms of column width, not cell width. You cannot adjust the width of an individual cell, only the width of the column that contains the cell. In Chapter 6 you will see how to change the width of both individual columns and a range of columns.

Entering Numbers

Excel gives you a lot of flexibility in entering numbers. You can enter numbers with commas, dollar signs, percent signs, and scientific notation. Excel converts your entry into a number with up to 15 significant places. You can then format the cell to display the number in any way you choose, no matter how you entered it.

Try entering several numbers now.

1. Press HOME and then press DOWN ARROW four times. The active cell moves to A5.

2. Type **1,234,567** including the commas. The number appears in the edit area.

3. Press DOWN ARROW. The number disappears from the edit area, and 1,234,567 appears in A5. If you entered the same number with an added digit—1,234,567.8, for example (you must do this on a new entry; editing the entry just made will round the decimal to 1,234,568)—it would be too wide to fit in the standard column width. The cell would fill with a series of number signs (#). The edit area would display the full number, with the exception of the commas. Unlike text, numbers do

not hang over the adjacent cell when they are too big for the column they are in. The column must be widened for the number to show.

4. Type **3.25** and press RIGHT ARROW. The number 3.25 appears in A6 as entered.

5. Type **$3.25** and press RIGHT ARROW. The number $3.25 appears in B6.

6. Type **3.25%** and press RIGHT ARROW. The number 3.25% appears in C6.

7. Type **3 1/4** and press RIGHT ARROW. The number 3 1/4 appears in D6.

8. Type **32.5E-1** and press RIGHT ARROW. The number 3.25E+00 appears in E6.

9. Type **=e6** and press ENTER. The number 3.25E+00 appears in F6. You entered a formula by placing = in front of a cell reference, and you used it to put up the contents of cell E6 in cell F6.

Figure 4-5 shows how your screen should look when you have completed these entries.

Being able to enter commas, dollar signs, percent signs, and fractions is an important capability, even if you must change them later. When you enter numbers that you are copying from a source that has dollar signs, commas, and so on, you might naturally type the symbols as well as the numbers. In

4

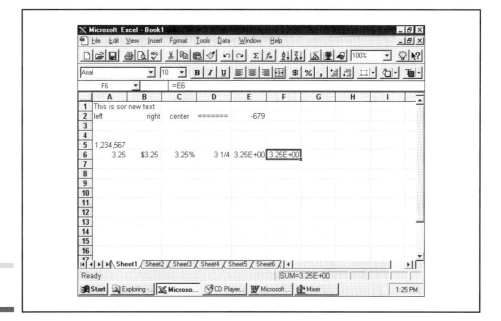

Text entries

Figure 4-5.

some spreadsheet packages you would get an error with such an entry. Excel gives you the flexibility to enter numbers with or without symbols.

Some formatting symbols can be entered by clicking on the Formatting tools in the toolbar. For example, if you type **325**, press ENTER, and then click on Currency Style (the $) in the Formatting toolbar, Excel will format the cell as $325.00. Convenient toolbar formatting is also available to apply the Percent and Comma styles and to increase or decrease the number of decimal places.

Using the Numeric Keypad

Although you were not told to do so, it is likely that you entered the numbers in the previous exercise using the numeric keys at the top of the typewriter keyboard. Unless you are using a laptop or notebook computer, you also have a numeric keypad on the right of your keyboard. The numeric keypad performs two functions: movement of the active cell when NUM LOCK is off and numeric entry when NUM LOCK is on. The NUM LOCK key is at the top of the numeric keypad. Most keyboards have a light to tell you if it is on or off, and Excel has a status indicator, NUM, that appears at the bottom of the window to tell you when NUM LOCK is on.

When NUM LOCK is on, the numeric keypad can be used for numeric entry like a 10-key adding machine. The direction keys on the numeric keypad are no longer available when NUM LOCK is on, unless you press and hold down SHIFT while pressing a direction key. Enhanced keyboards have a set of direction keys, separate from the numeric keypad, that can be used at any time. Throughout your work with Excel, you may use either set of keys for numeric entry without affecting the results.

Fixing the Number of Decimal Digits

If you are experienced using a 10-key adding machine or calculator and like the ability to enter numbers with a fixed number of decimal digits without typing the decimal point, you can do that with Excel. To set up a fixed number of decimal digits, follow these steps.

1. Select the Tools menu, choose Options, and then click on the Edit tab.
2. If there is no check mark next to the Fixed Decimal option, click on the check box. A check mark appears in the box.
3. To change the number of decimal digits after clicking on the Fixed Decimal option, simply click on the spinner until the number you want to use appears. The applicable part of your Options Edit dialog box should look like this:

4. Click on OK to close the dialog box and return to the sheet.

Remember that when you turn on this setting you have a fixed number of decimal digits in every number you type. Typing **6** gives you .06, and typing **3500** gives you 35. Excel remembers this the next time you start it up—it is a permanent setting until you turn it off. There is a status indicator, FIX, that appears in the Status bar to remind you that you have fixed the number of decimal digits.

4

Try it out now. Go to a blank cell, type a number like **3675**, and press ENTER. If you left 2 as the number of decimal places, you will get 36.75 without having to type the decimal point. For the sake of the work you do with this book, you need to turn the Fixed Decimal option *off*. Use the instructions above to do so now.

Completing an Entry and Moving to the Next Cell

As you saw in the previous examples, you can complete an entry either by pressing ENTER or by pressing one of the direction keys, depending on where you want to go next. If you use ENTER, the active cell remains the cell in which you made the entry (unless you did not turn off the Move Selection after Enter option described above). After using ENTER, you can then use one of the direction keys to move where you wish. If you want to go directly to another cell, you can save one keystroke by pressing a direction key to complete the entry.

You are not limited to the arrow keys. You can complete an entry using HOME or END plus arrow keys, or even PGUP, PGDN, CTRL-PGUP, or CTRL-PGDN—it just depends on where you want to go next.

Using AutoComplete

Excel 7 offers a handy feature, AutoComplete, that completes entries that have previously been entered. Excel keeps track of entries made in each column and as you type a new entry, any entry previously made in the same column that begins with the same first letters is automatically entered in the current cell. If there is more than one previous entry with the same beginning letter, the second character you type will focus the search to words that begin with the same two letters, and so on. For example, if you have previously entered the names Jones and Johnson, as you type a "J" Excel automatically enters the alphabetically first word that begins with a J, Johnson in this case. When you type the "o" nothing happens as you are still spelling Johnson correctly. If you now enter an "n" to repeat an entry for Jones, Excel automatically enters Jones as the now most specific match to your text entry.

If you want to avoid typing any characters altogether, right-click on the active cell to open the popup menu, and choose the Pick from list option. A list of previous entries drops from the bottom of the active cell from which you can choose an entry to be repeated in the active cell, as you can see here.

After the word is automatically entered, complete the entry by pressing ENTER or by one of the other methods previously discussed. You can turn off this feature, which is turned on by default, by clearing the check box Enable AutoComplete for Cell Values in the Edit tab of the Tools menu Options option.

Making Changes

Making changes to the information you are entering or have entered into Excel is a task at least equal in importance to making the initial entry. One of the beauties of an electronic spreadsheet is that changes can be made easily and often. You can make changes in four ways. First, you can replace a completed entry in a cell by typing over the original entry. The original entry disappears and the new entry takes its place. Second, you can edit an entry as you are entering it. Third, immediately after completing an entry you can remove it and restore the previous contents of the cell by pressing one of the Undo keys (ALT-BACKSPACE or CTRL-Z), clicking on the Undo tool in the Standard toolbar, or choosing Undo from the Edit menu. Fourth, with the cell you want to change selected as the active cell, you can edit a completed entry by pressing F2 or clicking in the edit area of the Formula bar. The next several sections explore the last three of these methods.

Editing During Entry

Editing during entry has a Simple mode that uses the BACKSPACE or ESC key and an Edit mode using the F2 (Edit) key. In the Simple mode, while you are entering data, press BACKSPACE to erase one or more characters to the left of the insertion point or press ESC to erase the entire entry. After pressing one of these keys, you can continue to type the corrected or new entry. When you press F2 (Edit), the mode indicator in the Status bar changes from Enter to Edit and you have full use of the Edit keys. (The Edit mode of editing is the same during and after entry, and is explained in the "Editing After Entry" section coming up shortly.) Now try simple mode editing.

1. Select the File menu, choose New, and click on OK to create a new workbook.
2. Type **Spring 92**. "Spring 92" appears in the edit area.
3. Press BACKSPACE and type **5**. "Spring 92" changes to "Spring 95" in the edit area.
4. Press ESC and type **Fall 95**. "Spring 95" changes to "Fall 95" in the edit area.
5. Press ENTER. The edit area closes and "Fall 95" is the final contents of cell A1.

4

Simple mode editing is just that, simple. You will use it frequently to correct the many small errors made during data entry.

Using Undo

The Undo option, which is available from the Edit menu, the Undo tool, and from its shortcut keys ALT-BACKSPACE or CTRL-Z, is a great lifesaver. It lets you remove the last thing you did and restore the sheet to the way it was before you did it. The definition of "the last thing you did" is usually whatever happened between two Ready modes, but there are exceptions. One important thing you *cannot* undo is the effect of recalculating the sheet. You can undo an Undo. When you are editing, you can use Undo to reverse the last change you made to a cell. Try that now.

1. Make sure the active cell is still the cell in which you last entered "Fall 95."
2. Type **Spring 96** and press ENTER. "Spring 96" replaces "Fall 95" in cell A1.
3. Click on the Undo tool in the Standard toolbar (or press ALT-BACKSPACE or CTRL-Z). "Fall 95" is restored in A1.

When you make a mistake that requires retyping, immediately choose Undo from the Edit menu, click on the Undo tool, or press ALT-BACKSPACE or CTRL-Z and see if it restores the sheet to its condition before the mistake. It cannot make the situation worse.

Editing After Entry

To edit a cell entry after it is completed, highlight the cell and press F2 (Edit). The Edit mode indicator is displayed, and in the cell the insertion point is blinking on the right of the entry. The LEFT ARROW, RIGHT ARROW, CTRL-LEFT ARROW, CTRL-RIGHT ARROW, HOME, and END keys all move the pointer within the entry so that individual characters can be changed. Pressing BACKSPACE removes the character to the left of the insertion point and pressing DEL removes the character to the right of the insertion point. Also, you can press INS to switch from *Insert mode,* which pushes existing characters to the right of new characters, to *Overtype mode,* which replaces existing characters with new ones at the insertion point. Try editing now.

1. Make sure the active cell still contains "Fall 95."

2. Press F2 (Edit). The edit area is activated (the Cancel box, Enter box, and Function Wizard appear in the Formula Bar) and the insertion point appears to the right of 95 in the cell.

3. Press HOME. The insertion point moves to the left of Fall.

4. Type **Summer/**. The entry becomes "Summer/Fall 95."

5. Press LEFT ARROW four times. The insertion point moves so it is between the two "m"s in Summer.

6. Press INS and the insertion point covers the second "m."

7. Type a period (.). The period replaces the second "m" in "Summer."

8. Press DEL twice. The "e" and "r" are removed from "Summer."

9. Press END and then LEFT ARROW three times. The insertion point moves to the right of the second "l" in "Fall."

10. Press INS and Excel returns to Insert mode.

11. Type **/Win.**. The entry now reads "Sum./Fall/Win. 95."

12. Press END. The insertion point moves to the right end of the entry.

13. Type **/96**. The entry now has "/96" at the right end. The top part of your screen should look like this:

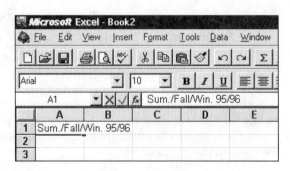

14. Press ENTER. The edit area closes and A1 reflects the final entry. Unlike in Enter mode, where you can press a direction key to finish editing a cell and move to a new cell, Edit mode requires you to press ENTER and then press a direction key to move to another cell.

Using AutoCorrect

There is an alternative to using any of the previously discussed editing methods, and that is letting Excel do the editing for you. AutoCorrect *edits* as you type any words that do not match a list of commonly misspelled, or more often, incorrectly typed, words. It also can check for the common mistake of capitalizing the second letter in a word that starts with a capital letter and make sure the days of the week start with a capital letter. The AutoCorrect option is on the Tools menu and when chosen opens a dialog box of the same name, shown here.

4

In the Replace Text as You Type section you can add words of your own to the starter collection of words supplied by Excel. For example, if you find yourself having a repetitive problem typing a word such as "type," enter the misspelled word, "tyupe" in the Replace text box and then the correctly spelled word in the With text box. Clicking on the Add command button will add that combination to the list of words and characters that are checked. The next time you enter "tyupe," Excel will replace it automatically with "type."

Edit Keys

The functions of the keys you can use while editing are summarized in the following table.

Key	Function
ALT	Activates Menu bar
ALT-ENTER	Inserts carriage return into cell
ALT-BACKSPACE, CTRL-Z	Undo previous action
BACKSPACE	Deletes the character to the left of the insertion point
CTRL-ALT-TAB	Inserts tab into cell
CTRL-LEFT ARROW or CTRL-RIGHT ARROW	Moves the insertion point one word to the left or right in the entry
CTRL-DELETE	Deletes text from the insertion point to the end of the current line
CTRL-'	Inserts the formula in the cell above the active cell at the insertion point
CTRL-`	Switches between displaying formulas and values in the active cell
CTRL-"	Inserts the value in the cell above the active cell at the insertion point
CTRL-;	Inserts the current date in your computer at the insertion point
CTRL-:	Inserts the current time in your computer at the insertion point
DEL	Deletes the character to the right of the insertion point
END, CTRL-END	Moves the insertion point to the right end of the current line of the entry
ENTER	Completes editing, closing the edit area and leaving the active cell where it was originally
ESC	Cancels any changes made during editing, closes the edit area, and returns the original contents to the active cell
F2	Activates the cell and edit area so you can do a character-by-character edit on the active cell
HOME, CTRL-HOME	Moves the insertion point to the left end of the current line of the entry

Key	Function
INS	Switches between Insert mode, in which newly typed characters push existing characters to the right, and Overtype mode, in which newly typed characters replace existing characters
LEFT ARROW or RIGHT ARROW	Moves the insertion point one character to the left or right in the entry
UP ARROW or DOWN ARROW	Moves the insertion point between lines in the edit area if the entry occupies more than one line; otherwise does nothing
SHIFT-LEFT ARROW or SHIFT-RIGHT ARROW	Selects the previous character or the next character
CTRL-SHIFT-RIGHT ARROW or CTRL-SHIFT-LEFT ARROW	Selects the next or previous word
SHIFT-TAB	Completes cell entry and moves to previous cell
TAB	Completes cell entry and moves to next cell

4

Editing with the Mouse

Editing with the keyboard is effective and often preferred if you are doing a lot of typing. However, the mouse has two benefits: you can jump immediately to the characters you want to change by clicking on the spot, and you can easily highlight characters to be deleted or otherwise changed by dragging across them. These benefits often make it worthwhile to take your hands off the keyboard to use the mouse. Try it now.

1. The workbook that you have on your screen should have "Sum./Fall/Win. 95/96" in cell A1.

2. Click on E12. The active cell moves to E12.

    Assume that you want to edit cell A1. If it were not in the home position, it would take at least two keystrokes to get there. With the mouse, it only takes one movement.

3. Click on A1. The active cell moves to A1.

4. Drag across "Sum./" in the edit area, *not* in the active cell. (Place the mouse pointer on the "S" in "Sum" in the edit area, not in cell A1. Press and hold the mouse button while dragging the mouse pointer across "Sum./," then release the mouse button.) "Sum./" in the edit area is highlighted.

Notice that the mouse pointer becomes an I-beam when you move it into the edit area. This allows you to click between characters in placing the insertion point. Notice, also, that you activated the edit area as soon as you pressed the mouse button while pointing anywhere in the edit area.

5. Press DEL. The edit area contains "Fall/Win. 95/96."

6. Drag across the period following Win. Type **ter**. The edit area now reads "Fall/Winter 95/96," as shown here:

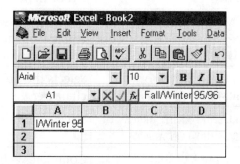

7. Click on E12 to carry on where you started.

The ability to jump quickly to a cell, make a change by clicking and dragging in the edit area, and then jump back to where you started is powerful. Use it for awhile and you will agree.

Using Menus

Menus are the primary means of having Excel perform tasks such as opening a file, copying a group of cells, printing a workbook, or creating a chart. All menu operations begin in one of three ways:

♦ Clicking on a menu name.

♦ Clicking the right mouse button or pressing SHIFT-F10 to access the popup menu.

♦ Pressing ALT, F10, or / to activate the Menu bar and then either typing the underlined letter in the menu name or pressing the direction keys to move to the correct menu name and pressing ENTER.

Any of these methods causes the selected menu to be displayed. Once a menu is displayed, you have three ways to choose an option:

♦ Clicking on an option name.

♦ Typing the underlined letter in the option name (this does not work in the popup menu, but you can type the first letter of the option, possibly several times if more than one option starts with the same letter, to highlight it and then press ENTER).

♦ Using the direction keys to highlight an option and pressing ENTER.

Once you have selected a menu and chosen an option, either the option immediately executes (as does Save in the File menu or Copy in the Edit menu, for example) or a dialog box opens. When you choose a menu option with an ellipsis (...) after it, a dialog box opens. Excel (and all Windows applications) uses a dialog box to get further information. Dialog boxes give you additional choices and provide the means for you to type in a name or some other information.

Take a look now at how the menu system works. In the following instructions the keyboard and mouse methods are intermixed to give you experience with both.

1. Press ALT. The File menu name in the Menu bar is highlighted if your document is not maximized. If it is, the document Control menu is highlighted. Notice that the Status bar at the bottom of the window gives you a brief description of the File (or Control) menu.

2. Press ENTER. The File menu opens.

3. Press DOWN ARROW, and then press it several more times. Notice that the Status bar provides a description of each option as you highlight it.

4. Press RIGHT ARROW. The File menu closes and the Edit menu opens.

   Some of the options in the Edit menu are light gray or dimmer than the other options. These options are not available because they are not applicable to the current situation. For example, some of the light gray options in the current Edit menu deal with pasting (copying something from the Clipboard to the sheet). To paste you must *first* cut or copy, both of which place something from the sheet onto the Clipboard.

5. Press RIGHT ARROW slowly several more times. Look at each of the menus in succession. Use DOWN ARROW to explore some of the options that interest you. Look at the Status bar to see the description of the option.

6. Press RIGHT ARROW until the Help menu is selected. Then press it once more. The highlight wraps around and opens first the Excel Control menu; then, if you keep pressing RIGHT ARROW, it opens the workbook Control menu and finally returns to the File menu where you started.

   If you continue to press RIGHT ARROW, you continue to move around the set of menus. If you press LEFT ARROW, you move the other way. If you press UP ARROW or DOWN ARROW, you move up or down through the options in the menu that is currently selected. The direction keys provide a sure way to move through the menu system.

7. Press ESC twice. The Menu bar is deactivated and you return to the sheet.

8. Click on A1, and it becomes the active cell. A1 should still contain Fall/Winter 95/96. If it doesn't, type anything in it (your first name, for example) so you have something to work with in the next set of instructions.

9. Click on Edit in the Menu bar. The Edit menu opens.

10. Click on Copy in the Edit menu. The Edit menu closes and a blinking *marquee* appears around the active cell, A1, telling you that a copy of the contents of A1 is ready to be placed in some other cell on the sheet.

11. Click on C5 to select it as the destination of the copy. Press ENTER to complete the copy. C5 now contains a copy of A1's contents.

12. Press ALT to activate the Menu bar (make sure the document window is not maximized; then maximize the window after the next step).

13. Press **E** to open the Edit menu.

14. Press **T** to choose the Cut option. The Edit menu closes and again a blinking marquee forms around the active cell, in this case C5. The contents of C5 are placed on the Clipboard.

15. Click on E9 and press ENTER. The contents of C5 are moved to E9. In other words, the contents of C5 are removed (cut) and placed (pasted) in E9.

16. Drag on the Edit menu until Undo Paste is highlighted (point on the Edit menu name in the Menu bar, press and hold the mouse button while dragging the highlight bar down to the Undo Paste option, and then release the mouse button). The contents of E9 are restored to C5 and a blinking marquee reappears. With Edit Undo Paste, you have completely undone step 15 and you are back where you were when you completed step 14, except that E9 is the active cell.

17. Drag to highlight cells C5, C6, C7, and C8 (place the mouse pointer on C5, press and hold the mouse button while dragging the mouse pointer over C6, C7, and C8, and then release the mouse button). Cells C5 through C8 are highlighted.

18. Click on the Edit menu to select it, and then point on Fill. A submenu is displayed. Click on Down. The contents of C5 are replicated in cells C6 through C8, as shown in Figure 4-6.

19. With the mouse pointer in the C5 through C8 highlighted range, click the right mouse button to display the popup menu. Click on Clear Contents. The contents of C5 through C8 are cleared from the screen. (If you find the highlight disappearing from the screen when you bring

Results of
choosing Fill
Down from
the Edit menu
Figure 4-6.

up the popup menu, you have not placed the cursor in cells C5 through
C8 before pressing the right mouse button.)

20. Click on the Edit menu to select it, and then click on Undo (the word
    Clear is added to the Undo option to let you know which command you
    are restoring). The screen returns to its original look, as in Figure 4-6.

Cut, Paste, Copy, and Undo all have tools in the Standard toolbar that can
easily and quickly be used instead of the Edit or popup menu.

The majority of menu options are discussed in later chapters of this book.
The same procedures are used throughout the book to open a menu and
choose an option. The ease and flexibility with which you can make a menu
selection and choose an option constitute one of Excel's and Windows'
greatest strengths. Most instructions in this book do not tell you to use one
method or the other when using the menus; you can choose the method
you prefer.

Using Zoom

Another feature is Zoom. Much like a camera lens, Zoom allows you to
increase or decrease the magnification of the sheet. You can choose from
five magnifications provided by Excel or create your own, anywhere from 10

to 400% of normal (normal being 100%). Zoom changes only the size of the sheet; the window that contains the sheet stays the same.

The Zoom option is available both from the View menu and with the Zoom Control tool on the Standard toolbar. Try some zooming exercises now.

1. Click on the View menu, and then click on the Zoom option. The Zoom dialog box appears. Choose 200% magnification by clicking on its option button, and then click on the OK button. The sheet is enlarged as shown in Figure 4-7.

2. Again, click on the View menu, choose Zoom, but this time choose the Custom option button. Type **40** and click on the OK button to display the sheet in Figure 4-8.

3. Return to the original sheet magnification by clicking on the Zoom Control tool on the Standard toolbar. Click on 100% to return the sheet to its normal magnification as seen earlier in Figure 4-6.

Using Files

Files provide a permanent record of the workbooks you build. To create a file, you must save the workbook on a disk. If a workbook is not saved, it is

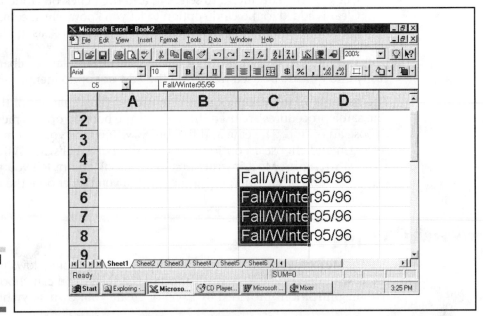

Sheet enlarged
in size
Figure 4-7.

Sheet reduced
in size
Figure 4-8.

4

lost when you leave Excel or turn off the computer (although you will
receive a warning if you try to leave Excel without saving an open workbook).

Naming Files

When you save a file you must give it a name. The full name of a file has three
components: a path, a filename, and an extension. The *path* is made up of
the drive letter (for example, C: or A:) and one or more folder names—for
example, \WINDOWS\ or \EXCEL\PLAN\. The drive letter is a single letter
followed by a colon, and a folder name can be up to 255 characters enclosed
in backslashes. In a tree structure set of directories, several folder (or subfolder)
names make up the path, as in \PLAN\SALES\1995\.

A *filename* can also be up to 255 characters long. A filename can consist of
any combination of letters, numbers, and spaces, but cannot include the
following special characters:

> / \ ? : * " < > |

The filename *extension* is optional, but highly recommended. It begins with a
period and can be up to three characters long. Unless you override it, Excel
automatically adds an extension to all files. The extensions and the types of
files they are applied to are summarized in Table 4-1.

Extension	File Type
.CSV	Comma-separated values
.DBF	dBASE II/III/IV
.DIF	Data Interchange Format (VisiCalc)
.SLK	Symbolic Link (SYLK) (MultiPlan)
.TXT	Text
.WKS, .WK1, .WK3, .WK4, .FMT, or .FM3	Lotus 1-2-3
.XLA	Macro Add-ins
.XLB	Toolbar
.XLC	Chart (Excel 4)
.XLL	Commercial Add-ins
.XLM	Macro sheet (Excel 4)
.XLS	Workbook or Excel 2.1, 3, or 4 Worksheet
.XLT	Templates
.XLW	Workbook (Excel 4)
.WQ1	QuattroPro/DOS
.PRN	Formatted Text (space-delimited Lotus print format)

Default Filename Extensions Created by Excel
Table 4-1.

Saving Files

You already saved a file when you worked through some steps in Chapter 3. That example required only a minimum of explanation, so use the following instructions to save another file now (even though there is not much in the workbook to save).

1. Click on File. The File menu opens, as shown here:

2. Click on Save As. The Save As dialog box opens, asking for the name of the file you want to save, as shown here:

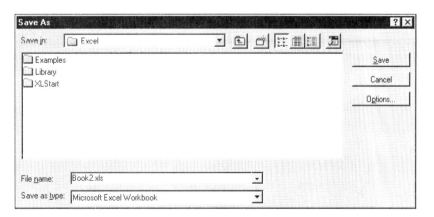

3. Type **ch4**. The name CH4 goes into the File name text box of the Save As dialog box. Excel automatically adds the workbook extension .XLS (the current drive and folder are used if no others are specified, as described in the next section, "Using Folders").

4. Click on Save. A second dialog box, Properties, is displayed which allows summary information to be entered. Type **Test Sheet** for the Title and click on OK. The sheet is saved in a file named CH4.XLS, and Excel returns to Ready mode.

Using Folders

In the previous example, you saved a file without specifying a drive or folder. When you do that, Excel uses the current drive and folder. Unless you have changed your default drive and folder (which can be done in the General tab of the Tools menu Options option), the current drive and folder on your computer are the ones in which you installed Excel. In other words, you store your workbook files in the same folder as your programs are stored.

While there is nothing inherently wrong with using the program folder to store data files, it is not a good idea for files that are important. You should not keep data and program files together because you can end up erasing the data files that you want to save along with all the program files that you want to erase when you install a new release of the program. Also, the number of Excel program files in the folder makes it hard to find your data files.

It is recommended that you create one or more separate folders to hold your data files. You can then specify one of these folders when saving files. Chapter 1 describes creating a folder named Sheet in which you can store the sample files created in this book. If you have not done that, it is recommended that you turn to Chapter 1 now and do it. In the remaining chapters of this book, it is assumed that you are using a path of \Sheet\ for your files.

You can make the Sheet folder the default folder by selecting the Tools menu, choosing Options, and then the General tab. Type the path to your Sheet folder in the Default File Location text box. The next time you choose Open or Save As from the File menu, the Sheet folder's files will be displayed.

Retrieving Files

Retrieving files is similar to saving files. You select the File menu and then choose Open. A dialog box opens that asks you for the filename, and a list of files in the current directory is displayed. Try that now with the following instructions.

1. Click on the File menu. The File menu opens.
2. Click on Open. The Open dialog box opens, as shown here:

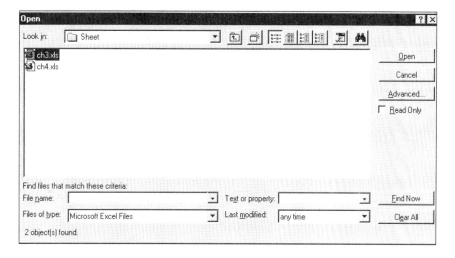

3. Double-click on ch3.xls in the Files List box. The file CH3.XLS opens.

If you don't know a filename, you can use the two *wildcard characters,* ? and *. To replace a single character, use ?; to replace any number of consecutive characters, use *. For example, ?QTRPLAN.XLS refers to 1QTRPLAN.XLS, 2QTRPLAN.XLS, 3QTRPLAN.XLS, and so on, while *.XLS refers to all files with an .XLS extension.

4

It is important to note that when Excel opens a file, it creates a new workbook window that is added to the other workbook or document windows you have open. You can find out what document windows are open by opening the Window menu.

You can see that you currently have three windows open. If you want to go to another window, choose that window from the Window menu or click on the window if you can see it on the screen. To display all windows currently open, choose Arrange from the Window menu, click on the Tiled option button, and then click on the OK button. With the current windows available, this will produce a screen that looks like Figure 4-9.

Quitting Excel

When you are done using Excel, you should formally leave it—rather than just turn off your computer—either by choosing Exit from the File menu, Close from Excel's Control menu, double-clicking on Excel's Control Menu icon, or by clicking on the Close button in the upper-right corner of the Excel window. The main reason for this is that if you have forgotten to save a file, using one of the formal exiting options reminds you as part of the

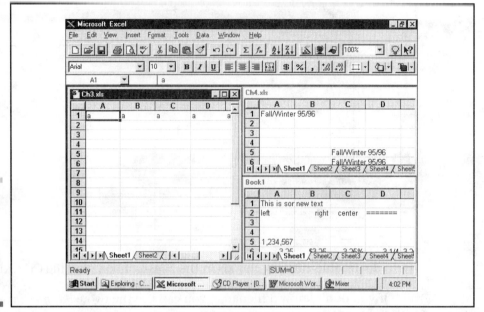

quitting process. Also, with the formal options, Excel erases any temporary files it has written, thus keeping your hard disk from getting filled with them. Use the following steps to leave Excel.

1. Click on Excel's Close button.

   The Save Changes dialog box asks if you want to save changes in Book1 and gives you three command buttons to choose from: Yes, No, and Cancel. Choosing Yes saves Book1 in a file named BOOK1.XLS in the current directory. Choosing No exits Excel without saving Book1—in essence throwing away Book1. Choosing Cancel interrupts the quitting process and puts you back in Ready mode. You can then look at Book1 and determine if you want to save it. Since you want to throw away Book1, choose No.

2. Click on No to leave Excel without saving Book1.

3. Click on the Start menu Shut Down option to leave Windows.

4. Click on Yes to end your Windows session.

Excel and Windows shut themselves down, erasing any temporary files. You can now safely turn off your computer when told it is safe to do so.

Creating a Spreadsheet

5

Creating a spreadsheet is a primary function in Excel, and it is the one thing every user of Excel does. The importance of learning how to do this well, and becoming familiar with as many spreadsheet tricks and shortcuts as possible, cannot be overemphasized. This chapter provides the foundation for that learning process by taking you through the actual construction of a spreadsheet. Chapter 6 builds upon this foundation to demonstrate additional spreadsheet capabilities in Excel.

You will benefit from following along on your computer as you read this chapter. It is not absolutely necessary to do this—there are plenty of figures and illustrations to show you what is going on—but you will learn far more by actually seeing for yourself what is happening as the spreadsheet progresses. More importantly, you will learn how to untangle yourself from the many small mistakes that everyone makes but are impossible to predict in a book.

Creating a spreadsheet has a number of steps. This chapter covers planning the spreadsheet, placing headings and titles, entering numbers and formulas, copying formulas, and completing and saving the workbook that contains the spreadsheet.

Planning a Spreadsheet

You *could* start building a spreadsheet by simply entering the necessary headings, labels, and numbers or formulas. If you need an extra row or column, you could just insert it and delete those you do not need. A great number of spreadsheets—probably the majority—are built that way. As with most things, however, a little planning up front saves considerable time as you go along. Planning involves simply visualizing what the spreadsheet will look like and making a note of it so you have something to follow as you build the spreadsheet. This takes only a few minutes and can save more time later.

Figure 5-1 shows a layout for a third-quarter budget spreadsheet that you will build in this chapter. This layout was done using Excel, but most are simply sketched on a piece of paper. To construct this layout, you first need to answer four questions: How many revenue, cost of sales, and expense accounts are to be included? How many time periods are covered? What assumptions are involved? How many organizational units are to be separately included?

Layout for a
third-quarter
budget
Figure 5-1.

The answers to these questions allow you to make the following
determinations regarding the layout in Figure 5-1.

- A title will appear at the top of each sheet with a blank line under it.

- There will be three assumptions, one each for the growth of revenue,
  cost of sales, and expenses. Each requires a row, and there will be a blank
  line following the third assumption.

- Each column heading will take two rows and have a blank line below it.

- The row headings will be in columns A and B and take 17 rows, 10
  through 26 (five for revenue, four for cost of sales and gross income, six
  for expense, and two for net income).

- The data area will occupy six columns: C through H (two for quarters,
  three for months, and one for the percent growth).

- Three stores will each have their own budget, each taking a sheet, plus a
  total company budget sheet, so that there will be four sheets altogether.

If you cannot visualize the spreadsheet from the layout in Figure 5-1 and these decisions, don't feel bad. Sneak a look at the finished product in Figure 5-19 at the end of the chapter. As you build more spreadsheets, you will be able to visualize them more easily before you start them.

That's all there is to the planning process: constructing a rough layout of what will go where in the workbook after making a series of decisions about what is to be included and how much room it will take. Use the plan to begin building the spreadsheet by placing headings and other elements where you have decided they belong.

Placing Labels, Headings, and Titles

Where you begin a spreadsheet probably has as much to do with how you visualize or create it in your mind as with anything else. It is important to minimize the number of keystrokes (and therefore the traveling you must do around the spreadsheet), but trying to reach the absolute minimum path is more trouble than it's worth and does not allow for possible errors. Therefore, start where you like and don't worry about it. Here, after preparing to use multiple sheets, you will start with the row labels, knowing that you will have to go back and enter the title and assumptions.

Setting Up Similar Sheets

Since you will be creating four sheets that will be the same except for the numbers they contain, you can save yourself some time by entering the common information on all the sheets at the same time. You do that by initially selecting the sheets to work on and then entering the common information on one of them. Select the sheets now with these steps.

1. Turn on your computer and load Windows and Excel so that a blank workbook is on your screen with Sheet1 selected as the active sheet.

2. Press and hold SHIFT while clicking on the tab for Sheet4.

   This will select sheets 1 through 4. If you want to select a set of sheets that are not next to each other, press and hold CTRL while clicking on the sheet tabs. As you are working on this chapter, make sure these four sheets remain selected until you are told to deselect them and to begin work on just one sheet. This is especially important to remember if you leave this project and/or Excel and then return.

When you have multiple sheets selected, if you want to work on just one of them you need to first click on another sheet and then back on the sheet you want to work on, or right-click on the sheet you want to use and choose Ungroup Sheets from the popup menu. For now, though, leave all four sheets grouped.

Entering a Column of Labels

You are now ready to begin entering information that will be placed on all four sheets. Begin by using the following instructions to enter a column of labels (you should be on Sheet1).

1. Click on A10 to move the active cell to A10.
2. Type **REVENUE** and press DOWN ARROW. All capital letters are used to set off an account title. If you make a mistake in typing before pressing DOWN ARROW, use BACKSPACE or ESC to correct it. If you notice a mistake after pressing DOWN ARROW, ignore it. You will come back later and edit the labels.
3. Press SPACEBAR four times. This indents a detail account.
4. Type **Forms** and press DOWN ARROW.
5. Indent (press SPACEBAR four times), type **Supplies**, and press DOWN ARROW.
6. Type **Total Revenue** and press DOWN ARROW twice. When you complete this instruction, you should be in A15.

Using this process, type the remaining row labels as shown in Figure 5-2. Use BACKSPACE to correct any errors you notice prior to completing an entry, but ignore errors you notice after completion. Leave the space between P/R Taxes and Other Expenses to allow for its use later. Press ENTER when you complete Net Income since it is the last account.

 Note: Your screen might display more or less rows and columns than the examples in the figures. Just scroll your document window using the horizontal and vertical scroll bars to see any hidden data.

Editing Completed Entries

Look over the row labels carefully for any typing errors. Then read through the following steps that show you how to correct any errors that you have

5

Completed
row labels
Figure 5-2.

made or might make in the future. (As an example, assume that the second "a" in "Salaries" has been left out.)

1. Click on the entry to be corrected (A20 for Salaries).

2. Move the mouse pointer to the edit area, place the I-beam at or to the right of the error (between the "l" and "r" if the second "a" is missing in "Salaries"), and click to place the insertion point. Excel enters Edit mode.

3. Correct the error. If you need to delete an incorrect character, press DEL to delete a character to the right of the insertion point, or use BACKSPACE to delete a character to the left. Then type the correction. In the case of Salaries, type the missing **a**.

4. Press ENTER. Excel returns to Ready mode.

Correct all of the errors you see in the row labels this same way: move the active cell to the incorrect label, go into Edit mode (you can press F2 as well as click in the edit area), get to the incorrect character using the mouse or the arrow keys, use BACKSPACE or DEL to remove characters you do not want, type characters that need to be added, and press ENTER to complete the editing.

Spelling The Spelling tool on the Standard toolbar or the option on the Tools menu provides an easier (and often more accurate!) way to edit misspelled words than the method just described. Your entire workbook is checked by default unless you select a range, a word, or an embedded chart, in which case only the smaller object is spell checked. The Spelling dialog box, shown here, offers suggested alternative spellings to words it does not find in the standard dictionary.

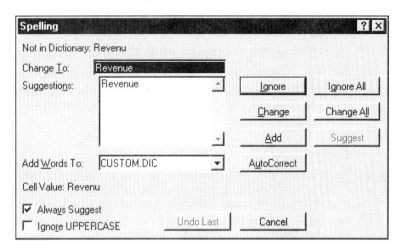

Spelling starts spell checking the workbook from your selected cell. You can replace a misspelled word in your workbook with the suggested word in the Change To box by clicking on the Change All button (Change All changes all occurrences of the misspelled word). If you prefer one of the words in the Suggestions box, click on the word, and then click on the Change button. You can change the present use of the word or choose to change all instances throughout the workbook. Additionally, you can add to the custom dictionary commonly used words, acronyms, or abbreviations unique to your work. If you set up Excel as part of Microsoft Office, you will find the custom dictionary is used also by Word and PowerPoint. Finally, after you have made your selections, Excel will ask you if you want to continue spell checking the workbook from its beginning, or stop and return to the workbook. Try the following exercise to get a feeling for the use of Spelling.

1. Click on cell A10 to move the active cell to A10.
2. Press F2 to change to Edit mode.
3. Press BACKSPACE once to delete the "E" and change "REVENUE" to "REVENU."
4. Click on the Enter box in the editing area.
5. Press DOWN ARROW three times. Repeat steps 2 through 4 to change "Total Revenue" to "Total Revenu."

6. Click on the Spelling tool in the Standard toolbar or click on the Tools menu and then choose the Spelling option.

7. Click on "Revenue" in the Suggestions box. "Revenue" becomes highlighted.

8. Click on the Change All button. Excel substitutes the proper spelling of Revenue for the misspelled contents of cell A13; then it asks if you want to continue checking from the beginning of the workbook.

9. Click on the Yes button since "REVENU" in cell A10 is still misspelled.

10. Excel automatically corrects the spelling of "REVENU" in A10 and on the other sheets. Excel lets you know spell checking is finished. Click on OK. Since the Spelling dialog box did not reappear, there are no additional misspelled words.

Long Labels

As you look at the row labels, notice that many are longer than the width of column A. They hang over into the next column. This works fine while there is nothing in the column. As you saw in Chapter 4, if you place a label or number in the cell to the right of the long label, the label will appear to be truncated. This workbook was laid out with that in mind, providing a blank column B. In Chapter 6 you will see how columns can be widened to accommodate long labels and numbers, eliminating the need for a blank column beside them.

Centering a Title

The second step is to add a title to the sheet: Third Quarter Budget. You want to center it across the width of the sheet. Excel has the capability to center text across several columns. In this example, the title will fill columns D and E and part of F, leaving G and H on the right balanced against A and B on the left.

Follow these steps to add the title.

1. Press CTRL-HOME to move the active cell to A1.

2. Press CAPS LOCK for uppercase letters.

3. Type **THIRD QUARTER BUDGET**. Check your entry for mistakes. If you made any, either press BACKSPACE or click in the edit area to correct them. When you are satisfied, press ENTER to complete the title.

4. Drag across row 1, from column A through column H. (Move the mouse pointer to A1, press and hold the mouse button while moving the mouse to H9, and then release the mouse button.) Row 1 from cell A through cell H is highlighted.

5. Click on the Format menu and the Cells option

6. The Format Cells dialog box opens. Click on the Alignment tab and then on the Center across selection option button, and then on OK. (Alternatively, you can click on the Center Across Columns tool next to the dollar sign in the Formatting toolbar.)

7. Click on cell A1 and then press CAPS LOCK to turn off uppercase letters.

8. The top of your screen should look like this:

	A	B	C	D	E	F	G	H	I	
1				THIRD QUARTER BUDGET						
2										
3										

Entering a Row of Headings

Each column of data on this sheet needs a heading. Two rows have been left for this purpose, plus one row for a double line under the headings. Enter these now.

1. Click on C7 to make that the active cell.

2. Type **Second** and press DOWN ARROW.

3. Type **Quarter** and press RIGHT ARROW.

4. Type **July** and press RIGHT ARROW.

5. Type **August** and press RIGHT ARROW.

Use Figure 5-3 as a guide to finish the remaining column headings.

Placing a Border

In this exercise, you'll separate your row labels and column headings with a border. With Excel you can format a cell or range of cells to have a border on any or all of its four sides. This is different from using a string of hyphens, equal signs, or vertical lines to produce a border. It is actual formatting of a cell to include a line on one or more of its sides while keeping its text or number(s) intact. The border is placed on the grid lines, so adjoining cells share a border.

To create a double line, it's easiest to make one of the borders on a cell a double line. The line will be on the edge of the cell, not centered within it. To center a double line, you need to place a top and bottom border on a row and then reduce the height of the row to the space you want between the lines. You cannot read anything else contained in that row.

5

	A	B	C	D	E	F	G	H	I
5									
6									
7			Second				Third	Percent	
8			Quarter	July	August	Sept.	Quarter	Growth	
9									
10	REVENUE								
11	Forms								
12	Supplies								
13	Total Revenue								

Completed
column
headings
Figure 5-3.

Add a double-line border across row 9 using the second method and a single-line border between columns B and C with the following instructions.

1. Drag across row 9 from column A through column H. (Move the mouse pointer to A9, press and hold the mouse button while moving the mouse to H9, and then release the mouse button.) In row 9, columns A through H are highlighted.

2. Click on the Format menu, the Cells option, and the Border tab. The Border dialog box opens.

3. Click on Top and Bottom in the Border dialog box. The thin solid line should already be selected, as shown in Figure 5-4.

4. Click OK. The dialog box closes and a top and bottom border is placed across the selected cells in row 9.

5. Point on the row numbers on the left of the window at the intersection of rows 9 and 10. The mouse pointer becomes a vertical two-headed arrow with a bar in the middle. This allows you to change the height of a row.

6. Press and hold the mouse button while dragging the mouse upward to reduce the height of row 9 to roughly 1/16 inch, as shown here:

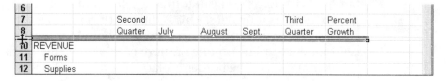

7. Drag down column B from row 10 through row 26. B10 through B26 are highlighted.

8. Click on the drop-down arrow of the Borders palette, which is the third tool from the right in the Formatting toolbar. The Borders palette will open.

9. Click on the right-hand vertical line, which is the fourth line style in the top row, to add a single-line border down the right side of B10 through B26. After deselecting the range, Figure 5-5 shows the results.

Creating a
double-line
border
Figure 5-4.

You can also add shading to groups of cells with the Format Cell Patterns
dialog box. Figure 5-1 is an example of how such shading can be used.

5

Horizontal
and vertical
borders in
place
Figure 5-5.

Saving the Workbook

You have now done a fair amount of work in the workbook that you probably would not want to redo. It is a good idea to save your workbooks early and often, so save this workbook now.

1. Click on the File menu and Save As option. The Save As dialog box opens.

2. Type **c:\sheet\qtr3bud** in the File name text box. (The path C:\SHEET\ is the path example discussed in Chapter 1. If your path is different, use your path.) The Save As dialog box looks like this:

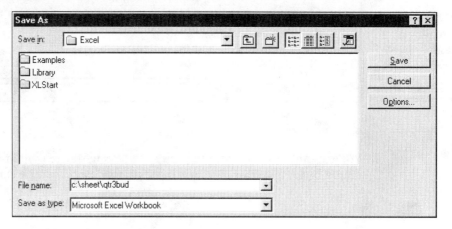

3. Click on Save and the file's Properties dialog box opens. Give the file a title if you want and press OK, or just press Cancel. The workbook is saved on your hard disk and Excel returns to Ready mode.

Saving a file is simple and should be done often to prevent losing your work from a power failure or human error. As you will see later in this chapter, once you have saved a file, you can resave it with the File Save command without reentering the filename.

Entering Numbers and Formulas

Your next task is to enter the body of the spreadsheet—the numbers and formulas that make up the budget proper. Most budgets are projections based on actual sets of numbers. In this example, you'll start with an actual second quarter to project the third quarter. In other words, the second quarter is an actual set of numbers, while each month of the third quarter contains a formula that calculates its value based on values from the second quarter. Start by entering the second quarter actuals.

Entering a Column of Numbers

You enter a column of numbers just as you entered the column of labels earlier: you type one number and press DOWN ARROW to move to the next one. If you enter the numbers with commas, you will get automatic comma formatting. Follow these steps to enter the column of numbers.

1. Click on C11. The active cell moves to C11.

2. Type **87,000** and press DOWN ARROW. If you make a mistake while typing, use BACKSPACE or ESC to correct it. If you see a mistake after completing an entry, wait until you finish the column to correct it.

   If you got 870 instead of 87,000, you have the fixed decimal feature turned on (you will see the status indicator FIX in the right corner of the Status bar). Choose Options from the Tools menu, click on the Edit tab, and then click on Fixed Decimal to turn it off. Finally, click on OK to close the Options dialog box.

3. Type **147,300** and press DOWN ARROW.

4. Type **234,300** and press DOWN ARROW twice.

In a similar manner, complete the column of numbers shown in Figure 5-6. When you reach the Net Income number, cell C26, press ENTER instead of DOWN ARROW.

5

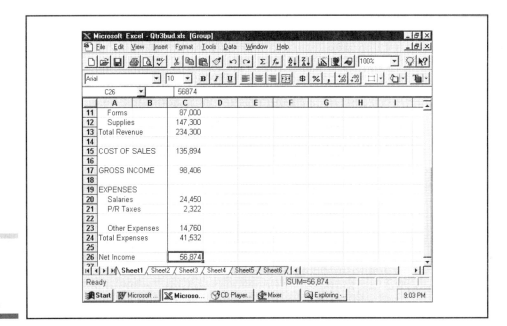

Completed column of numbers
Figure 5-6.

Editing and Completing the Column

When you finish entering the numbers, look back over them and compare what you see to Figure 5-6. It is important that the numbers be accurate because the rest of the spreadsheet is based on them. If you see an error, use the following instructions to correct it. (As an example, assume that Other Expenses was entered as 14,660 instead of 14,760.)

1. Click on the cell in error (for example, C23 for Other Expenses).
2. Click or drag on the edit area to highlight the error. The mode indicator changes to Edit. In this example, you would drag across the left 6 in 14,660.
3. After dragging over any number(s) to be replaced, type the replacement number(s). For this example, type **7**. You can also use BACKSPACE or DEL to remove unwanted characters and type correct ones.
4. Press ENTER. The correct number is placed on the sheet, and Excel returns to Ready mode.

Use this procedure to correct as many errors as you have, moving up the list as you go. For the next section, you must be near the top of the list.

Building Formulas

The next three columns (D, E, and F) represent the projected amounts for July, August, and September. The amounts for each month are totally derived, using formulas based on the actual second quarter. There are 11 figures per month (including one for the blank after P/R Taxes) and three months. This means you have 33 formulas, which is a lot if you had to enter them all. Thankfully, the copying facility for formulas is very powerful in Excel, so most of the work will be done for you.

If you look ahead a month and think about the formulas there, you will notice that four of the formulas are based on other numbers in the same column—the summation formulas for Total Revenue, GROSS INCOME, Total Expenses, and Net Income. They are the same formulas for all three months. It would be worthwhile doing them first in July so they can be copied to the other months.

In building the formulas, you can use + and – from either above the typewriter keyboard or on the right of the numerical keypad, and you can use either uppercase or lowercase letters. As you are building the formulas, check them carefully. It is easier to catch an error and correct it as formulas are being built rather than after the fact. The following steps build the first formula.

1. Click on D13, Total Revenue for July.

2. Type **=d11+d12** and the formula appears in the edit area and in D13. The formula adds Forms (D11) to Supplies (D12) to get Total Revenue.

3. Press ENTER. Excel returns to Ready mode.

On the sheet, you'll see only a 0 in D13, but in the edit area you'll see the formula. When numbers are available in D11 and D12, D13 will reflect them.

Pointing Versus Typing

When entering the first formula, you directly typed it as you would text or a number. This works fine when you can see on the screen the cell addresses that you want to use in the formula. Excel has another method of entering formulas that works even if the cell is not on the screen.

The process is to start a formula with an equal sign (=), use the mouse or direction keys to point to the first cell in the formula, type one of the following arithmetic symbols

> $+ - * / \char94 \% \& : , ( )$

and then point to the second cell, and so on to complete the formula. The following instructions demonstrate this.

5

1. Click on D17, GROSS INCOME for July.

2. Type = and = appears in the edit area. The mode indicator changes to Enter.

3. Click on D13. A blinking dotted line appears around D13. D13 is displayed in the formula under construction in the edit area and in the cell, and the mode indicator changes to Point.

4. Type - and - appears in the formula after D13. The blinking dotted line disappears from D13.

5. Click on D15. A blinking dotted line appears around D15, and D15 goes into the formula in the edit area and the cell. Your screen should look like that shown in Figure 5-7.

6. Press ENTER. The formula is completed, and Excel returns to Ready mode.

Again you see only a 0 on the sheet, but the formula appears in the edit area. The process of entering an arithmetic symbol and pointing at a cell can go on as long as you want up to a maximum of 255 characters in a formula. Also, there are shortcuts for formulas, as you are about to see.

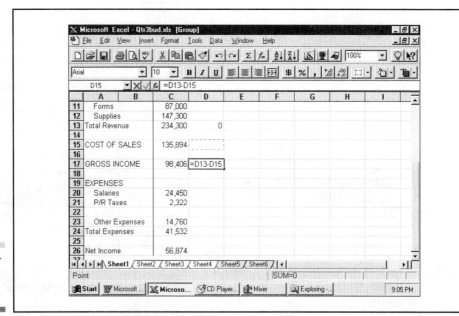

Formula under
construction
Figure 5-7.

Functions Versus Formulas

The next formula is for Total Expenses in D24. This is the sum: D20+D21+D22+D23. You *can* type in such a formula; with an = in front, it is 16 keystrokes. You also can point to the four cells and type + four times. Alternatively, you can use the SUM function that Excel uses for summing. Instead of identifying each cell, you identify (type or point to) the range encompassing the cells to be summed. Here is how it is done.

1. Click on D24. The active cell moves to D24, Total Expenses for July.

2. Type **=sum(** which will appear in the edit area and the cell. The ENTER indicator comes on.

3. Click on D20. The blinking dotted line appears around D20. D20 is displayed in the formula under construction and the mode indicator changes to Point.

4. Type **:** to indicate a range, and the starting address of a range is anchored at D20. The EXT keyboard indicator comes on.

5. Click on D23. The blinking dotted line appears around the range D20:D23, and the formula includes that range, as shown in Figure 5-8.

6. Type **)** and press ENTER. The completed formula is placed in D24, and you can see it in the edit area. (For future reference, you don't need to type the ending parenthesis in simple SUM formulas, just press ENTER and Excel will add it automatically.)

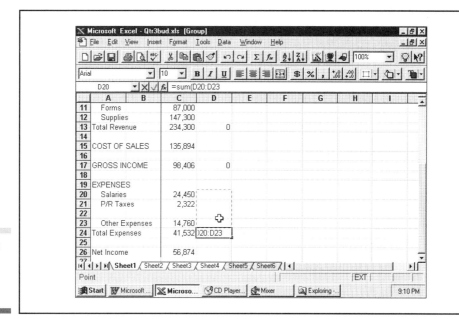

SUM formula
under
construction
Figure 5-8.

The SUM function is the most heavily used Excel function. You will find it
very useful. A rule of thumb is to use SUM if you are summing three or more
cells, and to individually add if you are summing two cells. Depending on
how big the cell addresses are, you may not save keystrokes with SUM on
three cells, but it provides another benefit—it is expandable. Later in the
chapter you will see an even easier way to sum a range of cells for a quick
onscreen total.

When you insert a row or column between cells that are being summed, the
summation adjusts so you are still summing the same cells you originally
identified, but you do not add the new cell in between. For example, if your
original formula is =C4+C5+C6 and you insert a new row between rows 4
and 5, the formula adjusts to become =C4+C6+C7. The formula is still the
way you specified it—the old C5 has become C6 and is so recognized in the
formula. The problem is that the new C5 is not included, and usually when
you insert a new cell in a range, you want that cell included in the
summation. If you use SUM, the new cell *is* included. In the previous
example, the original formula is =SUM(C4:C6). After inserting the new row,
the formula becomes =SUM(C4:C7) and includes the new C5.

Finishing the Columnar Formulas

One columnar formula is left—Net Income in D26. Use these instructions to
enter it.

1. Click on D26. The active cell moves to D26.

2. Type = and the mode indicator changes to Enter. The = goes into the cell and the edit area.

3. Click on D17. The blinking dotted line appears around D17, GROSS INCOME. D17 is reflected in the formula, and the mode indicator changes to Point.

4. Type – and the blinking dotted line disappears from D17.

5. Click on D24. The blinking dotted line appears around D24, Total Expenses, and D24 is reflected in the formula.

6. Press ENTER. The formula is completed, and Excel returns to Ready mode.

Copying Formulas

You have now completed the four columnar formulas and are ready to copy them to the columns for the other two months. You could copy the same formulas to the Third Quarter total in column G, but you will handle that differently. Also, you will be copying other formulas from August to September and you can include the totals in that copy. Therefore, the copying you do here is just from July to August, columns D to E.

You might wonder how you can copy a formula from column D—for example, =D11+D12—to column E and have it work. It would need to be changed to =E11+E12. Excel knows that and, unless you tell it otherwise, it automatically changes the formula *relative* to the location to which it is copied. Follow these steps to copy one formula, and look at it for yourself (the active cell should be D26).

1. Click on the Edit menu and the Copy option. A blinking marquee appears around D26, indicating that it is the source of the copy.

2. Click on E26. The active cell moves to E26, indicating that E26 is the destination of the copy.

3. Press ENTER. The copy finishes by placing the copied formula in E26.

Look now at the formula from E26 in the edit area. It is =E17-E24, as you can see here:

In the process of copying from D26 to E26, the formula automatically changed from =D17~–D24 to =E17~–E24.

Relative Addressing

This ability to adjust a formula from one location to another, as you just did, is called *relative addressing*. The formula is always adjusted relative to its location. This means that the Net Income formula within Excel is

="the cell 9 cells up"-"the cell 2 cells up"

Such a formula will work anywhere in the workbook. Of course, sometimes you want to fix one or more parts of an address. If the entire address is fixed—locked on to a particular cell no matter where you copy it—the addressing scheme is called *absolute addressing*. If some parts of the address are fixed and some are not, the addressing scheme is called *mixed addressing*. Mixed and absolute addressing will be discussed shortly.

Copying the Rest of the Columnar Formulas

You have seen how to copy formulas using the Edit Copy option. Now you can use the drag-and-drop feature to copy the rest of the columnar formulas with the mouse by following these instructions (E26 should still be the active cell).

5

1. First, you may have to activate Cell Drag and Drop if it isn't already activated. Click on Tools, Options, and Edit; then click on the Allow Cell Drag and Drop check box if a check mark does not already fill the check box. Click on OK. The active cell, E26, will now contain a small box in its lower-right corner, called the *fill handle*.
2. Drag on D13 through D24 (point on D13, and then press and hold the mouse button while dragging down to D24). The range D13:D24 is highlighted.
3. Position the mouse pointer on the right border of the highlighted range. Ensure the mouse pointer becomes an arrow.
4. Press and hold CTRL while you drag (by holding down the mouse button) the range D13:D24 to range E13:E24. When you have the shaded border in position over the range E13:E24, release first the mouse button and then CTRL. The contents of range D13:D24 are copied to E13:E24, as shown in Figure 5-9.

The three remaining columnar formulas are thus copied from column D to E and adjusted relative to their new location. You can now calculate all of the totals for July and August.

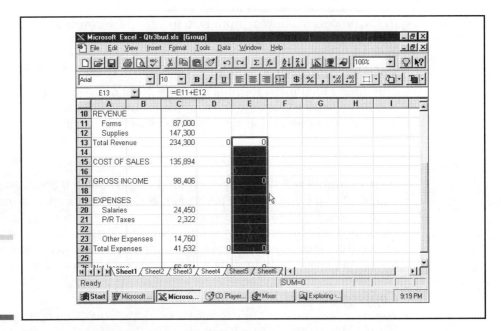

Copying a
column of
formulas
Figure 5-9.

When you pressed CTRL, you probably noticed the mouse pointer changed,
as shown here:

	A	B	C	D	E	F
8			Quarter	July	August	Sept.
10	REVENUE					
11	Forms		87,000			
12	Supplies		147,300			
13	Total Revenue		234,300	0	0	
14						
15	COST OF SALES		135,894			
16						
17	GROSS INCOME		98,406	0	0	
18						

Pressing CTRL while using drag and drop *copies* the contents of a cell or range
to a new location. Using drag and drop without pressing CTRL *moves* the
contents to a new location and the original cell or range contents are
cleared. Copy and move indicators are displayed in the message area of
the Status bar.

Drag and drop is a powerful Excel feature. In the remaining chapters of this
book, it is assumed you are using drag and drop.

Using Assumptions

The formulas used for projection in this model are simple growth formulas that use an assumption for the rate of growth. This assumption can be built into the formula, but if you want to change it, you must edit each formula that uses the assumption. Even in this small budget, that is a lot of formulas. Also, when an assumption is buried in a formula, you cannot see it without moving the active cell to the formula. A better technique is to have all assumptions in a separate table that you can see and easily change. Then the formulas that use these assumptions can reference the table.

The next step, then, is to build a table of assumptions. It consists of three growth factors, one each for revenue, cost of sales, and expenses. Enter these assumptions now with the following instructions.

1. Press CTRL-HOME once and DOWN ARROW twice. The active cell moves to A3.
2. Type **Revenue Growth/Mo.** and press DOWN ARROW.
3. Type **C O S Growth/Mo.** and press DOWN ARROW.
4. Type **Expense Growth/Mo.** and press ENTER.
5. Click on C3. The active cell moves to C3.
6. Type **.012** and press DOWN ARROW.
7. Type **.013** and press DOWN ARROW.
8. Type **.01** and press ENTER.

5

When you finish the last assumption, the upper-left corner of your screen should look like this:

	A	B	C	D
1				THIRD QUAR'
2				
3	Revenue Growth/Mo.		0.012	✛
4	C O S Growth/Mo.		0.013	
5	Expense Growth/Mo.		0.01	
6				

Absolute Addressing

The formula that you use to project July from the second quarter divides the quarter by 3 (to get a monthly value) and then multiplies by 1 plus the growth rate. It is the same formula for all accounts: revenue, cost of sales, and expenses. The only difference is in the growth rate you use. For the two revenue accounts, the growth rate is the same. Therefore, when you copy the formula from D11 to D12, if you do not use absolute addressing (which you'll learn more about in a moment) for the growth rate, it is changed by the copy and points to the growth rate for cost of sales. The growth rate in the formula, then, must use an absolute address. Use the following instructions to build a formula for projecting July Forms revenue with an absolute address for the growth rate and then copy it for use in projecting July Supplies revenue.

1. Click on D11, Forms revenue for July.

2. Type **=** and press LEFT ARROW. The mode indicator changes to Point, and =C11 is placed in the formula.

3. Type **/3*(1+** which is added to the formula under construction.

4. Click on C3. The blinking dotted line appears around C3, the revenue growth rate, and C3 is added to the formula.

5. Press F4 (Absolute). The address C3 in the edit area is changed to $C$3, an absolute address. The upper-left section of your screen should look like this:

C3		=C11/3*(1+$C$3			
A	**B**	**C**	**D**	**E**	**F**
2					
3 Revenue Growth/Mo.		0.012			
4 C O S Growth/Mo.		0.013			
5 Expense Growth/Mo.		0.01			
6					
7		Second			
8		Quarter	July	August	Sept.
10 REVENUE					
11 Forms		87,000	=C11/3*(1+$C$3		
12 Supplies		147,300			

6. Type **)** (you need to type the parenthesis here) and press ENTER. The formula is completed and placed in D11, which becomes the active cell. Note that the totals immediately reflect the number.

7. Press CTRL to start drag and drop and place the mouse pointer on the lower border of D11.

8. While holding down CTRL, drag D11 to D12.

9. Release first the mouse button and then CTRL to complete drag and drop. The copy operation is completed; the formula in D11 is copied to

D12 and the active cell moves to D12, so you can see the resulting formula in the edit area. It should look like this:

In the formula in D12, the reference to the second quarter has changed from C11 to C12, but the reference to the growth rate has remained C3. The $ in front of each part of the growth rate address means that it is an absolute reference and remains the same no matter where it is copied.

Types of Mixed Addresses
When you make an address absolute, each part of the address—the column and the row—is fixed. You also can have various combinations of fixed and relative. These are called mixed addresses. To get a mixed address, press $ repeatedly to cycle through all four possible combinations, as shown in the following table.

If You Have	Pressing F4 Will Give You	Type of Address
C3	$C$3	Absolute address
$C$3	C$3	Mixed (fixed row)
C$3	$C3	Mixed (fixed column)
$C3	C3	Relative

F4 (Absolute) always cycles through the alternatives in the same order, independent of where you start.

Editing Formulas
The formulas for projecting cost of sales and expenses are relatively the same as the formulas for projecting revenue, except for the growth rate. You can easily copy the revenue formula to cost of sales and expenses and then edit the formula. Once the first expense account is corrected, it can be copied to the other expense accounts. Use these steps to do the copying and editing of July's formulas. Your active cell should be D12.

1. Press CTRL and drag and drop D12 to D15. The active cell moves to D15 along with a copy of the contents of D12.

2. Press CTRL and drag and drop D15 to D20. D15 is copied to D20 and the active cell moves to D20.

3. Drag across the rightmost 3 in the formula in the edit area. Excel goes into Edit mode, and the row reference to the growth rate is highlighted.

4. Type **5**. The formula reference, previously referring to the growth rate in C3, is changed to C5, as shown here:

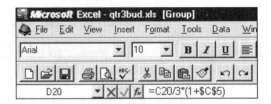

5. Press ENTER. The correct formula is placed in D20, and Excel returns to Ready mode.

6. Drag D20 through D23. The range D20:D23 is highlighted.

7. Click on the Edit menu, then point on Fill, and finally click on Down. The formula in D20 is copied to D21, D22, and D23, as shown in Figure 5-10.

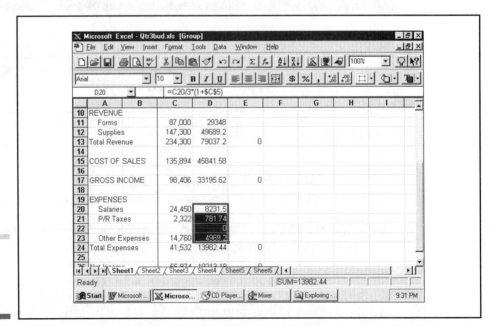

Copying
expense
formulas
Figure 5-10.

As you can see, Fill is a fast way to copy when you have a range immediately next to the area to which you want to copy.

8. Click on D15 and drag across the rightmost 3 in the formula in the edit area.

9. Type **4** and the formula reference to the growth rate in C3 is changed to C4.

10. Press ENTER. The correct formula is placed in D15, and Excel returns to Ready mode.

A similar situation exists in the formulas that project July and those that project August. In the formulas used in July, the second-quarter amounts (in the cell to the left) were divided by 3 to get a monthly amount and then multiplied by the growth factor. In the formulas for August, you will multiply the July amounts (in the cell to the left) by the same growth factor. The only difference is that for July, you divide the cell to the left by 3 and for August you do not. You can copy the July formulas to August and edit out the /3. Follow these steps to build the projection formulas for August.

1. Click on D11.

2. Press CTRL and drag and drop D11 to E11. D11 is copied to E11.

3. Drag across /3 in the formula in the edit area, press DEL and then press ENTER. The formula for projecting August Forms revenue in E11 is modified to remove the division by 3, as shown here:

5

E11		=D11*(1+$C$3)			
	A	B	C	D	E	F
7			Second			
8			Quarter	July	August	Sept.
10	REVENUE					
11	Forms		87,000	29348	29700.18	
12	Supplies		147,300	49689.2		

4. Press CTRL and drag and drop E11 to E12. E11 is copied to E12.

5. Click on D15.

6. Press CTRL and drag and drop D15 to E15. D15 is copied to E15.

7. Drag across /3 in the formula in the edit area, press DEL, and press ENTER. August Cost of Sales in E15 is modified to remove the division by 3.

8. Click on D20.

9. Press CTRL and drag and drop D20 to E20. D20 is copied to E20.

10. Drag across /3 in the formula in the edit area, press DEL, and press ENTER. E20 is modified to remove the division by 3.

Next use drag and drop to fill a contiguous range. This feature is called *AutoFill* and uses the little square in the lower-right corner of the active cell border.

11. Point on the lower-right corner of the active cell border on E20. The mouse pointer will become a plus sign.

12. With the mouse in the lower-right corner of E20, drag down through E23. The range E20:E23 is highlighted and the formula in E20 is copied to E21 through E23.

Your screen should look like the one shown in Figure 5-11. What AutoFill accomplished by dragging the lower-right corner is very handy, as you can see.

Copying a Column of Formulas

Once the August projection is completed, you can copy the entire month to September. There are no differences between the relative formulas as they are now constructed in August and what is needed for September. Use the following instructions to produce September's projection.

1. Drag from E11 through E26. The entire range of Revenue, Cost of Sales, and Expense (E11:E26) is highlighted.

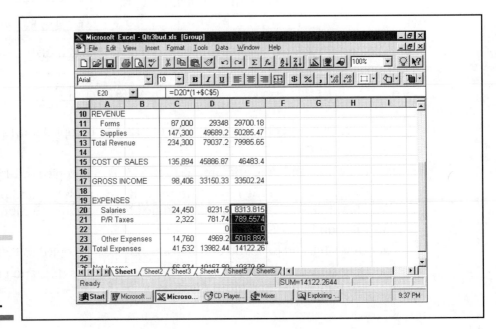

Completed
August
projection
Figure 5-11.

2. Press CTRL and drag and drop E11:E26 to F11:F26. E11:E26 is copied to F11:F26, as shown in Figure 5-12.

Here again you see the power of the Copy command. If you want to build an annual budget by month, all you have to do is build one month and copy it to the other eleven.

Copying

The copying capability is extremely valuable and quite simple. As you have seen, there are three types of copying. With the Copy option, you identify a range you want to copy from—the *source range*—choose the Copy option from the Edit menu, and then specify the range you want to copy to—the *destination range*. With the Fill option, you identify both the source and destination ranges and then choose the command from the Edit menu. The Copy option can do the same type of copying as the Fill options, but the Fill options do it faster with fewer steps. Finally, you can use drag and drop for both copying and filling.

For all types of copying, the mouse is by far the easiest means of identifying both the source and destination ranges. The keyboard can, however, also be used. Using the direction keys, first move the active cell to one of the corners of the range, and then press and hold SHIFT while using the direction keys to expand the highlight to the other cells in the range.

5

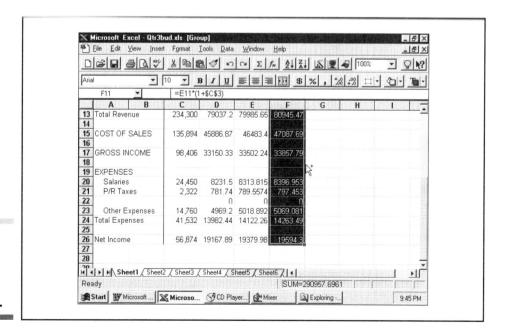

Copying August formulas to September

Figure 5-12.

There are four copy range combinations that work:

♦ Copying a single column to a range spanning several columns. The destination is a single row—the top row of the receiving columns.

♦ Copying a single row to a range spanning several rows. The destination is a single column—the left column of the receiving rows.

♦ Copying a single cell to another single cell, to a row of cells, to a column of cells, or to a block of cells. The destination is another cell, a row, a column, or a block.

♦ Copying a block to a second block. The destination is a single cell—the upper-left corner of the receiving range.

Figure 5-13 shows these four copy range combinations.

Completing the Spreadsheet

The basic three-month projection is now complete. Still to be added, however, are the Quarterly Total and Percentage Growth columns. Also, you will customize the individual stores, do the total company sheet, and spruce up the spreadsheet a bit before finishing this chapter.

Producing a Total

The Quarterly Total is just the sum of the three months. Use the SUM function again to produce a quarterly total.

1. Click on G11. The active cell moves to G11.

2. Click on the AutoSum tool in the toolbar. The edit area contains =SUM(C11:F11), as shown here:

	A	B	C	D	E	F	G	H
8			Quarter	July	August	Sept.	Quarter	Growth
10	REVENUE							
11	Forms		87,000	29348	29700.18	30056.58	=SUM(C11:F11)	
12	Supplies		147,300	49689.2	50285.47	50888.9		
13	Total Revenue		234,300	79037.2	79985.65	80945.47		
14								

The AutoSum tool automatically builds a SUM formula in the active cell based on a contiguous range of numbers, either above or to the left of the active cell. In this case, the contiguous range of numbers is to the

Copy a column to
range of columns:
copy-to range is a row

Copy a row to range
of rows: copy-to range
is a column

Copy a cell to a row,
column, or block:
copy-to range is a
cell, row,column, or block

Copy a block to
a block: copy-to
range is a cell

Four copy
range
combinations
Figure 5-13.

left and includes the second quarter, which you don't want. You
therefore need to revise the range to be summed.

3. Press RIGHT ARROW. The range in the SUM formula changes to just D11.

4. Press SHIFT-RIGHT ARROW twice. The range in the SUM formula becomes
   D11:F11, which is what you want to sum in the third quarter.

5. Pressing SHIFT and any arrow key extends the selection of cells in the
   direction of the arrow key. This is also true with HOME, END, PGDN, and

PGUP. Unless you press SHIFT, you will replace D11 with the new active cell instead of creating a range as you intended.

6. Press ENTER. The summation formula is completed, and Excel returns to Ready mode.

The summation formula will be copied down the Third Quarter summary column with the Percentage Growth formula in a moment.

Another way to produce a sum is with Excel's AutoCalculate feature, which displays on the Status bar in the large section at the left end of the mode indicators with the word SUM= and some value. You get an instantaneous, although temporary, sum of any range by just selecting the range and letting AutoCalculate produce the result. As soon as you deselect a particular range (or cell) you lose that sum and AutoCalculate produces a new sum based on the newly selected cells. Highlight the range D11:F11 and compare the number in G11 with the result displayed on the Status bar. AutoCalculate also can perform other commonly used functions, which are described in Chapter 8, "Working with a Database."

Calculating a Percentage

The Percentage Growth formula is the difference between the second and third quarters divided by the second quarter. Build that formula by following these instructions.

1. Click on H11.

2. Type =(and click on G11. The mode indicator changes to Enter and then to Point, and =(G11 is placed into the cell and the edit area.

3. Type - and click on C11. -C11 is added to the formula.

4. Type)/ and click on C11 again. The edit area now looks like this:

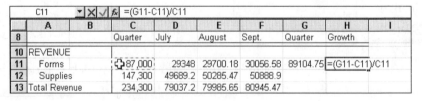

5. Press ENTER to complete the Percentage Growth formula.

Copying a Row of Formulas

The quarterly summation and percentage growth formulas now must be copied down their columns. There are three ways to do this. One way is to copy the formulas in five operations to the five segments that need them (Revenue, Cost of Sales, Gross Income, Expenses, and Net Income). The second method is to copy the formulas to the entire column at one time and then erase the four blank lines that divide the segments. Finally, you can use AutoFill to copy the quarterly summation and percentage growth formulas to the entire column. As you have seen, AutoFill allows you to create a filled range of fixed values (as in this case) or extend a *series* by incrementing numbers or dates. (Series will be discussed in Chapter 7.) In this example, you will still need to erase the four blank lines that divide the segments, but now the copy operation can be done in a single mouse operation. Use AutoFill in the following exercise.

1. Drag across G11 and H11 and point on the fill handle in the lower-right corner of the highlighted range G11:H11. The mouse pointer will again become a plus sign, as you can see in the following:

5

2. Keeping the mouse a plus sign, drag the mouse pointer down the right border of the range G11:H26. Release the mouse button when the highlighted area covers the range. Columns G and H are filled with figures, as shown in Figure 5-14.

On the unused rows, like 14, you get the message #DIV/0!. This is an error message stating you are dividing by zero. Don't let it bother you. You are going to erase or clear these next.

Clearing a Range of Cells

Clearing a range (which, you remember, can be a cell, a column, a row, or a block) is very easy: highlight the range, and press DEL. Do that next for row 14.

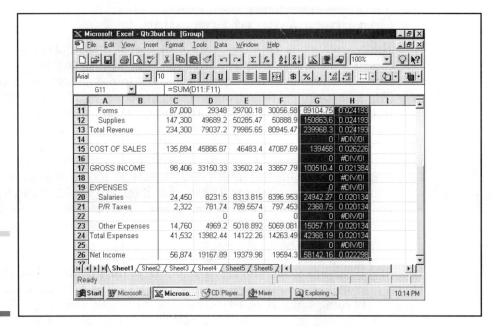

Completed
totals and
percentages
Figure 5-14.

1. Drag across G14 and H14. The range G14:H14 is highlighted.

2. Press DEL. G14 and H14 are cleared, as shown here:

If you want a little more control over what you are deleting, you can use the Clear option in the Edit menu. When you do that, you get a chance to clear everything in the cell, or clear just the formats, contents, or notes. Try that next.

3. Drag across G16 and H16. Then click on the Edit menu and on the Clear option. A submenu opens up, like this:

The options that are available on the Clear submenu and their results are as follows.

♦ *All*   Erases everything (contents, formats, and notes) from the cell and returns it to the General format.

♦ *Formats*   Erases only the formats, leaving the contents and notes. The cell is returned to the General format.

♦ *Contents*   Erases only the contents, leaving the formats and notes.

♦ *Notes*   Erases only the notes, leaving the contents and formats.

4. Click on All to clear everything in G16 and H16.

5. Use either the DEL key or Edit Clear option to erase rows 18, 19 (which can be done together), and 25. Leave row 22 for the moment.

Inserting a Row

To make the sheet easier to read, you will now insert a line between the expense and revenue totals and the detail accounts above them. To do this, you insert a blank row and then copy a line across it.

1. Drag across A13 through H13.

5

2. Click on the Insert menu and on the Cells option. The Insert dialog box opens, as shown here:

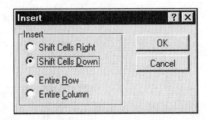

The Insert dialog box gives you four options: Shift Cells Right, Shift Cells Down—which is what you want here—Entire Row, or Entire Column. Since Shift Cells Down is the default, you need only click on OK.

3. Click on OK. A new, blank row 13 is inserted, and all the cells below A13:H13 are shifted down.

4. Click on C13, type -, and press ENTER. C13 contains a single hyphen.

5. Click on the Format menu, the Cells option, and the Alignment tab. The Alignment dialog box opens.

6. Click on Fill and OK. The dialog box closes, and C13 fills with hyphens.

7. Drag C13 through H13. Click on the Edit menu and the Fill Right option. The line in C13 is copied across the range D13:H13, as shown here:

	A	B	C	D	E	F	G	H	I
11	Forms		87,000	29348	29700.18	30056.58	89104.75	0.024193	
12	Supplies		147,300	49689.2	50285.47	50888.9	150863.6	0.024193	
13			-----------	-------------	-------------	-------------	-------------	-------------	
14	Total Revenue		234,300	79037.2	79985.65	80945.47	239968.3	0.024193	
15									

Go down to A25 and, following the previous instructions, insert a new row and copy a line across columns C through H. Note that in both cases the total formulas remain unaffected by the new rows.

Deleting a Row

You have been hanging on to what is now row 23 with the idea that you will do something with it. You will, you'll delete it. Row 23 was added to demonstrate deleting a row in a SUM range. Do that now by following these instructions.

1. Drag across A23 through H23.

2. Click the right mouse button (popup menu) and the Delete option. The Delete dialog box opens with the options Shift Cells Left (to delete columns) or Shift Cells Up (to delete rows), as shown in Figure 5-15. The default, Shift Cells Up, is what you want. Therefore, you need only click on OK.

3. Click on OK. The range A23:H23 is deleted and all the cells below that row shift up. Note that the row deletion did not change the Total Expenses or Net Income amounts.

Inserting and Deleting

Inserting and deleting rows and columns are simultaneously very powerful and potentially dangerous operations. They are powerful because they allow you to easily change the structure of a spreadsheet after it is built by, for example, adding new or forgotten accounts or deleting unwanted elements. Inserting and (especially) deleting can also be dangerous because, under certain circumstances, you can cause a formula to become incorrect.

Excel has many safeguards against causing a formula error with an insertion or a deletion. You have seen how both cell-by-cell addition and SUM formulas are not affected by inserting rows. Even an absolute range is correctly adjusted if an inserted row changes its position. For example, if a

5

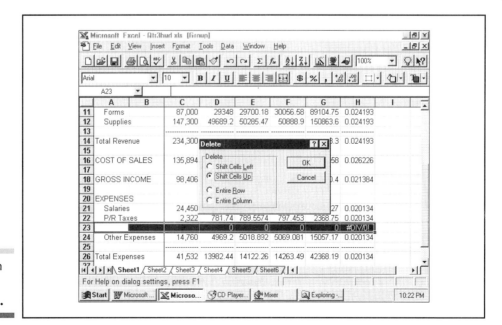

Row deletion in progress
Figure 5-15.

row is inserted between rows 2 and 3, pushing the assumptions in C3 through C5 down a row, the absolute references to those cells are corrected automatically.

One safeguard is that both inserts and deletes can be undone if you choose Undo from the Edit menu or press CTRL-Z or ALT-BACKSPACE before you carry out another operation that takes Excel out of Ready mode. You can look at a formula, but do not try to edit it, which will take it out of Ready mode. Get into the habit of pausing after doing an insert or delete and looking around the sheet. Highlight several formulas to see if they have been correctly changed, thereby giving yourself a chance to use Undo if necessary.

Excel's formulas are extremely flexible, especially SUM. Not only can you insert or delete cells in the middle of a summation range, but you can also delete the named first and last cells in a summation and the formula will be correctly adjusted.

When you do an insert or delete, it is handy to think of it as inserting or deleting rows or columns. However, there is good reason for Excel's not using this terminology in its dialog boxes: you insert or delete only the specific cells you previously highlighted. You do not insert or delete a row or column across or down the entire sheet.

While it may be obvious that to delete three rows, you need to highlight three rows, it is not so obvious that to insert three rows, you need to highlight three rows. The number of rows highlighted is inserted immediately above the top row highlighted. For columns, the number of columns highlighted is inserted immediately to the left of the leftmost column highlighted.

Making Corrections

This completes the work you will do on the spreadsheet in this chapter. Your screen should now look like the one shown in Figure 5-16. If your numbers are different, you may have an error in one of your formulas. Although it is a bit of a pain, you might want to look for it just to see how a search is done. Go down columns D and E, highlighting each cell. Also, look at cells G11 and H11. Compare the cell contents in the edit area with various figures and descriptions in this chapter. It should not take long to find the error. A good rule is to thoroughly check formulas as you are building them to avoid having to go back and correct them later.

Customizing Individual Sheets

All of the work you have done so far in this chapter has been entered onto four sheets. All the titles and headings and all of the numbers and formulas

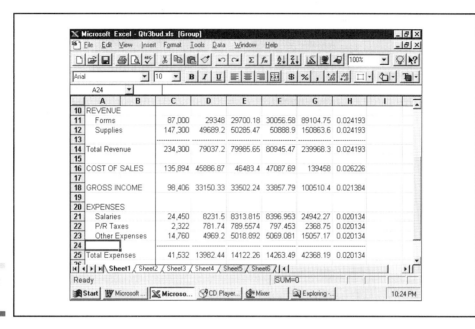

Finished sheet
Figure 5-16.

that you have entered or created on Sheet1 have been automatically duplicated on Sheet2 through Sheet4. It is now time to unlink the four sheets and customize each sheet. In a real-world situation, this would entail, at a minimum, putting an identifying title on each sheet and customizing the assumptions and the starting numbers. In addition, you need to change Sheet4 so that it sums the other sheets. For this exercise, you will customize only two of the sheet titles and change Sheet4 so that it is a summary. You have already changed enough numbers that you do not need further practice in that.

Begin the customization with these instructions for unlinking the sheets and changing the titles.

1. Click on Sheet5 to select that sheet and in the process unlink the other four sheets.

2. Click on Sheet1 to select just that sheet. Note after you select Sheet1, Sheet2 through Sheet4 are no longer selected.

3. Press CTRL-HOME to go to cell A1, which contains the title.

4. Click in the edit area of the Formula bar to the left of the "T" in "THIRD."

5. Type **5TH AVENUE STORE** - and press ENTER. The title will change and be recentered automatically.

6. In order to tell which sheet is which, also change the name on the sheet tab by double-clicking on the tab, as shown in Figure 5-17, and typing **5th Ave**.

7. Click on OK to complete changing the sheet tab.

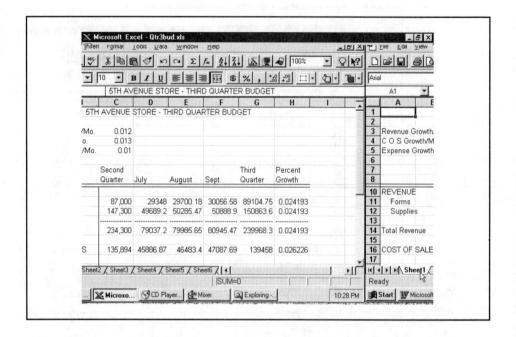

If you wish, click individually on Sheet2 and Sheet3 and change their titles and sheet tabs to include a store name (Main Street Store and University Store, for example) using the above instructions.

Sheet Summarizing Formulas

Summarizing a group of sheets is very similar to summarizing any other group of cells—you can even use the mouse to identify the cells on the various sheets that you want to summarize. The major difference in formulas that span sheets is that the references must include a sheet name prior to each cell reference and be separated from the cell reference by an exclamation point. For example, if you want to refer to the range C4:D8 on Sheet2, you would write it Sheet2!C4:D8. Also, the Excel functions work as well across sheets as they do across any other range.

See how sheet summarization works by entering formulas to summarize Sheet1 through Sheet3 on Sheet4. Enter the title for Sheet4, change the sheet tab, and use the AutoSum tool to build the formulas, following these instructions.

1. Double-click on the sheet tab for Sheet4 to select that sheet and open the renaming dialog box.

2. Type **Total** and press ENTER to create a new tab name.

3. Press CTRL-HOME, click to the left of "THIRD" in the edit area, type **TOTAL COMPANY** - , and press ENTER to change the title.

4. Click on C11, which will contain the first formula summarizing the other sheets.

5. Click on the AutoSum tool in the Standard toolbar to create a SUM formula.

6. Click on Sheet1 (5th Ave) and press and hold SHIFT while clicking on Sheet3 (Univer.) to select the range of sheets.

7. Click on C11 to select that as the cell to summarize on all three sheets as shown here:

	A	B	C	D	E	F
1			5TH AVENUE STORE - THIRD QUARTER BUD(			
2						
3	Revenue Growth/Mo.		0.012			
4	C O S Growth/Mo.		0.013			
5	Expense Growth/Mo.		0.01			
6						
7			Second			
8			Quarter	July	August	Sept.
10	REVENUE					
11	Forms		87,000	29348	29700.18	30056.58
12	Supplies		147,300	49689.2	50285.47	50888.9

C11   =SUM('5th Ave:Univer.'!C11)

8. Press ENTER to complete the formula building process.

9. Use drag and drop with CTRL to copy C11 to C12, C14, C16, C18, C21:23, C25, and C27. Make sure you are firmly holding down CTRL before dragging or you will move the formula instead of copying it. If you do that, you will change the percentage formula in column H, and you will need to correct it before completing the sheet.

10. Drag down C11:C27 and use AutoFill with CTRL (drag on the lower-right corner of the range) to copy the formulas in that range to columns D, E, F, and G. (Column H, the percentages, needs to use its original formulas to calculate the percent growth.) When you are done, your screen should look like Figure 5-18.

5

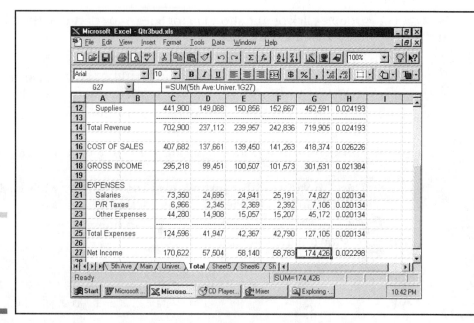

Completed
Total
Company
sheet
Figure 5-18.

As you can see, summing over sheets is both easy and very powerful. With Excel 7, you truly have a full three-dimensional work area.

Saving and Quitting Excel

The only task remaining is to save the workbook and leave Excel. Use the following instructions for that purpose.

1. Click on the Save tool (the third tool from the left in the Standard toolbar). The file is saved under the name you originally gave it: QTR3BUD.

   As a default, when Excel saves a file it simply copies over the last copy of the same file on disk. The save you just completed copied over the file that you created by saving the workbook early in the chapter. You can also have Excel make a new file each time you save a file. Since you can have only one file with a given name, Excel automatically renames the old file by changing its extension to .BAK (for backup). The third time you save a file, the first copy is deleted and the second copy is given the .BAK extension.

2. To have Excel make a backup, use the Options button in the File Save As dialog box, as shown in the following steps.

3. Click on the File menu and click on Save As. The File Save As dialog box opens. Make sure the path to the QTR3BUD.XLS file is to your Sheet folder. Change the path if necessary.

4. Click on the Options button in the File Save As dialog box. A new dialog box opens, as shown here:

5. Click on the Always Create Backup check box, click on OK, and then click on Save. The Options and the File Save As dialog boxes close, and another dialog box opens asking if you want to replace the existing QTR3BUD.XLS file.

   5

   Click on Yes. The Summary tab to the file's Properties dialog box opens. Click on OK after making any changes or click on Cancel to accept the information in the tab.

   The previous file, which was called QTR3BUD.XLS, is now renamed QTR3BUD.BAK, and a new file named QTR3BUD.XLS will be created. You now have two files on disk. The file backup capability is handy if you need to reuse the earlier file for any reason.

   You are done with Excel and Windows for this chapter. Therefore, shut them both down now.

6. Double-click on Excel's Control-menu icon and then on the Start button. Choose Shut Down and click on Yes to end your Windows session.

Total

TOTAL COMPANY - THIRD QUARTER BUDGET

Revenue Growth/Mo.	0.012					
C O S Growth/Mo.	0.013					
Expense Growth/Mo.	0.01					

	Second Quarter	July	August	Sept.	Third Quarter	Percent Growth
REVENUE						
Forms	261,000	88,044	89,101	90,170	267,314	0.024193
Supplies	441,900	149,068	150,856	152,667	452,591	0.024193
Total Revenue	702,900	237,112	239,957	242,836	719,905	0.024193
COST OF SALES	407,682	137,661	139,450	141,263	418,374	0.026226
GROSS INCOME	295,218	99,451	100,507	101,573	301,531	0.021384
EXPENSES						
Salaries	73,350	24,695	24,941	25,191	74,827	0.020134
P/R Taxes	6,966	2,345	2,369	2,392	7,106	0.020134
Other Expenses	44,280	14,908	15,057	15,207	45,172	0.020134
Total Expenses	124,596	41,947	42,367	42,790	127,105	0.020134
Net Income	170,622	57,504	58,140	58,783	174,426	0.022298

Printed
spreadsheet
Figure 5-19.

At this point, the spreadsheet in printed form is not particularly pretty without the grid, as shown in Figure 5-19. The formatting of the numbers is messy and the columns seem to run together. Making it look better in a number of ways, as well as printing it, will be covered in Chapter 6.

Enhancing a Workbook

6

In Chapter 5 you created a workbook for preparing a third-quarter budget. The results were usable, but they were difficult to read and not particularly attractive. In this chapter, you'll use a number of techniques to make the budget easier to read and more attractive. The techniques include changing the formatting of numbers and headings and moving, deleting, and erasing sections of the workbook. You will also set the parameters for and print the workbook. Finally, you'll change the Third-Quarter Budget workbook into a template that can be used to set up any quarterly budget.

Loading a Workbook

To begin working on the budget workbook, you must load the file that holds it on the disk. Remember that the last thing you did in Chapter 5 before leaving Excel was to save the file. You must now load that file back into memory so you can work on it. Start your computer, load Excel (if necessary), and use the following instructions:

1. Click on the File menu and the Open option. The File menu opens, followed by the Open dialog box, similar to what is seen here:

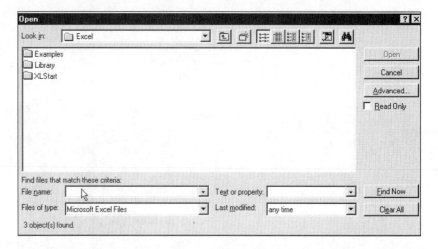

If you continued here directly from Chapter 5 without leaving Excel, you are probably looking at the correct folder and can skip the next two steps. However, if you closed Excel and Windows as suggested in Chapter 5 and restarted both here, the folder you are looking at in the Open dialog box is probably the \EXCEL program folder, not the \SHEET folder where you stored QTR3BUD. Your first task, then, is to change folders. Make the necessary changes with the following steps.

2. Open the Look in drop-down list box and click on C: to view the folders in your C drive.

3. Double-click on "Sheet" in the large list box that occupies most of the dialog box. If you do not see "Sheet," use the horizontal scroll bar (click on the right end of the scroll bar) to find it. In the list box, QTR3BUD.XLS should appear, as shown here:

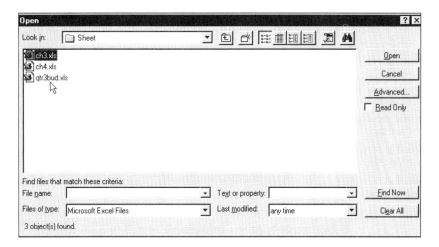

If you don't see the file extension XLS (the three characters to the right of the decimal point in a filename) it's because you have not told Windows 95 you want to view file extensions of files that are *registered*. Registered files are those that Windows associates with a program, so when you double-click on them in the Explorer or My Computer, their parent program opens with the file loaded. You can choose to view the extensions of registered files in the Explorer View menu Options dialog box. In the View tab, clear the check box Hide MS-DOS file extensions for file types that are registered.

4. Double-click on QTR3BUD.XLS in the list box.

The third-quarter budget opens on your screen, as shown in Figure 6-1. You can now begin working on it.

Formatting

Excel lets you *format* (change the appearance of) individual characters and cells as well as groups of cells, an entire sheet, or even an entire workbook. After formatting a group of cells with the most common format in that group of cells, you can come back and change specific cells that you want to be different from the overall format. You can also set overall formats for

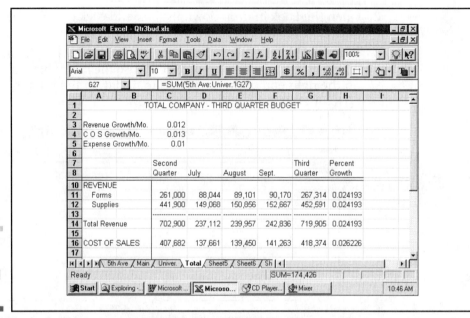

Third-quarter
budget as
initially loaded

Figure 6-1.

several aspects of the workbook, but here you will set the overall format just
for numbers and for the width of columns.

Overall Number Format

The overall number format determines how numbers appear on a sheet,
both on the screen and when printed. Most of the numbers in the workbook
are formatted with the General format, which is the format Excel starts with.
It is the most versatile format in terms of the variety of numbers it can
display, but it looks the least appealing. Let's first see how to change the
Number format and then look at some of the formatting alternatives.
Start out by reselecting the four sheets and then highlighting the area
to be formatted.

1. Click on the sheet tab for the 5th Avenue store (old Sheet1).

2. Press and hold SHIFT while clicking on the sheet tab for the Total
   Company (Sheet4) to reselect all four sheets together. Your Title bar
   should now include the word "Group" to indicate more than one sheet
   is selected.

3. On the 5th Avenue sheet (Sheet1), drag the mouse from C10 through
   H27 to highlight that area, as shown in Figure 6-2. Alternatively, you

can select the range by clicking on C10, pressing the SHIFT key while you scroll your screen so you can see H27, and then clicking on H27.

4. Click on the Format menu, the Cells option, and the Number tab, if necessary. The Format Cells dialog box opens to the Number tab, as shown here.

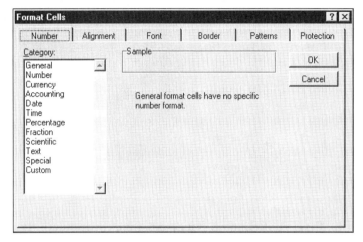

5. Click on Custom, the last entry in the Category list box. The Number tab changes to include a list of formatting codes.

6. Double-click on the fourth alternative (#,##0) in the Type list box. The Format command finishes, and the workbook is rcdisplayed in the new format.

6

Your screen should now look like the one in Figure 6-3. Don't be concerned that all of the percentages disappeared. When you selected #,##0 from the Format Cells dialog box, you told Excel to format the numbers without decimal places (you'll see how this works in a moment). Excel took this literally and displayed no decimal places even when decimals were all you had. You will come back soon to override the overall format with a specific percentage format for column H. Additionally, you will see that for the majority of your number formatting needs, Excel 7 provides a simple means to set the number of decimal places, foregoing completely the use of format codes.

You might wonder why you use the format chosen when the majority of numbers in the workbook are currency. If you use a currency format, the sheets become cluttered with dollar signs. Later in this chapter you will format just the total lines at the bottom of each sheet as currency. That sets the totals off from the rest of the numbers and doesn't clutter the entire page with dollar signs.

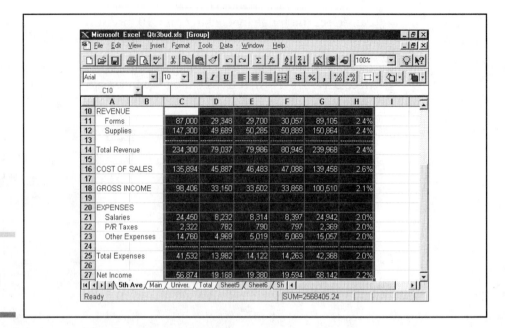

Highlighting
the range to
be formatted
Figure 6-2.

Formatting Alternatives

The Format Cells dialog box Number tab offers many formatting
alternatives, and you can also construct your own format. This chapter

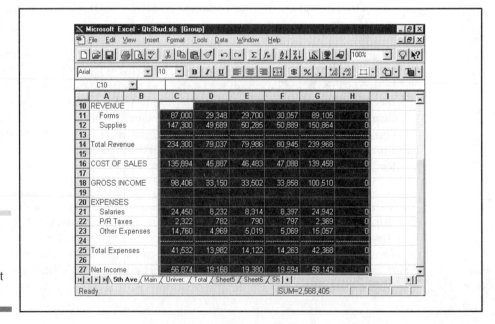

Third-quarter
budget after
setting the
overall format
Figure 6-3.

discusses the built-in formats, selecting formatting options such as the number of decimal places, and how you can construct a format of your own.

In Excel, numbers are stored with as many significant digits as the column width allows. All significant digits can be displayed, and can be all to the left or all to the right of the decimal point, or some combination. Of course, the column must be wide enough. For all formats except the General format, the column must be wide enough to display all of the whole digits to the left of the decimal point, the number of decimal digits specified, and any other characters such as dollar signs, commas, or periods that are part of the format. If the column is not wide enough, it is filled with # symbols.

There are three ways Excel allows you to add formatting to your workbook: by using the Format menu, by selecting formatting tools from the Formatting toolbar, and by choosing the automatic formats provided by Excel (AutoFormat). There are advantages to each method in making your workbook more attractive. You will learn more about each of these in the exercises in this chapter.

Format Symbols

You communicate to Excel the type of format you want to use with symbols. The symbols describe such things as the number of decimal places; whether or not a dollar sign, percent sign, or comma should be used; and how to handle negative numbers, zero values, and text. Excel provides many built-in *format codes,* including the General format. Excel divides these format codes into 12 *categories,* as follows: General, Number, Currency, Accounting, Date, Time, Percentage, Fraction, Scientific, Text, Special, and Custom. Each category has a number of the total format codes. For example, the Date category has 11 codes, as shown here:

6

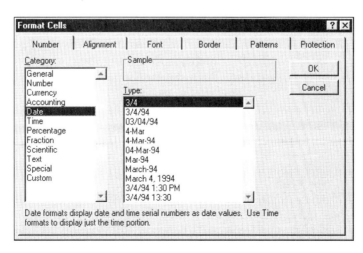

Each of these built-in format codes, plus any that you build, use the formatting symbols shown in Table 6-1 to communicate their formats. Note that the first three symbols in Table 6-1, 0, #, and ?, are placeholders that may be filled with numbers if there are numbers available for that place. If there is no number to fill 0, a 0 will take the place; if there is no number to fill #, nothing takes its place and no space is left; if there is no number to fill ?, a blank space takes its place.

Symbol	Usage
0	Specifies the number of *fixed* decimal places to the right of the decimal point and the minimum digits to the left of the decimal point. For example, with the built-in format 0.00, you always have two decimal places to the right of the decimal point and at least one digit to the left of the decimal point. With the 0.00 format, the following numbers are formatted as shown: **Entry** **Display** .456 0.46 45 45.00
#	Specifies the number of *optional* digits on either side of the decimal point. If there are more digits in the number than there are #'s to the left of the decimal point, the digits will be displayed, but on the right side of the decimal point the decimal digits will be rounded to the number of #'s in that part of the format. For example, in the built-in format #,##0 the # provides the optional digits surrounding the comma, which is used as a thousands separator. If there are not enough digits to fill the number of places, these will be blank and space will not be left. You want the first place to be a 0 and not a #, so you will get at least a 0 printed if you have a decimal too small to round to 1. With the #,##0 format, the following entries are formatted as shown: **Entry** **Display** 46.67 47 12345 12,345

Formatting
Symbols
Table 6-1.

Symbol	Usage
?	Specifies the number of spaces to leave on either side of the decimal point in order to align the decimal point with fewer digits. For example, the built-in format # ??/?? provides space for six characters to the right of the decimal place (one to separate the whole number from the fraction, two for the denominator, two for the numerator, and one for /). Space is always left for each ?. With the # ??/?? format, the following entries are formatted as shown: **Entry** **Display** 5.8125 5 13/16 5.25 5 1/4
. (period)	Specifies where a decimal point is to be placed.
, (comma)	Specifies that the thousands separator is a comma if a comma is surrounded by zeros or # symbols, for example, #,##0. One or more commas on the right of a format will scale the resulting number by a thousand for each comma. For example, formatting 5,650,000 by typing **0.00,,** in the Type text box would produce the number 5.65.
;	Separates sections of a format. You can have up to four sections. The first, or leftmost, specifies how to format positive numbers, the second section specifies how to format negative numbers, the third specifies how to format zero, and the fourth section specifies how to handle text. All numbers are handled the same way if there is only one section. With two sections, positive and zero values are formatted with the first, and negative numbers are formatted with the second. Text is not given special treatment with only three sections. An example of using a semicolon is shown with the next set of symbols.
_ (underline)	Specifies that a space be left that is equal in width to the character immediately following the underline. For example, in the built-in format $#,##0_);($#,##0), the "_)" shifts positive numbers to the left an amount equal to the width of a ")". This aligns positive and negative numbers by leaving room for the ")".

6

Formatting
Symbols
(*continued*)
Table 6-1.

Symbol	Usage
$ + – ( ) / : space	Specifies a literal character to be displayed. For example, the built-in format $#,##0_);($#,##0) places a $ to the left of the leftmost number and ( ) around negative numbers. With the $#,##0_);($#,##0) format, the following numbers are formatted as shown: **Entry** **Display** –45.67 ($46) 1234 $1,234 If you want to enter a literal character other than $ + – ( ) / : or space, precede the character with a backslash (\) or enclose one or more of the characters in double quotation marks (" "). These are explained shortly.
"text"	Specifies that whatever is between the " " is displayed. As an example, $#,##0"DB" ;$#,##0"CR";0 places DB after positive numbers, CR after negative numbers, and 0 for zero values.
\	Specifies that the character following the \ is displayed. This is the same as enclosing a single character in " ". For some characters, you do not have to enter the \ because Excel will automatically do it for you. These characters are ~! ^ & ` ' = { } < >. +  For example, you can enter the format `#,##0'! and Excel will in effect (but not on the screen) change it to \ `#,##0\'\!. If you format the number 45 with this format you will get `45'!.
@	Specifies where any text in a cell is placed in a format. For example, 0.00 ;@ formats all numbers with 0.00 and displays any text appearing in the cell. (0.00 by itself does the same thing.)

Formatting
Symbols
(*continued*)
Table 6-1.

Symbol	Usage
*	Specifies that the character following the * is repeated to fill any unused space in the cell. For example, $**#,##0 places a $ in the leftmost position in a cell, fills any intervening space with *, and right aligns the number in the cell as usual. You see this on computer printed checks. With the $**#,##0 format, the following numbers are formatted as shown: **Entry** **Display** 45 $*******45 1234 $****1,234 You cannot have more than one sequence beginning with an asterisk in one section of a format.
%	Specifies that a number is multiplied by 100 and a % placed to the right. For example, the built-in format 0.00% multiplies the number by 100 and places a % after a pair of decimal points. With the 0.00% format, the following numbers are formatted as shown: **Entry** **Display** .07 7.00% .4575 45.75% −0.067 −6.70%
E+ E− e+e−	Specifies that the scientific format is used if either a # or a 0 precedes either E or e. If a − is specified, only negative numbers have a sign. With a +, both positive and negative numbers have a sign. For example, the built-in format 0.00E+00 uses a capital E and both plus and minus signs for the scientific format. With the 0.00E+00 format, the following numbers are formatted as shown: **Entry** **Display** 4567 4.57E+03 −1234 −1.23E+04 .0045 4.50E−03

6

Formatting
Symbols
(*continued*)
Table 6-1.

Symbol	Usage
m mm mmm mmmm	Specifies that a month is displayed as a number without a leading zero (m) or with a leading zero (mm), as a three-letter abbreviation like Apr or Sep(mmm), or as a full name (mmmm). If m or mm follows h or hh, it specifies minutes rather than a month.
d dd ddd dddd	Specifies that a day is displayed as a number (1 - 31) without a leading zero (d), with a leading zero (dd), as a three-letter abbreviation like Tue or Thu(ddd), or as a full name of the day of the week (dddd).
yy yyyy	Specifies that a year is displayed as either a two-digit (94) or four-digit number (1994).
h hh	Specifies that an hour is displayed as a number either without a leading zero (4) or with a leading zero (04).
m mm	Specifies that a minute is displayed as a number either without a leading zero (5) or with a leading zero (05). If the m or mm does not appear after an h or hh, the month is displayed.
s ss	Specifies that a second is displayed as a number either without a leading zero (6) or with a leading zero (06).
AM/PM am/pm A/P a/p	Specifies that time is displayed using a 12-hour clock with AM, am, A, or a (times before noon) and PM, pm, P, or p (from noon to midnight).
[color]	Specifies that the characters in the cell should be displayed in a color. The colors available are black, white, red, green, blue, yellow, magenta, and cyan or [color $n0$] where $n0$ is a number from 1 through 56 indicating one of the 56 colors in the Format Cells Patterns tab's custom color palette . For example, the built-in format #,##0_); [Red](#,##0) displays negative numbers in red.
[condition value]	Lets you define what values fall in each section of a format code. *Condition* is one of the logical operators < > = <= >= <> (the last operator means *not*) and *value* is any number. For example, using the comma format, if you wanted values above 10,000 to be green, values between 0 and 10,000 to be yellow, and values below 0 to be red, you would use the following format: [Green][>10000]#,##0_);[Yellow][>=0]#,##0_);[Red](#,##0)

Formatting Symbols (*continued*)

Table 6-1.

When you have a fixed number of decimal places, the decimal digits are rounded to fit the format. Also, if you have blank format sections (semicolons with nothing between them), that type of number is not displayed. For example, 0.00;;;@ displays and formats positive numbers and text, but does not display negative numbers and zero values.

General Format

Every time you create a new workbook, all cells are automatically formatted with the General format. The General format displays numbers with a variable number of decimal places, no thousands separators, a minus sign if the number is negative, and a leading zero if the number is less than 1. If the column is not wide enough to display all of the decimal digits, they are rounded to the nearest digit that can be displayed. If the column is not wide enough to display all of the whole digits to the left of the decimal point, the number is converted to scientific notation.

Here are some examples of General formatting with the standard column width of 8.43 characters:

Entry	Display
1234567.89	1234568
1234567890	1.23E+09
−4567.89	−4567.89
.8956	0.8956

Setting Overall Column Width

6

Excel starts with a standard column width of 8.43 characters. This allows you to display eight or nine text characters or a number with eight characters in it (a blank character always remains on the left of a right-aligned number). A column's width can be set from 0 to 255 characters.

To change the width of a column on a sheet, you can either drag the intersection between two column headings to the right of the column whose width you want to change, or use the Column Width dialog box. You can change single or multiple columns with either method. Try the dialog box next with the following steps.

1. If columns C through H are not currently highlighted (it doesn't matter what rows), drag across C11 through H11.

2. Click on the Format menu, point on the Column option, and click on the Width suboption. The Column Width dialog box opens, as shown in the following illustration:

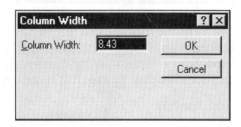

3. Type **10** and press ENTER. All columns in the C through H range are widened to ten characters, as shown in Figure 6-4. Compare with Figure 6-3 to see the effect of the widened columns.

Now compare this dialog box method with dragging the width of multiple columns.

1. Click on the Edit menu and the Undo Column Width option to restore the original width to columns C through H.

2. Drag across the column *headings* (not the individual cells) for columns C through H. Six entire columns will be highlighted.

3. Point on the line between the column headings C and D. The mouse pointer becomes a two-headed arrow with a bar in the middle. This allows you to change the column width.

4. Drag the right edge of column C's heading until "Width: 10.00" appears on the left side of the Formula bar, as shown here:

Width:10.00 ▼			
	A	**B**	**C** ⊕ **D**
10	REVENUE		
11	Forms		87,000 29,348
12	Supplies		147,300 49,689

Columns C through H will be widened to ten characters.

The dragging method is not only slightly easier, but you can also see exactly how wide the column will be.

Detail Formatting

You have now set the overall format and column width. Next you will tailor specific areas with the formatting that makes them look best. In the following sections, your formatting tasks include recovering the percentages that disappeared, formatting the summary lines in the budget as currency, and centering and embolding the column headings in their columns.

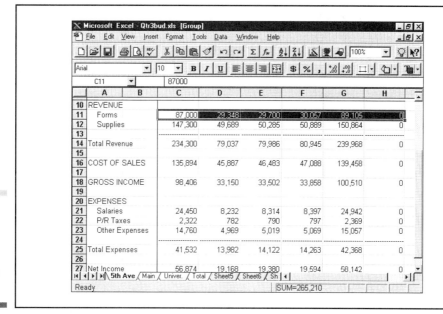

Effect of
widening
columns C
through H to
ten characters
Figure 6-4.

Creating a Percentage Format

The percentages disappeared when the overall format was set with no
decimal places. With the General format the percentages were not easy to
read. A format with the % symbol, which multiplies a number by 100 and
adds a percent sign, is a better way to display percentages. Two areas or
groups of cells in the workbook require this kind of format: the percent
growth in column H and the assumptions in the upper part of column C.

Excel 7 provides several decimal places to the right of the decimal point for
percentage formatting. This is a major improvement over previous versions
of Excel that required you to create custom formatting codes for anything
but a few built-in codes. Format the two areas that need to display
percentages in the following steps.

6

1. Drag from cell H11 through H27 to highlight the first area to be
   formatted.
2. While pointing in the highlighted area, press the right mouse button to
   display the popup menu, click on the Format Cells option, and, if
   necessary, click on the Number tab.
3. Click on the Percentage category, and then click on the up arrow in the
   Decimal Places spinner so a 1 appears in the numeric entry box.

Your Number tab should look like this:

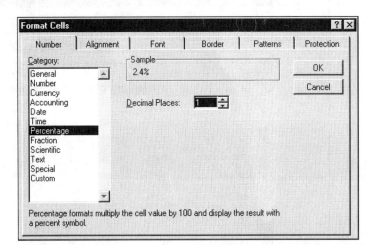

4. Click on OK. The Format Cells dialog box closes, and the percentage growth numbers in column H are formatted as shown in Figure 6-5.

5. Scroll your sheet up and to the left and then select C3 through C5.

Growth
percentages
formatted with
a single
decimal place
Figure 6-5.

6. Click the right mouse button on one of the selected cells to open the popup menu and then click on the Format Cells option. The Number tab should already be selected.

7. Click on the Percentage category and choose one decimal place to create a single decimal format. The three growth assumptions are formatted into percentages, as shown here:

Adding Currency Formatting

To set off the total lines from the rest of the budget, you can format them as currency, which places a dollar sign in front of each number. There are four total lines: Total Revenue, GROSS INCOME, Total Expenses, and Net Income. Use these instructions to format the first of the lines.

1. Drag across C14 through G14. The two quarterly and three monthly totals are highlighted.

2. Click on the Format menu and the Cells option. The Format Cells dialog box opens with the Number tab displayed.

3. Click on Currency in the Category list box.   **6**

The Currency category, like the Number category, allows you to specify several decimal places. In our example, we do not want any decimal places so the default of zero is fine. The Use $ check box should be checked so a dollar sign appears to the left of the number. If you have negative numbers in a spreadsheet, Excel provides four formats from which to choose.

Most of your general formatting needs can be satisfied by the choices available in the tab. However, if you want to customize the format beyond the limits of the options in the tab you can choose the Custom category, select a format comprised of the codes used in Table 6-1, and format your spreadsheet as you see fit. For example, the first currency format in the Custom category (denoted by the leading dollar sign), shown next, shifts the number one character to the left, leaving a blank space on the right.

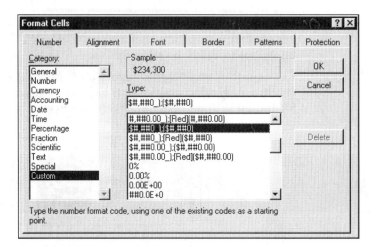

This is because the formats contain a _) on the right of the positive number section so positive numbers will align with negative numbers that have parentheses around them.

4. Return to the Currency category, if needed, and click on OK. The Total Revenue amounts are now formatted with dollar signs.

5. You could use the above procedure to format the remaining total lines. Excel, though, has a copy format tool, called Format Painter, that allows you to quickly repeat a format you have already applied. Try that now to complete the currency formatting.

6. With C14:G14 still selected, click on the Format Painter tool (the paintbrush); a marquee appears around C14:G14 and the mouse pointer now includes a paintbrush.

7. Drag across C18 through G18 and you will see the new format applied.

8. With C18:G18 still selected, again click on the Format Painter tool, and then drag across C25 through G27 (three rows). Both Total Expenses and Net Income are formatted with the currency format and your screen should look like the one shown in Figure 6-6.

The Format Painter is extremely powerful, and you will find many uses for it.

Centering and Embolding Headings

The final item of detail formatting that you need to do is to center each column heading within its columns and make it bold. Remember from Chapter 4 that Excel automatically left-aligns text. Unless you or someone else changed your third-quarter budget, all of the headings are left-aligned.

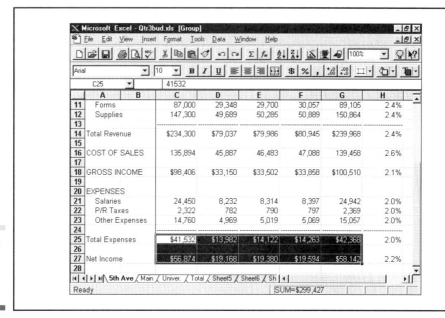

Formatting the
totals as
currency

Figure 6-6.

Centering the column headings and making them bold improves their look and is easy to do with the Formatting toolbar displayed. Use it now to do this formatting.

1. Scroll the screen up so you can see C7 through H8 and then drag across that range.

2. Click first on the Center tool and then on Bold (the "B"), as shown here: **6**

The Formatting Toolbar

The Formatting toolbar provides convenient access to many of the common formatting techniques most people often use. You can change the font and font size; apply bold, italic, and underline styles; align the cell contents on the left, center, right, or over a group of columns; apply the default currency, percent, or comma format; and increase or decrease the number of decimal digits as well as add background color, cell borders, and type color.

On the faint chance that none of the formatting tools interest you, you can turn off the Formatting toolbar to see more rows of your sheet and make the area above the sheet less "busy." Try the following instructions to remove the Formatting toolbar from the screen.

1. Click the right mouse button on one of the toolbars. The Toolbar popup menu opens with the Standard and Formatting toolbars checked, as shown here:

2. Click on Formatting. The Formatting toolbar is removed from the screen, and the area displaying your workbook expands by two rows.
3. Repeat the two preceding steps to restore the Formatting toolbar.
4. Click on the Save tool in the Standard toolbar to save your work.

N ote: When you restore the Formatting toolbar, it might be above the Standard toolbar, unlike its normal position below it.

The rest of this book assumes that you have left the Formatting toolbar displayed and can make use of it.

AutoFormat

AutoFormat allows you to automatically format your workbook. From a list of 6 formatting styles and a total of 16 formats, you can make choices that will change the appearance of any selected group of cells, or even an entire workbook, to give your work a professionally designed look.

In the previous formatting exercises, you learned how to use several formats to give the third-quarter budget a more personalized appearance. In this process, you were offered a number of individual options with which to format the workbook. This greater flexibility carries with it the extra burden of the time it takes to design and construct the final appearance of the workbook. AutoFormat provides 16 formats—each of which is a combination of number formats, fonts, alignment, borders, patterns, color, column widths, and row heights—that have been preselected for you. When you select one of the 16 formats, AutoFormat displays a sample of it and allows you to see the immediate effect of changing the formatting combinations.

The best way to appreciate AutoFormat is to use it. In the following instructions you will change your workbook a number of times. In order to restore the workbook to the way it looked before you applied the AutoFormat changes, you will use the Undo feature. Undo is a lifesaver, as you will see. The key is to use it *immediately* after making the change (or mistake). If you do anything that causes Excel to leave Ready mode, Undo undoes only to that point. Note that you can choose Undo from the Edit menu as well as use one of the two shortcuts, CTRL-Z or ALT-BACKSPACE. Try AutoFormat now.

1. Press CTRL-HOME and then CTRL-SHIFT-END to select the entire sheet.

2. Click on the Format menu and choose AutoFormat.

3. The AutoFormat dialog box appears, as shown here:

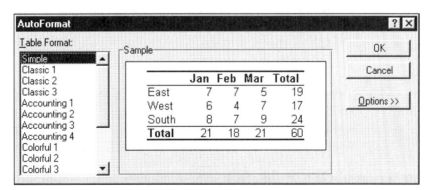

6

4. Take a moment to click on each format in the Table Format list box and see the different appearances you can choose.

5. Click on the Classic 3 format.

6. Click on the Options button.

   Six formats are displayed in the Formats to Apply section, with a check box next to each one, as shown here:

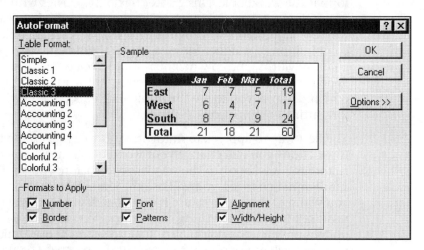

   Initially, all formats are selected.

7. Click on the Border check box. Notice how the borders are removed from the sample.

8. Click on the Width/Height check box; the column widths are expanded.

   When you clear formats from the Formats to Apply box, AutoFormat deletes the effect of those formats on the Table format and retains any previous formatting you may have applied to the selected group of cells or sheet.

9. Click on Cancel to return to the sheet.

Next see how AutoFormat can change the third-quarter budget. Since experimentation with AutoFormat is part of the exercise, your workbook will need to be preserved in its present appearance so you can continue the remainder of the chapter. This is easily done by saving the file now.

1. Click on the File menu and choose Save. The file QTR3BUD.XLS is saved to disk. You can now use AutoFormat freely, without worrying about making unrestorable changes.

2. Click on the Format menu and AutoFormat.

3. Click on Classic 3 and then on OK.

4. When you return to the sheet, click on the View menu and on the Full Screen option. The sheet expands to fill as much of the screen as

possible. To see the layout without obstructions, drag the Full Screen button to the right and click in the lower-right corner of your sheet to remove the highlight. Figure 6-7 shows what you should see.

5. Click on the Edit menu and Undo to clear AutoFormat.

    Continue to experiment with different AutoFormat formats and then try different selected ranges to get a sense of what AutoFormat can and cannot do. Also, turn off Full Screen view and use the Formatting toolbar to customize some of the AutoFormat settings. As you will discover, AutoFormat works best on a simple table, as in the samples. Depending on the structure of your workbook, it may be easier to do the formatting yourself, without using AutoFormat, or by using a combination of individual and automatic formats. Now, return to the third-quarter budget workbook without AutoFormat changes.

6. Click on the File menu and Close. Excel will ask if you want to save changes to QTR3BUD.XLS. Click on No.

7. You will return to a blank document window. Click on the File menu and then click on the first file in the list of four files at the bottom of the menu. This is the last saved version of file QTR3BUD.XLS.

8. If you haven't already, click on the Full Screen button to return to the normal screen layout.

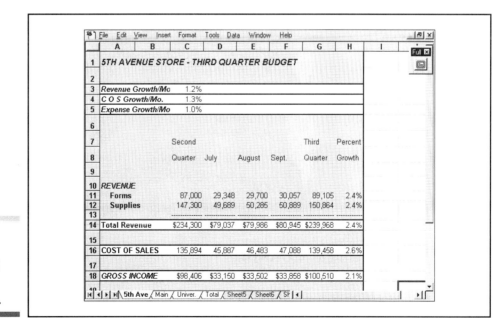

Effect of applying AutoFormat Classic 3

Figure 6-7.

6

Changing the Layout

Now you can make some changes to the workbook. The biggest change is deleting column B. To facilitate that, you'll move the assumptions over one column. Then you'll widen column A, narrow column H, and recenter the title. To make the formulas more understandable, you'll add some notes to them. Finally, you'll erase the previous month in preparation for the next quarter, but, remembering that you have not printed the workbook yet, you'll undo the erasure.

Moving Formulas

You need to move the growth assumptions from column C to column D so the assumption labels still have enough room when column B is deleted. When the contents of a cell are moved, any formula that refers to that cell is changed to reflect the move, even if it has an absolute reference. This gives you significant flexibility.

1. Drag down C3 through C5. The assumptions are highlighted.
2. Point on the right border of range C3:C5. The cursor turns into an arrow. Drag and drop the range to its new position, D3:D5. The assumptions are moved.
3. Click on D11 to look at the formula.

The reference to the assumption in the formula in D11 used to be $C$3. It has now changed to $D$3, as shown here:

D11		=C11/3*(1+$D$3)		
	A	**B**	**C**	**D**	**E**
1			5TH AVENUE STORE - THIRD QUAR
2					
3	Revenue Growth/Mo.			1.2%	
4	C O S Growth/Mo.			1.3%	
5	Expense Growth/Mo.			1.0%	
6					
7			Second		
8			Quarter	July	August
10	REVENUE				
11	Forms		87,000	29,348	29,700
12	Supplies		147,300	49,689	50,285

Deleting a Column

Column B of the third-quarter budget was used to provide room for the row labels without changing the column width. Now that you can change the column width, there is no longer a reason to keep column B. Using these instructions, delete column B.

1. Click on the column heading for column B.

2. Click on the right mouse button to display the popup menu and click on Delete.

When column B is deleted, the remaining columns to the right are relettered, as shown in Figure 6-8. Also, all formulas are revised accordingly. Look at several formulas that used to refer to the old column C, and you'll see they now refer to column B.

Adjusting Individual Column Width

Now that column B is gone, you need to widen column A so you can read the row labels. Do that by following these steps.

1. Place the mouse pointer in the column heading at the intersection of columns A and B. The mouse pointer turns into a two-headed arrow with a line in the middle, as shown here:

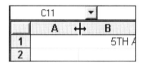

2. Drag the column intersection to the right until you are almost over the intersection of columns B and C—you are making column A about

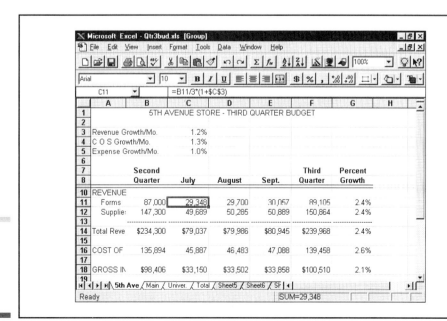

The effect of deleting the original column B

Figure 6-8.

6

equal to the sum of the old columns A and B. Notice in the Formula bar how the column width is increasing. Size the column to 17.57.

The second column sizing you will do narrows the percentage growth column to about seven and a half characters.

1. Place the mouse pointer in the column heading at the intersection of columns G and H.

2. Drag the column intersection to the left until the width in the Formula bar reads 7.57. Your workbook should look like the one shown in Figure 6-9.

Adding Notes to Cells

After a period of time has passed, it is sometimes difficult to remember why, for example, you built a formula the way you did, or who gave you a certain figure. This is a problem that becomes more important if you give your workbook to someone else to use. Excel has a feature that allows you to add notes to cells to explain their contents. You can put a note on only one sheet at a time. For the following exercise, you will deselect the four sheets and then reselect the 5th Avenue store's sheet (Sheet1) on which to place the note. Do this with the following steps and then add a couple of notes to your workbook.

After column resizing is completed
Figure 6-9.

1. Click on the tab for Sheet5 and then click on the 5th Ave tab to select just that sheet.
2. Click on C11. The active cell moves to C11.
3. Click on the Insert menu and the Note option. The Cell Note dialog box opens, as shown here:

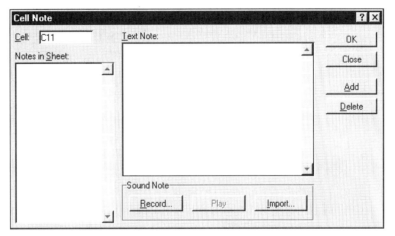

4. Type **Previous Quarter / 3 * (1 + Growth Rate)** and click on OK. This note is added to cell C11.
5. Click on C3. The active cell moves to C3.
6. Click on the Insert menu and the Note option. The Cell Note dialog box opens.
7. Type **From George Brown** and click on OK. This note is added to cell C3.

You can tell that a note is in a cell by the small red (or black on monochrome monitors) mark in the upper-right corner of the cell. To read a note, point on a cell with a note and the note appears in a popup box. Alternatively, you can move the active cell to a cell with a note and press SHIFT-F2. The same Cell Note dialog box will open, where you can also edit the note. You can also print notes by selecting the appropriate option on the Sheet tab of the Page Setup dialog box from the File menu.

Excel also allows you to record and play back a sound note and add it to the active cell. To use this feature, you need to have the appropriate hardware installed in your computer, such as a sound board and microphone. From the Cell Note dialog box, you can choose to record a new sound note, play back an existing note, or import a prerecorded sound.

194

Erasing a Group of Cells

The third-quarter budget is now complete. You can turn it into another quarter's budget by changing the previous quarter's actuals and growth rates. All the formulas are based on those two sets of numbers. A simple way to change the actuals is to erase them and enter new ones. Use the following steps to save the workbook twice, once under its current name and once under a name for the new quarter. Then, in the new quarter's workbook, select the first three sheets (you don't want to erase the totals), and erase the second-quarter actuals.

1. Click on the File menu and the Save option. The workbook is saved under its current name, QTR3BUD.XLS.

2. Click on the File menu and the Save As option, edit the File name text box so it reads QTRBUD instead of QTR3BUD (delete the 3), and press ENTER. The workbook is saved again under the name QTRBUD.XLS.

3. With 5th Ave (Sheet1) selected, press and hold SHIFT while clicking on the Sheet3 (or Univer.) tab to select the first three sheets.

4. Drag down column B from B11 through B27. The second quarter actuals are highlighted.

5. Press DEL. The second quarter actuals disappear, as shown in Figure 6-10.

Erasing the second-quarter actuals

Figure 6-10.

Notice that most of the formulas that depended on the second quarter actuals have changed to 0. The exception is the percentage growth amounts, which changed to #DIV/0!, indicating you are trying to divide by zero. All of the formulas, including the percentages, will change back to legitimate values as soon as you enter a new set of actuals. However, don't do that yet.

Using Undo

We forgot to print the workbook before erasing column B. Luckily, Excel has a feature that can restore the column, as long as you have done nothing since you erased it.

1. Press CTRL-Z or ALT-BACKSPACE (Undo) now. Your workbook should be restored to the way it was before you erased column B.

   Undo even restores a full workbook erase. (Remember, the key is to use it *immediately* after making a mistake.)

   If, for some reason, your workbook is not restored, restore it from disk by doing the following.

2. Click on the File menu and the Open option, type **\sheet\qtr3bud**, and press ENTER. Your workbook is restored to its original condition.

Printing the Workbook

So far, you have seen your budget results only on the screen. The screen version may give you the information you need, but it does not allow you to share the information easily with others—for that you must print the budget. To print, you must give Excel information about what and how to print. In other words, you must set some parameters for Excel to use while printing. Once you have set the parameters, you can do the actual printing. The options for both setting parameters and doing the printing are contained on several menus and dialog boxes, discussed in the next several sections. Begin the printing process by determining the area to be printed and by entering the settings on the Page Setup dialog box.

6

Setting the Parameters

If you specified your printer correctly when you installed Windows, the only required parameter for printing is the area in the workbook that you want to print. To give the printed output the same polish you did to the screen image, you can add a heading and check the page margins and length. Excel has a number of other parameters that can be set, but these are the ones most people use.

Identifying the Print Area

For this example you'll want to print the first sheet—everything you have done for the 5th Avenue store. Excel's default is just that—to print everything that has been entered on the currently selected sheet. You do not need to identify what to print here; it's done for you in this case. In other circumstances you might want to print only a section of a sheet. In that case, you'll need to specify that specific cells be printed. See how this is done in the following example.

1. Click on the tab for Sheet5 and then click on the 5th Ave tab to select just that sheet.

2. Click on the vertical scroll bar to see the top of Sheet1 (5th Ave).

3. Click on the File menu Page Setup option, then on the Sheet tab, and finally in the Print Area text box.

4. If necessary, drag the Title bar of the dialog box so you can see cell A1 of the sheet; then, on the sheet, drag from A1 through G27 to highlight that area. The Page Setup dialog box will reflect this selection as you can see in Figure 6-11.

   Whenever possible, print using the default of the entire sheet instead of specifying the print area. The reason for this is that if you modify your workbook by adding columns or rows and you have specified a print area, you will have to modify the print area to incorporate the new columns or rows. Once you have defined a print area, you can get rid of it by

Highlighting
the print range
Figure 6-11.

deleting the entry in the Print Area text box of the Page Setup dialog box.

5. Click on Cancel to restore whole sheet printing.

Setting Up a Page for Printing

You also use the Page Setup dialog box to specify the major facets of the page to be printed. Through this dialog box you can enter a header and/or footer to be printed on the page, set the page margins, and turn the row and column headings and gridlines on or off.

1. Click on the File menu and the Page Setup option; the Sheet tab of the Page Setup dialog box should again appear.

   Besides the Print Area, you can specify the rows and columns that are repeated on each page by clicking in the text box and dragging on the sheet as you did for the Print Area. The Print check boxes turn on and off the printing of a grid between each cell, the printing of cell notes, and the printing of the row and column headings. The buttons are also used for selecting draft quality and forcing the output to be black and white.

   Additionally, on the Sheet tab you can determine how you print a multipage workbook—*down* the sheet, one page wide until the end and then over to the next set of columns, or *across* the sheet, one page long to the end and then down. For most applications, the default page order of printing down first before moving to the right is what you want to use.

   For the third-quarter budget, the only change you want to make on the Sheet tab is to turn off the gridlines. Do that next and then open the Page settings of the Page Setup dialog box.

2. If necessary, click on Gridlines to turn it off (not checked).

3. Click on the Page tab to display the Page settings shown here:

6

Most of the settings under the Page tab are obvious. One of the handiest options, and maybe not so obvious, is the Fit to option under Scaling. If you select this, Excel will automatically scale the area you want to be printed to the number of pages you specify. This is particularly helpful when you find you have a sheet just a little too large for a given number of pages. For the third-quarter budget, you do not need to change the default settings.

You can also use the settings under the Page tab to change the orientation of what you are printing and the paper size. There are two orientations: *portrait*, in which the long side of an 8.5 x 11-inch page is vertical (the normal way a page is held), and *landscape*, in which the long side is horizontal. Not all printers can support various paper sizes and/or landscape printing. If yours doesn't, these options will be dimmed or colored light gray.

Entering a Header   A *header* is text that is added to the top of every printed page. It often contains a page number, the date of printing, and a descriptive line of text (like a company name). A *footer* is a line of text added to the bottom of every printed page. Excel provides a default header and footer that you can customize, or you can enter your own. In either case you can specify the alignment, use of bold or italic fonts, and the inclusion of such things as the date and page number. Look at the Header/Footer tab next.

1. Click on the Header/Footer tab to display this dialog box:

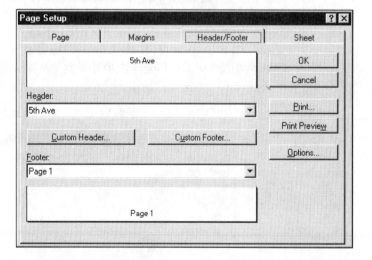

As you can see, the default header is the sheet name shown in the sheet's tab, "5th Ave" in the case of Sheet1 of the quarterly budget. The default footer is the word "Page" and the page number. By clicking on the drop-down list boxes, you can choose several other ready-made headers and footers. Most people, though, want to create their own headers and footers, and that is what you will do here.

Add a header containing the date, company name, and page number to the printout of the third-quarter budget, as well as a footer that says "Company Confidential" with the following steps.

2. Click on the Custom Header button to display the Header dialog box shown here:

A header or footer can have up to three segments: a left-aligned segment, a centered segment, and a right-aligned segment. Each of the three segments has its own text box or section. All left-aligned text is typed in the Left Section, center-aligned text in the Center Section, and right-aligned text in the Right Section.

The seven buttons in the middle of the dialog box perform the following functions in any of the sections:

Button	Name	Function
A	Font	Opens the Font dialog box that allows you to change the font, style, and size of text that you have previously selected
[#]	Page	Inserts the current page number
[+]	Pages	Inserts the total number of pages in the document
[date]	Date	Inserts the current date in the computer
[time]	Time	Inserts the current time in the computer

6

Button	Name	Function
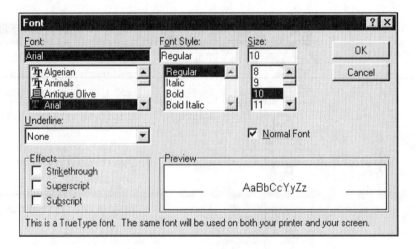	File	Inserts the workbook filename
	Tab	Inserts the sheet name entered on the sheet's tab

Try these buttons next. Note that the insertion point (the blinking vertical line) is in the Left Section, so that is where you will begin by placing the date there.

3. Click on the Date button (in the middle). In the Left Section, &[Date] appears, telling Excel to place the current computer date on the left of the header when the sheet is printed.

4. Press TAB to move the insertion point to the Center Section and highlight the current contents—the sheet (tab) name. Type **MORNINGSIDE SPECIALTIES**. This enters the company name and deletes the existing code. Don't worry that it is on two lines in the text box. It will be on one line when it is printed, unless you make the font size very large.

5. Drag across both words of the company name to highlight them and then press the Font button on the left. The Font dialog box opens as shown here:

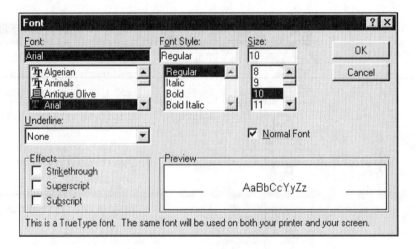

6. Click on bold, scroll the size box until you see 12, and then click on it and, finally, on OK. The company name is made bold and enlarged to 12 points.

7. Press TAB one more time to move to the Right Section. Type **Page**, press SPACEBAR once, and click on the Page Number button (second from the left). Click on OK.

8. You are returned to the Page Setup dialog box. Click on the Custom Footer button.

9. Press TAB, and type **COMPANY CONFIDENTIAL** in the Center Section to replace the default footer with these words.

10. Press SHIFT-HOME to select the words, click on the Font button, again select bold and 12-point size, and click on OK twice to complete both the Font dialog box as well as the Footer dialog box.

Your completed Header/Footer tab of the Page Setup dialog box should look like this:

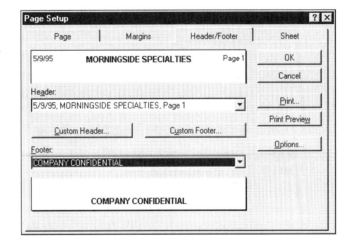

Setting the Margins   Margins are the distances in inches from the edge of the page to the printed data or chart on four sides: top, bottom, left, and right. Look at the Margins tab and set the margins for the third-quarter budget with the following steps.

1. Click on the Margins tab. The Page Setup dialog box opens, as you can see here:

6

As can see in the little Preview in the center of the dialog box, the default margins cause the sheet you want to print to be offset up and to the left of center. You could change the top and left margins until the sheet was centered, but you can have Excel automatically center it for you by using the Center on Page check boxes in the lower left of the dialog box.

2. Click on Horizontally and on Vertically to center the sheet in both directions. Notice how the little Preview in the center mirrors what you do.

3. Click on OK to close the Page Setup dialog box.

Doing the Printing

The actual printing is anticlimactic after setting up the page, but you still must perform several steps, such as readying your printer, setting some final printing parameters, and, finally, telling Excel to print.

The steps to prepare your printer are governed by the printer you are using. All printers must be turned on and placed online. In most printers, the paper must be aligned so the upper-left corner is correctly positioned. Also, your printer must be correctly cabled to your computer. Finally, you should have installed your printer with the Windows Setup program or by using the Printers folder in the Start menu, Settings option, or the Control Panel. (If you do not know whether your printer is installed correctly, try printing. If it works, you have an affirmative answer.) Take any other steps necessary to ensure that your printer is ready to print.

Once your printer is ready, start printing with the Print option from the File menu. The Print option does not begin the printing directly, but rather opens another dialog box that asks you several more questions. Look at that dialog box next and then do the actual printing.

1. Click on the File menu and the Print option. The Print dialog box opens, as shown here:

This Print dialog box is for the HP LaserJet 4M printer. If you are using a different printer, your dialog box may be slightly different, but should have most of the options shown. Importantly, this is where you determine what is to be printed: a selected print area, selected sheets, or the entire workbook. Also, in this dialog box you have the ability to specify the number of copies you want and to print all or only selected pages.

6

Before you actual print to paper, it often saves you time and money to preview the output on your screen. Look at this option before you print.

2. Close the Print dialog box by clicking on Cancel.

3. Click on the Print Preview button (fifth from the left on the Standard toolbar) or select the File menu and choose Print Preview. The workbook clears from your screen and a small representation of the printed sheet appears, as shown in Figure 6-12.

On most displays you cannot easily read the image on the preview screen, but you can tell a lot about placement on the page and how good a guess you made on the margins. You can also zoom in and see a particular area. Do that next.

4. Move the mouse pointer, which you notice has become a magnifying glass, to the approximate center of the sheet and click. The image expands to clearly show the center of the sheet, as you can see in Figure 6-13.

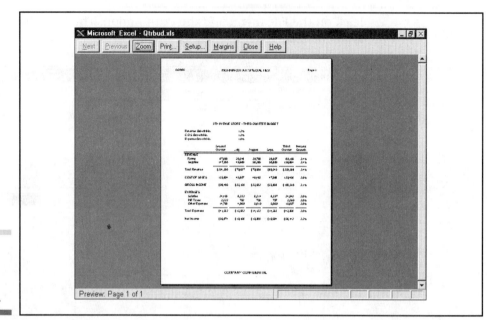

Preview of
printed
worksheet
Figure 6-12.

5. Use the horizontal and vertical scroll bars to look around the sheet and the header and footer.

   Notice that when you deleted column B, you got rid of the vertical line you placed between the old columns B and C. This is what Print Preview is for—it lets you find problems before printing. Go back now and replace the line and then come back and print.

6. Click on Close to return to the sheet. Select the four sheets by pressing and holding SHIFT while clicking on the Total tab, scroll your sheet so you can see rows 10 through 27 (or as many as your screen allows), and then drag down column A from rows 10 through 27. Open the Borders tool in the Formatting toolbar and select the right-hand border in the top-right corner of the palette. Deselect all but the 5th Ave sheet by clicking on Sheet5 and then on the 5th Ave tab. Finally, click on the Print Preview button. You now have the vertical line as you intended.

7. With the preview the way you want it, click on the Print command button to open the Print dialog box and click on OK to actually print, or click on the Print tool, fourth tool from the left on the Standard toolbar. The Print tool prints one copy of whatever Print dialog settings are currently in effect. Your final printed output should look like Figure 6-14.

8. If you want to stop printing once you have started, click on the Cancel button in the Printing message box, as shown here:

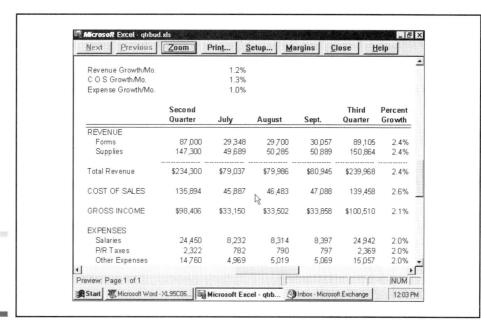

Preview
zoomed in on
the center
Figure 6-13.

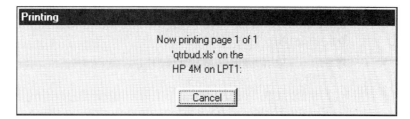

When you tell Excel to print, it creates a print job in memory containing all of the information to be printed, and sends it to the Windows Print Manager. You can then go back to work while, in the background, the Print Manager is actually doing the printing. You can have several print jobs in memory waiting to be printed. The Print Manager gives you the ability to cancel a job after it has left Excel and to rearrange the priority of the jobs waiting to be printed. For a small sheet like the one you built here, the advantage of the Print Manager is not very evident, but with a large multipage print job it offers a significant benefit.

Trial and Error

Your printout probably did not come out exactly the way you wanted it—or maybe it did not come out at all. Using a printer is almost always a

6

5TH AVENUE STORE - THIRD QUARTER BUDGET

Revenue Growth/Mo.		1.2%				
C O S Growth/Mo.		1.3%				
Expense Growth/Mo.		1.0%				

	Second Quarter	July	August	Sept.	Third Quarter	Percent Growth
REVENUE						
Forms	87,000	29,348	29,700	30,057	89,105	2.4%
Supplies	147,300	49,689	50,285	50,889	150,864	2.4%
Total Revenue	$234,300	$79,037	$79,986	$80,945	$239,968	2.4%
COST OF SALES	135,894	45,887	46,483	47,088	139,458	2.6%
GROSS INCOME	$98,406	$33,150	$33,502	$33,858	$100,510	2.1%
EXPENSES						
Salaries	24,450	8,232	8,314	8,397	24,942	2.0%
P/R Taxes	2,322	782	790	797	2,369	2.0%
Other Expenses	14,760	4,969	5,019	5,069	15,057	2.0%
Total Expenses	$41,532	$13,982	$14,122	$14,263	$42,368	2.0%
Net Income	$56,874	$19,168	$19,380	$19,594	$58,142	2.2%

Printed sheet
Figure 6-14.

trial-and-error process. Be persistent and you should get it to work. To cure several common types of problems, try the following suggestions. (If you leave Excel, choose Save from the File menu to save the workbook on disk before leaving.)

If you could not print at all, try these steps.

1. Start at the printer end. Is the printer plugged in, turned on, and set online? Does it have adequate paper and a ribbon? Is there a cable connecting the printer to the computer?

2. Look at the computer. To which port is the printer connected (LPT1, COM1, COM2)? Are any other devices interfering with the printer port? (For example, are both a printer and a modem connected to the same port?)

3. Double-click on the Printers folder in the Start menu Settings option, and make sure your printer name is correctly specified and that the port to which it is connected is the correct one.

4. Look at the print settings you have specified. Go through the steps of setting the parameters again, checking each against the figures and illustrations in this book.

If the budget printed but it is not the way you want it, try these steps.

1. Adjust the print settings to fit your particular situation. For example, if the margins are not correct, change them until the sheet is located on the page the way you want it.

2. Make sure your printer is not set through its console for some particular type of printing (for example, compressed printing when you want to print at full size).

3. Adjust the layout and formatting so it pleases you. For example, you may want the title to be bold and a larger or even different font. If so, use the techniques you used earlier with the Formatting toolbar to select the title and make the changes.

4. Click on the Print tool (the printer, fourth from the left) in the Standard toolbar to reprint the sheet until you are satisfied.

Saving the Workbook

When you are satisfied with your printout, you need to resave the workbook to capture the print settings you entered. Click on the Save tool (the disk, third from the left) in the Standard toolbar.

Making a Template

After building the third-quarter budget, you can use it for the fourth quarter and other future quarters. None of the formulas need to be changed. You must change only the titles and the previous quarter actuals. When you make this workbook more general purpose, it becomes a *template* (a type of form or structural pattern) for use with any quarter. The remainder of the chapter discusses how this is done.

6

Changing Titles

To make the titles general purpose, you need to remove the references to the third quarter. With the following instructions, edit the titles to make them generic.

1. Select just the 5th Ave sheet (if it isn't already selected) by clicking on Sheet5 and then on the 5th Ave sheet (since you have individualized the titles, you must change them one by one).

2. Click on cell A1 and drag across the word "Third" and its following space in the edit area and press DEL. The word "Third" is removed.

3. Click immediately after the word "QUARTER," type **LY**, and press ENTER.

4. Repeat this process for the other three sheets and then select all four sheets for the remaining changes.

5. Click on B7. The active cell moves to the first column heading.

6. Type **Previous** and press ENTER. "Second" is changed to "Previous," but remains centered in the column and bold.

7. Press DOWN ARROW and RIGHT ARROW. The active cell moves to the July column heading.

8. Type **Month 1** and press ENTER. "July" is changed to "Month 1" and centered in the column.

Change the second and third months by using AutoFill (drag the AutoFill box in the lower-right corner of C8 to E8) and then the third-quarter total, so the column headings are as shown here:

	A	B	C	D	E	F	G	H
1		5TH AVENUE STORE - QUARTERLY BUDGET						
2								
3	Revenue Growth/Mo.		1.2%					
4	C O S Growth/Mo.		1.3%					
5	Expense Growth/Mo.		1.0%					
6								
7		Previous				Current	Percent	
8		Quarter	Month 1	Month 2	Month 3	Quarter	Growth	
10	REVENUE							

Copying Values—Paste Special

There are several ways to change the previous quarter's actual values. One way is to erase the column and reenter the new numbers. Another way is either to edit or to type over the current numbers. A third way is to copy the current quarter's numbers to the previous quarter. These are not actuals *per se*. If you literally copy column F to column B, you would get a set of formulas that do not have any meaning. What you want to do is to copy the *values* produced by the formulas in F, but not the formulas themselves. To do this, use Excel's Paste Special command. Follow these steps to see how Paste Special works.

1. First deselect the four sheets and reselect only the first three since you do not want to change the Total sheet. Then drag on F11 through F27.

2. Press the right mouse button for the popup menu and click on Copy. A blinking marquee appears around the highlighted cells in column F.

3. Scroll your sheet up, and then click on B11, which you want to be the recipient of the copy.

4. Click on the Edit menu and the Paste Special option. The Paste Special dialog box opens, as shown here:

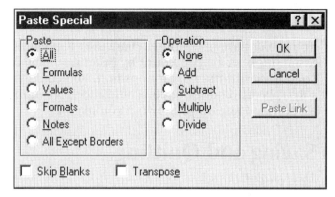

5. Click on Values and OK in the Paste Special dialog box. The dialog box closes. Now, only the values in column F are copied to column B. See Figure 6-15 for the result. Note the number in the Formula bar for B11 and how the number is changed by the cell formatting in B11.

6. The F11:F27 copy area is still selected to allow you to paste it in another location. Therefore, deselect it by pressing ESC.

One of the major benefits of using Paste or Paste Special from the menu (either Edit or popup), rather than the keyboard or toolbar, is that it does not deselect the copy area, so you can paste multiple times.

	A	B	C	D	E	F	G
10	REVENUE						
11	Forms	89,105	30,058	30,419	30,784	91,260	2.4%
12	Supplies	150,864	50,891	51,502	52,120	154,513	2.4%
13							
14	Total Revenue	$239,968	$80,949	$81,921	$82,904	$245,774	2.4%
15							
16	COST OF SALES	139,458	47,090	47,702	48,323	143,115	2.6%
17							
18	GROSS INCOME	$100,510	$33,859	$34,218	$34,581	$102,658	2.1%
19							
20	EXPENSES						
21	Salaries	24,942	8,397	8,481	8,566	25,444	2.0%
22	P/R Taxes	2,369	797	805	814	2,416	2.0%
23	Other Expenses	15,057	5,069	5,120	5,171	15,360	2.0%
24							
25	Total Expenses	$42,368	$14,264	$14,407	$14,551	$43,221	2.0%
26							
27	Net Income	$58,142	$19,595	$19,812	$20,030	$59,437	2.2%

Cell B11: 89104.754112

Microsoft Excel - Qtrbud.xls [Group]

Select destination and press ENTER or choose Paste   SUM=862,784

Results of copying values

Figure 6-15.

6

Other Modifications

You could make many other changes to this workbook. You could add an assumption for every account by inserting a new column to the left of column A with the assumptions in it. You could also add more accounts and subtotals of accounts, or you could add more months and quarterly totals for a year. Try these on your own if you like.

Saving and Quitting

The last step prior to leaving Excel is to save your work, even if you did it just a few moments earlier. In this case, you want to save the generalized version of the budget. Use these instructions to do that and then leave Excel.

6. Click on the Save tool in the Standard toolbar (third tool from the left).

7. Click on the Excel Close button to leave Excel and then click on the Start menu Shut Down option to turn off your computer.

Producing Charts

7

Excel charts are pictorial representations of data on a spreadsheet. They are another way of displaying the results a spreadsheet produces.

In this chapter you'll work with Excel's charting features. First you'll look at the menus and toolbars containing the charting commands. Then you'll go over the types of charts that are available and their subtypes and peculiarities. Finally, you'll build two types of charts, and then you'll see how to edit and customize them.

How a Chart Is Built

Producing charts in Excel is very simple: you create a range on a sheet, highlight that range, and tell Excel to create a new chart, using one of three techniques. This produces a standard chart based on the defaults set in Excel. You can then change any of these defaults and add many special features to customize the chart. You can create *chart sheets* that can be printed, viewed, or edited separately, or you can *embed* charts in your sheet so that they become a part of the sheet. Both embedded charts and chart sheets are updated as you change the data on the sheet.

There are three ways to create charts:

♦   The *Default Chart* tool, found on the Chart toolbar, is the easiest way to create an embedded chart. By clicking on the Default Chart tool, shown here, you can quickly see a chart displayed on the screen that is based on data you have highlighted. By default (which can be changed), this chart will be a Column (vertical Bar) chart.

♦   The *ChartWizard* tool, shown here, is found on both the Standard and Chart toolbars. It provides a step-by-step procedure for creating a chart. You can easily switch between 14 different chart types and their subtypes as you create an embedded chart on a sheet.

♦   The *Chart* option on the Insert menu displays a submenu that can be used to produce either an embedded chart on an existing sheet or a chart as a separate sheet. This is simply another way of starting the ChartWizard. The Chart option and submenu are shown in the following illustration.

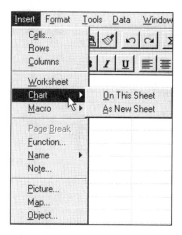

Chart Characteristics

A chart lets you see how data, or numbers on a sheet, look when they are plotted. For Excel to turn the data into a chart, the cells that contain them must adhere to certain guidelines. In addition, charts themselves have common elements that need to be defined.

Guidelines for Charting Data

The data that you intend to chart should be prepared with the following guidelines (use the data in Figure 7-1 as an example).

♦ The data must be in one or more rectangles or ranges (they don't have to be contiguous), with text labels in the topmost row and/or leftmost column. Otherwise, the range may contain numbers and text, but text is interpreted as zeros.

♦ Excel defines the first *data series—a range of numbers on a sheet that is comprised of related data points* to be plotted (points that would form, for example, a single line on a chart)—as beginning with the first cell in the upper-left corner of the highlighted range containing a number not formatted as a date and continuing across the rows and columns that are highlighted.

♦ Excel determines whether more rows or more columns are highlighted and, with the assumption that there will be more data points than data series, makes the larger of the two the data points. So, if you highlight six columns and three rows, each column will be a data point (a single number to be plotted) and each row a data series.

♦ Additional data series can be included in the range by highlighting additional rows or columns, depending on whether you are building a

7

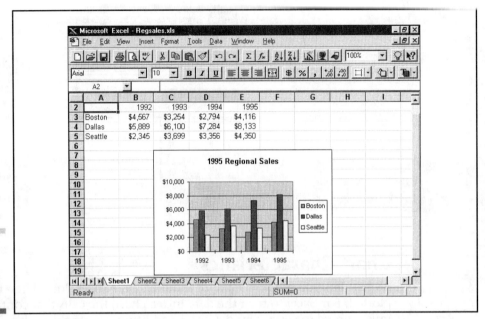

A data range
and its
resulting chart
Figure 7-1.

columnwise or *rowwise* chart. You can have ten or more data series, but the resulting chart may not be readable.

♦   If the first column or row of the highlighted range contains labels or date-formatted numbers and/or the cell in the upper-left corner is blank, the first column or row—depending on whether the data series are down columns (columnwise) or across rows (rowwise—is used for the X- or *category axis.*

♦   The numbers on the Y- or *value axis* are formatted with the same format that has been used with the data points on the sheet.

♦   The initial default is to produce a Column or Vertical Bar chart. This and other options can be easily changed.

Figure 7-1 contains a range of rowwise data series that fits the guidelines for a standard chart. Row 2 contains number-formatted dates that are used for the X- (category) axis; the next three rows are data series, each containing four numeric data points used to produce the Column chart shown in the lower part of the figure. The legend is taken from the first column.

Elements of a 2-D Chart

Charts have several common elements. Most of the chart elements can be changed or created apart from the creation of the chart itself. Figure 7-2 shows the elements of a 2-D chart; those for a 3-D chart will differ slightly, as you will see. The 2-D chart elements are as follows.

♦ *Y-axis* or value axis, which shows the value of the data points that are plotted.

♦ *X-axis* or category axis, which shows the categories of the data points that are plotted, such as years in Figure 7-2.

♦ *Chart title*, which can be taken from a cell on the sheet or can be added directly to the chart.

♦ *Category names*, which identify the individual data points. They may be dates, locations, products, and so forth. The category names are taken from the topmost row or the leftmost column, depending on the orientation of the sheet.

♦ *Legend*, which is a set of labels that describe each of the data series. These labels are attached to a symbol, a color, or a pattern that is associated with the series and placed on the chart (initially to the right, but you can move it). It is used to distinguish one data series from another. The text for a legend is taken from a text row or column, depending on the orientation of the sheet.

♦ *Data marker*, which is used to distinguish one data series from another. It is the bar, line, column, or pie wedge on the chart.

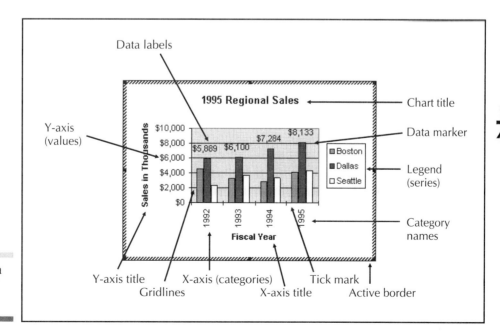

Elements of a
2-D chart
Figure 7-2.

◆ *Tick marks*, which are small lines used to divide the two axes and provide the scaling.

◆ *Gridlines*, which may be displayed for both axes to help read the value of individual data points. Gridlines are scaled according to the values on the axes and can be changed.

◆ *Data labels*, which are sometimes displayed to show the value of one data point.

◆ *Active border*, which identifies that a particular embedded chart is active and can be edited. An active border is a thicker gray line, as shown in Figure 7-2.

◆ *Selected border*, which identifies that a chart can be sized, moved, or deleted, and contains nodes or handles for that purpose. The chart in Figure 7-1 has a selected border.

Elements of a 3-D Chart

3-D charts have the following additional elements, which are shown in Figure 7-3.

◆ *Z-axis* or Value axis, which shows the value of the data points.

◆ *X-axis* or Category axis, which is the same as in 2-D charts.

◆ *Y-axis* or Series axis, which shows the individual series. It can be considered the depth or inward axis.

◆ *Wall*, which is the background of the plotted area.

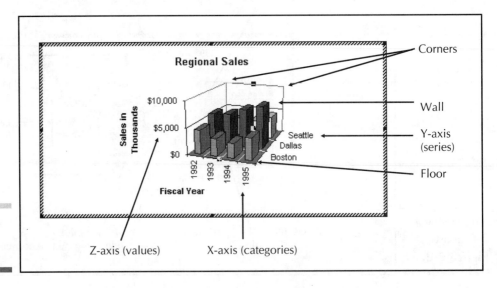

Elements of a
3-D chart
Figure 7-3.

♦ *Corners*, which are shown with nodes in Figure 7-3, and can be rotated to give you different views.

♦ *Floor*, which is the base upon which the series are plotted.

Each chart element can be accessed and either changed or used to change the chart in some way. You'll learn how later in the chapter.

Chart Tools and Menus

Excel provides an array of helpful tools and menus to build and customize charts. You will look at the more important of these with several hands-on exercises. Prepare for those exercises now by building a simple sheet of data that can be plotted.

1. If you don't have a new workbook on your screen, click on the File menu, and New option to create one now.

2. Type the data on the sheet as presented here:

	A	B	C	D	E	F
1						
2		1992	1993	1994	1995	
3	Boston	4567	3254	2794	4116	
4	Dallas	5889	6100	7284	8133	
5	Seattle	2345	3699	3356	4350	
6						

3. Save the workbook by clicking on the File menu, Save As option, and place it in the SHEET folder. Type the filename **regsales** and press ENTER. If the File Properties dialog box appears, press ENTER to bypass it.

This sheet will be used to demonstrate many of the charting tools and menus. The more complex ones will be explored later in the chapter.

7

The Insert Menu

To create a new chart sheet or an embedded chart, you can, after selecting the data to be plotted in the chart, use the Chart option on the Insert menu. The two-option submenu that you saw earlier in the chapter will be displayed.

If you select As New Sheet, a new sheet will be created entitled Chart1. You will be led through a series of dialog boxes to fully describe how you want the chart created. You will see how to create a chart sheet later in the section "Creating a New Chart Sheet with the Insert Menu."

If you select On This Sheet, the pointer will first turn into a crosshair pointer with a small bar chart next to it that you can use in either of two ways to define the area used by the embedded chart. First, you can simply click on the sheet containing the selected data and Excel will lay out the area as it sees fit, but which you can change later. Second, you can specifically define the chart area by dragging the pointer across the area you want to use. As you drag the pointer, a box will appear that defines the outer perimeter of the new chart. In either case, you will be led through a series of dialog boxes to describe how the chart is to be created. Figure 7-1 shows an embedded chart.

The Chart Toolbar

Whenever a chart is displayed on the screen, Excel places the Chart toolbar on the screen. Additionally, you can cause the Chart toolbar to be displayed from either the View or Toolbar popup menu. The Chart toolbar provides the following five charting tools:

Tool	Name	Description
	Chart Type	Selects different chart types
	Default Chart	Creates a default chart
	ChartWizard	Starts the ChartWizard
	Horizontal Gridlines	Switches horizontal gridlines on and off
	Legend	Switches a chart legend on and off

Like other toolbars, the name of an individual tool in the Chart toolbar can be seen in a small box beneath the tool whenever the pointer rests on it. Also, the Status bar describes the tool's function. To display the Chart toolbar, follow these steps.

1. From the View menu, select the Toolbars option.
2. Click on the Chart check box so that a check mark appears in it and click OK.

The Chart toolbar will then be displayed. The individual tools on the Chart toolbar are discussed next.

Note: You can move the Chart toolbar from the document window to the area where the Standard and Formatting toolbars are by dragging and dropping the Chart toolbar's Title bar to just below the Formatting toolbar. However, you will lose the display of your last two worksheet rows by moving it.

The Default Chart Tool

The Default Chart tool produces a quick look at the selected data range using the default chart type. Initially, the default chart type is the Column chart. Producing a default chart provides a starting point for a customized chart. The default chart is not meant to be a final, presentation-quality chart.

When you click on this tool, the pointer turns into a crosshair, which you can then use to precisely define the area in which the chart will be displayed.

Try it now with the sheet you have just entered by following these steps.

1. Highlight the sheet by dragging the pointer from A2 to E5, as shown here:

	A	B	C	D	E	F
1						
2		1992	1993	1994	1995	
3	Boston	4567	3254	2794	4116	
4	Dallas	5889	6100	7284	8133	
5	Seattle	2345	3699	3356	4350	
6						

2. Click on the Default Chart tool. A marquee appears around the selected data and the pointer turns into a crosshair.
3. Maximize your document window, if it isn't already, and drag the pointer from C7 to G16, as shown in Figure 7-4.

When you release the mouse button, the default Column chart will be displayed in the area you just defined. Your screen should look similar to Figure 7-1. There will be some differences—your chart will not have a Chart title and the X-axis category names may be oriented differently.

The Chart Type Tool

If you would like to see the chart you just produced in another format, then the first tool, the Chart Type tool, is what you need to use. The Chart Type tool opens a tear-off palette that you can leave permanently displayed and which you can drag anywhere in the document window as shown here:

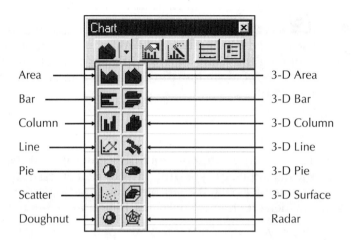

The Chart Type palette presents a choice of 14 chart types from which you can select. The 14 chart types—Area, Bar, Column, Line, Pie, Scatter, Doughnut, Radar, 3-D Surface, 3-D Pie, 3-D Line, 3-D Column, 3-D Bar, and 3-D Area—are described later in the chapter in "Deciding What to Chart."

You can replace one chart type with another by selecting the chart you want to change and clicking on one of the alternatives in the Chart Type palette. You can tell if the chart is selected if the border has nodes or handles on it. A

Dragging the pointer across a sheet for a default chart

Figure 7-4.

chart is selected in lieu of an active cell and the reference area of the Formula bar displays the word "Chart" and a number if a chart is selected. Follow these steps to replace one chart type with another.

1. If your chart is not selected (doesn't have nodes or resizing handles), click on it. The reference area of your Formula bar should say Chart 1.

2. Click on the arrow beside the Chart Type tool. The Chart Type palette will open. If you wish, drag it off to the right side by dragging on the border.

3. Click on the Line chart type (fourth down in the left column).

The Column chart is immediately replaced by a Line chart, as shown in Figure 7-5. Later, you can use this data to explore each of the chart types as they are discussed in the book.

ChartWizard

The ChartWizard, which is the third tool in the Chart toolbar, is also in the Standard toolbar. The ChartWizard leads you through the creation of a chart and prompts you to identify the size of the chart you want to create, the sheet range you want to use to supply the data, the chart type to use, and the descriptive text to add to the chart. You will learn about the ChartWizard in depth later in this chapter.

Line chart replacing the Column chart

Figure 7-5.

Horizontal Gridlines Tool

The Horizontal Gridlines tool is an off and on switch that displays horizontal gridlines in the chart or turns them off. Whether gridlines can be displayed depends upon the type of chart being displayed. For example, horizontal gridlines are especially meaningful with charts such as Bar, Column, or Line. They are not meaningful with Pie or Doughnut charts.

To see how this tool works, follow these steps.

1. If your chart is not selected, click on it.
2. Make sure that the chart is either a Line chart or a Column chart.
3. Click on the Horizontal Gridlines tool. The gridlines will disappear. Click again to see the gridlines reappear.

Legend Tool

Similarly, the Legend tool switches the legend in the chart on and off. If you want to turn off the legend (for example, because you are creating a custom legend), you would use the following steps.

1. Again, ensure that your chart is selected.
2. Click on the Legend tool to make the legend disappear. Click on it again to make it reappear.

Deciding What to Chart

The first step in creating a chart is deciding what to chart; this step may be one of the hardest. It is easy to pick a set of numbers to put on a chart, but do those numbers tell the story that you believe is in them?

These questions are not easy to answer, and there are probably several substantially different opinions. The best answer comes from asking yourself if the chart tells the story you are trying to tell. In later sections of this chapter, you will build charts based on simple sheets. For each, you can decide how well the chart tells the story that is in the numbers.

Selecting the Type of Chart

The type of chart to use is as much a subjective decision as what to chart. As mentioned above, Excel offers 14 types of charts plus several variations on each type and the ability to combine types. The choice of which type suits your data best depends on what you like, but there are also some rules of thumb. The next sections discuss each of Excel's chart types and when to use them. You also see what variations are available for each type of chart and how each uses particular options in the menus.

Area Charts

An Area chart shows the magnitude of change over time. It is particularly useful when several components are changing and you are interested in the sum of those components. Area charts let you see the change in the individual components as well as the change in the total. For example, in the Area chart shown in Figure 7-6, you can see the change in the sales of three products as well as the change in total sales, which is the sum of the three products.

An Area chart is a stacked line chart, with the area between the lines filled in with color or shading. An Area chart plots one data series above another. Assume, for example, that you have two data series in an Area chart. If the first data point of the first series is 50 and the first data point of the second series is 60, the data points would be plotted at 50 and 110. In a normal Line chart, the points would be plotted at 50 and 60. In Figure 7-6, desktop units are added to floor units and laptop units are added to the sum of the first two. The top line on the chart represents total sales, and each layer is that product's share of those sales.

A variation of the Area chart is the 3-D Area chart shown in Figure 7-7. While this chart has a certain "gee whiz" factor, it does not have one of the major features of an Area chart—the ability to show the total as well as the individual components.

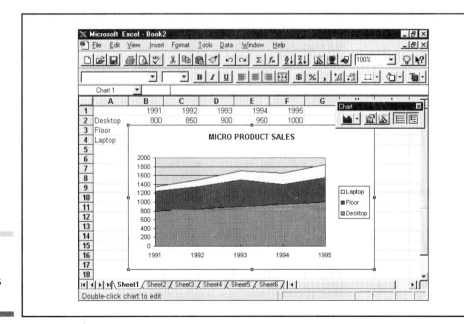

Area chart
showing
product sales
Figure 7-6.

7

Bar Charts

A Bar chart consists of a series of horizontal bars that allow comparison of the relative size of two or more items at one point in time. For example, the Bar chart shown in Figure 7-8 compares the sales for each of three products in each of five years. Each bar in a Bar chart is a single data point or number on the sheet. The set of numbers (or data points) for a single set of bars is a data series (for example, the five bars for Laptop sales make up one data series). The Bar chart in Figure 7-8 contains three data series representing the sales for three product lines.

Bar Chart Variations or Subtypes

The Bar chart has three primary subtypes: the Stacked Bar chart, the 100% Bar chart, and the 3-D Bar chart. The Stacked Bar chart displays additional data series as multiple segments within a single bar. With the product sales data and the Stacked Bar chart variation, you get the chart shown in Figure 7-9. The same data with the 100% Stacked Bar chart type produces the chart shown in Figure 7-10. In both cases, each of the three products is contained in a separate data series. Figure 7-11 shows the same data using the 3-D Bar chart type which simply adds depth to a standard Bar chart and does not have a third dimension.

In the Stacked Bar chart, the total length of the bar is the sum of the segments (total company sales, in the example). Therefore, the size of each segment is relative to both the total and to the other segments. The Stacked Bar chart has a similar visual effect as the Area chart.

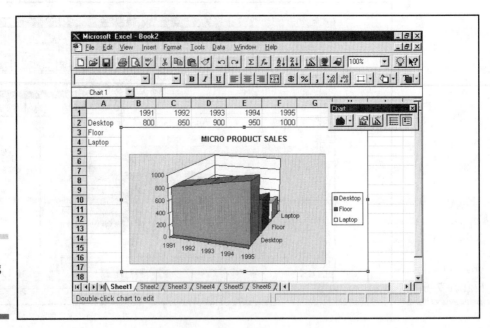

3-D Area chart showing product sales

Figure 7-7.

In the 100% Bar chart, all bars become the same height, representing 100 percent. The segments then become their percentage of the total instead of their numerical number, as shown in Figure 7-10. The 3-D Bar chart, in Figure 7-11, provides 3-D markers in place of 2-D horizontal bars.

7

100% Stacked
Bar chart
showing
product sales
Figure 7-10.

Column Charts

A Column chart consists of a series of vertical columns that allow
comparison of the relative size of two or more items, often over time. For

3-D Bar chart
showing
product sales
Figure 7-11.

example, the Column chart shown in Figure 7-12 compares annual sales by presenting a column for each year's sales. Each column in a Column chart is a single data point or number on the sheet. The set of numbers for a single set of columns is a data series. For example, the Column chart in Figure 7-12 contains three data series, each bar showing the annual sales for one office.

Column charts have the same variations as Bar charts: Stacked Column, 100% Stacked Column, and 3-D Column, the last of which is shown in Figure 7-13.

Line Charts

A Line chart is used to show trends over time. For example, the Line chart in Figure 7-14 shows that sales and expenses are not following each other, forcing earnings to be negative when expenses are not controlled during revenue declines. With Line charts, the reader can make a projection into the future—maybe inappropriately.

In a Line chart, each data series is used to produce a line on the chart, with each number in the range producing a data point on the line. There are three data series in Figure 7-14—Sales, Expenses, and Earnings—with 12 data points in each series.

There are two significant variations to the Line chart, a 3-D Line chart, shown in Figure 7-15, and a High-Low-Close chart, discussed next.

7

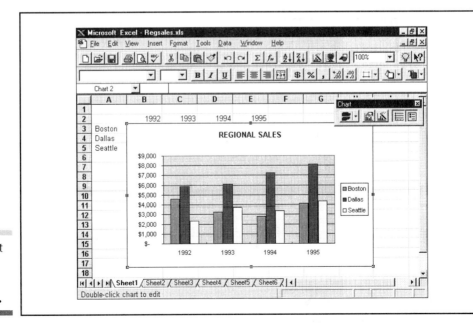

Column chart showing annual sales
Figure 7-12.

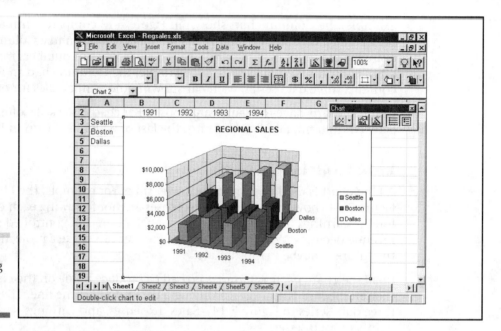

3-D Column
chart showing
annual sales
Figure 7-13.

High-Low-Close Charts

A High-Low-Close chart is a Line chart with three data series used to display
a stock's high, low, and closing prices for a given time period.

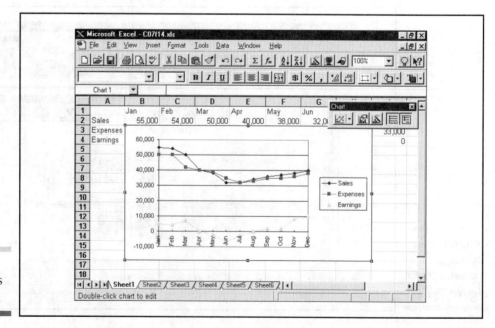

Line chart
showing sales
Figure 7-14.

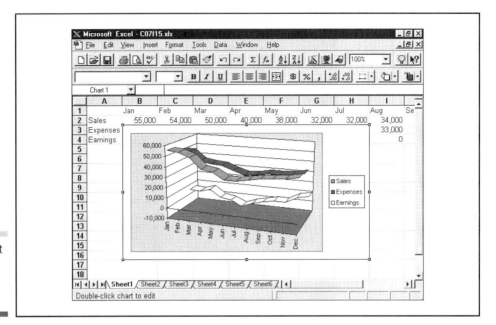

3-D Line chart showing monthly sales

Figure 7-15.

High-Low-Close charts also work well for commodity prices, currency exchange rates, and temperature and pressure measurements.

Figure 7-16 shows a High-Low-Close chart for stock prices. It contains three data series for the high, low, and closing prices of a stock issue on a given day each month for six months. The vertical lines are formed by drawing a line between the high and the low data points while the tick mark is the closing price.

Pie Charts

A Pie chart is best used for comparing the percentages of a sum that several numbers represent. The full pie is the sum, and each number is represented by a wedge or slice. Figure 7-17 shows an example of a Pie chart. Each slice represents the percentage of total sales for a given product category. There is only one data series in a Pie chart. If more than one series is selected, Excel plots the first one. In the example in Figure 7-17, three numbers are in the data series, one for each product category, and they represent the sales of each category for one year only. Excel automatically adds the numbers together and calculates the percentages to produce the chart.

In Figure 7-18, you may notice that the Pie chart is *exploded*—that is, one of the slices is separated from the other slices. This is very easy to do. You simply click on the slice and drag it away from the others. When you click

7

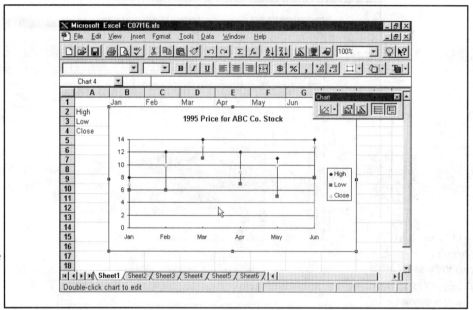

High-Low-Close chart
Figure 7-16.

on a slice, notice that black selection boxes appear around it, meaning it can be moved, as shown in Figure 7-18.

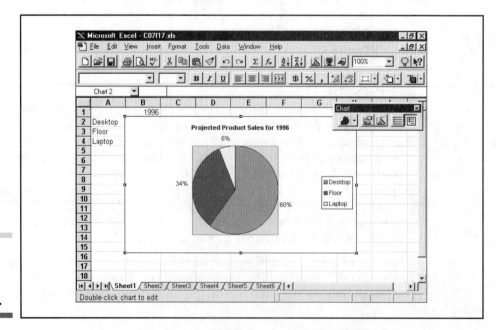

Pie chart for product comparison
Figure 7-17.

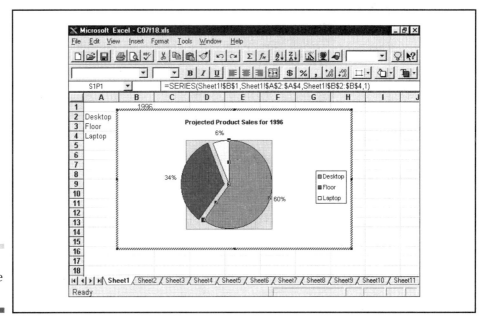

Pie chart with
a selected slice
Figure 7-18.

A 3-D Pie chart, which is the only significant variation, is shown next. A 3-D Pie chart can also be exploded in the same way a regular Pie chart can be—by dragging.

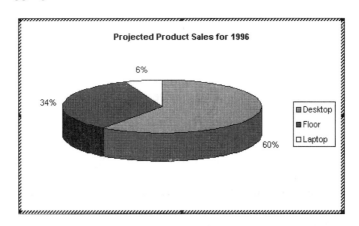

Doughnut Charts

The Doughnut chart is similar to the Pie chart. However, the Pie Chart is restricted to one data series while the Doughnut chart is not. A Doughnut Chart with 1996 data on the inside and 1997 on the outside is shown in Figure 7-19.

Radar Charts

Radar charts show how data changes in relation to a center point and to other data. The value axis of each category radiates from the center point. Data from the same series is connected by lines.

You can use the Radar chart to plot several interrelated series and easily make visual comparisons. For example, if you have three machines containing the same five parts, you can plot the wear index of each part on each machine on a Radar chart, as shown in Figure 7-20. The machine with the largest area has the highest cumulative wear index.

Scatter Charts

Scatter or XY charts show the relationship between pairs of numbers and the trends they present. For each pair, one of the numbers is plotted on the X-axis and the other number is plotted on the Y-axis. Where the two meet, a symbol is placed on the chart. When a number of such pairs is plotted, a pattern may emerge, as shown in Figure 7-21.

The Scatter chart in Figure 7-21 shows the hypothetical correlation between hours of sleep on the X-axis and units of production on the Y-axis. This is a typical example of how a Scatter chart is used.

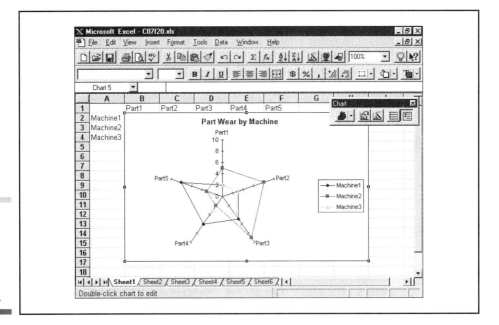

Radar chart
comparing
part wear on
several
machines
Figure 7-20.

3-D Surface Charts

There are two types of 3-D Surface charts: color charts that look like a
flexible sheet draped over a 3-D Column chart, and charts without color that
look like a wireframe chart.

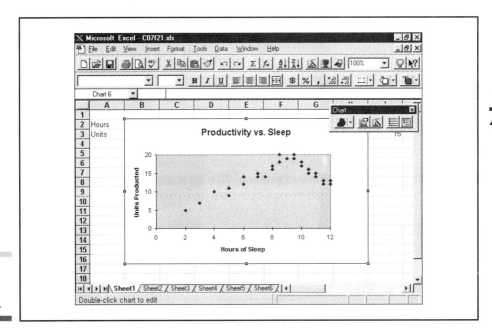

Scatter or XY
chart
Figure 7-21.

7

Both types are useful for showing the optimum combinations of two sets of data. On color charts, areas of the same height are shown as the same color. An example of the use of 3-D Surface charts would be bodybuilding: muscle is developed by lifting varying amounts of weight a repetitive number of times. A 3-D Surface chart shows the combinations of weight and repetitions that produce the greatest muscle development, as you can see in Figure 7-22.

Creating a Line Chart

Next, you will create two charts, one as a separate sheet using the Chart option on the Insert menu, and the second as an embedded chart using the ChartWizard. These two exercises will provide you with a good understanding of how a chart is created and what the options are in doing it.

To create these charts, begin with another simple sheet, named SALESCOM.XLS, that shows the sales commissions earned by five salespeople. Remembering that a Line chart is best at showing trends, start with a Line chart that shows the sales commissions for each sales person for the four quarters of 1995.

1. Close any open workbooks without saving.
2. Click on the File menu, New option. Click OK for the Workbook.

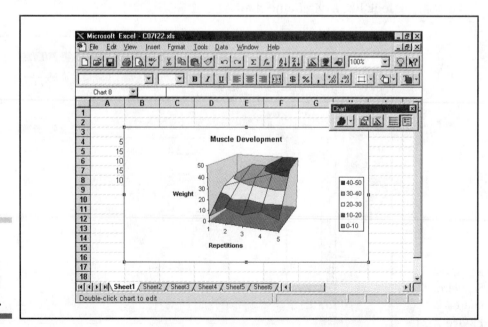

3-D Surface chart of muscle development

Figure 7-22.

3. Enter the following data on a sheet:

	A	B	C	D	E	F	G
1		1st Qtr	2nd Qtr	3rd Qtr	4th Qtr	Total	
2	Abbott, J	5000	18000	12000	15000	50000	
3	Crowley, C	5000	15000	5500	7000	32500	
4	Gerald, S	3000	10000	5000	7000	25000	
5	Marcus, M	8000	12000	10000	18000	48000	
6	Steel, N	15000	14000	16000	10000	55000	
7							

4. Use the File menu Save option to save the data with the name SALESCOM.XLS.

Selecting the Ranges to Plot

As you have already seen, your first step in building a chart is to select the range or ranges on the sheet that you want to plot. For this Line chart, you want to select the range A1 through E6. Within this range you have five data series—one for each sales person, and each series has four data points—one for each quarter. The category labels for the X-axis are the four quarters in 1995 located in B1 through E1 and the legend labels are the five salespeople located in A2 through A6.

1. Select or highlight A1 through E6 (do not include the Total column).

Incidentally, you may find that you have several ranges on a sheet that you want to plot on a single chart, but the ranges are not joined to each other in one unbroken rectangle. Ranges that you are going to plot on a chart may be separated from one another by several intervening rows or columns. These are called *nonadjacent sections*. Even though there are several noncontiguous sections, the overall shape of all the sections must still be rectangular. You can select multiple independent ranges by holding down CTRL as you highlight each range.

7

Creating a New Chart Sheet with the Insert Menu

To create a new chart sheet, you will use the Chart option on the Insert menu. The Chart option gives you two choices, as you will recall. You can create a chart either as a separate sheet or as an embedded chart. Use the following instructions to create a separate chart sheet.

1. From the Insert menu, choose Chart. The submenu showing the two options will open.

2. Click on As New Sheet. The first of five ChartWizard dialog boxes will open, which verifies that the range is defined as $A$1:$E$6, as shown here:

3. Click on Next. The second ChartWizard dialog box will be displayed.

   The second ChartWizard dialog box asks for the chart type to be plotted and contains 15 alternatives from which you can choose. These are the 14 alternatives that you saw in the Chart Type palette plus one for making Combination charts. You want the Line chart type, as shown in Figure 7-23.

4. Click on the Line chart and then on Next. The third ChartWizard dialog box will be displayed, as shown here:

   The third ChartWizard dialog box offers ten variations of the Line chart from which you can choose. You want the fourth variation, the format with the gridlines and the plot points, which is the default.

5. Click on Next to accept the default. The fourth ChartWizard dialog box will be displayed.

   A sample of the chart is displayed in the fourth dialog box, in which you can change the chart's orientation. In other words, this dialog box gives you the opportunity to determine if the Y- and X-axes are correctly labeled and if the legend is correct. In this chart, the orientation and legend are NOT correctly identified. The salespeople are

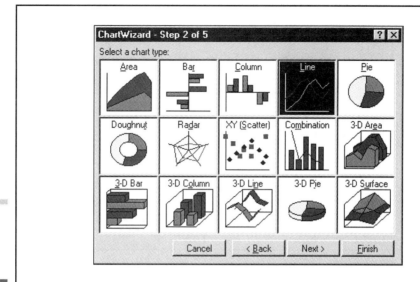

ChartWizard
Chart Type
dialog box
Figure 7-23.

considered to be data points and the quarters are considered to be data series, which is reversed from what you want.

You'll remember that one of the items Excel looks at when automatically preparing a chart is whether or not there are more rows or columns in the selected range; Excel assumes that whichever are more are the data points and the other are the data series. If they're the same, Excel assumes the columns are data points and the rows are data series. In this case you fooled Excel by having more series than points.

6. Click on Data Series in Rows. Instantly the chart will be changed and now make more sense, as shown in Figure 7-24.

   Now the legend shows the salespeople's names and the category names; the four quarters are on the X-axis. Also, you can tell by quarters which salesperson did best and what the trend has been over the year.

7. Click on Next. The last dialog box will be displayed. It allows you to fill in titles and other identifying text.

   At the top of the dialog box you have the opportunity to suppress the legend if you wish. You do not want to do this, so accept the Yes default. You do want to add chart and axis titles, so continue along with these instructions.

8. Press TAB to move the insertion point to the Chart Title text box.

7

The fourth
ChartWizard
dialog box
allows you to
change the
chart
orientation
Figure 7-24.

9. In the Chart Title text box, type **Sales Commissions for 1995**. You will see the title reflected on the sample chart as soon as you have typed it.

10. Press TAB to move the insertion point to the Category Axis Title text box. This is where you enter the text to appear under the X-axis.

11. Type **1995** and press TAB to move to the Value Axis Title text box. This is where you enter the text to appear to the left of the Y-axis.

12. Type **Sales Commissions**. The completed dialog box is shown in Figure 7-25.

13. Click on Finish. A chart sheet named Chart1 will appear.

Final
ChartWizard
dialog box for
the Line chart
Figure 7-25.

Saving, Printing, and Closing

You have now completed the Line chart. Save it, and then print and close it with the following steps.

1. Click on the Save tool in the Standard toolbar to save the workbook with Chart1.

2. Click on the Print tool in the Standard toolbar to print the Line chart. When it is finished, it should look like Figure 7-26. Later, you will see how you can use different patterns, markers, orientations, and colors to make your chart look different.

Using ChartWizard to Create Embedded Charts

The ChartWizard tool, located on both the Standard and the Chart toolbars, opens the same dialog boxes as the menu approach you just went through. However, you do not have to go through the menu, and in this case you will be creating an embedded chart.

Follow these steps to create a Bar chart from the SALESCOM.XLS data.

1. Click on Sheet1 to display that sheet again.

   If the cells of the sheet are not already selected, select them, A1 to E6; do *not* select the Total column.

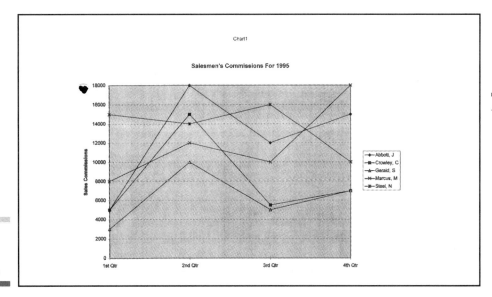

Printed Line
chart
Figure 7-26.

7

2. Click on the ChartWizard tool in the Standard toolbar to begin creating the embedded chart.

3. With the pointer that has become a crosshair, drag over the range in which you want to place the chart, from about B2 to H16.

4. When you release the mouse button, the first ChartWizard dialog box will be displayed.

5. Verify that the range of the data is correct, $A$1:$E$6, and click on Next to accept it. The second ChartWizard dialog box will be displayed.

6. Click on the Bar chart option, as shown in Figure 7-27. Then click on Next. The third ChartWizard dialog box will be displayed showing the several variations of the Bar chart from which you can choose.

7. Click on Next to accept the default format (number 6) that provides individual bars and a grid, as shown here:

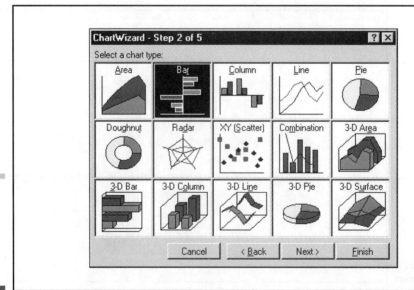

Bar chart selected from the Chart Types dialog box

Figure 7-27.

The fourth dialog box will be displayed. It contains a sample of the chart as it would display right now. This is where you can change the orientation of the chart by redefining the role of the rows and columns.

You'll notice that again the data series are assumed to be in columns. You could switch the data-series orientation as you did on the Line chart and have the salespeople identified in the legend and have the quarters as categories. However, it is easier to see the differences between salespeople the way it is.

8. Click on Next to accept the orientation of the chart. The final ChartWizard dialog box will be displayed. On it you can add chart and axis titles.

9. Press TAB to move to the Chart Title text box and type **SALES COMMISSIONS FOR 1995**. The title will appear on the sample chart.

10. Click on Finish. The chart will appear on Sheet1 as shown in Figure 7-28.

When you are done creating a chart, you may want to change some parts of it. Excel has considerable capability to edit and modify its charts using the ChartWizard, the Chart toolbar, and special chart menus. You have already seen how the Chart toolbar can be used, so look next at the ChartWizard's ability to edit.

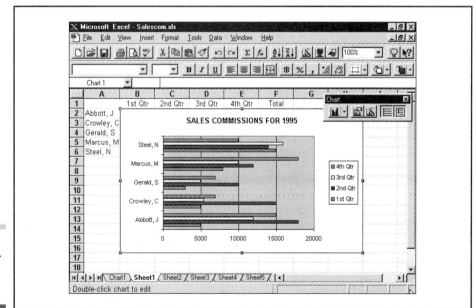

Final embedded Bar chart

Figure 7-28.

7

Using ChartWizard to Change the Chart

When you clicked on the ChartWizard to create a chart, five dialog boxes were displayed to guide you through this process. When you click on the ChartWizard with an existing chart selected, you get only two of the dialog boxes: the first one, in which you can change the definition of the data range, and the fourth one, in which you can change the chart orientation. Try these now.

1. With the current embedded chart showing and selected, click on the ChartWizard. The first ChartWizard dialog box will be displayed. If you want to add more rows or columns to your sheet, for example, this gives you a quick way to do it.

2. Click on Next for the second dialog box. The second dialog box in Editing mode is the same as the fourth one that appears when you are creating a chart. It allows you to change the orientation of the chart. You can change the references for data series, the X axis, and for legends.

3. Click on OK to accept the original settings.

To make other changes to the chart, you must directly modify the chart itself. In the next section, you'll find out how.

Modifying Charts Directly and With Menus

Once you have a chart defined, you can edit or modify it directly and through menus. In either case, before you can change a chart, it must be *activated*, not merely selected as it has been up until this point.

Activating a Chart

An embedded chart must be activated before it can be modified. You will know when a chart has been activated by its border. It has a thicker blue or gray border around it, as compared to the thin border with nodes of a selected chart. Figure 7-28 shows an example of a selected chart, Figure 7-29 shows an activated chart.

Compare selecting and activating a chart with these steps.

1. If the chart is not already selected, click anywhere on the chart to select it. The select nodes or handles will appear.

2. Double-click on the chart to activate it (it does not have to be selected first). The border will change to a gray or blue, thicker line.

Now you can edit or change the chart either by using special chart menus or directly. You will first look at what you can do with the menus.

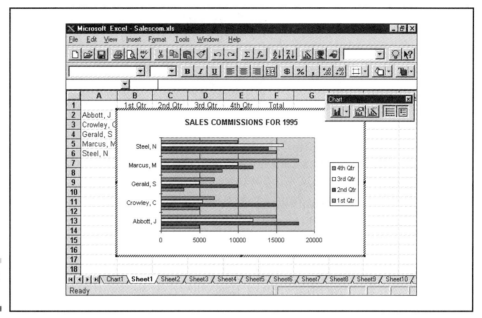

Activated chart
Figure 7-29.

Using the Insert Menu to Change a Chart

Once a chart is activated, the Insert menu contains options for editing it, as
shown here:

These special chart options are not available from the menu until a chart has
been activated. You will quickly see how you may change the chart with
these options.

Titles When you click on the Titles option of the Insert menu, you will
see this dialog box:

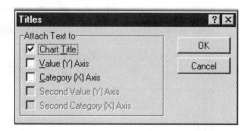

The Titles option allows you to suppress or display a Chart or Axis Title. If the check box contains a check mark, you will see a title. If there is no check mark, the title will not be displayed.

To see how this works, turn off the Chart Title and then redisplay it by doing the following.

1. Click on the Insert menu and then the Titles option, and the Titles dialog box will be displayed.

2. Click on the Chart Title check box so that the check mark is no longer in the box and then click on OK. The title will disappear from the activated chart.

3. Click on the Insert menu, Titles option, and then on the Chart Title check box to redisplay a title. Click on OK.

Now the title, "Title," is displayed. You will change the text later using the direct editing method.

Now you will add some data labels to the Bar chart.

Data Labels   The Data Labels option on the Insert menu allows you to place a label (the name of the salesperson) or the value (the quarterly dollar amount) by each of the bars. Place value labels on the chart with these steps.

1. Click on the Insert menu and then the Data Labels option. This dialog box will be displayed:

Currently there are no data labels.

2. Click on the Show Value option button and then click OK.

The value labels will be placed on the chart. They are difficult to read, but you'll change that shortly.

Next, you look at Legends.

Legends   When you select the Legend option on the Insert menu, you are simply telling Excel to display a legend. If no legend is showing and you click on this option, a legend will be inserted in the chart. In this case, the Legend option has no effect since you have a legend already showing.

Axes   When you select the Axes option on the Insert menu, you are shown this dialog box:

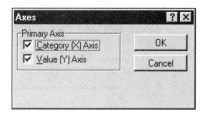

Both the X- and Y-axes labels are showing on the chart and both check boxes are checked in the dialog box. If you remove a check mark by clicking on a check box, the labels for that axis will be removed. You do not want to do that now. If you displayed the dialog box, click on Cancel.

Move on to the Gridlines option.

Gridlines   The Gridlines option on the Insert menu, like the Axes option, allows you to display or remove the gridlines on the chart. If you select the Gridlines option, you will see this dialog box:

7

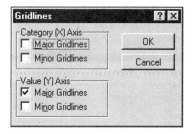

You can see that only the major gridlines for the Y-axis are displayed. Insert minor gridlines also for that axis:

1. Click on the Insert menu and the Gridlines option.
2. Click on Minor Gridlines for the Y-axis so that a check mark is in its box. Click on OK.

You'll see in the activated chart the effects of the minor gridlines. Now you can more precisely estimate the commissions for each of the salespeople.

Picture   The Picture option on the Insert menu allows you to insert a graphic object, such as a logo, into the chart. You do not want to use this right now. However, the dialog box that is displayed simply asks for the folder and filename of the picture file, as you would expect.

New Data   The New Data option on the Insert menu allows you to attach additional data to an existing chart. When you select this option the following dialog box is displayed:

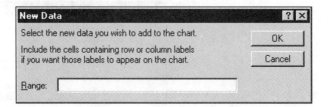

You simply fill in the range of the new data to be added to the chart, or drag across the range on the sheet, and click on OK. The chart will be redisplayed with a new bar appearing with the existing bars. Click on Cancel if you opened the New Data dialog box.

You have now seen how data can be changed through the Insert menu options. Next, look at how you can change charts through the Format menu options.

Using the Format Menu to Change a Chart

When a chart is active, the Format menu also changes to incorporate several special menu options, as shown here:

These include changing a selected object, changing the chart type, AutoFormatting a chart, and formatting a particular data group. Start by looking at the Selected Object option.

Selected Object Selected Object is shown grayed if nothing on the chart is selected. In this example, the legend on the chart was selected. If you selected another object in the chart, it would be the selected item, such as Selected Axis, or Selected Data Labels. If this menu item is then selected, options pertaining to the selected item would be made available.

Chart Type When you click on this option, you are shown 2-D or 3-D chart types, depending on your current activated chart structure. For the current Bar chart, you see the 2-D alternatives shown in Figure 7-30.

You can change from 2-D to 3-D and see a different selection of chart formats displayed. The alternatives allow you to change the major chart type. If you click the Options button in the Chart Type dialog box, you will open the Format Bar Group dialog box, which is also opened by the last option on the Format menu: 1 Bar Group.

Format Bar Group The Format Bar Group dialog box, which is opened either from the Format menu or from the Chart Type dialog box, allows you to access four groups of formatting options that are shown in Figures 7-31 through 7-34.

In Figure 7-31, you can see the major Subtypes available for the Bar chart: individual bars, stacked bars, and 100% stacked bars.

Chart Type selection from the Format menu
Figure 7-30.

7

Subtype tab of
the Format Bar
Group dialog
box
Figure 7-31.

By clicking the Series Order tab, you get the dialog box shown in Figure 7-32
where you can change the order of how the data series are displayed. For
example, instead of displaying the 1st Qtr first, you might want to show the
3rd Qtr first.

Series Order
tab of the
Format Bar
Group dialog
box
Figure 7-32.

Options tab of
the Format Bar
Group dialog
box
Figure 7-33.

In the Options tab, shown in Figure 7-33, you can set the distance between bars and how colors are varied.

Finally, Figure 7-34 shows the Axis option, which allows you to change the axis upon which the chart is plotted. In this case, you cannot change either (both of the axes options are dim) because the chart would have no meaning if an axis were turned off.

If you have displayed these dialog boxes on the screen, press Cancel now.

AutoFormat *AutoFormat* for charts is like AutoFormat for sheets. Several formats are predefined for each type of chart and are presented for your choice. Each format contains selected settings for such elements as label placement, font and point size selection, titles, colors, gridlines, patterns, and others. For example, if you select AutoFormat from the Format menu, you would get the dialog box shown in Figure 7-35 that shows the autoformats available for Bar charts. If you were to click on one of the other chart types in the Galleries display box, you would see the autoformats available for that chart type.

You can also custom design your own format and save it so that it can be selected just like one of the autoformats.

7

Axis tab of the
Format Bar
Group dialog
box
Figure 7-34.

Changing Charts with Direct Edits

Excel gives you extraordinary direct control over the details of a chart. You
can modify or edit all aspects of a chart by simply clicking on the element or
area you want changed and then selecting an option or typing text directly
onto the chart. Excel refers to the editing or modifications as *formatting*.

Format menu
AutoFormat
options
Figure 7-35.

When you click on a chart element, you select it and, depending on what the element is, you can move, size, or edit the element in that state. If you double-click on an element, a Format dialog box opens and certain options, shown in Table 7-1, become available. Which options are available depends on the element. For example, the Patterns, Font, and Alignment options are available if you double-click on text elements such as titles. For other elements, there are Number, Scale, Placement, Axis, Data Labels, Names and Values, and Y-Error Bars options.

In a 2-D chart, you can double-click on ten elements or areas that will result in one or more dialog boxes being displayed. These elements and areas are as follows.

♦ *Chart Title,* which can be formatted for Font, Patterns, and Alignment

♦ *Axis,* which can be formatted for Patterns, Scale, Font, Number, and Alignment

♦ *Axis Title,* which can be formatted for Patterns, Font, and Alignment

♦ *Data Label,* which can be formatted for Font, Patterns, Number, and Alignment

Option	Use
Patterns	Changes the border line width, style, and color as well as the foreground and background pattern and color
Font	Selects the typeface, size, style, and color
Alignment	Adjusts the alignment and position of text
Scale	Sets the minimum, maximum, major, and minor increments as well as the type of scales used on each axis
Number	Formats numbers
Placement	Determines the placement of the legend
Axis	Sets the axis on which the data series is plotted
Data Labels	Turns on or off data labels (similar to the Data Label option on the Insert menu)
Names and Values	Selects the sheet ranges that are the sources for the names and values of a particular series
Y-Error Bars	Turns on or off Y-error bars, which show the range of possible error in a data point

Format Dialog
Box Options
Table 7-1.

7

- ◆ *Legend,* which can be formatted for Font, Patterns, and Placement
- ◆ *Chart Area,* which can be formatted for Patterns and Font
- ◆ *Plot Area,* which can be formatted for Patterns
- ◆ *Data Series,* which can be formatted for Patterns, Axis, Names and Values, Y-Error Bars, and Data Labels
- ◆ *Data Point,* which can be formatted for Data Labels and Patterns
- ◆ *Grid Lines,* which can be formatted for Patterns and Scale

Three-dimensional charts have all of the 2-D elements and areas plus the three additional ones: walls, corners, and floors, all of which can be formatted for Patterns.

Next, experiment with some of the formatting capabilities using the Bar chart now on your screen.

Changing Text in Titles and Labels

When you create a chart, you are given the opportunity to create titles, legends, and labels. Sometimes you want to change either the text itself or the font and typeface.

Text, as you enter it, is given a default format by Excel. The title is formatted as 10-point bold Arial. The data values are formatted as 8-point regular Arial. You can change this formatting as you desire.

Changing the Chart Title   At the top of your screen is a Chart title, the original text of which has been replaced with the word "Title." In addition, you can see that the data labels are too big for the chart; they cannot be easily read. You will change the text in the title and the typeface of the data labels. Follow these steps.

1. Make sure Sheet1 is showing with the SALESCOM.XLS workbook and the Bar chart on the screen. The chart should be activated, with the distinguishing gray or blue border around it.
2. Click once on the Chart title. The word "Title" will be selected and a box with nodes or handles on it will surround it, like this:

3. As you place the pointer inside the box, you'll find that it turns from an arrow to an I-beam. Drag the I-beam pointer across the letters, highlighting all letters of the title, like this:

Title

4. Type **SALES COMMISSIONS FOR 1995**. The title text will be replaced with the new title.

   Next, add a background for the Chart title.

5. Double-click on the Chart title background. (Be careful. The pointer must be an arrow, not the I-beam, and the area clicked on must be the title area. Otherwise, you'll get the Chart Area dialog box, not the Format Chart Title dialog box. It may be easier to deselect the title by clicking somewhere else in the chart and then double-clicking on the title.)

   The Format Chart Title dialog box will be displayed.

6. Click on the Patterns tab. The Patterns dialog box will open.

   The Patterns dialog box for the Chart title lets you place a border around the title, select among a number of alternatives for that border, and select from among a number of colors and patterns for the area behind the title. What you want to do with the Bar chart is place a shadow in the background of the title.

7. Click on the light gray color (second from the right in the second row of the Color palette). Click on OK. The title reappears with the gray background as shown here:

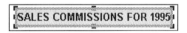

You can also change the background of the whole chart in the same way. You can do this by clicking on a blank area of the chart, verifying the selected object is the chart by seeing Chart in the Formula bar reference area, and getting the Format Chart Area dialog box with the same options.

Changing the Data Labels   Currently the data labels are values placed to the right of the bars in the chart. The values are difficult to read. You will make them bold italic.

7

When you select a data label, you will click on one number, but all numbers for that data series will be selected. Then you will select the numbers for the three other data series as well.

1. Double-click on one of the data labels. The values will be selected and the Format Data Label dialog box will open. Click on the Font tab and the dialog box shown in Figure 7-36 will be displayed.

2. Under Font Style, click on Bold Italic, as shown here:

3. Click OK. The data labels for that series will be made bold italic.

4. Select data labels from each of the other three data series. Press CTRL-Y to select each data label, and make them bold italic as well.

5. Click anywhere in the chart to end the text selection. Figure 7-37 shows the results.

Changing Colors and Adding Patterns   Although you can see the color of the bars perfectly fine on the screen, when they print on your printer, some of the colors will be hard to distinguish. You need to add a pattern to some of the bars. Follow these steps.

1. Double-click on one of the bars that you would like to see changed. Selecting one bar selects all bars for that data series. For example, double-clicking on one of the bottom bars selects all 1st Qtr bars.

   The Format Data Series dialog box opens, offering you a number of options for changing the formats of a data series. You want to change the patterns.

2. Click on the Patterns tab to display the dialog box shown in Figure 7-38.

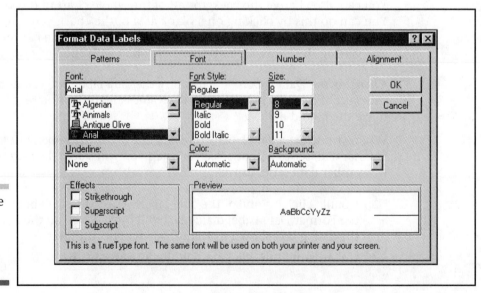

Font tab in the Format Data Label dialog box

Figure 7-36.

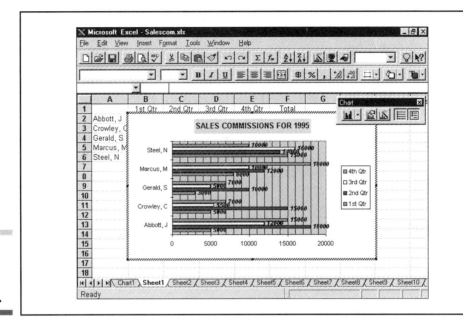

Chart after
changing the
text
Figure 7-37.

3. Click on the Pattern drop-down list box and a pop-up palette of
   patterns and colors will open. Click on the widely spaced dots in the
   upper-right corner of the patterns section and click on OK.

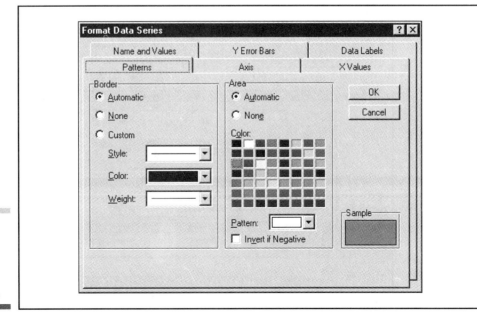

Format Data
Series dialog
box, Patterns
tab
Figure 7-38.

7

4. Select another data series by double-clicking on a bar. Then again choose a pattern and click on OK. Figure 7-39 shows one possible way you might reformat your bars.

You can see how the direct method works. You simply double-click on an element in a chart and Excel presents a dialog box with choices that you can use to change the format of the chart.

Continue to experiment with the chart. Double-click on the chart elements and see the dialog boxes that are presented to you. When you are finished, you will need to save and print the chart.

Saving and Printing the Chart

You are now done with the Bar chart, so you need to save it and then print it. Follow these instructions.

1. Click on the Save tool. SALESCOM.XLS will be saved.

2. Click on the Print tool to print the Bar chart.

Closing a Chart

While you can leave the Bar chart open on the desktop, it serves no real purpose to do so. Close it by clicking on the Bar chart's Close button. When

Final Bar chart
as reformatted
Figure 7-39.

the Bar chart closes, the previous sheet will be shown on the screen. You do not have to save it. Click on its Close button. When Excel asks whether you want to save the change, click on No.

Leaving Excel

Since you have saved or released all the sheets used in this chapter, none need to be resaved. You need only leave Excel and Windows. Do that now with these steps.

1. Click on Excel's Close button to close Excel.
2. Click on the Start button, the Shut Down option, and click on Yes to close Windows and prepare your computer to be turned off.

In this chapter, you have experimented with the many charting features of Excel. Now try some of these features on your own. In no time at all, your own charts will take on a more professional look.

7

Working with a Database

8

A database is a list—a phone list, a list of products, a list of parts, a list of customers—a set of related information organized into the row-and-column structure of Excel. In this chapter, you build two databases or tables. You then sort the tables, summarize them, extract information from them, analyze the information, and build a pivot table and a lookup table.

Databases are the third of Excel's three components (spreadsheets and charts are the other two). A database is a natural adjunct to Excel because Excel's row-and-column structure lends itself to storing information in a database. Each entry in the database, called a *record,* is placed across one row. In a phone list containing names and phone numbers, a record is a single name and phone number combination. Each part of a record (for example, the name or the phone number) is called a *field* and is entered in a column. Thus, a direct relationship exists between rows and columns on a spreadsheet and records and fields in a database.

A database must be contained on a single sheet. A single sheet can contain several databases, but only one of them at a time may be active and available for performing any of several predefined operations. It is generally better to put separate databases on separate sheets and to separate a database by one blank row and one blank column from other data on the same sheet. This separation allows Excel to automatically select the database. The first row of a database must contain *field names*—the labels in each column of a database that name the field in that column. The maximum size of a database in Excel is 256 fields in 16,383 records (the maximum number of columns in a sheet, and the maximum number of rows less one row to accommodate the field names).

A database can contain any information you want to organize into fields and records. However, it is a good idea to have *at least one blank row at the bottom* of the database to allow for expansion. (You can insert a new record above the last record, and the database range will automatically expand to include the new record.) All of the field names in a database must be unique—they cannot be duplicated—and field names cannot be numbers, logical values, error values, blank cells, or formulas.

Building a Database

Building a database involves little more than typing. You enter a set of field names and then enter the records, and that's all there is to it. Later you will learn some tricks to speed up the entry process, but otherwise it is simply typing. Of course, you can also import data into a database, as you'll see in Chapter 9.

Entering Field Names

The first database for you to build is a list of six sales offices. The record for each office contains an office number, a location, a manager's name, a quota, and a commission rate. The first step in building the database is entering the field names. Your computer should be on and Excel loaded, and you should have a blank workbook on your screen with A1 as the active cell.

1. Type **Number** and press RIGHT ARROW. "Number" is entered in A1, and the active cell moves to B1.
2. Type **Office** and press RIGHT ARROW. "Office" is entered in B1, and the active cell moves to C1.

Complete the remaining field names as shown in the following illustration, using a similar procedure. In column E press ENTER instead of RIGHT ARROW.

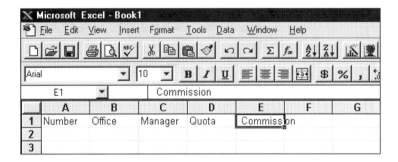

Numbering with a Series

When you have to enter almost any sort of consecutive numbers or dates, you can get help from Excel's Edit Fill Series option. To use this option you must specify the range you want to fill and then enter a start number, an increment or step number, and, optionally, a stop number. For example, if you want a list of numbers from 1 to 10 in column A, beginning in A1, you enter **1** as the start number, highlight the range, and enter (or accept the default of) **1** as the step number. You get 1 in A1, 2 in A2, 3 in A3, and so on to 10 in cell A10.

The start number must be entered on the sheet in the first cell of the row or column you want to fill. Excel uses 1 as the default for the step number and stop number, respectively, if you do not enter them. You can enter any number as the start number, including dates (in a recognizable format), negative numbers, or formulas that evaluate to one of those. The step or stop value must be a recognizable number, not a formula or range name. You can

8

use fractional numbers for the step and stop values, and the stop number may be a date (in a recognizable format).

Either the stop number or the end of the range can stop the series operation. If a stop number stops the series, it does so just before the stop number is exceeded. There are special considerations for series, which are discussed later in this chapter.

Even though you have only six numbers to enter, the Edit Fill Series option makes short work of it. Try it with these steps.

1. Click on A2. The active cell moves to A2.

2. Type **250** and press ENTER. The start value of 250 is entered in A2.

3. Highlight the range A2 through A7.

4. From the Edit menu, point on Fill and then select Series from the submenu. The Series dialog box opens, as shown here:

You can see in the Series dialog box that Excel has detected you want the series to go down a column. The default Type setting is Linear, which is what you want. The other Type options are *Growth*, which multiplies the last cell by the step value, *Date*, which produces a series of date values, and *AutoFill*, which will be discussed in the next section. If you choose Date, the Date Unit option becomes available (in the illustrated dialog box this option is grayed) and allows you to choose whether the date increment is Day, Weekday, Month, or Year.

5. Type **5** for the step value and press ENTER. The dialog box closes and the series of numbers appears in column A. Notice that the range size was used to stop the fill operation.

Numbering with AutoFill

AutoFill looks at the values in the highlighted cells and makes an intelligent decision on how to extend those values in a series that fills the remainder of the highlighted cells. As you saw in Chapter 5, AutoFill allows you to create or extend a series either by dragging the fill handle across the sheet in any direction or by selecting an option from the Series dialog box. Creating a series by dragging provides a faster, real-time display of the results, while using the Series dialog box offers greater flexibility in defining the range and incremental values.

To start a series, enter the first two values in two adjacent cells or choose a value with a known increment, such as a date. For example, if you highlight the range C2:D2 and enter **50** in C2 and **100** in D2, you could then simply drag the fill handle of C2:D2 to the right to extend the series. The value 150 would automatically be placed in E2, 200 in F2, and so on. Unlike with the Series dialog box, there is no way to set a stop value; the series is extended as long as you continue dragging. The Formula bar reference area displays the prospective values of the active cells as they are dragged. Try the following instructions to see how AutoFill works by dragging the fill handle.

1. Highlight A2:A7 (if it isn't already) and press DEL. The series you previously made is deleted.
2. Make sure that Cell Drag and Drop is turned on in the Tools Options dialog box Edit tab, then highlight A2:A3. Type **250** in the active cell, A2, and press ENTER.
3. Type **255** and press ENTER to establish the series increment in cell A3.
4. Drag the A2:A3 fill handle down column A to A7. Notice how the numbers increase in the Formula bar's reference area as you drag.

Continue to experiment with AutoFill by dragging the fill handle up and down column A. Click on a single cell in column A. Drag its fill handle to the right. The adjacent cells are filled in with the same values since there is no incrementing detected by AutoFill. When you are through experimenting with AutoFill, erase your experimentation so you have only the field names in the first row and the series in column A.

Entering Records

Entering the remaining parts of the records is just simple typing. You can either type down a column or across a row, whichever is easier for you. Do that now, entering all of the information shown in Figure 8-1. Enter the quota figures without the comma and enter the commission amounts as decimals (without the leading zero—Excel adds it) instead of percentages (for example, entering **.04** instead of 4%). You will format both the quota figures and commission amounts in the next series of steps.

8

Making the Database Easier to Read
The rightmost pair of columns could benefit from formatting, so do that now.

1. Drag on D2 through D7.

	A	B	C	D	E	F
1	Number	Office	Manager	Quota	Commission	
2	250	Boston	Kauffman	50000	0.04	
3	255	Atlanta	Pearson	65000	0.045	
4	260	Denver	Fisher	45000	0.035	
5	265	Chicago	Colby	70000	0.05	
6	270	Seattle	Burke	40000	0.03	
7	275	Phoenix	Shepard	60000	0.045	
8						

Completed
sales office
database
Figure 8-1.

2. Choose Cells from the Format menu, click the Number tab (if necessary), and then choose the Number category by clicking on it.

3. Click on the Decimal Places spinner to set it to zero decimal places, click on the Use 1000 Separator (,) check box to select it, and on OK. The quotas in column D are formatted with a comma.

4. Drag on E2 through E7, choose Format Cells from the popup menu. The Number tab will again be displayed.

5. Click on the Percentage category, click on the Decimal Places spinner to set it to one decimal place, and press ENTER. The percentages in column E are formatted with a single decimal.

The result of formatting the right pair of columns is shown in Figure 8-2.

Columns
D and E
formatted
Figure 8-2.

Sorting a Database

Sorting a database rearranges the records in the database to produce a specific order to the records. You must identify the range or database you want sorted and then specify the key or keys you want to sort on. The keys are one or more fields that you want ordered. Unlike some of the other Data commands, Data Sort does not require the field names, and they should *not* be included in the data range. That means you can sort anything in an Excel workbook, not just a database. When you use Data Sort, each record (which can be a row or a column) within the range you specify is reordered along with the key fields in that record.

Selecting the Sort Range

There are several ways to sort the database you just built; for now, you will consider an alphabetic sort by either office or manager. Start by sorting the table by Office. The basic procedure is to highlight a range of records to be sorted, choose Sort from the Data menu, enter the keys on which to sort, and start the sort by clicking on OK. Begin that procedure with these instructions.

1. Select the range A2 through E7, as shown here:

	A	B	C	D	E	F
1	Number	Office	Manager	Quota	Commission	
2	250	Boston	Kauffman	50,000	4.0%	
3	255	Atlanta	Pearson	65,000	4.5%	
4	260	Denver	Fisher	45,000	3.5%	
5	265	Chicago	Colby	70,000	5.0%	
6	270	Seattle	Burke	40,000	3.0%	
7	275	Phoenix	Shepard	60,000	4.5%	
8						

2. Choose Sort from the Data menu. The following Sort dialog box opens:

8

The Sort dialog box shows that Excel has guessed correctly that you have a set of field names (a Header Row) just above the selected range and Excel is using the names in that row to name the column(s) on which to sort. Excel assumes that you are sorting by rows. This means that all the cells in one row within the highlight are moved together as the sort is carried out. This makes sense in terms of the database because one row is a single record and, while you want to rearrange the records, you want any given record to remain intact.

Identifying a Sort Key

The sort key, when sorting by rows, is the column containing the field you want sorted. In this example, you want the records sorted by offices, so you want to select Office as the sort key. You can do this by typing **Office** in the first (top) sort key or by opening the drop-down list and selecting it. If necessary, you can move the dialog box to see the sheet.

Click on the top drop-down list box to open it and then click on Office. Figure 8-3 shows how your screen should look.

You have entered the first sort key, which is all you want to sort on in this example. You might wonder what happens in a larger database when you have duplicates in the key you are sorting on. If you specify only one key, duplicates are left in the same order in which they started. However, you can

Sort key
selected for
sorting by
Office

Figure 8-3.

specify a second key to sort records with duplicate first keys, and even a third key to sort duplicate second keys. You even can sort on more than three keys by doing more than one sort, using the lowest priority keys first and the highest priority keys last.

Ascending Versus Descending

Once you have specified the sort key, you can specify the sort order—ascending or descending. That is, you indicate whether you want to sort in normal *ascending* alphabetical order (A first, Z last) or the reverse of that, *descending* order.

The normal alphabetic sequence (A, B, C,...Z) has been extended to include numbers, blanks, symbols, and logical and error values. Microsoft has established a specific sort order that is followed in all cases. The ascending sequence of this sort order is as follows.

1. Numbers entered as values from the largest negative number to the largest positive number, including dates and times from the earliest to the most recent

2. Text, ignoring capitalization and including numbers entered as text, in this sequence:

   0 1 2 3 4 5 6 7 8 9 Space ! " # $ % & ' ( ) * + , - . / : ; < = > ? @ [\ ] ^ _ `
   { | } ~ (and all other special characters) a b c d e f g h i j k l m n o p q r s t u v w x y z

3. Logical values, False first and then True

4. Error values (with no particular sort order)

5. Blank cells

The descending order is the reverse of the order just shown, except that in both ascending and descending order, blank cells are always sorted last. The ascending sort order for text given above is for United States English and may be different with other languages.

In this example, you are dealing with simple alphabetic letters. You want to sort from A to Z, which is ascending order; this is the default and is already selected. If you want to change the sort order, you would click on Descending.

8

Doing the Sort

The actual sorting is anticlimactic, just click on OK. The dialog box closes, and the database is sorted alphabetically by office, as shown here:

	A	B	C	D	E	F
1	Number	Office	Manager	Quota	Commission	
2	255	Atlanta	Pearson	65,000	4.5%	
3	250	Boston	Kauffman	50,000	4.0%	
4	265	Chicago	Colby	70,000	5.0%	
5	260	Denver	Fisher	45,000	3.5%	
6	275	Phoenix	Shepard	60,000	4.5%	
7	270	Seattle	Burke	40,000	3.0%	
8						

Changing and Re-sorting

Once sorted, the database can be re-sorted on a different sort key in a few quick steps. One reason to have a numbered column in the database is that you can re-sort the list on the numbers and return the database to the original order in which it was entered. You could do that with this database. Instead, sort on the Manager column using the sort tools in the Standard toolbar.

The sort tools immediately sort the selected rows in either ascending order or descending order, using the active cell to identify the column to sort on. As a matter of fact, you do not even have to select a range you want to sort if the active cell is in the range and there are either sheet edges or blank rows and columns all around the range. Under many circumstances, Excel can even tell if you have a row of field names or not and if you do, they will not be included in the sort. See how it works with these instructions.

1. Click on C1 to deselect the sort range and place the active cell in the column you want to sort on.
2. Click on the ascending sort tool (A to Z). The database is sorted alphabetically by Manager, as shown in Figure 8-4.

The automatic selection of the sort range is impressive, especially the determination of the field names or header row. It is not foolproof, though, and if you want that degree of certainty you should take the extra step of selecting the cells to be sorted.

Selecting Information from a Database

A database is primarily an ordered storage place for information. You place information in a database to make it easier to analyze the information or to select particular records. After building a second database, you will spend the remainder of this chapter selecting or analyzing information in one or both of the databases.

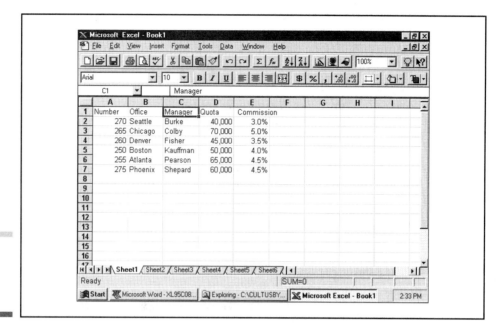

Database
sorted by
Manager
Figure 8-4.

Building a Second Database

The second database contains the weekly sales amounts for three of the offices for the month of April. The fields will be the office number and name, the week the figures are for, the number of sales, and the total dollar amount of sales. Enter the field names for this table with the following instructions.

1. Click on the vertical scroll bar below the scroll box, and click on A21 to move your active cell to A21.

2. Type the five field names shown here, but don't type the dates yet:

	A	B	C	D	E	F
21	Number	Office	Week	Sales	Amount	
22						
23						
24						

Entering Dates as a Series

One of the fields is an identifier for the week of the month for each record. Instead of typing this sequence of dates, you can use the Series dialog box to enter them automatically. For the start number, you enter the starting date; for the step number, you enter a calendar increment (day, weekday, month, or year); and for the stop number, you enter the ending date. The starting

8

and ending dates can be in any recognizable Excel date format. The step number can be a decimal—1.5, for instance. Its units depend on the date units you select: days, weekdays, months, or years. Since you cannot display fractional days without also displaying the time (which you can do), the entries for this database are rounded to the closest whole day.

For the April sales database, enter the weeks in column C, beginning with April 8, 1996, and ending May 8, 1996. Do that with these steps.

1. Click on C22, type **4/8/96**, and press ENTER. Notice that Excel recognized this as a numeric date because it right-aligned the figure in the cell and changed 96 to 1996 in the Formula bar.

2. Choose Fill Series from the Edit menu, type **7** for a step value of seven days, press TAB to move to the Stop Value field, type **5/6/96**, and click on Columns for the direction of the series. Date and Day have already been selected by Excel, which recognizes that the active cell contains a date. The Series dialog box looks like this when you are done:

3. Click on OK. The dialog box closes and the dates appear on your sheet like this:

	A	B	C	D	E	F
21	Number	Office	Week	Sales	Amount	
22			4/8/96			
23			4/15/96			
24			4/22/96			
25			4/29/96			
26			5/6/96			
27						

The dates could use a little formatting, so do that next.

4. Select the range C22 through C26.

5. Choose Cells from the Format menu and click on the Number tab if it isn't already selected. The Number tab displays with the Date category selected.

6. We want the dates to appear in a month-day format, but there is no prebuilt format. Create a custom format in the following steps.

7. Click on the Custom category and select the closest format to the one you want, d-mmm, approximately half-way through the Type list. The format appears in the Type text box.

8. Edit the format in the Type text box from d-mmm to mmm-d by selecting and deleting d-, and then typing **-d** after mmm. Your dialog box should look like this:

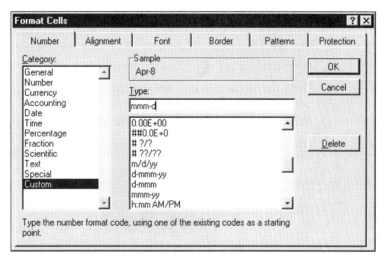

Notice the date in the Sample section appears in the correct format.

9. Click on OK. The date sequence is formatted as shown here:

	A	B	C	D	E	F
21	Number	Office	Week	Sales	Amount	
22			Apr-8			
23			Apr-15			
24			Apr-22			
25			Apr-29			
26			May-6			
27						

Completing Data Entry

8

The table of sales amounts that you must enter is for five weeks and three sales offices—a total of fifteen entries. The dates that you just entered are for one sales office and therefore need to be copied twice more down column C. Each sales office (Boston, Denver, and Seattle) and its corresponding number must be entered five times, once for each of the weeks covered here. Finally, you must enter the sales quantities and amounts. Perform these tasks with the following steps. The week beginning dates should still be highlighted. Begin by copying the dates twice using drag and drop.

1. Press CTRL and drag the lower border of C26 to C31. The dates are copied to C27:C31.

2. Again, press CTRL, and now drag the lower border of C31 to C36. The dates are copied a second time, as shown in Figure 8-5.

    Next, copy the sales office number and name.

3. Drag the vertical scroll bar upward and stop when the popup box indicates row 5, and drag across the two cells containing "250 Boston" (A5:B5 if the first database is still sorted by Manager).

4. Press CTRL-C to copy "250 Boston" to the clipboard.

5. Drag the vertical scroll bar downward until row 22 (or the closest it will come to row 22) appears in the popup box, drag A22 through B26, and press ENTER. "250 Boston" is copied five times, as shown here:

	A	B	C	D
21	Number	Office	Week	Sales
22	250	Boston	Apr-8	
23	250	Boston	Apr-15	
24	250	Boston	Apr-22	
25	250	Boston	Apr-29	
26	250	Boston	May-6	
27			Apr-8	

Dates as copied

Figure 8-5.

6. Repeat steps 3 through 5 to copy "260 Denver" to A27:B31 and "270 Seattle" to A32:B36.

   Enter and copy a formula to calculate the sales amount from the sale units, and then enter those units to complete the database.

7. Click on E22, type **=D22*145.95**, press ENTER, and format E22 with a comma and no decimals (#,##0) by clicking on the Comma format tool once and the Decrease Decimal tool twice. (Since 145.95 is the average value of a sale, you can derive the total sales amount by multiplying the number of sales by this average. You'll enter the sales figures in column D in a minute.)

8. Drag the E22 fill handle through E36 to copy the formula down the column.

9. Type the sales figures in D22 through D36 as indicated in Figure 8-6, which shows the finished database.

   Carefully check your work against Figure 8-6. This April Sales database is used for the remainder of the chapter. Entry errors could cause considerable confusion in subsequent sections. When you are satisfied with your database, save it before going on.

10. Choose Save As from the File menu, type **c:\sheet\salesapr**, and press ENTER. The file is saved. If you are using a different folder, make the appropriate changes.

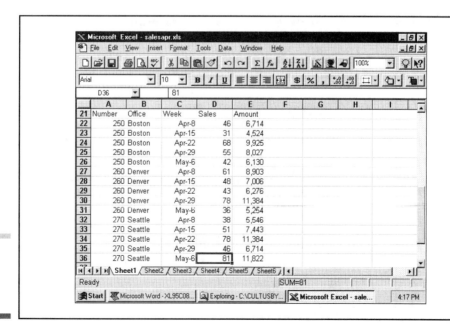

Completed April Sales database

Figure 8-6.

8

Subtotaling a List

The first thing you want to do with the April Sales database is find the monthly total for each sales office. You could go through, insert blank rows, and add SUM functions yourself. Excel, though, has the ability to do this for you and in the process put the list or database in an Excel outline that allows you to see just the subtotals. Try that next with these instructions (the active cell must be in the April Sales database).

1. Open the Data menu and choose Subtotals. The April Sales database is automatically selected and the Subtotal dialog box appears as shown in Figure 8-7.

   You can see from the dialog box that Excel has figured out a lot for you. First, it has looked at your database and seen that the first column periodically changes and guessed that you might want to subtotal on that. Since the first column is the office number and you want to subtotal by office, subtotaling on the first column is fine. You could also subtotal on the second column with the same result. Second, since the SUM function is the one most frequently used, Excel has guessed that using SUM is what you want to do here. You could also count, or calculate the average, among many other functions. Finally, Excel has guessed that you want to subtotal the Amount field. This is a good guess. In this case,

Subtotaling automatically selects the list with the active cell and opens the Subtotal dialog box

Figure 8-7.

you want to also subtotal on the Sales field. The only change you need to make is to additionally select Sales in the Add Subtotal to list.

2. Click on Sales in the Add Subtotal to list and then click on OK.

3. Choose Full Screen from the View menu to see all the subtotals. Your screen should look like Figure 8-8.

Totals have been added in new rows for the Total sales and amount in each office as well as a Grand Total. Just as valuable, your list has been placed in an Excel outline that allows you to display just the subtotals or Grand Total. You will see how the outline works in a moment. First make the one following change to your list.

The subtotals would be more informative if they showed the city (office) name instead of the number. Make that correction next.

4. Again open the Data menu and the Subtotal dialog box. In the top drop-down list, select Office. Make sure that Replace Current Subtotals is checked at the bottom of the dialog box and then click on OK.

The subtotal headings change to now reflect the city instead of the number, making them more understandable.

Outline
structure and
subtotals
added

Figure 8-8.

	A	B	C	D	E	F	G	H	
21	Number	Office	Week	Sales	Amount				
22	250	Boston	Apr-8	46	6,714				
23	250	Boston	Apr-15	31	4,524				
24	250	Boston	Apr-22	68	9,925				
25	250	Boston	Apr-29	55	8,027				
26	250	Boston	May-6	42	6,130				
27	250 Total			242	35,320				
28	260	Denver	Apr-8	61	8,903				
29	260	Denver	Apr-15	48	7,006				
30	260	Denver	Apr-22	43	6,276				
31	260	Denver	Apr-29	78	11,384				
32	260	Denver	May-6	36	5,254				
33	260 Total			266	38,823				
34	270	Seattle	Apr-8	38	5,546				
35	270	Seattle	Apr-15	51	7,443				
36	270	Seattle	Apr-22	78	11,384				
37	270	Seattle	Apr-29	46	6,714				
38	270	Seattle	May-6	81	11,822				
39	270 Total			294	42,909				
40	Grand Total			802	117,052				

8

Using an Excel Outline

The outline structure produced by Excel is very powerful. By simply clicking on the little buttons, you can hide or display various levels of the outline. Try that with these instructions.

1. Click on the minus button to the left of row 27, the Boston total. The Boston detail is hidden like this:

	A	B	C	D	E	F
21	Number	Office	Week	Sales	Amount	
27		**Boston Total**		242	35,320	
28	260	Denver	Apr-8	61	8,903	
29	260	Denver	Apr-15	48	7,006	
30	260	Denver	Apr-22	43	6,276	
31	260	Denver	Apr-29	78	11,384	
32	260	Denver	May-6	36	5,254	

(File Edit View Insert Format Tools Data Window Help)

2. Click on the second level button at the top-left of your screen. All of the detail records are hidden leaving only the subtotals and Grand Total, as you can see here:

	A	B	C	D	E	F
21	Number	Office	Week	Sales	Amount	
27		**Boston Total**		242	35,320	
33		**Denver Total**		266	38,823	
39		**Seattle Total**		294	42,909	
40		**Grand Total**		802	117,052	
41						

(File Edit View Insert Format Tools Data Window Help)

3. Click on the first level button and everything is hidden except the Grand Total.

4. Click on the third level button and all your information is redisplayed.

5. Click on the various outline buttons until you are comfortable with the operation. (It is a very useful feature of Excel.) When you are done, leave the outline fully displayed.

6. Again choose Subtotals for the Data menu and click on Remove All to return April Sales to the database you entered. Also, click on the Full Screen button to return to the normal Excel display.

Adding a Full Screen Tool

The full screen view is useful and deserves its own tool to quickly switch to that view. As an example of how you can customize the toolbars to your own needs, remove the Drawing tool and replace it with the Full Screen tool. The Drawing tool allows you to display or hide the Drawing toolbar. You can easily display or hide the Drawing toolbar from the View menu Toolbars option, so it is a good candidate for replacement. Also, at the end of this section you'll see how to restore your toolbars to their original content.

1. Click with the right mouse button on a toolbar to open the Toolbar popup menu and click on Customize. The Customize dialog box will open as you can see here:

While the Customize dialog box is open, you can drag tools on and off toolbars that are displayed. The dialog box itself displays tools in categories that you can add to the displayed toolbars. You can find out what a tool in the dialog box does by clicking on it and looking at the description at the bottom of the dialog box.

2. Drag the Drawing tool off the top of the Standard toolbar (first tool to the left of the Zoom Control drop-down list box). The Drawing tool disappears.

3. Click on Utility in the Categories list box. In the lower right of the set of tools or buttons you will see what looks like a tiny screen. Click on it and you will see the description "Toggles Full Screen."

4. Drag the Full Screen tool up to the Standard toolbar, to the approximate location from which you removed the Drawing tool. The tools to the right of where you drag the new tool will move to the right to provide room for it as shown in Figure 8-9.

5. Click on Close to close the Customize dialog box.

If you want to restore the Standard toolbar to its original configuration, you can do so very easily with these steps.

1. Click the right mouse button on a toolbar to open the Toolbar popup menu and click on Toolbars. The Toolbars dialog box opens.

8

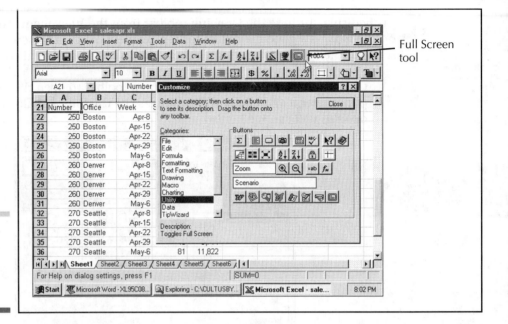

2. Ensure the Standard toolbar is selected and then click on Reset and the Drawing tool reappears and the Full Screen tool disappears.

Filtering a Database

Most databases are built with the objective that users will be able to find or select information they contain. In Excel, the process of finding and selecting information is called *filtering*. You create a filter that removes (hides—it's still in the workbook) all the information you don't want and leaves only what you want. Excel provides an AutoFilter for doing this simply and an Advanced Filter that handles more complex situations. In this and the next sections you will try both of these techniques. Begin by looking at the AutoFilter with these instructions.

1. Click anywhere in the April Sales database (A21:E36) to move the active cell there if it isn't already.

2. Open the Data menu, point on Filter, and then click on AutoFilter from the submenu that opens. Drop-down list arrows appear next to each of the field names, like this:

	A	B	C	D	E	F
21	Number ▾	Office ▾	Week ▾	Sales ▾	Amount ▾	
22	250	Boston	Apr-8	46	6,714	
23	250	Boston	Apr-15	31	4,524	
24	250	Boston	Apr-22	68	9,925	

3. Click on the drop-down arrow to the right of Week. A drop-down list box opens with all the weeks as you see here:

	A	B	C	D	E	F
21	Number ▾	Office ▾	Week ▾	Sales ▾	Amount ▾	
22		250 Boston	(All)		46	6,714	
23		250 Boston	(Top 10...) (Custom...)		31	4,524	
24		250 Boston	Apr-8		68	9,925	
25		250 Boston	Apr-15		55	8,027	
26		250 Boston	Apr-22		42	6,130	
27		260 Denver	Apr-29 May-6		61	8,903	
28		260 Denver	Apr-15		48	7,006	

4. Click on Apr 8. All database entries but the three for the week of April 8th disappear as shown here:

	A	B	C	D	E	F
21	Number ▾	Office ▾	Week ▾	Sales ▾	Amount ▾	
22		250 Boston	Apr-8	46	6,714	
27		260 Denver	Apr-8	61	8,903	
32		270 Seattle	Apr-8	38	5,546	
37						

You have created a filter based on the Weeks field and selected only the entries with "Apr 8" in that field. The other entries were then hidden so you see only the entries you want. This is a very quick way to select just the entries for that one week. Notice the color of the drop-down arrow next to Week changes to indicate that Week is the field being filtered. Also, the records (rows) that are displayed as a result of the filtering have their row numbers appear in a different color.

5. Again click on the drop-down arrow next to Week and, after scrolling to the top of the drop-down list box, click on All to redisplay all of the entries in the database.

6. Click on the drop-down arrow next to Sales and click on Custom in the drop-down list box that appears. The Custom AutoFilter dialog box opens like this:

8

The Custom AutoFilter dialog box lets you create a filter or a *criteria* for selecting other than an existing cell entry. For example, picking one cell entry in the Sales field, like 61, would not have much meaning, but specifying a range of sales, like all weekly sales above 60, would be meaningful. Try that and see.

7. Click on the drop-down arrow on the top-left and a list box opens with various relational operators. Click on greater-than (>).

8. Press TAB to move to the text box on the right, type **60**, and press ENTER. The dialog box closes and you see the list filtered to show only those entries with sales above 60, as shown here:

	A	B	C	D	E	F
21	Number	Office	Week	Sales	Amount	
24	250	Boston	Apr-22	68	9,925	
27	260	Denver	Apr-8	61	8,903	
30	260	Denver	Apr-29	78	11,384	
34	270	Seattle	Apr-22	78	11,384	
36	270	Seattle	May-6	81	11,822	
37						

The relational operators that you can use in the Custom AutoFilter dialog box have the following meanings:

Operator	Meaning
=	Equal to
>	Greater than
<	Less than
>=	Greater than or equal to
<=	Less than or equal to
<>	Not equal to

These operators can be used with both text and numbers, and the sort order discussed earlier in the chapter determines the relationship of text. Numbers are matched without regard to their format. For example, the number 54 matches $54, 5400%, 5.40E+01, and 54.00. With text, you can use wildcard characters (? for any single character and * for any group of characters) to find inexact matches. For example, entering **pea**? as the criterion selects "peak," "peal," and "pear," while entering **for*** selects "for," "foray," "forecast," and "forest." You can combine wildcard characters. For example, AM??DC* might be used with part numbers in an inventory system to select all parts from a given manufacturer (the AM) for a particular machine (the DC).

You can enter two criteria in the Custom AutoFilter dialog box and combine them with either AND or OR. If you use AND, both criteria must be met; but with OR, only one of the criteria has to be satisfied. For example, if you want all the records with sales above 50 but below 70 you would use AND between the criteria: >50 AND <70. If you want all the records of sales in either Boston or Seattle, you would use OR with the criteria: =Boston OR =Seattle.

9. Open the Sales drop-down list box and click on Custom. In the Custom AutoFilter dialog box, type **50**, click on And, select < in the bottom-left drop-down list, press TAB, type **70**, and click on OK. You get a new selection that looks like this:

	A	B	C	D	E	F
21	Number ▾	Office ▾	Week ▾	Sales ▾	Amount ▾	
24	250	Boston	Apr-22	68	9,925	
25	250	Boston	Apr-29	55	8,027	
27	260	Denver	Apr-8	61	8,903	
33	270	Seattle	Apr-15	51	7,443	
37						

Another handy filtering technique that AutoFilter offers is a search of the top or bottom items or percent of items in a field. You can adjust the number of records that are displayed, from one to as many records as you have in your database.

1. Again, open the Sales drop-down list box and click on Top 10. In the Top 10 AutoFilter dialog box, shown next, open the leftmost drop down list box and choose Bottom, click on the spinner in the middle of the dialog box to choose two items, and then click on OK. The two records with the smallest sales number are displayed.

2. Open the Data menu, choose Filter, and click on AutoFilter to turn it off. Your database is restored to its original appearance without the drop-down arrows.

8

Using the Advanced Filter

As powerful as AutoFilter is, there are situations where you have complex criteria, especially computed criteria, with which AutoFilter will not work. In those instances, you must use the Advanced Filter option. To use the Advanced Filter, you must identify two or three ranges. The first range is the database itself and is required by all operations using the Advanced Filter. The database (or list) range is the source for selecting records on which you will operate. The second range is the criteria range and is also required. The criteria range contains the criteria on which the selections are made. The third range is the Copy to range and is required only if you want to copy the selected records to a location different from the original database. The Copy to range will contain a new database of the selected records.

Defining the Database   To define the database, you have the choice of selecting it either before or after you start the Advanced Filter or of typing the coordinates or a range name into the Advanced Filter dialog box. The database range must contain the full set of records from which you want to select, as well as the field names for those records. Since you will be using this range in many operations throughout the chapter, it is best to name the range now and have it over with. If you name the range "Database," Excel will automatically identify the first row as a set of field names. To create a name, you can either use the Name Define option on the Insert menu or type the name in the reference area on the left of the Formula bar. Define the database range for the April Sales database using the Insert menu and these steps.

1. Drag from A21 through E36 to highlight the database.
2. Choose Name from the Insert menu and click on Define in the submenu. The Define Name dialog box will open.
3. Type **Database** as the name in the dialog box, as shown in Figure 8-10.
4. Click on OK. The highlighted range is given the name "Database," and you are returned to Ready mode.

You can tell that the database has been named because as long as it is selected, the name will appear in the reference area of the Formula bar.

Establishing the Selection Criteria   Establishing the selection criteria requires that you identify a criteria range in the workbook. The criteria range is a small database. The first row of the criteria range must contain some or all of the field names from the database you want the criteria to work with. The rest of the criteria range contains the criteria that will be the basis of your selection.

You can build the criteria range in any blank area of the workbook, but it is usually best not to build it directly below the database so there is room for the database to expand. The field names in the criteria range must be exact copies of the field names in the database. Frequently, the full set of field names is copied from the database with the Copy option.

Defining the
name of the
April Sales
database
Figure 8-10.

The criteria directly relate to the field name under which they are entered. For example, if you want to select all of the records for the Boston sales office in the April Sales database, you'll build a two-cell criteria range. The top cell has the field name "Office"; the bottom cell contains "Boston." The selection process searches for "Boston" in the Office field. This process gives you the matches between the criterion and the records in the database. A criterion of "Boston" also gives you a match with "Bostonian." If you want just "Boston" you must enter the formula **="=Boston"**, including the quotation marks. You can use text, numbers, or formulas as criteria for matching.

You can also use text, numbers, or formulas that cause Excel to search for records that are not matches. For example, if you want all records from the April Sales database that have more than 60 sales, as you did with the AutoFilter, you build a criteria range with Sales as the field name and >60 as the criterion. Do that now, and identify it as the criteria range with the following instructions. Since you want the field name in the criterion to be exactly the same as the field name in the database, copy the database field name.

8

1. Click on D21, click on the Copy tool in the Standard toolbar, click on G21, and press ENTER. The word "Sales" is copied from D21 to G21.

2. Click on G22, type **>60**, and press ENTER. The field name and criterion are entered.

3. Drag on G21 through G22, click in the reference area of the Formula
   bar, type **Criteria**, and press ENTER. The criterion is identified as
   shown here:

F	G	H
	Sales	
	>60	

Like the AutoFilter, the >60 criterion entered in the example is just one of
many ways to specify criteria. Some rules on specifying criteria follow.

♦ Use relational operators, numbers, text, and wildcard characters as
   defined for the AutoFilter.

♦ Formulas that refer to fields in the database range should use relative
   addresses. Formulas that refer to fields outside the database range should
   use absolute addresses. For example, the formula =SALES>=AMOUNT/150 is
   the same as =D22>=E22/150 and uses relative addressing to refer to fields
   within the database range of the April Sales database. On the other hand,
   =SALES>=$H$23 uses absolute addressing to refer to an address outside
   the database range.

♦ Usually a criterion refers to the field name under which it has been entered.
   If the criterion is a formula that relates to the total record instead of a
   specific field (as =SALES>= AMOUNT/150), then you need to use a field
   name in the criterion not used in the database. For example, "Formula"
   might be such a field name.

♦ You can use the database field names in a criterion formula (for example,
   =SALES>=AMOUNT/150) without defining them with the Formula
   Define Names option. You will get the error message #NAME? in the
   criterion cell, but the formula is utilized correctly for database selection.
   An example of an error message resulting from a field name formula is
   shown here:

F	G	H
	Formula	
	#NAME?	

♦ If you put criteria in multiple columns but only one row of a criteria
   range, *all* of the criteria must be satisfied for a record in the database
   range to be selected. It is as if you had put a logical AND between the
   fields. For example, if you create a criteria range with field names of
   "Sales" and "Amount" and enter **>60** under Sales and **>8000** under

Amount, only records that have both greater than 60 in sales and greater than $8,000 in the amount are selected. If either of those conditions is not met, the record is not selected. This is an AND criteria range:

F	G	H
	Sales	Amount
	>60	>8000

♦ If you put criteria in multiple rows of a criteria range, satisfying *either* of the criteria causes a record in the database range to be selected. It is as if you had put a logical OR between the fields. For example, if you enter **>60** under Sales in row 1 and **>8000** under Amount in row 2, records that satisfy either criterion are selected. This is an OR criteria range:

F	G	H
	Sales	Amount
	>60	
		>8000

♦ If you have a blank row in a criteria range, all of the records in the database are selected. You can combine as many rows and as many columns as necessary to specify the criteria you need, but do not include a blank row unless you want to select all records.

♦ You can select records that fall within a range for a given field. For example, select all records that have greater than 50 sales and fewer than 70 sales by creating two criteria columns (both with the same field name) and entering the **>50** in one column and **<70** in the other, as shown here:

F	G	H	I
	Sales	Sales	
	>60	<70	

Selecting Records   Once you have specified both the database range and the criteria range, you can use the Advanced Filter to identify selected records in the database range that meet the criteria. Try the Advanced Filter with the following instructions (your criteria should still be Sales, >60).

8

1. Click inside the database range so the active cell is within A21:E36.

2. Open the Data menu, point on Filter, and click on Advanced Filter. The Advanced Filter dialog box opens with the correct ranges identified, as shown in Figure 8-11.

Advanced
Filter dialog
box with the
database and
criteria ranges
identified
Figure 8-11.

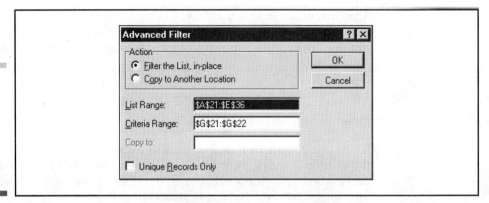

3. Click on OK and the database is filtered just as it was with the AutoFilter.
   (Don't worry about row 22 containing the criteria disappearing—it will
   return in a minute.)

4. Open the Data menu, choose the Filter option, and click on Show All to
   return the database to its original state.

Copying Selected Records   If you wish, with the Advanced Filter you can
copy selected records and selected fields from the database and place them
in another location on the sheet. To do this, you must define a range to
receive the selected records. Like the criteria range, this Copy to range must
have a row containing one or more field names that exactly match the field
names in the database range. If you want to limit the number of rows that
Excel can fill with selected records, then you need to highlight that number
of rows in addition to the row of field names when you define the Copy to
range. If you want Excel to define the number of rows it needs, then
highlight only the row of field names when you define the Copy to range.
With the following steps, define a Copy to range, change the criteria to a
more complex one, and then use the Advanced Filter to copy selected
records within the range you defined with these steps.

1. Click on G26, type **Office**, press RIGHT ARROW, type **Week,** and press
   ENTER. The labels "Office" and "Week" will be placed in G26 and H26,
   respectively.

2. Drag G26 through H26 to highlight the cells to be used as the range,
   click in the reference area of the Formula bar, and type **Extract**.

3. Click on G21, type **Formula**, press DOWN ARROW, and type
   =Amount*.05>$I$22 to look for commissions that are greater than
   the amount in I22, and press ENTER to redefine the criteria.

4. Click on I22, type **500**, and press ENTER to enter the reference value for the criteria.

5. Point on Filter from the Data menu and click on Advanced Filter. The Advanced Filter dialog box opens.

6. Click on the Copy to Another Location option button, click in the Copy to text box and drag across the G26:H26 range (if the reference isn't already there), as shown in Figure 8-12.

   The Advanced Filter dialog box allows you to select all records that match the criteria or only unique records, thus eliminating duplicates. Here, you select all records.

7. Click on OK. The Copy to operation executes, placing information extracted from three records in the Copy to range, as shown in Figure 8-13.

If you select a fixed area beneath the Copy to field names and the copying selects more records than can fit in that area, you get an error message to that effect. Enlarge the area or highlight only the field names and repeat the process.

Be aware that if you specify only a one-row Copy to range and thereby allow Excel to use as much room as it needs for selected records, any other information in the rows under the field names of this range is cleared or written over. *All rows below the Copy to range are cleared, whether or not they are used for extracted data. You cannot undo the Advanced Filter Copy operation!*

Defining
the Copy to
range in the
Advanced
Filter
Figure 8-12.

8

Results of
copying
selected
records to
another range
Figure 8-13.

Analyzing Information from a Database

In addition to selecting and extracting information, the other primary
reason for building a database is to analyze the information it contains.
Analyzing includes summarizing, averaging, counting, grouping, and
calculating the standard deviation and variance. The next few sections cover
several functions and options within Excel that are used for analyzing
information in databases.

Using Database Statistical Functions

In previous chapters, you used the SUM function to add a set of numbers in
a range. SUM has the general form, or syntax, of

SUM(reference)

where *reference* is any set of reference names or addresses. Other functions
include AVERAGE, which calculates the average of a reference; COUNT, which
counts the number of items in a reference; and MIN and MAX, which identify
the minimum and maximum numbers in a reference. They have similar syntaxes:

AVERAGE(reference)
COUNT(reference)
MAX(reference)
MIN(reference)

Excel has another set of functions called *database statistical functions*. Among them are DSUM, DAVERAGE, and DCOUNT. They have the same general purposes as statistical functions: they sum, average, and count. Database statistical functions, however, are meant to operate on specific fields in a database and to perform only on records that match criteria. Each database statistical function has a syntax similar to

   DSUM(database,field,criteria)

where *database* is a range in the workbook containing the field, *field* identifies a field name or column in the database on which you want to operate (sum, average, count), and *criteria* is a criteria range used to select the particular records you want to use in the calculation.

The primary difference between SUM and DSUM or between statistical and database statistical functions is that statistical functions operate on a group of cells without any selection. Database statistical functions select both a particular column (field) within a larger range and particular records (cells in the column) on which to operate. DSUM is the same as SUM if the database is a single column you want to sum and the criteria range is blank.

All of the information you have learned about database ranges and criteria ranges as they apply to the Advanced Filter applies to database statistical functions. The *database* can be the addresses of a range in the workbook (A21:E36, for example), or the name of a range you have defined with Insert Name or by typing a name in the reference area.

The *field* can be a field name, a field number, or the address of a cell that contains a field name or number. If a field name is used, it should be in quotation marks and should match the field name in the database range exactly. The number determines the column within the database table, beginning with the leftmost column as 1. The number for the second column is 2, and so on.

The *criteria* can be the addresses of a range in the workbook (G21:G22, for example), or a name you have defined with Insert Name or by typing a name in the reference area.

All of the following formulas do the same thing: sum the selected sales units in the April Sales database you entered into A21:E36 using the criteria you entered into G21:G22.

8

```
=DSUM(A21:E36,4,G21:G22)
=DSUM(Database,"Sales",Criteria)
=DSUM(April,D21,Top) if you have defined the names "April" as A21:E36 and "Top"
as G21:G22
```

Creating Names

You have already named the database and criteria ranges of the April Sales database using the Insert Name option and by typing in the reference area of the Formula bar. Once you have created a name, you can use it anywhere to represent a group of cells in the current workbook. You can have only one range with a given range name, so you can have only one range named "Database" and one range named "Criteria." As you work with database statistical functions, you are going to want to use ranges other than those defined as Database and Criteria. For these other ranges you can use either addresses or names.

There are two and sometimes three reasons to use names over addresses. First, and most compelling, is that a name always accurately reflects changes you make to a workbook. When you use a name in several functions, all those functions are updated when you change the range referred to by the name. Secondly, names are often easier to remember and almost always are more recognizable than the addresses they represent. Third, in some cases a short name is easier to enter than a long set of addresses. Since you will be building several database statistical functions with the same database and criteria ranges, get some practice naming a couple of ranges even though you could use the name already attached to one of those ranges. Use these instructions for that purpose.

1. Highlight the range A21:E36 (the database), open the Insert menu, point on Name, and click on Define. The Define Name dialog box opens, as shown here:

Notice that Criteria, Database, and Extract are listed as names already existing in the workbook. Also, the range that you highlighted is shown as the range to which the new name you enter will be attached. "Number," which came from the first cell of the highlighted range, is shown as a default name, but you want a different name for the range.

2. Type **April** and press ENTER. The database is now named April, as well as Database.

3. Highlight the range A38:A39, which you will use as a second criteria range, click in the reference area on the left of the Formula bar, type **Loc** (short for location), and press ENTER to name the range.

   Next, prepare an area on the sheet for entering database statistical functions by entering several titles.

4. Click on A38 and type **Office**. Press RIGHT ARROW twice to move to C38 and type **Number**. Press RIGHT ARROW and type **Total #**, press RIGHT ARROW and type **Total $**, press RIGHT ARROW and type **Average #**, press RIGHT ARROW and type **Average $**, and then press ENTER.

The bottom few lines of your screen should look like this:

37						
38	Office		Number	Total #	Total $	Average # Average $
39						
40						

Building the Formulas

Under each of the titles (Number, Total #, and so on), you will enter a database statistical function. (Use Office as a criteria range field, not a title for a database statistical function.) The titles are not necessary for the database statistical functions, but they are informative. After the formulas are entered, only their result is displayed. The formulas you enter are DCOUNT, to count the number of cells containing numbers in a field in the records of the database range that match the criteria; DSUM, to sum a field in the records of the database range that match the criteria; and DAVERAGE, to average a field in the records of the database range that match the criteria. Initially, you leave the criteria blank to select all of the records in the database range.

When you enter a function, you can either type the function or use the Function Wizard to lead you through it. If you type the function, do not include spaces anywhere except in a literal enclosed in quotation marks. Also, be sure to include the = symbol and both parentheses (although in many cases the last parenthesis will automatically be provided for you). With these rules in mind, enter several database statistical functions with the following steps.

1. Click on C39. The active cell moves to C39.

2. Type **=dcount(april,"number",loc** and press ENTER. The result, 15, appears in C39, as shown in Figure 8-14. The DCOUNT function counts the number of cells containing numbers in the Number field of the April database that match the criteria in Loc.

8

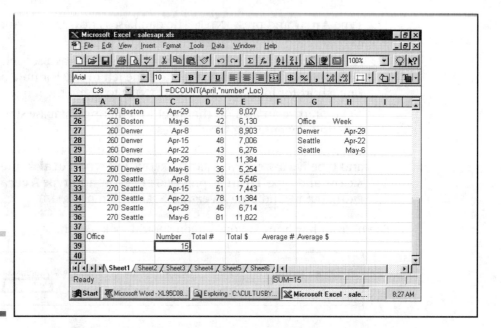

DCOUNT
function
completed
Figure 8-14.

When typing a function, it is a good idea to use lowercase letters. That
way you can tell if Excel recognizes what you are typing. If it does, the
functions automatically change to all uppercase, and range names
change to leading caps. Excel acts like a spelling checker.

3. Click on cell D39 and then click on the Function Wizard tool next to
AutoSum in the Standard toolbar. The Function Wizard dialog box
opens as you can see here:

4. Click on Database in the Function Category list, click on DSUM in the Function Name list, and click on Next. The second Function Wizard dialog box opens like this:

5. Type **april**, press TAB, type **"sales"** (including the quotation marks), press TAB, and type **loc**. Notice that as you are typing, as soon as Excel recognizes the name it appears on the right of the text box. Also, as soon as you complete typing the criteria, the value appears in the upper right of the dialog box as shown here:

6. Click on Finish and the result, 802, appears in D39. This DSUM function adds all the numbers in the Sales field of the April database that match the criteria in Loc.

The Function Wizard does three things for you: first, it presents the list of functions from which you can choose; second, it saves you a little typing by supplying the equal sign, function name, parentheses, and commas; third, and probably most important, it provides a list of arguments for you to fill in. Depending on how good your memory is and how often you use functions, you may or may not find the Function Wizard helpful.

8

7. Press RIGHT ARROW, and in the next three cells use the Function Wizard or type the following formulas. Press RIGHT ARROW after the first two and ENTER after the last.

   =dsum(april,"amount",loc)
   =daverage(april,"sales",loc)
   =daverage(april,"amount",loc)

8. Drag across C39:G39, click on the Comma tool, and then click twice on the Decrease Decimal tool in the Formatting toolbar. The row of database statistical functions is formatted with the comma format and no decimal places. Figure 8-15 shows the results.

Of course, for a such a small database it would be much faster to use the AutoCalculate feature to find these sums, averages, and counts. AutoCalculate is fine for calculating solutions that you want to see quickly and that you are not concerned about saving as a permanent part of the database.

You are now in a position to change the criteria and immediately see the result—called a *what-if* situation. The formulas in C39:G39 reflect the criterion in A39. Enter a new criterion, and the formulas reflect the result. Currently, the blank criteria range means that the formulas are utilizing the entire database range. If you enter **Boston** in the criteria range, the formulas utilize only records with Boston in the Office field. Try that next with these instructions.

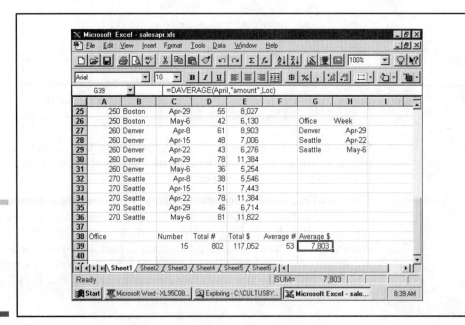

Database statistical functions entered and formatted
Figure 8-15.

9. Click on A39, type **Boston**, and press ENTER. "Boston" is entered in the criteria range, and the formulas recalculate to reflect that, as shown here:

37						
38	Office		Number	Total #	Total $	Average #	Average $
39	Boston		5	242	35,320	48	7,064
40							

Note that the criteria are not case-sensitive. You could enter **boston** or **BOSTON** and get the same results. Also note that amounts in the Total # and Total $ fields are the same as the Boston subtotals shown in Figure 8-8.

Creating a Data Table

As powerful as the criteria and formula combination is, Excel has a better way to perform its task—a *data table*. A data table shows the results of one or more formulas when one or two variables in the formulas are varied. As an example, a data table can show the results of the five database statistical functions entered in the last section for all of the three sales offices at one time. The variable in this case is the criteria, and the three offices are the variations. This is known as a *one-input data table*.

A one-input data table is a specially configured range on a sheet. It can be configured in rows or columns, but rows are most common. For the row configuration, the top row contains as many formulas as you want to use. C39:G39 would be such a row. Then, in the column to the left of the first formula and beginning one row beneath it, you would enter as many variables as you want applied to those formulas. Here, you will enter the three cities **Boston**, **Denver**, and **Seattle**. Each formula needs to refer to one cell where the variable is substituted. This cell is known as the *input cell*, and is A39 in this example. Build this data table now, and observe how it works. A39 should still be the active cell.

1. Press DEL. The criterion (Boston) is erased and the database statistical functions once again show the totals in the database range.

2. Click on B40 and type **Boston**, **Denver**, and **Seattle**, pressing DOWN ARROW after the first two and ENTER after the last.

3. Highlight B39 through G42 as your data table range, which is shown here:

8

37							
38	Office		Number	Total #	Total $	Average #	Average $
39			15	802	117,052	53	7,803
40		Boston					
41		Denver					
42		Seattle					
43							

4. Choose Table from the Data menu. The Table dialog box opens, as shown here:

The Table dialog box asks you for a row input cell and/or a column input cell. Since you have only one variable (the cities) and it is in a column, you only need to enter a column input cell.

5. Press TAB to move from Row Input Cell to Column Input Cell, click on A39 (or type **$A$39**), and click on OK. The data table is then calculated, as shown here. (Although A39 is blank, it is used by Excel during the calculation of the table to hold each of the criteria as they are used.)

			Number	Total #	Total $	Average #	Average $
37							
38	Office		Number	Total #	Total $	Average #	Average $
39			15	802	117,052	53	7,803
40		Boston	5	242	35320	48.4	7064
41		Denver	5	266	38823	53.2	7764.6
42		Seattle	5	294	42909	58.8	8581.8
43							

6. Format the data table with the comma format and no decimal places as you did with the original database statistical functions above.

Working with Two-Input Data Tables

The data table you just used is called a one-input data table because there is one variable (the criteria). It can have multiple formulas, but only one variable. The other type of data table is a *two-input data tables*. It has two variables, but only one formula. In a two-input data table, one variable is in a column, as the sales offices were in the previous example, and the other variable is in a row. The formula is in the upper-left corner cell that is the intersection between the row variables and the column variables.

For an example of a two-input data table, assume you are a sales manager and want to look at the kind of money your salespeople can earn with varying commission rates and varying monthly sales. The formula for this would be to multiply the monthly sales by the commission rate by 12 to get annual income. The two variables are commission rates, which vary from 3 percent through 6 percent, and monthly sales, which normally fall between $40,000 and $100,000. The steps to build such a table follow.

1. Click on the downward vertical scroll arrow beneath the scroll box to get a blank area on your sheet.

2. Click on C45, type **Commission Rate**, press DOWN ARROW, type **Monthly Sales**, and press ENTER.

3. Click on B48, type 3%, press ENTER, point on Fill from the Edit menu, click on Series, type **.5%** for the step value, press TAB, type **6%** for the stop value, and press ENTER. The row variables appear across columns B through H.

4. Highlight B48 through H48 and click once on the Increase Decimal tool in the Formatting toolbar. The row variables are now formatted.

5. Click on A48, type **=e45*e46*12**, and press DOWN ARROW to enter the formula you want to vary.

6. Type **40,000**, press ENTER, point on Fill from the Edit menu, click on Series, type **10,000**, press TAB, type **100,000**, click on Columns, and click on OK. The column variables are entered.

7. Highlight A48 through H55, choose Table from the Data menu, click on E45 for the row input cell, press TAB, click on E46 for the column input cell, and click on OK. Your commission table is produced.

8. Format the body of the Commission table (A49:H55) with the comma format and no decimal places and move the active cell to A48. Your screen should look like that shown in Figure 8-16.

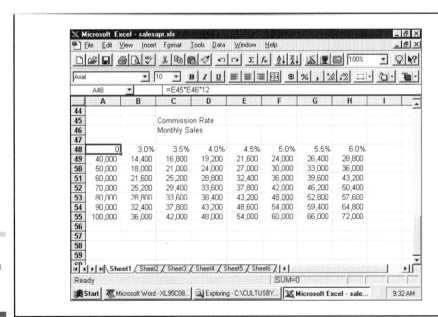

Completed
two-input data
table
Figure 8-16.

8

This table is equivalent to repeating the formula 49 times (seven rates and seven amounts). As you can see, a data table is a valuable analysis tool.

Creating Pivot Tables

A *pivot table* is a table in which you can interactively exchange the rows and columns to look at the data in different ways. Normally, the table shows summary information that is grouped in several ways with row and column totals and grand totals, like this:

	A	B	C	D	E	F	G	H	I	J
57										
58			Week							
59	Office	Data	4/8/96	4/15/96	4/22/96	4/29/96	5/6/96	Grand Total		
60	Boston	Sum of Sales	46	31	68	55	42	242		
61		Sum of Amount	6,714	4,524	9,925	8,027	6,130	35,320		
62	Denver	Sum of Sales	61	48	43	78	36	266		
63		Sum of Amount	8,903	7,006	6,276	11,384	5,254	38,823		
64	Seattle	Sum of Sales	38	51	78	46	81	294		
65		Sum of Amount	5,546	7,443	11,384	6,714	11,822	42,909		
66	Total Sum of Sales		145	130	189	179	159	802		
67	Total Sum of Amount		21,163	18,973	27,585	26,125	23,206	117,052		
68										
69										

Excel has a PivotTable Wizard that will help you build a pivot table from an existing Excel database or external database if you tell the Wizard various facts about the data. For your April database, a pivot table might total each office by week and then total each weekly figure to get the office total for the month. At the same time, you can get a total each week for all sales offices and do this for both sales and sales amounts. In this, each major row is a sales office and each column is a week, as shown in the previous illustration. Each cell totals the sales or the sales amounts for an office in a week. The total of each row is the total for an office in April, and the total for a column is the weekly total for all sales offices. The grand total is the total sales for all offices for the month. See for yourself how the PivotTable Wizard works with these instructions.

1. Open the Data menu and choose PivotTable. The PivotTable Wizard's first dialog box appears as shown in Figure 8-17.

   In the PivotTable Wizard's first dialog box you select the source of the data for the pivot table. In this case, you want the default already selected—a single Excel database (option one). The alternatives are an external (non-Excel) database (option two), multiple Excel databases or ranges (option three), or another pivot table (option four).

PivotTable
Wizard's first
screen
Figure 8-17.

2. Click on Next. The second PivotTable Wizard dialog box opens, which you can see here:

Excel has identified the range named Database as the potential range from which to build the pivot table. Since that is what you want, you have nothing to do in this second dialog box.

3. Click on Next. The third PivotTable Wizard dialog opens as shown in Figure 8-18.

The third dialog box allows you to drag the various database fields to where you want them in the table. See how that is done and it will become clearer what this means.

4. Drag the Office button to the ROW area so that the three offices become row headings.

5. Drag the Week button to the COLUMN area so that the weeks become column headings.

8

PivotTable's
third dialog
box
Figure 8-18.

6. Drag first the Sales and then the Amount buttons to the DATA area so they become the body of the table. Your completed third dialog box should look like Figure 8-19.

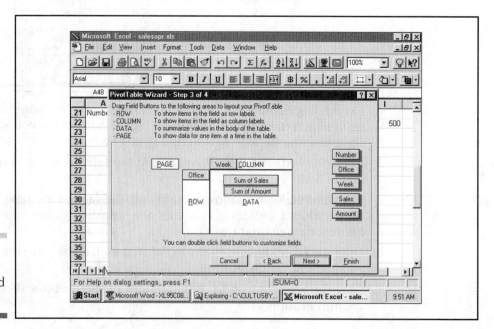

PivotTable's
third dialog
box completed
Figure 8-19.

7. Click on Next. The final PivotTable Wizard dialog box opens, as shown here:

8. Click on A58 (scroll your screen first if necessary) to identify the starting cell for the pivot table. You want all the other options that are already selected, so click on Finish.

The pivot table is displayed, as you can see in Figure 8-20. The dates across the top of the pivot table are text, so you cannot reformat them; if you want to change them, you must reenter them. The numbers in the pivot table can

Completed
pivot table
Figure 8-20.

8

be formatted for better readability. If you use the comma format with no decimal places, you will get the pivot table report shown at the beginning of this section. The problem is that the formats will go away each time you refresh the data (see below for how this is done). You can get around this by applying an AutoFormat to the table that will automatically get reapplied each time you refresh the data. Unfortunately, though, there is no AutoFormat that matches what you want here (those available have dollar signs and/or decimal points where you don't want them).

The PivotTable Wizard saves you a great deal of work in building what is in essence a summary sheet. If you want to do that in your work, it would be worthwhile to try the Wizard on your own.

Using a Pivot Table

As powerful as the PivotTable Wizard is, the real power in a pivot table is in what you can do with it after it is built. Notice in the completed pivot table that there are three buttons: one for Weeks, one for Data, and one for Office. By dragging these buttons, you can reorder the pivot table. Try that next.

1. Drag the Office button up so it is on top of the Week button and toward the left side of the Week button. The table is reordered like this:

	A	B	C	D	E	F	G	H	I	J
56										
57										
58		Office	Week							
59		Boston					Boston Total	Denver		
60	Data	4/8/96	4/15/96	4/22/96	4/29/96	5/6/96		4/8/96	4/15/96	4/22/96	4/2
61	Sum of Sales	46	31	68	55	42	242	61	48	43
62	Sum of Amount	6714	4524	9925	8027	6130	35320	8903	7006	6276	1
63										
64										

2. Drag the Week button to the other side of the Office button. Again the table is reordered as you see here:

	A	B	C	D	E	F	G	H	I	J
56										
57										
58		Week	Office							
59		4/8/96			4/8/96 Total	4/15/96			4/15/96 Total	4/22/96
60	Data	Boston	Denver	Seattle		Boston	Denver	Seattle		Boston
61	Sum of Sales	46	61	38	145	31	48	51	130	68
62	Sum of Amount	6714	8903	5546	21163	4524	7006	7443	18973	9925
63										
64										

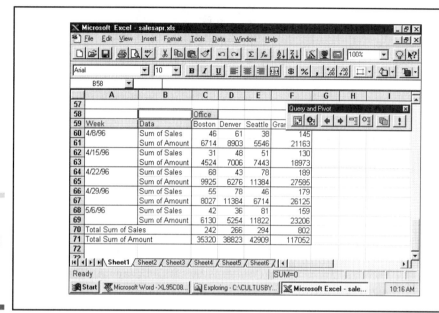

Pivot table
after it has
been reordered
for the third
time

Figure 8-21.

3. Drag the Week button down so it is on top of the Data button. The
   table is reordered for a final time. Your screen should look like that
   shown in Figure 8-21.

There are, of course, several other combinations of the three buttons that
you can try out on your own. The point is that there is exceptional flexibility
in a pivot table that allows you to look at data in any way that you want; all
you have to do is drag elements around with the mouse.

In addition to dragging the buttons around the pivot table, you can get rid
of either Office or Week by simply dragging them off the table—a large "X"
appears in them as you drag them off. You can also go back to the PivotTable
Wizard and revise your selections either by again choosing PivotTable from
the Data menu or by clicking on the PivotTable Wizard tool on the left of
the Query and Pivot toolbar that appears with a pivot table.

You can reorder the table through a dialog box instead of dragging by first
selecting the field to change and then either choosing PivotTable Field in the
Data menu or clicking on the second tool in the Query and Pivot toolbar. In
the PivotTable Field dialog box that appears and on the next pages, you can
determine in which position the field is to appear, how it is to be subtotaled,
and whether any of the entries are to be hidden.

8

You can create groups of items by simply dragging across the items to highlight them and then clicking on the Group (right arrow) tool in the Query and Pivot toolbar. For example, if you wanted to group the weeks of April 8 and April 15 together, you would drag across these dates and click on the Group tool. You will get a new level as shown here (after rearranging the applicable buttons):

	A	B	C	D	E	F	G	H	I
57									
58			Week2	Week					
59			Group1		4/22/96	4/29/96	5/6/96	Grand Total	
60	Office	Data	4/8/96	4/15/96	4/22/96	4/29/96	5/6/96		
61	Boston	Sum of Sales	46	31	68	55	42	242	
62		Sum of Amount	6714	4524	9925	8027	6130	35320	

After grouping and creating a second level, you can get rid of the original level by dragging it off the table. If you want to restore the original level and ungroup what was grouped, click on the Ungroup (left arrow) tool in the Query and Pivot toolbar. If you want to just hide the detail within one grouping instead of dragging an entire level off the table, select the items to be hidden and click on the Hide Detail (minus sign) tool in the Query and Pivot toolbar. You can reverse that operation with the Show Detail (plus sign) tool.

There is an additional level, called Pages, that is available with a pivot table, but not used in the example shown in this chapter. If you use that additional level, you still see only one page on a sheet, but you have a drop-down list box to select the other pages. If you want to print the other pages, you need to display each of them on a sheet and then select those sheets to be printed. To do that, select the location for receiving a page from the table and then click on the Show Pages (sheets of paper) tool in the Query and Pivot toolbar. A dialog box will open and you can select the page to be placed on the current sheet.

A pivot table is not directly tied to the source data by formulas on the sheet. In other words, the numbers that you see are values—not formulas—that reference the original data. If you make a change to the original data, your pivot table will not automatically be updated; you will need to update or refresh the numbers in the pivot table. You can do that either by choosing Refresh Data in the Data menu or by clicking on the Refresh Data (exclamation point) tool in the Query and Pivot toolbar.

Using Lookup Functions

Excel has two functions that, while not database functions, are related to using databases. These are the horizontal and vertical table lookup functions HLOOKUP and VLOOKUP. You use these two functions to search a two-dimensional range for an item, based on finding a match in another item that is in the first row (horizontal lookup) or the first column (vertical lookup) and an index that tells Excel how many rows down (horizontal lookup) or across (vertical lookup) to move to find the sought-after item. These functions have three arguments:

♦   A value (x) to look for in the first row or column

♦   A range or database in which to look

♦   An index to determine how far down or across to look in the range to find the item sought

The formats of these functions are

    HLOOKUP (x,range.index)

where x is the value to look for in the first row, and

    VLOOKUP(x,range,index)

where x is the value to look for in the first column.

Use the vertical lookup function with the second database you built (April Sales) to calculate commissions earned based on the commission rates in the first database you built. The function uses the office number in each record of the second database as the value to search for in the leftmost column of the first database, which is the range of the function. An index of 5 is used since the commissions are in the fifth column. The values in the first column must be in numerical order, so the first step is to re-sort the first database by

8

office number. Do that and then build the formulas with vertical lookup functions using these instructions:

1. Press CTRL-HOME to go to the top of the sheet so you can see the first database you built.

2. Highlight A2 through E7, choose Sort from the Data menu, select Number to sort by, and click on OK to accept the remaining defaults. Your database is sorted.

3. Click on the vertical scroll bar below the scroll box and click on F22.

4. Type **=e22*vlookup(a22,a2:e7,5)** and press ENTER. The formula is calculated with the result of 268.56 (4% of 6,714), as shown here:

	A	B	C	D	E	F	G	H
20								
21	Number	Office	Week	Sales	Amount		Formula	
22	250	Boston	Apr-8	46	6,714	268.56	#NAME?	
23	250	Boston	Apr-15	31	4,524			

The lookup function took the office number (250) in A22, searched the left column (because you used the vertical function) of the first database (A2:E7), and then, in the row in which it found 250, it went over five cells to find 4%. The 4% was then multiplied by the amount in E22. In searching for the 250 in the first database, Excel picks the first value that equals or exceeds the value for which it is searching. For that reason, it is imperative that the range be sorted on the first column or row. The A2:E7 range needs to be absolute because you will be copying it down the database and you do not want it to vary, as you do A22 and E22. To complete the April Sales database, format cell F22 and copy it to the remaining entries in the database.

5. Format the number with a comma and no decimal places.

6. Drag the F22 fill handle through F36. The formula is copied down the rest of the database, as shown in Figure 8-22.

To be sure that the lookup function is working, check several of the numbers. For example, Denver's April 15 sales of 7,006 times 3.5% is 245, and Seattle's April 22 sales of 11,384 times 3% is 342. Remember that both the sales amount and the commission are rounded to the nearest whole number. You should find that the vertical lookup function is working perfectly.

Like several other features of Excel's database capabilities, the vertical and horizontal lookup functions are very powerful. As you have seen in the example here, they allow you to combine two databases to perform certain functions.

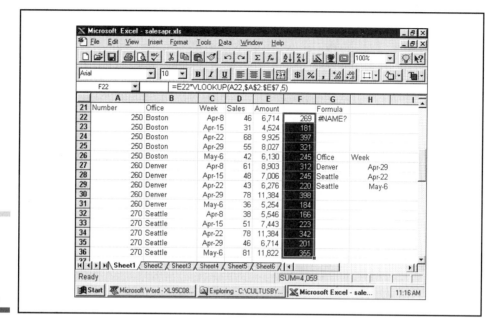

Vertical
lookup
commission
calculated
Figure 8-22.

As a final step in this chapter, save your workbook and, if you wish, leave
Excel and Windows by following these steps.

1. Choose Save from the File menu. The file is saved under its current
   name, replacing the version previously saved.
2. Click on Excel's Close button, and then click on the Start button and
   choose Shut Down. Click on Yes to close Windows and prepare your
   computer to be turned off.

Linking Workbooks and Using External Files

Establishing a link to and exchanging information between workbooks is the major topic in this chapter. The chapter covers the process of combining several workbooks into one, including using external-reference formulas, copying from one workbook to another, adding ranges from different workbooks, and linking workbooks with external-reference arrays. Also, the procedure for exporting and importing non-Excel text and number files is discussed.

Linking Workbooks

Even with Excel's multiple-sheet capability, there are many instances where you will want to use information in another workbook or transfer information between workbooks. Any time different people create and contribute information to a central organization or project, as in a budgeting process, for example, this capability is needed. Each department or other company segment can create and maintain its own workbook, which can then be combined at the corporate level.

Another common situation is where you are working on a large project and it is easier and safer to compartmentalize various aspects of the project in separate workbooks and then combine their results in still another workbook. Multiple workbooks have a safety aspect. With a single large workbook, you have to worry about what effect inserting and deleting rows, columns, and sheets will have on surrounding sections of the workbook. With multiple workbooks, you have a physical separation that protects you. Additionally, the multiple-workbook structure often makes intuitive sense and simplifies the layout of a complex project. Build a multiple-workbook project now and see for yourself.

Creating Multiple Workbooks

In the examples in this chapter, you use a set of simple departmental budgets for the marketing area of a corporation. Three departments—customer relations, public relations, and advertising—are summed into the total marketing budget. Each department and the total have exactly the same workbook format. You can therefore build one master workbook, copy it to the other three, and then come back and customize each of them. They could very easily be separate sheets in one workbook, but since you want to work with separate books in this chapter, you'll put each department in a separate book. Prepare these workbooks now with the following instructions. Your computer should be on, Windows and Excel loaded, and a blank workbook on your screen.

1. Enter, center, and make bold the titles and column headings across columns A to G as shown here (column A has been widened to 17 spaces, or approximately two normal column widths):

	A	B	C	D	E	F	G	H
1			QUARTERLY BUDGET					
2								
3								
4	Description		Assump.	1st Qtr	2nd Qtr	3rd Qtr	4th Qtr	Total
5								
6								

2. Select the column headings and, using the Borders tool on the right of the Formatting toolbar, add a double bottom border with the leftmost style in the second row of the Borders palette.

3. Maximize the workbook (if necessary), enter the row headings, and make them bold, as shown in Figure 9-1.

   These departmental budgets are based on a headcount, which varies by department; on an assumption (Assump.) for the average cost per head for each of the expense items, which also varies by department; and on a quarterly growth percentage, which is common to all departments. The formula, then, for all expense items, is headcount times assumption times 1+ growth.

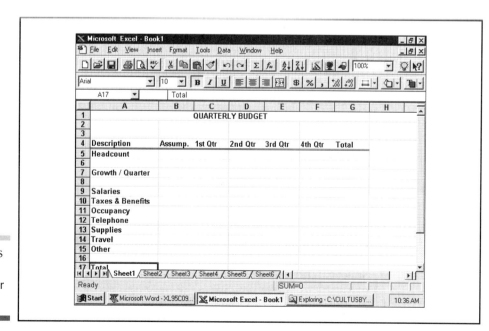

Row headings and double bottom border

Figure 9-1.

9

4. Enter the three growth percentages in D7:F7, format them with a single decimal place, and enter the first formula in C9 as **=C$5*$B9*(1+C$7)**, as shown here:

	A	B	C	D	E	F	G	H
1			QUARTERLY BUDGET					
2								
3								
4	Description	Assump.	1st Qtr	2nd Qtr	3rd Qtr	4th Qtr	Total	
5	Headcount							
6								
7	Growth / Quarter			1.5%	3.0%	5.0%		
8								
9	Salaries		=C$5*$B9*(1+C$7)					
10	Taxes & Benefits							

Note the mixed references on all the cell addresses. These are very important since you will be copying this one formula to all the other quarters and expense items. Remember that the easiest way to get absolute and mixed references is by pressing F4 immediately after pointing to or typing a cell address. The first time you press F4 you get an absolute reference ($C$5), the second time you press F4 you get a mixed reference with the row fixed (C$5), and the third time you press F4 you get a mixed reference with the column fixed ($C5). You do not have to remember the order because you can continue to press F4 until you get the reference you want.

5. By dragging on the AutoFill handle in the lower-right corner of the cell, drag C9 down to C15. Then, again with the AutoFill handle, drag C9:C15 to F9:F15 to copy the formula in C9 to the other quarters and expense items.

6. Select C9:G17 and click on the AutoSum tool to build the totals in G9:G15 and C17:G17 in one very swift stroke.

7. Select B9:G17 and format it with a thousands separator and no decimals. When you are done your master workbook should look like Figure 9-2.

Copying Across Workbooks

With the master workbook complete, follow these steps to build the other three workbooks and copy the master workbook to each of them.

1. Select Sheet2 through Sheet16 (click on Sheet2, press and hold SHIFT and click on the End-sheet button just to the left of the Sheet1 tab and then on Sheet16), click the right mouse button on a Sheet tab to open the Sheet tab popup menu, click on Delete, and click on OK to delete the extra sheets. Since you are using only one sheet, there is no sense in carrying the extra baggage with you.

Completed
master
workbook
Figure 9-2.

2. Open the Tools menu, choose Options, and click on the General tab. Then drag across the Sheets in New Workbook, type **1**, and click on OK. This way, the new workbooks you create will have only one sheet.

3. Select A1:G17 and choose Copy from the Edit menu (or press CTRL-C).

4. Click on the New Workbook tool in the far left of the Standard toolbar, click on the Paste tool (also in the Standard toolbar), and click on column A and widen it to 17 spaces.

5. Repeat step 4 for a third and fourth workbook. When you are done, click on the document window Restore/Maximize button to reduce the size of your workbooks so you can see all of them; your screen will look like Figure 9-3.

Handling Multiple Workbooks

The display that you have on your screen and that is shown in Figure 9-3 is one of several ways to look at multiple workbooks. This current display is called overlapping workbooks. If you see only one window, it is probably because you still have a maximized view—see step 5 immediately above.

Remember that one way to get around with multiple workbooks is by clicking on the book you want to go to. The default display, shown in Figure 9-3, provides the ability to click on all the other books if you are looking at Book4, but you cannot click on any other book if you are looking at Book1.

9

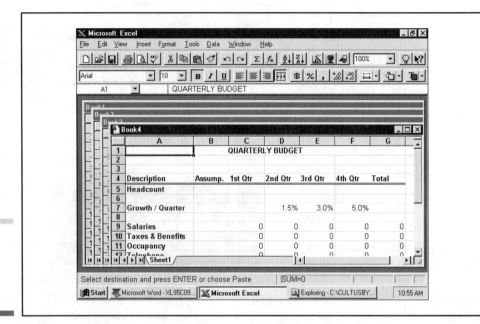

The first step, then, is to pull the right edge of each workbook to the left so the workbooks are stairstepped in the reverse order, as shown in Figure 9-4.

1. Drag the upper-right corner of Book3 to the left approximately one-half the width of the vertical scroll bar on Book4. Repeat this procedure for Book2 and Book1, dragging them to the left the approximate one-half the width of the previous workbook's scroll bar. Alternatively, use the Size option on each workbook's Control menu to do this operation with the keyboard.

   Next try switching between books, first with the mouse and then with the Window menu.

2. Click successively on workbooks 3, 2, and 1. Notice how the books are now stair-stepped on the right. Had you not done step 1, you would now be looking at only Book1.

3. Click randomly on the various workbooks. For example, click on Book3, Book4, Book1, and Book2. After a while you can tell which is which by their heights and if they are showing on the left or right.

4. Click on the Window menu. Notice how each workbook is listed and that the last workbook you clicked on, the *active workbook,* has a check mark beside it, as shown here:

5. Choose one or two of the workbook options from the Window menu. Notice how this method works exactly like clicking on a workbook. The benefits of using the menu are that there is never any question which workbook you are going to and the workbook does not have to be visible.

All of your work so far has been with overlapping windows. Another type of window view is called a *Tiled view,* which basically gives each window a small part of the screen. Look at that now.

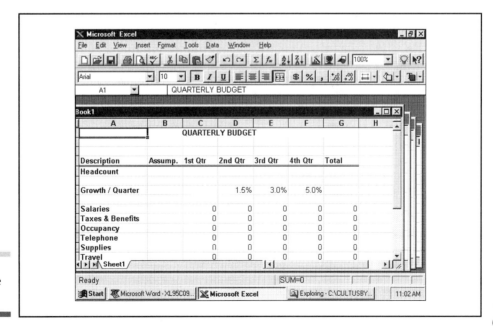

Stairstepping
the right edge
Figure 9-4.

6. Select Book1 by clicking on it and then choose Arrange from the Window menu. The Arrange Windows dialog box appears as shown:

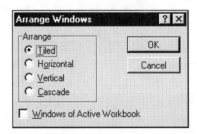

7. If it isn't already selected, click on Tiled in the Arrange list and then click on OK. The windows are resized so that a portion of all the windows you have open is displayed on the screen, as shown in Figure 9-5.

With the Tiled view, you can easily see what workbook you want to use, and then you can click on the Maximize/Restore button to actually use the workbook. When you restore the workbook to its original size with the Restore/Maximize button or the Restore option on the workbook's Control menu, you return to the Tiled view. If you want to get back to the overlapped view, you can choose Arrange from the Window menu and then click on Cascade.

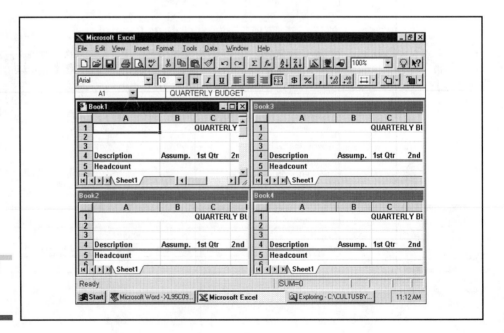

Tiled view of worksheets

Figure 9-5.

Customizing Individual Workbooks

Using the Tiled view, customize each workbook by following these three steps.

1. If it isn't already the active sheet, click on Book1 to make it so, and then click on its Maximize/Restore button so Book1 fills the Excel work area.

2. Enter the title, headcount, and assumptions on Book1, as shown in Figure 9-6. For the Taxes & Benefits assumption, enter **=14.5%*B9** in place of the amount shown in Figure 9-6. Click on Restore to return Book1 to its original size.

3. Repeat step 2 for Book2 and Book3, using Figures 9-7 and 9-8 for title, headcount, and assumptions.

If your Taxes & Benefits quarterly amounts are three or four dollars different than those shown here, you missed changing the assumption to =14.5%*B9.

Creating Linking Formulas

Book4 will be the total of the other three workbooks. You therefore want to replace the standard formulas in Book4 with formulas that sum the other three workbooks. The Tiled view and the mouse make short work of this. Follow these steps:

1. If you are not there already, return to the Tiled view so you can see all four workbooks.

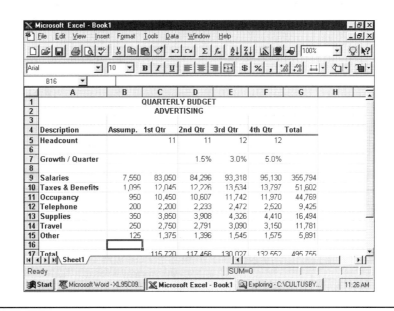

Headcount and assumptions for Book1

Figure 9-6.

9

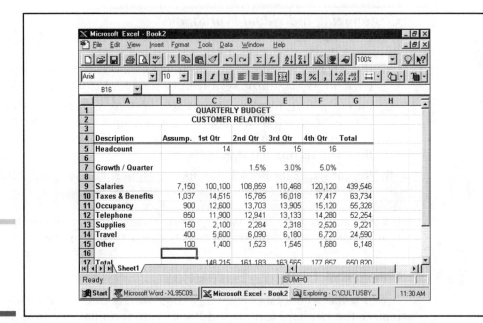

Headcount
and
assumptions
for Book2
Figure 9-7.

2. If necessary, scroll the books so that the first quarter headcount is visible in each window, and click on C5 in Book4 to make it the active cell and workbook, as shown in Figure 9-9.

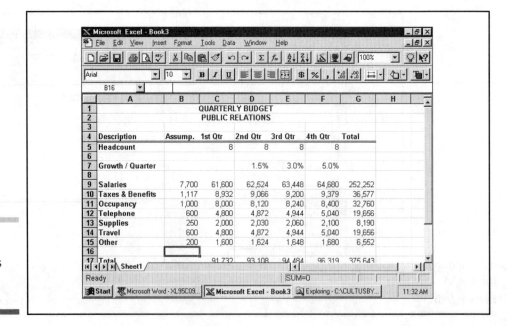

Headcount
and
assumptions
for Book3
Figure 9-8.

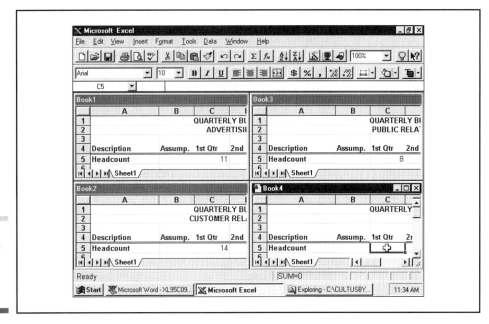

Each book
displaying the
1st Qtr
Headcount
Figure 9-9.

Type =, double-click on C5 in Book1, and press F4 three times to make
the reference relative. Type +, double-click on C5 in Book2, and press F4
three times. Type + again, double-click on C5 in Book3, press F4 three
times, and press ENTER.

You have created an *external reference formula,* shown in Figure 9-10.
Each part of the equation references a cell in a different workbook. This
is accomplished by including the full book name in square brackets
followed by the sheet name, an exclamation point (!), and the cell
reference. You need it to be relative so you can copy the same formula
to the other Headcount and expense cells.

4. Maximize Book4 and use AutoFill to copy the equation to the
   remaining Headcount cells.

5. With C5:F5 still selected, press CTRL-C to copy the selected cells, select
   C9:C15 on Book4, and press ENTER or press CTRL-V to paste the formulas
   into the expense cells.

6. Drag across the column headings for columns C through G, widen the
   columns slightly, and then reformat C9:F15 with the Comma format
   and no decimal places, as shown in Figure 9-11.

7. Type the title **MARKETING DEPARTMENT** in A2, make it bold, and
   center it across A2:G2 to finish the summary workbook.

9

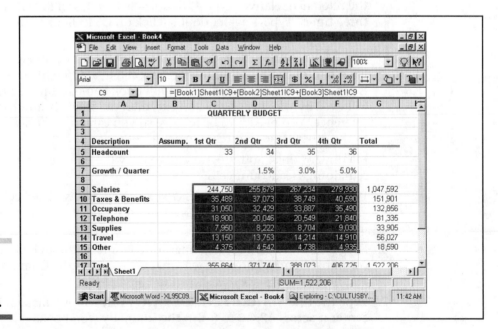

External
reference
formula
Figure 9-10.

Completed
summary
formulas
Figure 9-11.

Saving Multiple Workbooks

When you have a series of linked workbooks as you do here, it is very important that you save them in the proper sequence to maintain the linked formulas. Currently, the formulas have Book1, Book2, and so on for the filenames. If you were to save and close Book4 before saving Book1, Book2, and Book3, you would lose all your references. On the other hand, if you save Book1, Book2, and Book3 before saving Book4, the workbook references in Book4 automatically are replaced with the filenames. Excel has a fast way to do that with the Save Workspace command; it saves the group of workbooks and in the process prompts you to save the individual workbooks in the appropriate order. Try that next with the following steps.

1. Open the File menu and choose Save Workspace. In the dialog box that opens, select the C:\SHEET directory, type **qtrbud** for the filename, and click on Save.

2. When you are prompted about saving changes in Book1, click on Yes, type **qtrbudad** for the filename, and press ENTER to save Book1 as QTRBUDAD.

3. In a similar manner, save Book2 through Book4 as QTRBUDCR, QTRBUDPR, and QTRBUDTO, respectively.

4. Click on C5 and on QTRBUDTO or Book4 and look at the formula, which is also shown in Figure 9-12. Notice how the formula has been changed to reflect the new filename.

5. Restore QTRBUDTO to the size it was when tiled and then close each book (double-click on the Control-menu box) in the same order (start with QTRBUDAD or what was Book1, and end up with QTRBUDTO or Book4 last). Click on Yes to save changes to QTRBUDTO.

After closing QTRBUDAD (Book1), notice that the Headcount value in QTRBUDTO (Book4) remains 33. If you look at the formula in QTRBUDTO after closing the other two workbooks, you see it is still correct and now includes the full path name as well as the filename. All of the values on the workbook are also still correct, which means they are getting their information off your hard disk.

One consideration with external references is that names are even more important than they are in other workbook formulas. External reference formulas are not updated if you insert or delete rows or columns or move or cut cells in the workbook being referenced. If you use a range name, the range name is adjusted for the changes to the workbook and the external reference is correct.

9

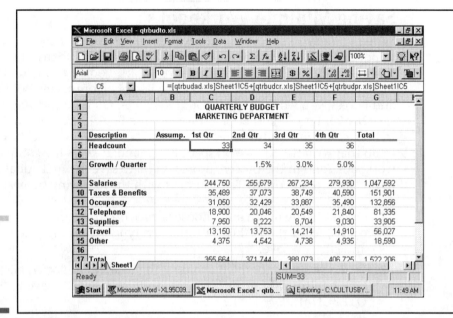

External
reference
formula with
filenames
Figure 9-12.

Combining Files

There are two other ways of combining workbooks: adding external ranges
and linking external ranges. These are the two ends of the technology
spectrum. Adding external ranges is the original way that several
spreadsheets were combined, and linking external ranges uses the newest
object linking technology. Using external reference formulas, as you did in
the first part of the chapter, is somewhere in the middle of the spectrum.
Look at both the adding and linking techniques in the following sections.

Adding External Ranges

Excel provides the means to mathematically combine a range in one
workbook with a similar range in another workbook using the Paste Special
option from the Edit menu. In other words, you can select and copy a range
in one workbook and then, through the Paste Special option, combine it
with a similar range on another workbook. The important phrase is *similar
range*. More accurately, the two ranges must be exactly alike, cell for cell,
because one entire range is overlaid on the other. The two workbooks also
have to be in memory together, although you can combine six workbooks
and have only two of them in memory at one time.

See how this works using the three workbooks created earlier in this chapter with a new total workbook. Build the new total workbook first with the normal Copy and Paste options and these steps.

1. Open the advertising department workbook QTRBUDAD, maximize it, select the range A1:H17, and click on the Copy tool in the Standard toolbar.

2. Create a new workbook, press ENTER or click on the Paste tool, widen column A, clear the contents in the range B5:F15, change the title to COMBINED TOTAL, and save the new workbook as QTRBUDCO in the SHEET directory.

   You now have a blank workbook, as shown in Figure 9-13, with the exact layout of the other three workbooks you built. You can use this new workbook to add the other three with the Paste Special option.

3. From the Window menu, activate QTRBUDAD, select C5:F15, and click on the Copy tool.

4. Activate QTRBUDCO, select C5, and choose Paste Special from the Edit menu. The following dialog box opens:

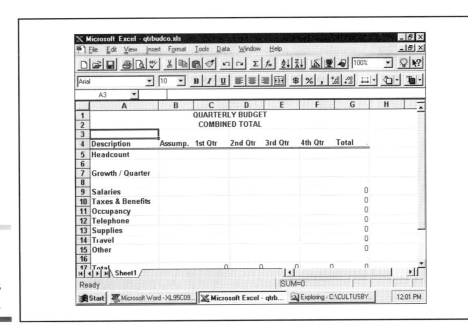

New worksheet ready for adding others

Figure 9-13.

9

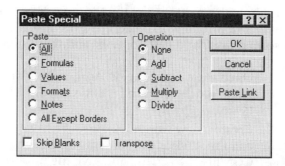

The Paste Special option allows you to paste only parts of the range you copied (the options on the left of the dialog box) and then to add, subtract, multiply, or divide the cells you copied to, from, by, or into the cells being pasted. As you are pasting, you can skip blank cells in the copied range so that you do not blank the contents of cells in the pasted range; you can also transpose rows and columns. In this example, you want to paste *only* the values, and you want to *add* them.

5. Choose Values and Add in the dialog box and click on OK. Your QTRBUDCO workbook now looks like Figure 9-14.

6. To make this example real, close the QTRBUDAD workbook by activating it and clicking on its Close button. You do not need to save any changes to QTRBUDAD.

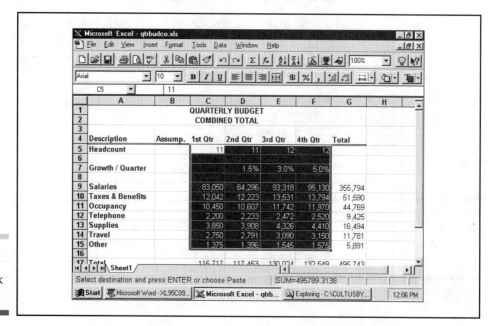

Results of pasting the first workbook

Figure 9-14.

Note that you cannot close QTRBUDAD before choosing Paste Special. If you do close QTRBUDAD, the Paste Special option will no longer have the ability to mathematically combine ranges.

7. Open QTRBUDCR, select C5:F15, choose Copy, activate QTRBUDCO, select C5 as the active cell, choose Paste Special, and then choose Values, Add, and OK. The second workbook is added to the contents of the first.

8. Close QTRBUDCR, open QTRBUDPR, and follow the same procedure outlined in step 7.

9. Clear the contents of the range C6:F8 on QTRBUDCO, since the added percentages are not meaningful. Drag across the column headings for columns C through G and then widen them slightly so all your numbers display. Your final COMBINED TOTAL workbook looks like Figure 9-15.

10. Close QTRBUDPR and save QTRBUDCO a second time.

If you compare this QTRBUDCO workbook with QTRBUDTO in Figure 9-12, you can see they are the same except for the growth percentages, which have been deleted in QTRBUDCO.

For the example in this chapter, and for most of your multiple workbook problems, the external reference formulas and the linking of ranges are better approaches than using Paste Special. Paste Special should be used only when

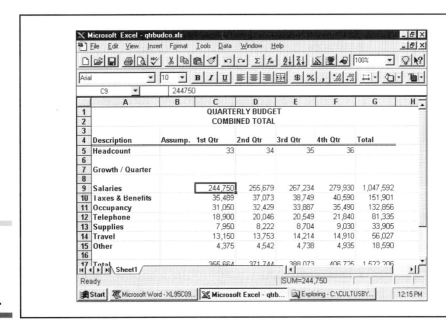

Final
COMBINED
TOTAL
workbook
Figure 9-15.

you are memory constrained. Paste Special is easier in that you do not have to build and copy the summing formulas. Of course, the big disadvantage is that the files must have exactly the same file layout. The numbers you want to add must be in the same cell positions on each workbook.

Dates and times generally should not be combined with Paste Special; the results are not meaningful. Also, blank cells are considered to be 0 by Paste Special unless you select Skip Blanks in the Paste Special dialog box.

The Paste Special option changes the current workbook by copying over or mathematically combining with its cells. Before using the Paste Special option, save your current workbook and carefully position the active cell. Also, if used soon enough, Edit Undo (CTRL-Z) can restore the current workbook to its contents prior to executing Paste Special.

Linking External Ranges

Linking external ranges consists of copying an external range and then pasting it in its own area in another workbook. In the process, a link is established between the original range and its copy, so that any changes in the original appear in the copy. Try this by linking separate Excel workbooks using the files you created earlier in the chapter and following these instructions.

1. With the COMBINED TOTAL workbook still on your screen, click your right mouse button on the Sheet tab, choose Insert, and click on OK to insert a new sheet. Alternatively, you can choose Worksheet from the Insert menu or press the shortcut keys SHIFT-F11 or ALT-SHIFT-F1.

2. Use any of the methods in step 1 to insert two more sheets. You should have a total of four sheets.

3. Choose Save As from the File menu, type **qtrbudle** (for *linked* and *embedded*), and click on Save to save your new workbook.

4. Click on the Open tool in the Standard toolbar and double-click on QRTBUDAD.XLS to open it.

5. Select A1:G17, click on the Copy tool, press CTRL-TAB to switch to QTRBUDLE, click with the right mouse button on cell A1 on Sheet4 of QTRBUDLE, and then choose Paste Special from the popup menu. The same Paste Special dialog box opens that you saw above.

6. Click on Paste Link. The range appears on Sheet4 as shown in Figure 9-16. Note the formula in A1 (you may have to click on A1 to see the formula). It is a group reference (or an *array*) to the source workbook. With it, any changes made to the source will appear here. The data needs a little formatting, but it is all here.

7. Press CTRL-TAB to return to the QTRBUDAD window, double-click on the document Control-menu icon to close QTRBUDAD.XLS, answering No to saving the large Clipboard data.

8. The range A1:G17 on Sheet4 of QTRBUDLE should still be selected (select it if it isn't) and visible to you. Select Sheets 4, 3, and 2 so the formatting you do will apply to all three detail sheets.

9. From the Tools menu, choose Options, click on View, click on Zero Values to turn off the display of zeros, and click on OK.

10. Widen column A to 17, make the data in column A and row 4 bold, format D7:F7 as percents with one decimal, and format B9:G17 with a thousands separator and no decimals.

    Unfortunately, you cannot center the two titles across columns A through G because the limitations of an array won't allow it. You also cannot do any editing within an array—you must go back to the original workbook for that.

11. Repeat steps 4 through 7 to paste links from QTRBUDCR.XLS and QTRBUDPR.XLS to Sheets 3 and 2, respectively, of QTRBUDLE. Click on Sheet1 to ungroup the sheets and then click on each sheet as you use it.

12. Click on Sheet1, click on C5, click on the AutoSum tool, click on Sheet4, press and hold SHIFT while clicking on Sheet2, click on C5 again, and press ENTER. The sheet summing formula will be produced.

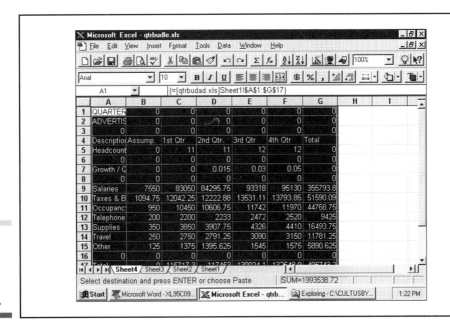

Pasted data linked to the original workbook

Figure 9-16.

9

13. Use the AutoFill handle to copy C5 to D5:F5. Leaving C5:F5 selected, press and hold CTRL while dragging across C9:F15, and then choose Fill and then Down from the Edit menu.

14. Select C9:F15 and format it with commas and no decimals. You have created a third copy of the departmental total, as shown in Figure 9-17.

   This third technique of summing linked sheets is probably the best for most applications where you need to combine workbooks. It is particularly effective across a network for summing information produced in several departments of a company. Every time you open QTRBUDLE it will be updated for any changes in the linked sheets. Try that now.

15. Save and close QTRBUDLE. Open QTRBUDAD, change C5 to 14, save and close QTRBUDAD, and reopen QTRBUDLE. You will get this message box:

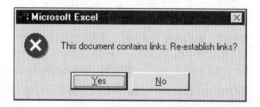

16. Click on Yes and QTRBUDLE will open. If you look on Sheet4, you will see the change. Close QTRBUDLE one last time.

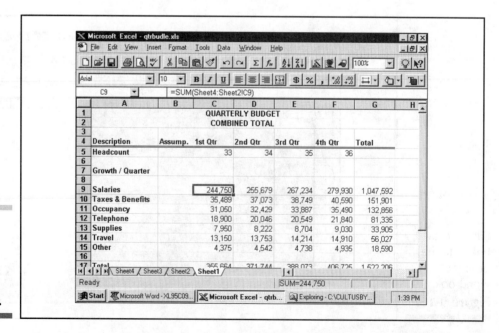

COMBINED
TOTAL
produced by
summing
linked sheets
Figure 9-17.

17. Click on the New Workbook tool. Open the Tools menu, choose Options, and click on the General tab. Then drag across the number of Sheets in New Workbook, type **16**, and click on OK to return this to its default setting.

Saving a Workbook as a Text File

Sometimes you want to get a range or a complete file out of Excel to use in another program. Most other programs cannot read an Excel file, but they can read a file that is written in the ASCII (American Standard Code for Information Interchange) format. Excel uses the File Save As option to accomplish this. The Save As dialog box has a Save as Type list box. When opened, the list box displays 26 different file formats in which you can save Excel files. These file formats are summarized in Table 9-1.

For your purposes here, you want either the Text or CSV format. For use in the body of a word-processed document, you use Text and then set tab stops in the word processor to re-create Excel's columns. For use in a database other than dBASE or for mail merging with word-processed documents, you use CSV. Save the QTRBUDCO file in both of these formats, and then exit Excel and look at the results by following the next set of instructions.

1. Open QTRBUDCO.XLS and then choose Save As from the File menu, open the Save as Type list box, click on Text (Tab delimited), and click on Save. The file QTRBUDCO.TXT is written to your active (SHEET) directory.

2. Choose Save As from the File menu, open the Save as Type list box, click on CSV (comma delimited), and click on Save.

   You have now created two new files: one in the ASCII text format with the filename extension .TXT and the second in ASCII comma delimited format with the extension .CSV. Next, close Excel and look at these files with the Windows accessory WordPad.

3. Click on the Excel Close button to close it. Click on No if asked to save QTRBUDCO.CSV.

4. Click on the Start button, point on Programs, then point on Accessories from the first submenu, and, finally, choose WordPad from the second submenu. Click on the Maximize/Restore button to expand WordPad to full-screen size.

5. Choose Open from the File menu, change the folder in Look in to \SHEET\ (or the folder you are using for Excel files), type in the filename QTRBUDCO.TXT, and click on Open.

   The quarterly budget COMBINED TOTAL workbook opens, as shown in Figure 9-18.

9

File Type	Description
Excel Workbook	Saves an entire workbook in the normal Excel 7 .XLS file format (which is the same as Excel 5 format).
Template	Saves an entire workbook in an Excel 7 .XLT template file format (which is the same as Excel 5 format). A template, which is a pattern for future workbooks, forces you to rename the file when you use it so you do not write over the template.
Formatted Text	Saves only the active sheet in the Lotus .PRN space delimited text file format.
Text	Saves only the active sheet in the ASCII .TXT file format with tabs between columns and carriage returns at the end of each row. This format is primarily used to bring a workbook into a word-processing package. All formulas are replaced by their values and, if a cell has a comma or a tab in it, the cell's value is enclosed in quotation marks.
CSV (Comma Separated Values)	Saves only the active sheet in the ASCII .CSV file format with commas between columns in place of tabs. Otherwise, it is the same as a text file. This is primarily used by database packages. It is sometimes called an *ASCII delimited file*.
Excel 4.0 Workbook	Saves sheets, chart sheets, and Excel 4 macro sheets in the Excel 4.0 .XLW file format.
Excel 4.0 Worksheet	Saves only the active sheet in the Excel 4.0 .XLS file format.
Excel 3.0	Saves only the active sheet in the Excel 3.0 .XLS file format.
Excel 2.1	Saves only the active sheet in either the Excel 2.1 for Windows or the Excel 2.2 for OS/2 .XLS file format.
WK4	Saves all sheets and chart sheets in the Lotus .WK4 format used with Lotus 1-2-3 Release 4.x.
WK3, FM3	Saves all sheets and chart sheets in the Lotus .WK3 format used with Lotus 1-2-3 Release 3.x.
WK1, FMT (ALL)	Saves only the active sheet in the Lotus .WK1 format used with Lotus 1-2-3 versions 2, 2.01, and 2.2.

The Various
File Formats in
Which You
Can Save
Excel Files
Table 9-1.

File Type	Description
WKS	Saves only the active sheet in the Lotus .WKS format used with Lotus 1-2-3 version 1A.
WQ1	Saves only the active sheet in the QuattroPro for DOS .WQ1 format.
DBF 4	Saves the currently defined database range in the format used by dBASE IV.
DBF 3	Saves the currently defined database range in the format used by dBASE III.
DBF 2	Saves the currently defined database range in the format used by dBASE II.
Text (Macintosh)	Saves only the active sheet in a tab delimited text format readable on the Apple Macintosh.
Text (OS/2 or DOS)	Saves only the active sheet in a tab delimited text format readable in either OS/2 or DOS.
CSV (Macintosh)	Saves only the active sheet in a comma delimited text format readable on the Apple Macintosh.
CSV (OS/2 or DOS)	Saves only the active sheet in a comma delimited text format readable in either OS/2 or DOS.
DIF	Saves only the active sheet in the Data Interchange Format used by VisiCalc. This format does not transfer formulas, only values.
SYLK	Saves only the active sheet in the SYLK (Symbolic Link) format used to transfer information among Microsoft workbook packages, including Multiplan.

The Various File Formats in Which You Can Save Excel Files (*continued*)
Table 9-1.

At this point the text file does not look great, but with very little work it can be markedly improved.

6. Choose Replace from the Edit menu, type " in Find what, and click on Replace All. This removes all quotation marks. Click on OK to acknowledge WordPad has finished searching the file. Click on the Close button of the Replace dialog box to close the dialog box.

7. Choose Ruler from the View menu, select all the text by dragging from the upper left to the lower right, and click in the space just below the ruler at 1.75", 2.5", 3.25", 4", 4.75", and 5.5" to set tab stops at those locations.

9

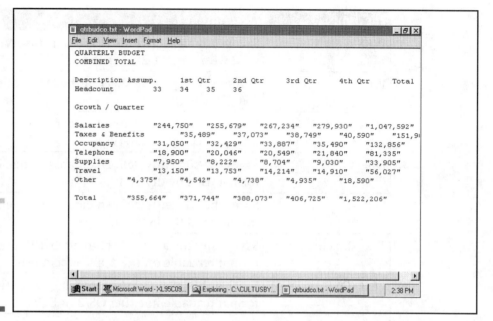

All of a sudden the exported workbook looks pretty good, as shown in
Figure 9-19. Additionally, since it uses tabs instead of spaces, the
workbook can be printed with a proportionally spaced font and not be
thrown out of alignment.

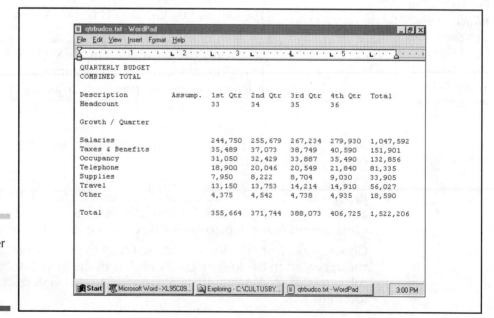

8. Choose Save As from the File menu and choose Word 6.0 format in the dialog box that appears as the format to save the file in. Change the filename extension to .DOC, and click on Save. The word-processing file will be saved with the default .DOC Word for Windows 6.0 extension.

9. Choose Open from the File menu, type **qtrbudco.csv**, and click on Open. The second text file opens, as shown in Figure 9-20.

You can see that the CSV file has replaced tabs with commas, but otherwise it looks very similar to the text file when you originally brought it in. The big difference is that you cannot simply set some tab stops and get a CSV file to line up properly. What you must do is replace the commas with tabs, which will cause a problem with commas used as the thousands separator in a number. In a word-processing package, the CSV format is not very useful except for mail merge. The standard text format with tabs is much more useful. The CSV format is primarily used for transferring files to database packages.

Importing ASCII Text Files

Just as you may need to get data out of Excel for use in other programs, you may need to get data into Excel from other programs in a format other than the Excel standard file format. The most common format is ASCII text in one

Comma separated (CSV) text file in WordPad
Figure 9-20.

9

of two types: nondelimited ASCII files that are continuous text strings and delimited ASCII files. A delimited ASCII file includes delimiters, usually commas, between fields or columns and often quotation marks around text. Delimiters can also be tabs for Excel's use, but most other programs recognize only commas or semicolons. Using ASCII delimited files with commas and quotation marks is the most common means of exchanging information among database programs. Many word-processing programs can also read ASCII delimited files and use them with their mail merge function.

Look at how Excel brings in each of the two text files (both the .TXT and the .CSV files) as well as a nondelimited text. While you are still in WordPad, create the nondelimited file from QTRBUDCO.CSV, which should still be on your screen.

1. Delete the first four lines down to but not including the Headcount line (select the lines and use the Cut option in the Edit menu or the DEL key), delete the three lines between Headcount and Salaries, and delete the line between Other and Total as well as any leading space in front of Total.

2. Select all of the remaining text, open the View menu, display the Toolbar and Format bar, and make sure Courier New is displayed in the Font list box. If it isn't, select it from the drop-down list box.

3. Select the first comma in the Headcount line, choose Replace from the Edit menu, type , (comma) in Find what, press SPACEBAR six times in Replace with, and click Replace. Continue to replace all commas in the first line with six spaces. Click on the Close button when through.

4. Using the Replace dialog box, change ,," to two spaces by typing ,," in Find what, pressing DEL in the Replace with text box, and clicking Replace All. Next, change all remaining commas to nothing by typing , in Find what, pressing DEL in the Replace With text box, and clicking Replace All. Change "" to two spaces, and change the remaining " to nothing. Click on Close.

5. Add and delete spaces so the numbers line up to the right, as shown in Figure 9-21. Then use Save As to save the file as text only with the filename TEST.TXT and change the Save File as Type to Text files.

6. Click on WordPad's Close button to close it. Finally, reopen Excel in your normal manner.

Opening Tab and Comma Delimited Text Files

Both the .TXT and .CSV files that you created are delimited text files. The .TXT file is delimited with tabs, and the .CSV file is delimited with commas. Both files have quotes around numbers that contain comma formatting so

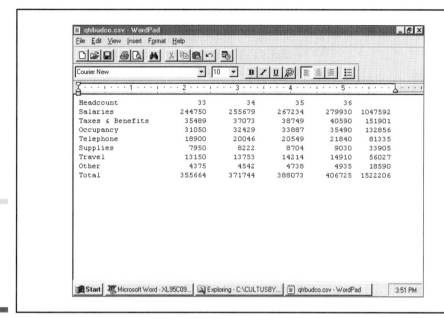

Nondelimited
ASCII text file
in WordPad
after being
cleaned up
Figure 9-21.

the commas will not be treated as delimiters. Bring each of the two delimited files back into Excel and see how they are split up into rows and columns with the following steps.

1. Click on the Open tool from the Standard toolbar, select C:\SHEET as your folder, choose Text Files in Files of type, and double-click on QTRBUDCO.TXT in the File name list box.

   The first Text Import Wizard dialog box opens as shown in Figure 9-22. The little black rectangles in the text are the delimiters (tabs in this case).

2. Click on Next. The second Text Import Wizard dialog box opens, showing you what it has determined to be the delimiters and how the text would be divided into columns.

3. Click on Next. The third Text Import Wizard dialog box opens, allowing you to select the overall formats by column.

4. Click on Finish to accept the default formatting. Figure 9-23 displays the tab delimited file back in Excel. When you click in individual cells, you see that everything is in place. About the only things you lost are the formulas and the centering and bold text formatting.

5. Click on its Close button to close the file called QTRBUDCO.TXT, and click on QTRBUDCO.CSV in the File menu.

9

First Text
Import Wizard
dialog box
Figure 9-22.

The CSV file is brought in immediately and everything is in its correct cell, with all that's lost being only the formulas, the title and column

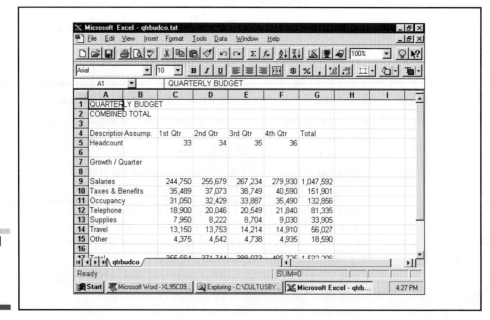

Tab delimited
file back in
Excel
Figure 9-23.

centering, and the extra width in column A, as it was with the tab delimiter. The ease with which these files come in is not deceptive. Any ASCII delimited file will come in as easily and as well behaved. If you are using commas as delimiters, use the .CSV extension when saving the file in another application. Excel will not as easily split the text into columns without this extension.

6. Click on its Close button to close the QTRBUDCO.CSV file.

Opening Nondelimited Text Files

Bringing a nondelimited text file into Excel, which used to be a major headache, is not much harder than bringing in a delimited file thanks to the Text Import Wizard. See for yourself by bringing in the TEST.TXT file you created in WordPad.

1. Choose Open from the File menu; if necessary reselect Text Files from the Files of type list, and double-click on TEST.TXT.

    The first Text Import Wizard dialog box opens, as shown in Figure 9-24. Note that the file has been correctly identified as a fixed-width file instead of delimited as you saw before. The dialog box is correct in all aspects.

2. Click on Next. The second Text Import Wizard dialog box opens, as you can see in Figure 9-25.

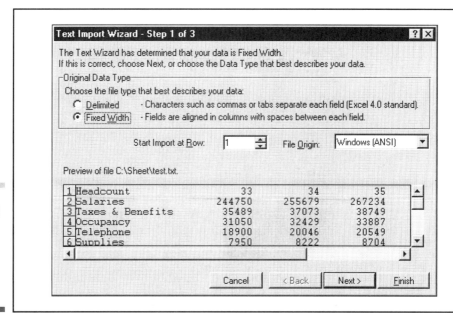

First Text Import Wizard dialog box with a nondelimited file

Figure 9-24.

9

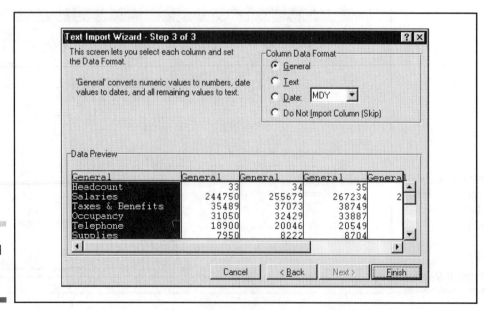

Second Text
Import Wizard
dialog box
Figure 9-25.

This dialog box lets you add, delete, and move column breaks. In this
case, though, all the column breaks are OK as is.

3. Click on Next. The third Text Import Wizard dialog box will open like
that shown in Figure 9-26.

Third Text
Import Wizard
dialog box
Figure 9-26.

The final dialog box allows you to set the overall formatting of each column and to skip (not bring in) a column if you wish. Once again, all the assumptions are correct as is.

4. Click on Finish.

The file comes into Excel perfectly laid out in rows and columns, as shown in Figure 9-27. Look at several cells in column A and then in other columns. You can see that each cell contains just the information (text or numbers) that it is supposed to and that numbers are actually numbers since they are right-aligned. If you wanted, you could do arithmetic operations on them and format them. The key to this was the alignment work that you did in WordPad. The Text Import Wizard was able to look at this text and quickly see what to do with it.

5. Click on the document's Close button to close the TEST.TXT file. There is no need to save it. Close Excel and Windows, if you are done computing.

Nondelimited text brought into Excel

Figure 9-27.

Dates, Functions, and Macros

10

This chapter brings together three subjects that do not fit easily into any other category: dates and times, functions, and macros. These three subjects need a forum of their own, in which it can be shown how their finishing touches—the "icing on the cake"—make a good spreadsheet a great spreadsheet.

Using Dates and Times

From schedules and dates on reports to time-related financial calculations, dates and times are important aspects of the problems Excel addresses. The sections that follow discuss how Excel handles dates and times internally, various ways Excel formats dates and times, and the date and time functions and arithmetic operations.

Dates and Excel

Dates do not form a nice, neat, linear progression: you cannot add 12 days to April 28th and get with certainty the proper date in May without knowing how many days there are in April. Microsoft has solved this problem by establishing a date serial number scheme. This scheme allocates one number for every day from January 1, 1900 (date serial number 1) to December 31, 2078 (date serial number 65380). Microsoft also provides formatting and formulas to convert the date serial number to a specific calendar date. Internally, Excel uses the unformatted date serial number. You can format the date serial number in several ways and get a normal looking calendar date from a serial number. For example, when formatted with the second Excel date format, the serial number 34948 becomes 9/6/95, as shown here:

B2	▼	9/6/1995	
A	**B**	**C**	**D**
1			
2	9/6/95		
3			
4			

In other words, simply typing 34948, pressing ENTER, and formatting the number with the date format m/d/yy produces the date 9/6/95. The following instructions demonstrate several date entry procedures. Your computer should be on, Excel should be loaded, and you should have a blank workbook on your screen.

1. Select B2:F2, choose Cells from the Format menu, click on the Number tab, select the Date category and the 3/4/94 type (second in the Type list), and click on OK. The range B2:F2 is formatted as m/d/yy dates.

2. Click on B2 and type **34963** and press RIGHT ARROW. The date 9/6/95 appears in B2.

10

3. Type **30638** and press RIGHT ARROW. The date 11/18/83 appears in C2.

4. Type **1**, press RIGHT ARROW, type **65380**, and press ENTER. The date 1/1/00 appears in D2, and E2 contains 12/31/78 as you can see here:

	A	B	C	D	E	F
				E2 ▼	12/31/2078	
1						
2		9/6/95	11/18/83	1/1/00	12/31/78	
3						
4						

Note that when you are working with dates in the next century, the two-digit year format can be confusing. Change the format next. (E2 should still be the active cell.)

5. Choose Cells from the Format menu, click on the Number tab, choose the Custom category, click after the last "y" in the Type text box (if the m/d/yy format is not in the Type text box, scroll down the list of types and select it), type **yy**, and click on OK. E2 fills with #'s because the date is now too big for the cell.

6. Drag on the intersection of columns E and F in the heading to widen the column slightly. The date 12/31/2078 appears in E2, like this:

	A	B	C	D	E	F
				E2 ▼	12/31/2078	
1						
2		9/6/95	11/18/83	1/1/00	12/31/2078	
3						
4						

There is one abnormality in Microsoft's date scheme. The year 1900 was not a leap year, even though the year was evenly divisible by four. Therefore, Excel assigns a date serial number to February 29, 1900, which didn't exist. The only impact of this is that date arithmetic spanning February 28, 1900 through March 1, 1900 is off by one day. All date serial numbers and calculated dates from March 1, 1900 onward are correct.

Times and Excel

Microsoft has also developed a scheme for calculating time: the time is added to the date serial number as a decimal fraction of a 24-hour day. Therefore, midnight is 0.000000, noon is 0.500000, and 11:59:59 PM is 0.999988. When the decimal fractions are formatted with Excel as times, they produce normal looking time numbers on either a 12-hour or 24-hour basis. The following steps show how several times are entered.

1. Select B2:F2, choose Clear from the Edit menu, and click on All to erase both the contents and formats of B2:F2.

2. Choose Cells from the Format menu, click on the Time category, select the second time type, 1:30 PM, and click on OK. The range B2:F2 is formatted with the second time type.

3. Click on B2 and type **.65** and press RIGHT ARROW. Cell B2 contains 3:36 PM, as shown here:

4. Type **.45** and press RIGHT ARROW. Cell C2 contains 10:48 AM.

5. Type **0**, press RIGHT ARROW, type **.9999**, and press ENTER. Cells D2 and E2 contain 12:00 AM and 11:59 PM, as you see here:

Dates and times are stored in one number. For example, 9:21:36 PM December, 21 1995, is stored as 35054.89 (the date on the left side of the decimal, the time on the right). In a single cell, you can display this as a date, as a time, or both, depending on the formatting.

Formatting Dates and Times

There are nine date formats, six time formats, and two combined date and time types built into Excel. The date formats use the integer part of a date serial number and the time formats use the decimal part. The decimal part of a number is ignored by a date format, and the integer part of a number is ignored by a time format. If a date format encounters a number that is negative or greater than 65380, the cell fills with #'s. If a time format encounters a negative number, the cell fills with #'s.

The 17 built-in date and time formats are shown in Figure 10-1. You can, of course, make your own. The components needed to construct your own formats are shown in Chapter 6. Some examples of custom date and time formats are shown in Figure 10-2.

The choice of which format to use is one of personal taste. Some formats require wider columns than others, which may have some bearing on your decision. Also, there is no reason you cannot mix formats in a workbook.

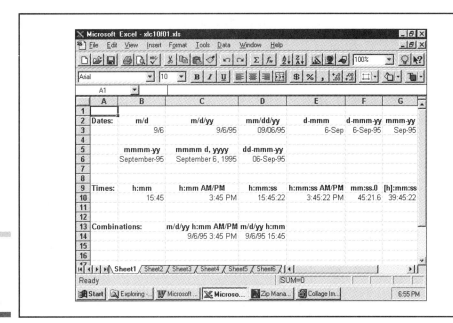

Built-in date
and time
formats
Figure 10-1.

Date and Time Functions

Date and time functions use the date serial number to calculate various date-
and time-related numbers. There are seven date and five time functions that

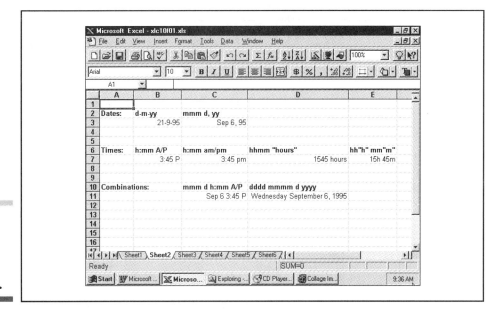

Examples of
custom date
and time
formats
Figure 10-2.

are used in date and time arithmetic. In addition, there are two functions that produce the current date and/or time. Of the fourteen functions, five produce a date or time serial number that must be formatted in order to be displayed properly. Any of the formats may be used with the functions.

Date Functions

The seven date functions are shown in Figure 10-3. The first two produce date serial numbers, shown in the middle column of Figure 10-3, that can be formatted as dates, shown in the third column. The next four functions transform a date serial number into part of a date. Note that a date for a day can be formatted into the name of the day with the format code dddd. The last function calculates the number of days between two dates using a 360-day year.

The DATE function takes three integers—one for the year, one for the month, and one for the day—and with these computes the date serial number. As with all functions, the three arguments (year, month, and day) can be integers that are entered directly into the function, or they can be addresses or reference names that refer to cells containing or computing integers suitable for the function. The DATE function is used when you break out a date for sorting or to use as a database criterion and you want to display the date that results from the combined parts.

DATEVALUE converts a date in text form to a date serial number. DATEVALUE looks for text as an argument. Therefore, a date that is directly entered into the function must be enclosed in quotation marks, as shown in Figure 10-3.

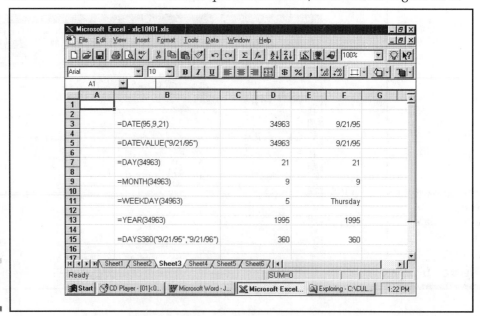

Date functions
Figure 10-3.

The next four date functions, DAY, MONTH, WEEKDAY, and YEAR, perform the opposite function of DATE: they split out the day, month, weekday, or year from the date serial number. WEEKDAY returns an integer from 1 for Sunday to 7 for Saturday.

Time Functions

The five time functions are shown in Figure 10-4. The first two produce the date serial numbers shown in the middle column of Figure 10-4, which can be formatted as the times shown in the third column. The last three functions transform a time serial number into the components of a time designation.

The TIME function uses three integers—one for hours, one for minutes, and one for seconds—to compute the time serial number (the decimal portion of a date serial number). TIME is used when you break out a time for sorting or for use as a database criterion and you want to display the time that results from the combined parts.

You use TIMEVALUE to convert a time that is entered as text to a time serial number. TIMEVALUE looks for a text as an argument. Therefore, a time that is directly entered into the function must be enclosed in quotation marks, as shown in Figure 10-4.

The next three date functions, HOUR, MINUTE, and SECOND, perform the opposite function of TIME: they split out the hour, minute, or second from the time serial number.

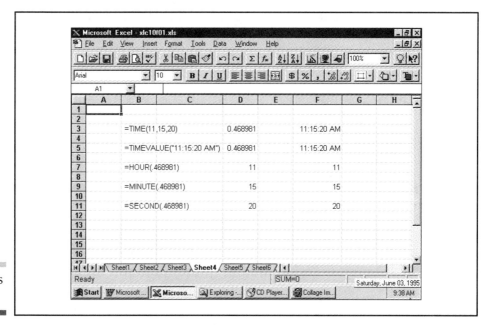

Time functions
Figure 10-4.

Current Date and Time Functions

The functions used to produce the current date and/or time are NOW and TODAY. Examples of their use are shown in Figure 10-5. These functions use the internal clock-calendar in your computer to determine the current date and time. NOW produces both the integer and decimal components needed for both date and time display. If you are using the current date in a formula or with another function, use TODAY to obtain the integer part of the current date. The decimal (time) part of NOW can cause inaccuracies in date calculations. If you simply are displaying the date, NOW by itself works. Date formats ignore the decimal part of the number.

Entering and Generating Dates and Times

You have just seen how you can enter dates and times either by entering the date serial number (which is not very practical because you don't know what it is in most instances) or by using one of the functions that convert a date or time to the date serial number. Also, you have seen how to generate the current date and/or time. You have two other ways to get dates and times into Excel. First, just typing a date or time on a sheet in an Excel format produces a date or time serial number. Second, the Data Series option generates a sequence of dates or times.

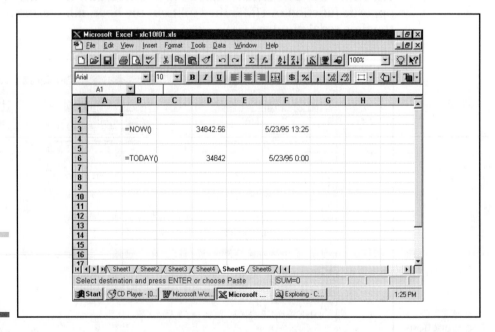

Current date and time functions

Figure 10-5.

Direct Entry of Dates and Times

You can enter a date or time directly into Excel in any recognized format and get a date or time serial number. It does not have to be one of the built-in formats. When you enter a date or time, it is automatically formatted as the first date or first time format, respectively. The following instructions provide some examples of direct entry of dates and times.

1. Choose New from the File menu, and click on OK for a new workbook.

2. Move the active cell to B3.

3. Type **9/21/95**, and it goes in the edit area, as shown here:

B3	▾ ✕ ✓ ƒₓ	9/21/95	
	A	**B**	**C**	**D**
1				
2				
3		9/21/95		
4				

4. Press ENTER. The date, 9/21/95, is converted internally by Excel to 34963, and the cell is automatically formatted and displayed as m/d/yy.

5. To confirm that 9/21/95 is in fact the date serial number 34963, click on B2, type **=B3**, press ENTER, and format B2 with the General format. Your results will look like this:

B2	▾	=B3	
	A	**B**	**C**	**D**
1				
2		34963		
3		9/21/95		
4				

6. Click on E3, type **9-21-95**, and press ENTER. The date is converted to 34963 and automatically formatted as 9/21/95.

7. If you want to enter a formula that looks like a date, you must put an equal sign in front of it.

8. Click on B5, type **3:45 pm**, and press ENTER. The time, 3:45 PM, is converted to 0.65625, and the cell is automatically formatted with h:mm AM/PM.

9. Prove that 3:45 PM is 0.65625 by clicking on B6, typing **=B5**, pressing ENTER, and formatting B6 with the General format.

10. Click on E5, type **3:45 p**, and press ENTER. The time, 3:45 p, is converted to 0.65625, and the cell is automatically formatted as 3:45 PM:

E5	▼		3:45:00 PM		
	A	B	C	D	E	F
1						
2		34963				
3		9/21/95			9/21/95	
4						
5		3:45 PM			3:45 PM	
6		0.65625				
7						

Generating a Series of Dates

In Chapter 8, you saw how you can generate dates with the Edit Fill Series option, which is a very capable and flexible tool. From any starting date to any ending date within the 178-year range of Excel's date scheme, you can generate as many dates as you can hold in the memory of your computer. If you are generating dates, you can increment them by a number of days, weekdays, months, years, or fractions thereof.

The following steps give several examples of generating dates and times with the Data Series option.

1. Delete what you entered above, or choose New from the File menu and click on OK to create a new workbook, or click on a different sheet.

2. Select B2:F13, choose Format Cells from the Cell popup menu, select the Date category, the m/d/yy (3/4/94) format, and click on OK to format the selected area.

3. Click on B2, type **1/31/96**, press ENTER, select B2:B13, point on Fill from the Edit menu, and click on Series. In the Series in and Type fields, Columns and Date should already be selected. Select Month for the unit. One month is the default step value, as shown here:

4. Press ENTER. B2:B13 fills with a series of dates that are one month apart, from 1/31/96 through 12/31/96.

This series provides the actual month-end date, 1/31, 2/29, 3/31, 4/30, and so on, not just 30- or 31-day intervals. It can be a very useful capability.

10

5. Click on D2, type **1/31/96**, press ENTER, select D2:D13, point on Fill from the Edit menu, click on Series, and type **7** for the step value. Seven days or one week is the intended step value.

6. Press ENTER. D2:D13 fills with a series of dates that are one week apart, from 1/31/96 through 4/17/96.

7. Click on F2 and do a third data series, using years as the increment from 1/31/96 to 1/31/2007. You also must reformat the column to display the dates in the next century.

When you are done, your screen should look like Figure 10-6. Column B shows a progression by month, column D shows a progression by week, and column F shows a progression by year.

Generating a Series of Times

Generating times with Excel is not much different from generating dates. Although there are no ready-made increments like hours, minutes, and seconds, you can use the standard time notation of hh:mm:ss to indicate a step value. For example, a step value of one second would be 00:00:01, one minute would be 00:01:00, and one hour would be 01:00:00.

The following steps demonstrate several data series that produce times.

Date series by month, week, and year

Figure 10-6.

1. Delete what you entered above, or choose New from the File menu and click on OK to create a new workbook, or click on a different sheet.

2. Select B3:F15, choose Format Cells from the Cell popup menu, select the Time category, 1:30:55 PM, and click on OK. The selected range is formatted with the h:mm:ss AM/PM time type.

3. Choose Column and then Width from the Format menu, type **12** for the new width, and click on OK. Columns B through F widen to 12 to handle the full time format.

4. Click on B3, type **11:00:00**, press ENTER, select B3:B15, point on Fill from the Edit menu, click on Series, type **00:00:01** as the step value, and press ENTER. B3:B15 fills with a series of times that are one second apart, from 11:00:00 through 11:00:12.

5. Click on D3, type **11:00:00**, press ENTER, select D3:D15, point on Fill from the Edit menu, click on Series, type **00:01:00** as the step value, and press ENTER. D3:D15 fills with a series of times that are one minute apart, from 11:00:00 through 11:12:00.

6. Click on F3, type **11:00:00**, press ENTER, select F3:F15, point on Fill from the Edit menu, click on Series, type **01:00:00** as the step value, and press ENTER. F3:F15 fills with a series of times that are one hour apart, from 11:00:00 AM through 11:00:00 PM.

When you are done, your screen should look like Figure 10-7. Column B shows a progression by second, column D shows a progression by minute, and column F shows a progression by hour, all formatted for a 12-hour clock.

Generating a List of Months or Weekdays

Often you find that you want a list of months or days of the week. For example, you might want months for row headings in a financial performance summary, as shown here:

		Sales	Expense	Net Income
1				
2		Sales	Expense	Net Income
3	January	1,805	1,516	289
4	February	4,368	3,669	699
5	March	7,330	6,157	1,173
6	April	9,449	7,937	1,512
7	May	8,956	7,523	1,433
8	June	6,961	5,847	1,114
9	July	6,000	5,040	960
10	August	2,807	2,358	449
11	September	7,692	6,461	1,231
12	October	3,182	2,673	509
13	November	9,272	7,788	1,484
14	December	2,553	2,144	408
15	Total	70,374	59,114	11,260
16				

10

Time series by
second,
minute, and
hour
Figure 10-7.

Alternatively, you might want days of the week for a daily lunch menu, like
this:

	A	B	C	D	E	F	G	H
1								
2			Monday	Tuesday	Wednesday	Thursday	Friday	
3		Menu	Hamburgers	Pizza	Spaghetti	Hot dogs	Fish & chips	
4								
5								

You could, of course, type the months or days of the week, but Excel has a
much easier way to do it with the AutoFill handle—just use the following
steps.

1. Type the first month or day, such as **January** or **Monday**, and press
   ENTER.

2. Drag the AutoFill handle over the number of months or days you want
   the series to fill.

That's it! The month and weekday lists are stored in the Custom Lists tab of
the Options dialog box that you open from the Tools menu, shown next:

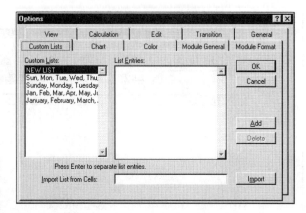

As you see, you can use the full name of the month and day of the week or their three-letter abbreviations.

You are not limited to these lists. You can build your own on a sheet and import it into the dialog box, or you can build it in the dialog box. Your lists can include a list of products, a list of salespeople, a list of accounts, or virtually anything you repeatedly use. For example, if you have a list of salespeople you frequently use, you might enter their names in the dialog box, as shown here:

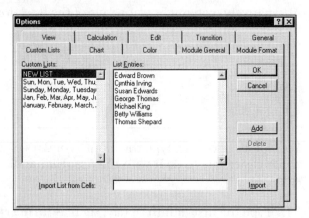

Then, by typing the first name (you must type the full name as you entered it) and dragging the fill handle, you will get a list of names like this:

Date and Time Arithmetic

One of the primary reasons Microsoft developed the date serial number was to allow easy date and time arithmetic. For example, you can add 1 to a date and get the day following, as shown in the next illustration:

C2			=B2+1	
	A	B	C	D
1				
2		4/30/96	5/1/96	
3				

You can add 30 days and get the appropriate day in the next month:

D2			=B2+30		
	A	B	C	D	E
1					
2		4/30/96	5/1/96	5/30/96	
3					

You can also subtract two dates and get the number of days between them.

E2			=D2-C2			
	A	B	C	D	E	F
1						
2		4/30/96	5/1/96	5/30/96	29	
3						

The date functions are useful in date arithmetic. For example, you can use YEAR to determine the number of years between two dates, as shown here:

D2			=YEAR(C2)-YEAR(B2)		
	A	B	C	D	E
1					
2		6/7/91	5/15/96	5	
3					

Time arithmetic is a little more complex in that you must add fractions. For example, the way to add one hour is to add 1/24th, as shown here:

C2			=B2+1/24	
	A	B	C	D
1				
2		9:25 AM	10:25 AM	
3				

Adding ten minutes requires the fraction 10/(24*60):

D2			=B2+10/(24*60)		
	A	B	C	D	E
1					
2		9:25 AM	10:25 AM	9:35 AM	
3					

Time functions are useful in time arithmetic. For example, you can determine the number of hours between two times with two HOUR functions, as shown here:

	E2	▾		=HOUR(C2)-HOUR(B2)		
	A	B	C	D	E	F
1						
2		9:25 AM	10:25 AM	9:35 AM	1	
3						

Functions

In earlier chapters you gained some familiarity with statistical functions, database statistical functions, and lookup functions, and you just learned about date and time functions in this chapter. Excel has six other types of functions: financial, mathematical (including matrix and trigonometric), text, logical, informational, and command. These will be discussed in this chapter, but first look at how functions are used and created.

Using Functions

Functions are ready-made formulas. They perform a previously assigned task that usually involves a calculation but may also include a nonarithmetic operation. Functions always produce a result in the cell in which they are entered. For example, SUM produces a value that is the arithmetic addition of a set of numbers, and UPPER produces a text string that is all uppercase. Functions provide a faster alternative to standard ways of accomplishing many tasks. For example, using SUM(*reference*) is quicker than adding each individual cell in the reference if the reference contains three or more cells. Functions are also the only way some tasks can be accomplished. For example, using NOW or TODAY is the only way you can read your computer's clock-calendar with Excel.

Specifying Arguments

In order to perform their tasks, many functions require specific pieces of information (for example, the reference in the SUM(*reference*) function). These pieces of information are called arguments. The number of arguments in a function varies, and the length of all arguments in a function is limited to 255 characters, including any quotation marks.

Arguments can be numbers, text, arrays, references, and logical or error values, as outlined here.

10

♦ Numbers used as arguments in a function can be numerals, numeric formulas, or addresses or reference names for cells that contain numbers or numeric formulas.

♦ Text is any sequence of letters, numbers, spaces, or symbols. Text in a function can be literal text enclosed in quotation marks, a text formula, or an address or reference name for a cell that contains literal text or a text formula.

♦ An array is a rectangular set of values (a range) that is treated in a special way. An array is enclosed in braces, { }, and has a semicolon between rows. For example, the array {5,6,7;3,4,5;1,2,3} is a 3-by-3 array, with three rows that each contain three columns. Arrays used as arguments in a function can be entered directly, result from a formula that evaluates to an array, or be a set of addresses or a reference name for a reference that contains an array or a formula that evaluates to an array.

♦ References can be addresses, reference names, or any formula that evaluates to an address or reference name.

♦ A logical value is either True or False. You can enter **True** and **False** in either uppercase or lowercase letters, but Excel converts them to uppercase. In a function, logical values may be entered directly, result from a logical formula that evaluates to either True or False, or be in a cell referenced by an address or reference name. A logical formula is one that contains one of these logical operators:

–	Equal to
>	Greater than
<	Less than
>=	Greater than or equal to
<=	Less than or equal to
<>	Not equal to

♦ Error values include #DIV/0!, #N/A, #NAME?, #NULL!, #NUM!, #REF!, and #VALUE!. In a function, error values may be entered directly, result from a formula, or be contained in a cell referenced by an address or reference name. A brief meaning of each of the error values is given here:

#DIV/0!	You tried to divide by zero
#N/A	No values are available
#NAME?	Excel does not recognize a name
#NULL!	Two group of cells you expected to intersect do not
#NUM!	Excel has a problem with a number
#REF!	Excel cannot find a reference to a cell or group of cells
#VALUE!	You used the wrong type of operand or argument

Entering Functions

There are many different functions, but they all have the same structure, or syntax. A *syntax* is a set of rules for consistently doing something in an orderly manner—in this case, entering functions. The syntax for entering functions is as follows:

◆ Every function begins with the = symbol, unless it is inside a formula (that is, not the first element of the formula) or another function.

◆ Functions can be entered in either uppercase or lowercase letters. They are displayed in uppercase by Excel. If you type a function in lowercase letters and Excel does not change it to uppercase or displays an error value, you know that you misspelled the function name or made some other mistake.

◆ Spaces cannot occur anywhere in a function, except within a literal string enclosed in quotation marks or immediately after a comma between arguments.

◆ The arguments of a function must be enclosed in parentheses. If one or more functions are used as arguments for other functions, the parentheses must be nested, with complete left and right sets of parentheses for each function. Even functions that do not have arguments must have a set of parentheses. For example, NOW( ).

◆ Two or more arguments within a function are separated by commas. You should not have more commas than there are arguments or two arguments without a comma between them.

◆ Blank cells referenced in a function are assigned the value 0.

◆ Functions can be used by themselves as a formula or as a part of another formula, function, or macro command.

10

Functions may be directly entered by typing them in a cell, following the syntax just described, or you can have Excel build the formula using the Function Wizard. To do the latter, make the cell in which you want the function placed the active cell and then click on the Function Wizard tool in the Standard toolbar. The first Function Wizard dialog box opens, as shown here:

In the first Function Wizard dialog box, functions are listed alphabetically, within 11 categories that include All and Most Recently Used. You can use the scroll bar to select first a category and then a function, or you can type the first letter of a function to quickly jump closer to it. Once you have chosen a function, click on Next to open the second Function Wizard dialog box, like this:

The second Function Wizard dialog box lists all the arguments and provides an explanation of those that are not obvious. You can enter a value, a reference, or another function for each argument by typing the value or reference or by clicking on the Function Wizard tool next to the argument name. Arguments that are required are bold, and those that are optional are not. When you are done entering the arguments you want to use, click on Finish and the completed function is transferred to the sheet.

Additional Functions

The next several sections of this chapter discuss some of the functions that have not been discussed elsewhere. They fall into five groups: financial, mathematical, text, logical, and informational. Because there are so many, not all of the individual functions are covered here. The following sections contain tips and suggestions for each of the five groups, along with one or two examples of functions within each group.

Financial Functions

Financial functions such as the following calculate amounts used in financing, budgeting, and depreciation. Optional arguments to the functions are in square brackets.

FV(*rate,term,payments*[*,pv,type*])	Returns the future value, given a series of equal payments, the interest rate, and the term. Optionally, you can enter the present value and/or whether the payment is made at the end of the period (the default, *type* = 0) or at the beginning of the period (*type* = 1).
IRR(*reference*[*,guess*])	Returns the internal rate of return for a series of cash flows contained in the reference. A guess may speed up the calculation. If you don't enter a guess, Excel uses 10%.
NPV(*rate,reference*)	Returns the net present value of a series of cash flows contained in the reference at a given interest rate.
PMT(*rate,term,principal*[*,fv,type*])	Returns the payment required for a loan amount (principal) given the interest rate and loan term. Optionally, you can enter the future value and/or whether the payment is made at the end of the period (the default, *type* = 0) or at the beginning of the period (*type* = 1).

PV(*rate,term,payment*[*,fv,type*])	Returns the present value, given a series of equal payments, the term, and the interest rate. Optionally, you can enter the future value and/or whether the payment is made at the end of the period (the default, *type* = 0) or at the beginning of the period (*type* = 1).
SLN(*cost,salvage,life*)	Calculates depreciation expense for an asset using the straight-line depreciation method.

When you use financial functions, the term and interest rate must be in the same time units. For example, if you want a result in months, the term must be in months and the interest rate must be in months. (See the first example in the "Examples" section that follows.)

The interest rate can be entered in a financial function as either a decimal (.108) or a percent (10.8%). Also, in many financial functions you must distinguish between cash outflow, which should be a negative number, and cash inflow, which should be a positive number (see the examples that follow).

Where a series of payments is used in a function, the payments are assumed to be equal and paid regularly at the end of each period. This is known as an *ordinary annuity*. If you want to change the payment to the beginning of the period, use the optional *type* argument with a value of 1.

Examples   To calculate the prospective monthly mortgage payment on a $140,000 30-year loan at 7.8% interest, use the following function:

```
=PMT(.078/12,30*12,140000) returns -$1,007.82/month
```

To calculate the annual rate of interest necessary for a $10,000 investment to grow to $24,000 over 10 years with monthly compounding, use the following function:

```
=RATE(10*12,0,-10000,24000)*12 returns 8.79%/year
```

Mathematical Functions
Mathematical functions such as the following calculate general, matrix, and trigonometric values.

ABS(*x*)	Returns the absolute value of a number
ATAN(*x*)	Returns the arctangent of a number
MINVERSE(*array*)	Returns the inverse of a matrix or array
RAND( )	Returns a random number between 0 and 1
ROUND(*x,n*)	Rounds a number off to a specific number of decimal places
SIN(*x*)	Returns the sine of an angle
SQRT(*x*)	Calculates the square root of a number

Angles used as arguments for COS, SIN, and TAN must be expressed in radians. To convert degrees to radians, multiply the degrees by PI/180. The angles that results from ACOS, ASIN, ATAN, and ATAN2 are in radians. To convert radians to degrees, multiply the radians by 180/PI.

Example   To calculate the length of a guy wire that is supporting a 150-foot antenna when the guy wire, attached to the top, makes a 55-degree angle with the ground, use the following function:

```
=150/SIN(55*PI/180) returns 183.12 feet
```

Text Functions
Text functions convert, parse, and manipulate text strings. Some of the text functions are as follows.

CHAR(*x*)	Returns the ASCII character corresponding to the number x
EXACT(*string1,string2*)	Compares two text strings and returns True if the two strings are the same and False if they differ
LEN(*string*)	Returns the number of characters in a text string
MID(*string,start-number,n*)	Returns the specified number of characters from within a text string beginning at a specified position
PROPER(*string*)	Converts the first character in each word of a text string to uppercase and the rest of the characters to lowercase, as in a proper name

TEXT(x,*format*)	Converts a number to text with a given numeric format

10

The offset number used in string functions always begins at 1. The first character in a string is 1, and the last character is the length of the string. Blank cells in a string function are still considered text, have a length of 0, and do not return an error code.

Example   To convert the date 4/19/96 in A1 to a text string that can be used in a title, use the following function:

```
=TEXT(A1,"mmmm d, yyyy")
```

This function returns April 19, 1996, which is text, not a value.

Logical Functions
Logical functions such as the following perform tests to determine if a condition is true.

AND(*condition 1,condition 2,...*)	Returns True if all conditions or logical statements are true
IF(*condition,true-result,false-result*)	Evaluates an equation or condition for true or false and takes one action for a true result and another action for a false result
TRUE	Returns a logical True

Example   When you calculate percentages, there are situations that result in dividing by 0, which produces a #DIV/0! error. To replace a possible error value with 0 in the formula =E15/C15, use the following formula in its place:

```
=IF(ISERROR(E15/C15),0,E15/C15)
```

Informational Functions
Informational functions such as the following provide information about cells and areas of the workbook, including the number of rows or columns in a reference, the formatting of a cell, and whether a cell is blank, contains text, or is a logical value.

COLUMNS(*reference*)	Returns the number of columns in a reference

ISBLANK(*value*)	Returns the logical value True if the value or cell is blank
ISERROR(*expression*)	Returns a value indicating whether an expression is an error value
ISTEXT(*value*)	Returns the logical value True if the value or cell is text
ROW(*reference*)	Returns the row number (not the number of rows) of the first row in the reference or an array of row numbers for all of the rows in the reference

Example It is often helpful to know the column width of a cell. You can choose Column Width from the Format menu, or you can use the function CELL("width"). CELL("width") returns a value that is rounded to the nearest whole number. For example, =CELL("width") returns 8 for the standard cell width of 8.43.

Macros

A *macro* is a shortcut. It is a way of accomplishing a set of Excel commands with fewer steps and a way to automate or speed up repetitive procedures. A macro is also a way to guide a less knowledgeable user through a complicated workbook.

There are two kinds of macros in Excel. A *command macro* is a series of Excel commands, and a *function macro* is a custom function that returns a result. An example of a command macro is one that saves your workbook, while an example of a function macro is one that calculates your local sales tax. You can have Excel execute a command macro by pressing only two keys. A function macro is executed by putting it in a workbook cell and recalculating the workbook. Almost all commands that you can perform from the keyboard, the mouse, or a menu can be stored in a macro and can be activated as you choose. In addition to keyboard and menu commands, a set of *macro commands* lets you perform built-in programming functions, such as repeating a sequence or accepting input from the keyboard. With macro commands, you can build custom menus and automate a workbook. You can see that command macros, which are custom procedures that you create to perform some function, and macro commands, which are used in command macros and supply the programming capability, are distinct—although they can be easily confused.

10

Anything that you do on a repetitive basis is a candidate for a macro. You can even create a library of macros that you can use with many workbooks, a way of making macros even more useful.

There are two ways in Excel 7 to create macros: using Visual Basic and using the Excel 4 macro language. Visual Basic is the wave of the future and is covered in considerable detail in Chapters 12 and 13. There are many applications written for Excel that use Excel 4 macros. For the balance of this chapter you'll see how the Excel 4 macro language gives you the ability to create or modify many macros.

Excel 4 Macro Basics

You have seen earlier in this book that formatting a number is important, but if your preferred number format is not preassigned to a tool in the Formatting toolbar, it might require up to six mouse clicks (for example, the Format menu, the Cells option, the Number tab, the category, the type, and OK), 11 keystrokes (ALT-O, E, one or more arrow keys to select the tab, ALT-C and several arrow keys to select the category, ALT-F and several arrow keys to select the type, and ENTER), or even more mouse clicks or keystrokes for custom formatting. This is not a lot of effort, but when you repeat it several times a day, it begins to add up. If you could replace the actions with easy keystrokes like CTRL-E, a single option in the Tools menu, or, better yet, a single tool in a toolbar, it would make a difference. Applying your preferred number format, then, is a candidate for a macro.

Recording a Macro

Built into Excel is the capability to record whatever you are doing on an Excel sheet and to store those steps on a macro sheet. Once stored, you can "play back" the steps and repeat what you were doing. The steps that are stored on the macro sheet comprise the macro, and playing them back is called *running the macro*. You turn on the Excel macro recorder by choosing Record Macro from the Tools menu. Do that now and record a macro that formats a preselected area of a workbook with these instructions.

1. Choose New from the File menu and click on OK to open a new workbook.

2. From the Tools menu, point on Record Macro and then choose Record New Macro from the submenu that opens. The Record New Macro dialog box opens, as shown here:

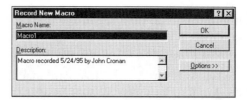

In this dialog box you can name the macro (which cannot contain spaces) and enter or edit a description. Here, you do want to name the macro, and you also need to enter some other options.

3. Type **Format_Number** in the Macro Name text box and then click on Options to open the rest of the dialog box, as shown here:

There are three ways you can store macros: in a special Personal Macro Workbook, on a macro sheet in the current workbook, or on a macro sheet in a new workbook. The Personal Macro Workbook is automatically opened each time you start Excel. This is generally the workbook to use for simple, frequently used utility macros because Excel will name, open, and save the workbook for you. If you use the current workbook, the macros are only available with it. If you create a new workbook, you will have to manually open it both to record to it and to run the macros once they are recorded, and you will have to save the workbook. Here, you will create and record a macro using the Personal Macro Workbook.

4. Click on Menu Item on Tools Menu and click in the text box under that and type **Format Number** to place the macro in the Tools menu.

5. Click on Shortcut Key and accept the CTRL-E that is shown. If you accept the keys that are shown, you will not use a shortcut key that is already assigned, as CTRL-A through CTRL-D are.

6. Click on Personal Macro Workbook in the Store in options group, click on MS Excel 4.0 Macro, and click on OK. The dialog box closes, and the Recording status message comes on in the Status bar.

10

The name of a macro can be any legitimate Excel name. It must start with a letter, can be up to 255 characters long, and can contain any combination of letters, numbers, and underscores. It should not look like a reference (either D3 or R3C4) and cannot contain spaces or punctuation marks. Since you cannot use spaces, underscores are used as word separators. An Excel name can be entered in either uppercase or lowercase letters—Excel does not distinguish between the two.

The shortcut key can be any single uppercase or lowercase letter. Uppercase and lowercase letters are considered two different characters and will not conflict with one another. You cannot use numbers as shortcut characters. If you use a shortcut key that has been previously assigned, you will be alerted to that fact, and you can choose whether to reassign the key. The shortcut keys you can possibly reassign include the ones like CTRL-C for copying and CTRL-S for saving. However, you want to think carefully about doing this.

7. Choose Cells from the Format menu and then click on Number. Select the Currency category, click on the Decimal Places spinner twice to indicate zero decimal places, ensure the Use $ check box is checked, choose the third Negative Numbers format, and click on OK. These are the steps you want to record.

8. Click on the Stop Recording tool in the little one-tool Stop Recording toolbar that looks like this:

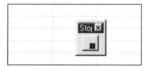

The Recording message disappears, as does the Stop Recording toolbar.

9. From the Window menu, choose Unhide. The Unhide dialog box opens, as shown here:

10. Double-click on PERSONAL.XLS. The Personal Macro Workbook that was automatically created in the previous steps becomes the active sheet, as shown here:

Personal.xls		
A	**B**	**C**
1 Format Number (e)		
2 =FORMAT.NUMBER(		
3 =RETURN()		
4		
5		

The Personal Macro Workbook looks just like a normal sheet except that the columns look a little wider. The macro itself is in the upper-left corner, in cells A1:A3. A1 contains the name and shortcut key you gave the macro. A2 and A3 are the macro commands that format the selected cells and return control to you. Macro commands are formulas—they always begin with an equal sign (=). A macro sheet always displays formulas, not the results they produce. Displaying formulas is an option on a normal sheet, but normally a sheet displays the results a formula produces. You can use the View tab in the Options dialog box reached from the Tools menu to turn off the formulas display on a macro sheet, but the resulting values are generally not informative. In this case, your macro commands in rows 2 and 3 are replaced with the word "FALSE."

When you are displaying formulas instead of their results, their placement on the sheet is left-aligned and cannot be changed with the Format alignment option. Otherwise, all formatting works on a macro sheet as it does on a sheet.

Documenting a Macro

As you create macros, you may find that after a while you forget what they do. Also, you may want to give one or more macros to someone else, who will need to know what the macros do. For this reason, you must document your macros when you create them.

You can document a macro in several ways. You have used a form of documentation already—giving the macro a descriptive name. Other ways include formatting the macro name on the Personal Macro Workbook so it stands out, adding one or more cell notes, and, most importantly, adding some comments beside the macro commands. Add some comments and format the macro name with these steps.

1. With A1 as the active cell, click on the Bold button in the Standard toolbar. The macro name should be made bold.

2. Click on B1, type **Formats selection**, press DOWN ARROW, type **$ format w/no decimals**, and press ENTER. After widening columns A and B, the upper-left corner of your macro sheet now looks like this:

	A	B	C
	Personal.xls		
1	Format_Number (e)	Formats selection	
2	=FORMAT.NUMBER("$#,##0_);($#,##0)")	$ format w/no decimals	
3	=RETURN()		
4			
5			

10

Running a Macro

Now that you have a finished and documented macro, you can run it in one of three ways. First and most simply, you can press CTRL-E, the shortcut key. Second, the Macro dialog box, reached by choosing Macro from the Tools menu, lists all the macros available on open macro sheets, so you can select the macro you want and click on OK. Third, the Tools menu now contains a new option named Format Number that you can choose. Try all of these methods using the following instructions.

1. From the Window menu, choose Book1 (or whichever new workbook you are using), type several numbers to format and make one of them negative, use the AutoFill handle to copy those numbers to four more rows so you have five sets of numbers, and then select the first set of numbers.

2. Press CTRL-E. The numbers are formatted.

3. Select the second set of numbers. Then, from the Tools menu, choose Macro. The Macro dialog box opens, as shown here:

The Macro dialog box lists the macro you have just created. By clicking on the entry in the list box and then on Run, you can run the macro. You can also just double-click on the entry.

4. Double-click on the entry. The second set of numbers is formatted.

5. Select the third set of numbers. Then, open the Tools menu. Notice a new option appears at the bottom of the menu, like this:

6. Click on Format Number and the third set of numbers is formatted.

   If you had any fears about macros, you can now set them aside. You have successfully created and run a macro!

7. Activate the Personal Macro Workbook by choosing it from the Window menu.

8. Close the Personal Macro Workbook by choosing Hide from the Window menu. When you exit Excel, a dialog box will ask if you want to save changes to the Personal Macro Workbook; click on Yes and the Personal Macro Workbook will be hidden, but working, in future Excel sessions.

If you exit Excel without both hiding the Personal Macro Workbook again and choosing Yes to save the changes to it, the Personal Macro Workbook will appear every time you start Excel until you choose to hide it and to save the changes on exiting.

Attaching a Macro to a Tool on a Toolbar

There is one more way to run a macro and that is to attach it to a tool on a toolbar. The tool can be either a custom tool that is not currently assigned to a function or an existing tool that has a built-in function it performs. For example, the Currency Style tool on the Formatting toolbar has a slightly different format from the one you choose in the macro. Assume that most of your currency formatting will be the new format, so you want to attach your macro to the Currency Style tool (you can easily reset it back to its original format). See how that is done with these steps.

1. Select the fourth set of numbers and click on the Currency tool in the Formatting toolbar. The numbers are formatted with the built-in format. If necessary, widen the columns to view the formatted numbers.

2. Click the right mouse button on a toolbar to open the Toolbar popup menu and choose Customize.

3. Click on the Currency Style tool on the Formatting toolbar to select it.

4. From the Tools menu, choose Assign Macro. The Assign Macro dialog box opens as shown here:

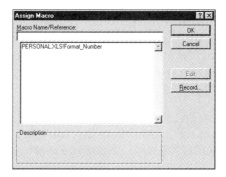

5. Double-click on the Format_Number macro and click on Close in the Customize dialog box.

6. Select the fifth set of numbers and click on the Currency Style tool. The numbers are once more formatted like this:

	A	B	C	D
1	$34,568	($87,654)	$53,479	
2	$34,568	($87,654)	$53,479	
3	$34,568	($87,654)	$53,479	
4	34,568.00	(07,054.00)	50,470.00	
5	$34,568	($87,654)	$53,479	
6				
7				

Attaching macros to tools is one of the most powerful features in Excel. By doing this, you can customize the toolbars to your needs. You can reset the tool to which you attached the macro in two ways: one restores just one tool to its original function, and the other resets all tools to their original function and tool face. If you want to reset all the tools, choose Toolbars from either the View menu or the Toolbar popup menu and click on Reset. If you want to restore just one tool to its original function, use these steps.

1. From the Toolbars popup menu, choose Customize.

2. Drag the tool to which you assigned the macro (Currency Style in this case) off the top of the screen.

3. From the Customize dialog box, select the category from which you want to select a tool (Formatting here) and then drag the tool you want from the Customize dialog box to the same position on the toolbar to which it belongs. The function of the tool will be restored.

Creating Additional Macros

Create several more simple and general-purpose macros. This time, however, watch the macros being built by reducing the size of the workbook you are working on and exposing most of the macro sheet, as shown in Figure 10-8. Do that with these steps.

1. Choose Unhide from the Window menu. The Unhide dialog box appears. Highlight PERSONAL.XLS, click on OK, and the file is opened.

2. Using the Window menu, toggle between the two documents, arrange and then size Book1 by dragging the upper-left corner of the Book1 window to reduce it to approximately the size shown in Figure 10-8.

When you create a second macro, Excel places it in A1 of a new macro sheet, unless you tell Excel otherwise (you'll see how in a minute). Since you have used Macro1, the next macro you create is placed in Macro2.

Move Macro

Assume that you have a number of entries on an Excel sheet that you want to move to the right by three columns. These entries are not all in one column so you can't easily move them together, you can't simply delete and insert columns to make it happen, and dragging won't work. There are enough cut and paste operations to make it worth a macro. To accomplish

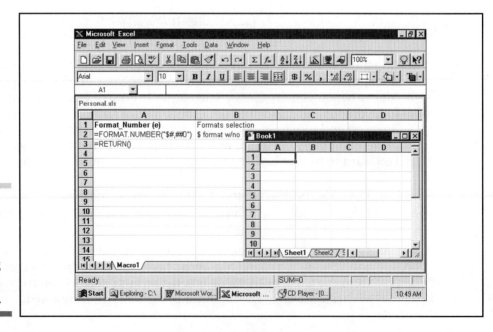

A small workbook window for watching macros being built

Figure 10-8.

this task quickly, make sure that Book1 is the active book and then record a macro to handle it, with these instructions.

1. From the Tools menu, point on Record Macro, then choose Record New Macro, type **Move_Selection**, click on Options, click on Shortcut Key, accept the suggested CTRL-H, click on Personal Macro Workbook, click on MS Excel 4.0 Macro, and click on OK. The Recording message comes on in the Status bar, and the name and shortcut key appear in C1 on the macro sheet.

2. Click once on PERSONAL.XLS to make it active and then on the Macro2 sheet to see the macro being developed. Choose Book1 from the Window menu to return your screen to the arrangement shown in Figure 10-9.

   Don't be concerned about the additional activation and selection commands that appear in the macro, you will remove them shortly.

   If you cannot see the Move_Selection macro name on Macro2, it is probably because you did not click on Personal Macro Workbook in step 1. It could also be that you did not set up your screen as described in the previous section. In either case, stop the macro recording by clicking on the Stop Recording tool, exit Excel *without* saving either the Personal Macro Workbook or Book1, restart Excel, set up your screen as shown in the previous section, and repeat step 1.

Move macro added to the macro sheet

Figure 10-9.

3. Press CTRL-X to cut the current selection to the Clipboard. The blinking marquee appears around A1 (or whatever cell you are pointing at) in Book1. The macro command =CUT( ) appears in A2 on the macro sheet.

4. Click three columns to the right in Book1 (D1 if you started in A1) and press ENTER to complete the steps you want to record. The macro commands =SELECT("R1C4") and =PASTE( ) appear in A3 and A4 on the macro sheet.

5. Click on the Stop Recording tool. The macro command =RETURN( ) appears in A5 on the macro sheet.

6. Select A2:A4, right-click on the selection to open the popup menu, choose Delete, and accept the default option of Shift Cells Up. Click on OK. Your screen should look like that shown in Figure 10-9.

7. Click on cell A1 in the macro sheet. Click on the Bold tool in the Formatting toolbar.

8. Click on B1, type **Copies selection**, and press ENTER. Your second macro is documented. Next, try it out.

9. From the Window menu, choose Book1. Type something in A4, press ENTER and press CTRL-H. What you typed in A4 has moved to D1.

   The concept for this macro was to move the contents of the selected cells to the right three columns. In other words, move the contents of A4 to D4, not D1 as just happened. You therefore have a problem.

   The reason for this is that the =SELECT macro command gave you an absolute reference ("R1C4"). The R1C4 stands for "row 1, column 4" and is the same as $D$1. If you want a relative reference, as you do when moving an active cell relative to its current position, place [ ] around the numbers. For example, =SELECT("RC[3]") moves the active cell three columns to the right without changing the row and =SELECT("R[-2]C[2]") moves the active cell up two rows and to the right two columns. If you want all your recorded references to be relative addresses, you can choose the Use Relative References suboption from the Record option of the Tools menu.

10. Click on Macro2 to activate it and then double-click on A3. Change R1C4 to RC[3] and press ENTER.

11. From the Window menu, choose Book1. Type something in A4, press ENTER, and press CTRL-H. Now, what you type in A4 is moved to D4, as shown in Figure 10-10 and as you wanted.

These steps of trying out and correcting a macro are called *debugging*—the trial and error process of correcting problems in a macro.

Setting a Recording Area

Your next macro would be placed on Macro3, unless you tell Excel otherwise. Since that is unnecessary, tell Excel you want it to begin in A8. You do that by clicking on this starting cell (A8 in Macro2), choosing the Mark Position for Recording suboption under Record Macro on the Tools menu, and then using the Record at Mark suboption from the regular sheet for the actual recording.

If you select a single cell in which to start the macro, Excel fills as many cells below that cell in the same column as necessary to complete the macro. If the macro reaches the bottom of the column, Excel redirects the macro to the top of the next vacant column with a GOTO macro command and then continues the macro in the next column. If you select a single cell and the single cell is not blank, Excel finds the last nonblank cell in the column and begins recording immediately below it. If the last nonblank cell has the RETURN macro command in it, RETURN is replaced by the first macro command of the new macro. In this way you can stop recording a macro and then later restart where you left off.

If you select an area in which to record a macro, the area becomes the limits within which the macro is contained. Excel starts the macro in the upper-left corner and continues to the lower-right corner, placing GOTO functions at the bottom of each column. If Excel reaches the limits of the area without completing the macro, you get a message that the area is full. Unlike when

The results
of the
Move_Selection
macro

Figure 10-10.

selecting a single cell, if you select an area and the upper-left cell in the area is not blank, Excel displays a message saying the area is full and cannot be used.

Set the starting cell for recording the next macro with these instructions.

1. Click on A8 of the macro sheet.
2. Point on Record Macro from the Tools menu and click on Mark Position for Recording.
3. Choose Book1 from the Window menu to return to your regular sheet.

Once you have set where you want to place your next macro, you must start the macro with the Record at Mark suboption of the Record Macro option of the Tools menu. Record at Mark, though, is meant to be used for adding to the last macro you have entered. Record at Mark does not ask you to name or enter a shortcut key for a macro. You can use it only if you have already used Record New Macro within an Excel session (after your most recent starting of Excel) or if you have used Mark Position for Recording to establish a starting cell. If you have started a macro with Record New Macro, you can use Stop Recording to quit macro recording and then restart with Record at Mark as if you had never quit; you need not use Mark Position for Recording.

Percentage Macro

The custom percent format 0.0% deserves a macro for quick use. Build it next and give it the shortcut key CTRL-J.

1. Point on Record Macro from the Tools menu and click on Record at Mark.
2. Choose Cells from the Format menu, click on the Number tab, click on Percentage, click on the Decimal Places spinner to indicated one decimal place, and click on OK.
3. Click on the Stop Recording tool to complete the macro. Click anywhere on Macro2 to activate it and widen column A to 20. Your macro sheet should look like this:

7	
8	=FORMAT.NUMBER("0.0%")
9	=RETURN()
10	
11	

You can see your new macro does not have a title or shortcut key as it should. Supply these next.

4. Click on cell A7, type **Percent_Format (j)**, press ENTER, and make it bold.

5. Open the Insert menu, point on Name, and then click on Define to open the Define Name dialog box shown here:

6. Drag across the __j in the Names in Workbook text box and press DEL. Click on Command under Macro, type **j** in the Key text box, and click on OK. Your percentage macro is defined.

   If you ever want to delete an Excel 4 macro, you must do it from the Define Name dialog box. You cannot do it from the Macro dialog box. The Delete button in the Macro dialog box works only with Visual Basic macros.

7. Click B7 in the macro sheet, type **0.0% Format**, and press ENTER to document the macro. Now try it out.

8. Click on Book1 in the Window menu, type a decimal number (**.345**) in A1, press ENTER, and press CTRL-J to format it. Your screen should look like Figure 10-11.

Date/Time Stamp Macro

You will often want to add the date and/or time to a sheet. To do so manually, you must type **=NOW( )**, format the cell, and then use Copy and Paste Special to convert the function to a permanent value that does not change every time the sheet is recalculated. It is easier to look at your watch or calendar and type the numbers as text so they do not have to be formatted. A macro takes this process down to two keystrokes that format the cell, enter the function, and convert it to a value. Create the macro following these steps.

1. Click on A3 in Book1 to make it the active cell.

2. Point on Record Macro from the Tools menu, click on Record New Macro, type **Date_Time_Stamp**, click on Options and Shortcut Key, accept K as the shortcut key, click on Personal Macro Workbook, click on MS Excel 4.0 Macro, and click on OK. The name appears in C1 of the

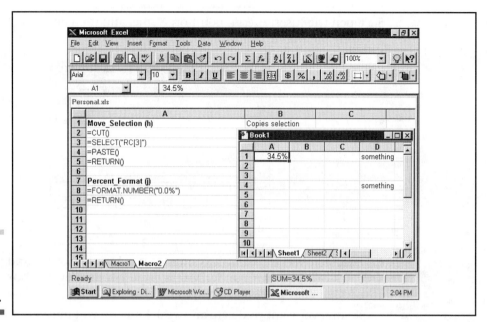

Percentage
macro and its
results
Figure 10-11.

macro sheet. Since you have used the Mark Position for Recording option, new macros are placed on the current macro sheet in the next available column to the right.

3. Type **=now()** and press ENTER. The date and time appear and are automatically formatted the way you want them.

4. Widen column A of the sheet by dragging on the intersection between columns A and B until column A is about half-again as large.

5. Click on the Copy tool, choose Paste Special from the Edit menu, click on Values and OK, and press ESC. The =NOW( ) formula is converted to a value and the copy marquee removed.

6. Click on the Stop Recording tool. Click on the Macro2 sheet, widen column C so you can see all of the macro, and make that column the leftmost one in the window. Then make the macro name bold and document your macro as shown in Figure 10-12.

7. Choose Book1 from the Window menu, click on B3, and press CTRL-K.

   The date and time are placed in B3, but the column is not widened. Go back to the macro sheet and see why.

8. Click on the macro sheet and click on C3, which contains the COLUMN.WIDTH macro command.

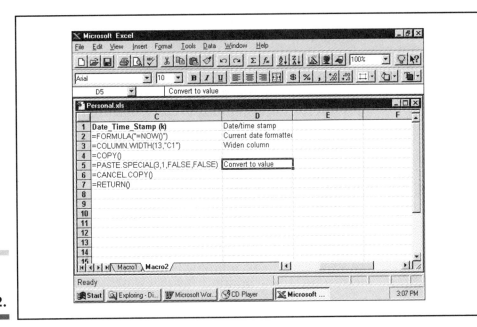

The COLUMN.WIDTH macro command has two arguments: the width
itself (your width may be different due to variations in dragging), and
an optional reference to the column to be widened. The reference
shown here, C1, does not mean column C, row 1, but rather "column
1." This is the problem. To make the Date/Time Stamp macro flexible,
you need to remove the column reference. Then the COLUMN.WIDTH
macro command will refer to the current selection, which is what you
want. If your width value is a number with many decimal places, edit
by rounding it to an even 14.

9. Edit C3 so that it contains =COLUMN.WIDTH(14).

10. Return to Book1 and try the macro again in C5. It now works the way it
should, as you can see in Figure 10-13.

Entering Macros

All the macros you have created so far have been recorded. You modified
two of the recorded macros to give you what you want. You can also directly
type in a macro. You can either use an existing macro sheet or create a new
one. You simply pick an area on the macro sheet and start typing the
necessary macro commands. Doing this, of course, takes some familiarity
with the macro commands and their arguments. Once you have written the
macro, you can name it with the Name Define option on the Insert menu.
Try that next by writing a macro to apply the #,##0 format. You can use the
Percent macro as a model.

1. Click on Macro2 and on C11. Type **Comma_Format (l)** and press DOWN ARROW.

2. Type **=format.number("#,##0")**, press DOWN ARROW, type **=return()**, and press UP ARROW twice.

3. Choose Name from the Insert menu, click on Define, drag across the __l and press DEL, click on Command as the macro type, press TAB, type **l** as the shortcut key, and click on OK.

4. Format the name on the macro sheet to make it bold, and enter the documentation as shown here:

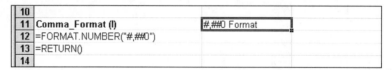

10		
11	**Comma_Format (l)**	#,##0 Format
12	=FORMAT.NUMBER("#,##0")	
13	=RETURN()	
14		

5. Try out the macro by returning to the Book1 sheet, typing **62503.60**, pressing ENTER, and pressing CTRL-L. It works!

You can see that while you can type in a macro, it is much easier to use the recorder. Even if you need to do some heavy modification, building an initial structure with the recorder is a substantial benefit. It not only saves time, but it also gives you the correct macro command name and argument set and saves you from having to look either of these up.

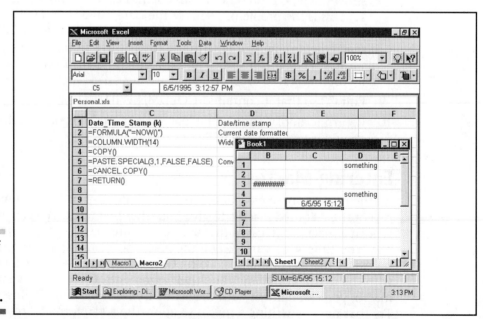

Final results of the Date/Time Stamp

Figure 10-13.

10

Rules for Macro Entry

All parts of a macro can be typed in either uppercase or lowercase. Excel converts it to uppercase if it is spelled correctly. A macro can occupy as many cells in a column as necessary. You can use both sheet functions and macro commands. Placing one function or command per cell makes the macros easier to read on the screen and easier to edit. As Excel is executing a macro and completing the instructions in one cell, it automatically goes to the cell immediately below and continues macro execution. Excel continues down a column in this manner until it reaches a terminating or redirecting macro command such as RETURN, GOTO, or HALT. During macro execution, Excel ignores a blank cell.

If a macro refers to one or more cells, it is better to name the reference than to use addresses. An address in a macro is not updated if the sheet is changed. A reference name, on the other hand, continues to track an address through changes in the workbook. Also, if you are working with multiple files, it is a good idea to precede a reference name with the filename in square brackets ([*filename*]).

Debugging Macros

When a macro does not behave the way you expect, you need to *debug* it, or correct it. Debugging can be as simple as correcting an obvious spelling error in a reference name. In many instances, however, the error is not so obvious, as with the COLUMN.NUMBER problem in the Date/Time Stamp macro.

Debugging begins by looking carefully at what happened when the macro was run. Were there any error messages, and what did they say? What happened on the sheet? Do you get the same result each time you run the macro?

Next, look at the macro itself. Are there any misspellings? Are there missing arguments, periods, or macro commands? If you recorded the macro, did the recorder supply some arguments you do not want? Did you use absolute addressing when you wanted relative, or vice versa? Have you defined the reference and macro names you are using?

Finally, go back and record the macro again to see if you get the same macro commands a second time. Carefully note all of your actions while you are recording the macro.

In most instances these steps identify the problem. If not, there is one further thing that can be done. You can use the Step command in the Macro dialog box to execute a macro one step (one macro command) at a time. Excel pauses after each step so you can see the effects of that step, and continues only when you give the command to do so. The Step command also allows you to permanently halt the macro after any step, so you can more fully explore the partial results of a macro.

Try the Step command now by clicking on Book1, if necessary, and choosing the DATE.TIME.STAMP macro from the Macro dialog box. Click on Step and the Single Step dialog box appears like this:

Arrange your screen so you can see both the Single Step dialog box and Book1. Keep clicking on Step Into to see the macro execute one step at a time.

Macro Commands

A macro command, when executed, performs a predefined function that may be available from the keyboard, the menus, or the mouse. Some macro commands, however, are for purposes of further automating a process and are not available in any other form. These macro commands cause the macro to accept input from the user, wait while the user does something, make a choice among several things, or loop through a set of macro commands multiple times. These are programming macro commands, which, due to the advent of Visual Basic, are replaced by it and discussed in Chapters 12 and 13.

Macro commands have a common syntax that must be followed in order for Excel to understand what to do. This syntax is exactly the same as that for sheet functions described earlier in this chapter.

Function Macros

Function macros are custom functions you create on a macro sheet and then use on a regular sheet to return a value or other result. You can distinguish function macros from command macros in two ways. First, command macros take some action like formatting, copying, or saving. Function macros take no action, but rather produce a result, as you might get from a calculation. Second, a command macro is wholly contained on the macro sheet and is executed with the shortcut key or the Macro option on the Tools menu. A function macro is created on a macro sheet, but to use it you must enter the resulting function on a regular sheet.

Function macros are generally calculations you have to perform over and over. They have arguments through which you supply values, and they use formulas and regular functions to calculate a result based on the values you supply. When you build a function macro, you must use three special macro commands that handle the arguments and the result. These commands, in the order in which they must be used, are described in the final three sections of the chapter.

RESULT

The RESULT command is used only if you need to change the data type of the result. The RESULT command has one argument, the data type number. If you have not used a RESULT command to change it, the data type is assumed to be a number, text, or a logical value. The possible data type numbers are listed here:

1	Number
2	Text
4	Logical
8	Reference
16	Error
64	Array

Data type numbers can be added together, except for the reference and array types. For example, the default of number, text, or logical is a type 7 (1+2+4) and the default RESULT command looks like this:

```
=RESULT(7)
```

ARGUMENT

You must have one ARGUMENT command for each argument in the function macro you are building, and the arguments must be in the order in which they are presented in the function macro. The ARGUMENT command can have up to three arguments of its own: a name, a data type, and a reference. You must have either a name or a reference. Whichever you specify, the other is optional. The data type is always optional. The name must be a legitimate Excel name and becomes defined by the ARGUMENT command. It can then be used by the formulas and regular functions that follow. If you do not specify a data type, Excel assumes it to be a number, text, or a logical value. If the value received by the ARGUMENT command is not a default type and you have not used the data type argument to change that, you will get a #VALUE! error. The reference argument is a reference to a cell or cells on the macro sheet where the value received by the ARGUMENT command is placed. If you use both a name and a reference, the reference is given the name and can be referred to by it. A typical ARGUMENT command with a name and a data type looks like this:

```
=ARGUMENT("amount",1)
```

RETURN

All function macros must end with the RETURN command. The RETURN command has one argument in a function macro—the cell on the macro sheet that contains the result.

The formulas and regular functions to be used in a function macro must be placed after the last ARGUMENT command and before the RETURN command. Any formulas and regular functions must result in a value being placed in a single cell that is referred to by the RETURN command. A typical RETURN command looks like this:

```
=RETURN(A9)
```

Function macros must be directly entered—they cannot be recorded. Build an example to see how they work. The example, call it Tax, calculates sales tax. It has two arguments: the amount on which to calculate the tax, and the tax rate. Enter the tax function macro on the open macro sheet in A6.

1. Click on the macro sheet and in A6. Type **Tax** and press ENTER. Format it as bold.

2. From the Insert menu, point on Name, and click on Define. Click on Function at the bottom and on OK.

3. Click on cell A7. Then type **=argument("amount",1)**, press DOWN ARROW, and then type **=argument("rate",1)**. Press DOWN ARROW again.

4. Type **=amount*rate**, press DOWN ARROW, type **=return(a9)**, and press ENTER.

5. Click on Book1 in the Window menu, then click on A5.

6. Click on the Function Wizard, and the first Function Wizard dialog box will open.

7. Scroll the Function Category list box and click on User Defined. The name you want, PERSONAL.XLS!Tax, is already selected, so click on Next. The second Function Wizard dialog box will open.

8. Type **100**, press TAB, type **8.1%**, and press ENTER.

The result, 8.1, appears in A5 in Book1, as shown in Figure 10-14. If an argument is missing when a function macro is used, the ARGUMENT command for that argument passes a value of #N/A to the formulas and functions that follow. To allow for optional arguments, you must trap the #N/A with an IF(ISNA( )) function. For example, if you want to include a default 8.1% rate and make the entry or a tax rate optional in the function macro you just built, you must change the formula in A9 to:

```
=amount*IF(ISNA(rate),8.1%,rate)
```

This way, if the rate is not entered, 8.1% would be used.

As you are going back and forth between the macro sheet and a regular sheet, be aware that the regular sheet is not recalculated by simply activating it. You must either make an entry to or edit a cell, or press F9, the Calculate Now key.

Depending on who is going to use your macros, especially function macros, you must consider their error-handling capability. If you are the only one who will be using the macros, they can probably be fairly insensitive to errors. If novice Excel users are going to handle them, the function macros must work with many different error conditions. You are now in the position of many programmers, whose hardest job is probably to figure out all the ways someone can use their programs. A basic ground rule is that if it can happen, it will, and if it cannot happen, it might anyway. Chapters 12 and 13 deal with writing macros in Visual Basic to automate a workbook so

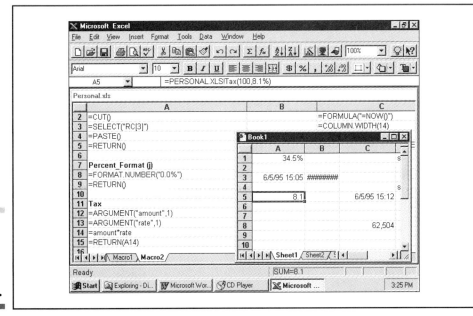

Function macro for calculating sales tax

Figure 10-14.

a novice can use it (and they do *not* consider every possible error that could occur!).

You are now left with a number of open sheets. Only the macro sheets have potential value. Save them, if you want, and tell Excel you do not want to save the other sheets. Exit both Excel and Windows.

Solver and Other Analysis Tools

11

One of the real powers of an electronic spreadsheet is the ability to change a number and have that change almost instantly reflected in all related numbers. This makes it possible to quickly look at many alternatives for a given situation. Keeping track of the alternatives and finding the "best" one, though, can still be a difficult job. Excel provides several tools to make such an analysis easier for you. These tools can help you quickly cycle through and organize different sets of values or scenarios. They can also help you determine what values will achieve a certain result. These tools are as follows.

♦ *Goal Seek,* which finds a solution for a formula by changing a single variable.

♦ *Scenario Manager,* which keeps track of different sets of values for you.

♦ *Solver,* which finds a solution for a formula by changing multiple variables, and allows you to set constraints on the variables. Solver also allows you to create several reports.

These tools will help you answer such questions as: How much money should I spend on advertising in order to maximize profit? If I only have a certain amount of dollars to spend on advertising, how should I allocate that money on a monthly basis in order to get the biggest return? What if the monthly growth ratios are different? How will that difference affect sales and income? Each of these tools will be discussed in the following sections.

Preparing for Analysis

Before you can use Excel's analysis tools, you need to set up a workbook on which the tools will operate. The workbook should contain formulas that express a situation. Make your workbook as easy to use and as understandable as possible. Write clear formulas and use a simple layout. It is helpful to name variables so they are easy to identify.

The workbook that you created in Chapters 5 and 6 can be used after you make a few modifications. You will change the formula for the monthly sales of forms to be dependent on advertising expense and a monthly growth ratio. It is important to have the cells that you are defining as variables related, either indirectly or directly through formulas, to the cell or cells for which you are trying to find values. Without this relationship, the analysis tools will not work.

1. Open the workbook QTR3BUD.XLS. Your screen should look like Figure 11-1. (You may need to scroll up the screen before you see the same rows.)

11

Beginning
workbook
using
QTR3BUD.XLS
Figure 11-1.

[Excel screenshot: Microsoft Excel - Qtr3bud.xls]

	A	B	C	D	E	F	G
1		5TH AVENUE STORE - THIRD QUARTER BUDGET					
2							
3	Revenue Growth/Mo.		1.2%				
4	C O S Growth/Mo.		1.3%				
5	Expense Growth/Mo.		1.0%				
6							
7		Second				Third	Percent
8		Quarter	July	August	Sept.	Quarter	Growth
10	REVENUE						
11	Forms	87,000	29,348	29,700	30,057	89,105	2.4%
12	Supplies	147,300	49,689	50,285	50,889	150,864	2.4%
13							
14	Total Revenue	$234,300	$79,037	$79,986	$80,945	$239,968	2.4%
15							
16	COST OF SALES	135,894	45,887	46,483	47,088	139,458	2.6%
17							

2. Click on C11. Type the formula **=290*(C3 * 100)*(C23 + 3000)^0.5** and press ENTER. This formula relates sales of forms (C11) to a monthly growth ratio (C3) and advertising expense (C23). You will change C23 to represent advertising shortly.

3. Select the range C11:E11.

4. Choose Fill from the Edit menu and then Right from the submenu. Cells D11 and E11 will change to zero. You will fix that next.

5. Click on D3. Type **1.4%** and press RIGHT ARROW. You are entering a monthly growth ratio for August.

6. Type **1.2%** and press ENTER. This is the monthly growth ratio for September.

7. Select D3:E3. Format as 0.0% by clicking on the Decrease Decimal tool in the Formatting toolbar.

8. Scroll your screen and click on A23. Indent (press SPACEBAR four times), type **Advertising**, and press ENTER.

9. Click on C23. Type **5000** as the beginning advertising value. Press ENTER.

10. Select C23:E23. Choose Fill from the Edit menu and Right from the submenu.

11. Click on the File menu and the Save As option.

	A	B	C	D	E	F	G	H
10	REVENUE							
11	Forms	87,000	31,126˙	36,314	31,126	98,566	13.3%	
12	Supplies	147,300	49,689	50,285	50,889	150,864	2.4%	
13								
14	Total Revenue	$234,300	$80,815	$86,599	$82,015	$249,429	6.5%	
15								
16	COST OF SALES	135,894	45,887	46,483	47,088	139,458	2.6%	
17								
18	GROSS INCOME	$98,406	$34,928	$40,116	$34,927	$109,971	11.8%	
19								
20	EXPENSES							
21	Salaries	24,450	8,232	8,314	8,397	24,942	2.0%	
22	P/R Taxes	2,322	782	790	797	2,369	2.0%	
23	Advertising	14,760	5,000	5,000	5,000	15,000	1.6%	
24								
25	Total Expenses	$41,532	$14,013	$14,103	$14,194	$42,311	1.9%	

Workbook
prepared for
analysis
Figure 11-2.

12. Type **SOLVEREX** in the File name box and press ENTER. If necessary, press ENTER again to bypass the Properties dialog box.

Your workbook should now look like Figure 11-2. Now that you have prepared your workbook, with cells related through formulas, you are ready to explore Excel's analysis tools.

Goal Seek

Goal Seek is one of Excel's simplest analysis tools. When you want a formula to equal a particular value, you specify a cell on which the formula is dependent; Goal Seek varies the value of that cell until the formula is the value you want. Goal Seek is useful when you want to solve a formula dependent on one variable. To see how Goal Seek works, use the workbook you just prepared to find out how much you need to spend on advertising in order to sell $40,000 worth of forms in July. In this case, the variable is cell C23 (advertising expense for July), and the formula we want to equal $40,000 is in cell C11 (sales of forms for July).

If you haven't already, scroll your workbook so you can see cells C11 and C23 simultaneously. Notice that C11 (sales of forms for July) contains the value 31,126. Notice also that C23 (advertising for July) contains the value 5,000.

1. Click on cell C11.

2. Open the Tools menu and choose the Goal Seek option. The Goal Seek dialog box opens, as shown in the following illustration. Set cell is automatically $C$11 because C11 is the active cell on the current sheet.

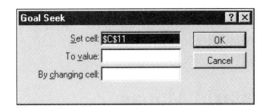

3. Press TAB and type **40,000** in the To value box.

4. Press TAB and type **C23** (advertising for July) in the By changing cell box. Click on OK.

5. If necessary, move the Goal Seek Status dialog box so that you can see both C11 and C23.

   Notice that C11 now contains the value 40,000, and cell C23 now contains 10,212, as seen in Figure 11-3. You now know that you would have to spend $10,212 on advertising in July to increase your sales of forms to $40,000 (assuming that the formula is valid!).

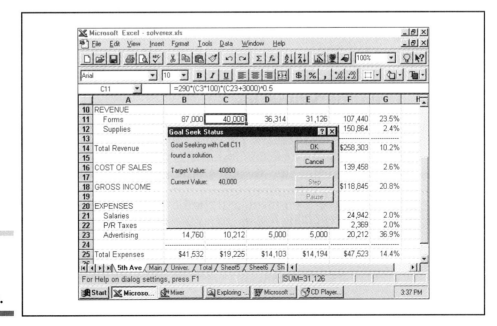

Workbook after Goal Seek

Figure 11-3.

6. Click on the Cancel button to restore values to what they were before. If you click on OK, the new values are saved in your workbook. If you choose OK by accident, and you want to restore your old values, immediately choose Undo Goal Seek from the Edit menu.

Goal Seek is useful if you want to know what a single value needs to be in order to cause a single formula to result in a particular value. Solver, discussed later in this chapter, is useful if you want to solve a problem with multiple variables.

Scenario Manager

Scenario Manager allows you to store different values for variables in your workbook. With Scenario Manager, you must explicitly enter all *sets* (specific combinations) of values you want to represent. Each combination or set of values is a *scenario*. You can have as many different scenarios for your workbook as you like. Each scenario is named and is a convenient way to organize your sets of values. Once you have entered all the scenarios in your workbook, you can print a report that compares the different scenarios by listing all the sets of input values and any affected cells you would like to appear on the report. With this report, you can easily compare the various scenarios you are analyzing. In summary, Scenario Manager allows you to

♦ Name and store as many scenarios as you like

♦ View existing scenarios

♦ Modify existing scenarios

♦ Delete scenarios

♦ Create a summary report of the different scenarios

Creating Scenarios

First, you'll want to create several scenarios in your workbook. You must explicitly enter a scenario for every combination of input values you want to examine. Make sure SOLVEREX.XLS is your active workbook and C3 your active cell, then follow these steps to create three new scenarios.

1. Open the Tools menu and choose the Scenarios option. The Scenario Manager dialog box opens, as shown here:

2. Click on Add. The Add Scenario dialog box opens:

3. In the Scenario Name box, type **Scenario1**.

4. In the Changing Cells box, type **C3:E3**. Click on OK.

    The Scenario Values dialog box will be displayed, where you identify the values of the changing cells, as shown here:

You want to retain the default values for this first scenario.

11

5. Click on Add. The first scenario is stored. Now you can add other scenarios in the same way. You will repeat filling in the name and changing the value for each scenario.

6. For the second scenario, type **Scenario2** in the Scenario Name box. The cells are correctly identified—no change is needed. Click on OK.

7. Type **0.011** in the $C$3 box and click on Add.

8. Type **Scenario3** in the Scenario Name box. Click on OK.

9. Type **0.015** in the $D$3 box and click on OK. The Scenario Manager dialog box reappears with the new scenarios that you just defined listed in the Scenarios list box, like this:

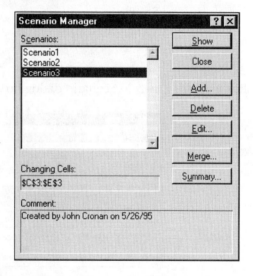

Viewing Existing Scenarios

You just added three scenarios. You can view the different scenarios by choosing the Show option in the Scenario Manager dialog box. When you show a scenario, Scenario Manager substitutes the values associated with that scenario into the variables in your workbook. Any cells containing formulas dependent on those variables are updated to new values. Follow these steps to see how this works.

1. Click on Scenario2, then click on the Show button.

   Watch how the values you assigned to the three variables in Scenario2 affect your workbook. You may need to move the dialog box. Now look at a different scenario.

2. Click on Scenario1, then click on Show. Examine the results in your workbook.

3. Click on Scenario3, then click on Show.

4. Practice going back and forth between the scenarios using Show.

You can see how easy it is to substitute sets of values into cells and to examine the effect they have in your workbook.

Modifying a Scenario

11

Scenario Manager provides a convenient way of storing and reviewing different scenarios. You can modify an existing scenario very easily. For example, you can change the value of E3 in the Scenario3 you just created by following these steps.

1. Click on Scenario3 in the Scenario Manager, then click on the Edit button. In the Edit Scenario dialog box, click on OK.

2. In the Scenario Values dialog box, change the value of $E$3 to 0.011 and click on OK.

3. Back in the Scenario Manager, click on the Show button to see the effect of your change.

Creating a Summary of Your Scenarios

Next create a summary report of your three scenarios. The summary report not only lists your various input values for your variables, it also allows you to specify other cells in the workbook you want included in the report, such as the cells that will change in each scenario. This gives you a convenient way to compare how different inputs give you different results.

1. Click on the Summary button.

2. The Scenario Summary dialog box appears, as seen here:

You want a Scenario Summary, which is the default report.

3. In the Result Cells box, type **C11:F11, C27:F27**. These cells, for forms sales and net income, respectively, contain formulas that are dependent on the values in cells C3:E3.

4. Click on OK.

A summary report is created on a new sheet in the workbook, as seen in Figure 11-4. You can save this summary as a separate workbook and print it out if you wish. You may want to chart the summary report to give you a comparison between the scenarios. Refer to Chapter 7 for information about how to build a chart. Figure 11-5 shows an example of a chart created from a Scenario Manager summary report. You can see at a glance the relationship between different growth ratios and sales figures.

5. When you have finished looking at the summary, activate SOLVEREX.XLS again, if you are not already in it, by clicking on the 5th Ave sheet tab.

Creating Other Reports

You can also create reports with the different scenarios using the Report Manager option on the View menu. The Report Manager option is an add-in and will only appear on the View menu if it has been installed. If it does not appear on your View menu, you can look at the Add-ins from the Tools menu to see if it is there. If Report Manager is on the Add-in list, you can simply click on it and then click on OK and Report Manager will be installed and appear on the View menu. If it is not on the list, you will have to install it from the Excel 7 or Office 95 distribution disks or CD.

Using Report Manager, you can print a single view (or scenario) of your workbook, or you can print a series of views in one step. Use the following

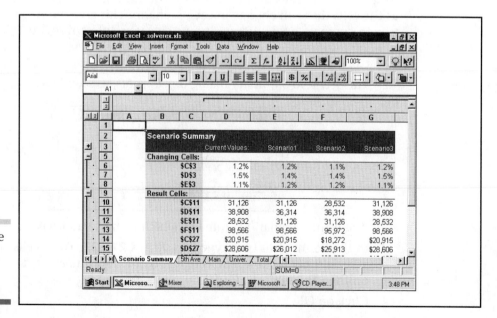

Printout of the summary report

Figure 11-4.

Chart from a
summary
report
Figure 11-5.

directions to print out a single view of your workbook using the Report
Manager option.

1. Open the View menu and choose the Report Manager option.
2. On the Report Manager dialog box, click on Add. The Add Report dialog
   box will be displayed, as shown here:

3. Click on the down arrow on the right end of the Scenario box, and click on Scenario1.

4. Click on the Report Name box, and type **Report1**.

5. Click on the Add button. Your Add Report dialog box should look like this:

6. Click on OK. On the Report Manager dialog box, click on Print, then click on OK in the Print dialog box for one copy. A report is generated as shown in Figure 11-6.

The power of the Report Manager feature is realized when you have many scenarios set up for your workbook and you want to print out a copy of your workbook for each scenario. Because this option allows you to print them all at once, it will save you a great deal of time.

Solver

Solver, another Add-in, is Excel's most sophisticated analysis tool. If you want to find a solution to a formula that has multiple variables, Solver is the right tool to use. Solver allows you to specify up to two hundred variables. It also allows you to define up to one hundred constraints on those variables. A *constraint* limits the values a variable can take on. For example, you could constrain a variable to be an integer, to be greater than zero, or no larger than a certain value. Solver tries to solve the formula to equal the value you specify by trying different values for the variables you defined within the constraints. Instead of specifying a single value you want the formula to equal, you can indicate that the formula should be a maximum or a minimum value.

11

```
                                              5th Ave


                      5TH AVENUE STORE - THIRD QUARTER BUDGET

          Revenue Growth/Mo.              1.2%      1.4%      1.2%
          C O S Growth/Mo.                1.3%
          Expense Growth/Mo.              1.0%
```

	Second Quarter	July	August	Sept.	Third Quarter	Percent Growth
REVENUE						
Forms	87,000	31,126	36,314	31,126	98,566	13.3%
Supplies	147,300	49,689	50,285	50,889	150,864	2.4%
Total Revenue	$234,300	$80,815	$86,599	$82,015	$249,429	6.5%
COST OF SALES	135,894	45,887	46,483	47,088	139,458	2.6%
GROSS INCOME	$98,406	$34,928	$40,116	$34,927	$109,971	11.8%
EXPENSES						
Salaries	24,450	8,232	8,314	8,397	24,942	2.0%
P/R Taxes	2,322	782	790	797	2,369	2.0%
Advertising	14,760	5,000	5,000	5,000	15,000	1.6%
Total Expenses	$41,532	$14,013	$14,103	$14,194	$42,311	1.9%
Net Income	$56,874	$20,915	$26,012	$20,733	$67,660	19.0%

The following example shows how to use Excel's Solver to maximize income for the quarter by figuring out how to best spend advertising dollars on a monthly basis. Make sure 5th Ave is the active sheet. Since Solver is an Add-in, you will have to make sure it has been installed in the same way as Report Manager above.

1. Scroll your workbook up, if necessary, click on C3, type **1.1%** if it isn't that value already, and press RIGHT ARROW.

2. Type **1.2%** and press RIGHT ARROW.

3. Type **1.4%** and press ENTER. You just entered three new monthly growth ratios for this exercise.

   Your workbook should now look like the one pictured in Figure 11-7.

4. Click on File, then click on Save. If you make a mistake in the following exercises, you can return to this point and start over.

Setting Up Solver

You are now ready to set up Solver.

1. Scroll your workbook so you can see C23:F23 and cell F27, as shown in Figure 11-8.

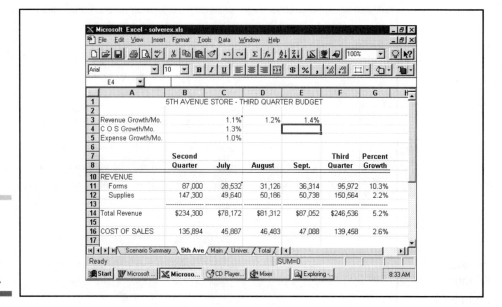

2. Open the Tools menu and choose Solver. The Solver Parameters dialog box opens, as shown here:

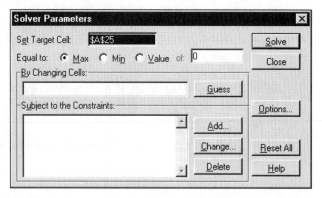

3. Type **F27** (net income for the quarter) in the Set Target Cell box. You want to maximize net income, and since Max is the default Equal to option button, you can TAB past the Equal to option.

4. Type **C23:E23** (monthly advertising expense) in the By Changing Cells box.

5. Click on the Solve button.

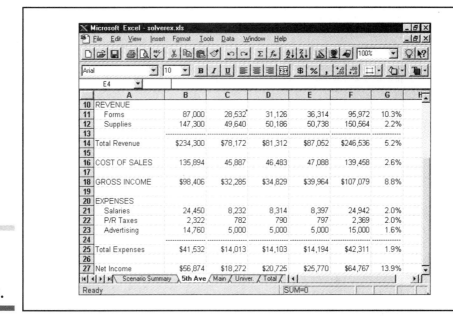

Workbook
ready for
Solver
Figure 11-8.

Notice that the values Excel is using to try to solve for in cell F27 appear
in the Status bar. It may take several seconds. Once a solution is found,
the Solver Results dialog box appears as shown here:

This dialog box allows you to restore the original values, keep the new
values, store the values using Scenario Manager, or print reports. For
now, you want to look at what happens when you keep the new values.

6. Make sure the Keep Solver Solution button is on, and click on OK.

Your workbook should now look like Figure 11-9. Compare Figure 11-8 with
Figure 11-9. Figure 11-8 shows what your workbook looked like before using
Solver, and Figure 11-9 shows your workbook after using Solver. Pay special
attention to cells C11:F11 (sales of forms), C23:F23 (advertising expenses),
and C27:F27 (income). Because all of these cells are related either directly or
indirectly through the formula in cell F27, when Solver maximized F27 by
changing advertising expenses, it also caused the sales for forms to increase.

After Solver is
run
Figure 11-9.

In this example, instead of spending $5,000 a month on advertising, Solver found that you could make the most money if you spend $22,440 in July, $27,276 in August, and $38,209 in September for advertising.

On the basis of the information you provided in your workbook, you have just determined how to make the most money possible by spending $87,925 on advertising. You could have used trial and error in order to determine this result, but that would have been a very tedious and time-consuming undertaking, with no guarantee that the answer you found would be the optimal solution. Solver is an extremely efficient and accurate problem solver that will provide you with invaluable information.

Constraining Variables

It's nice to say you can make the most money if you spend $87,925 on advertising, but what happens if you don't have $87,925? You need to set an upper limit, a *constraint* on the advertising budget. You can constrain a Solver problem in several ways. You can constrain variables to take on particular values, not to exceed or go lower than certain values, to be integers, to be positive numbers, and so on. You can also constrain the problem by limiting the time Solver can take to come up with a solution. If Solver takes too long to solve a problem and you want to interrupt the process, you can stop Solver by pressing ESC.

If your advertising funds are limited, you can constrain the problem to take this into consideration. Say you are going to limit the amount of money you allocate to advertising to $20,000 for the quarter; now, let Solver determine how best to spend this money on a monthly basis in order to maximize profits.

1. Open the Tools menu and choose the Solver option.
2. Type **F27** in the Set Cell box (if $F$27 isn't already there).
3. Make sure the Max button is selected.
4. Type **C23:E23** in the By Changing Cells box (if it isn't there already).
5. Click on the Add button to add a constraint. The Add Constraint dialog box appears, as shown here:

6. Type **F23** in the Cell Reference box. The <= (less than or equal to) comparison operator is the one you want, so you don't need to change it.
7. Type **20,000** in the Constraint box. Click on Add to add a second constraint.
8. Type **C23:E23** in the Cell Reference box and click on the arrow to display the comparison operators. Select >= (greater than or equal to), type **3,000** in the Constraint box, and click on OK to add the constraint and close the Add Constraint dialog box.

   The Solver Parameters dialog box is now displayed. It shows the constraints you have now set up.

9. Click on the Solve button. Solver again searches several seconds for a solution. When it finds one, the Solver Results dialog box reappears.

   Your workbook should now look like Figure 11-10. Notice that Solver determined how to optimally spend your quarterly advertising budget in order to maximize your income. If you don't enter the second constraint (C23:E23 >= 3,000), it is possible that the formulas in C11:E11 will go negative. Since you cannot take the square root of a negative number (the formulas in C11:E11 take the square root), you will get an error condition that will stop the Solver.

11

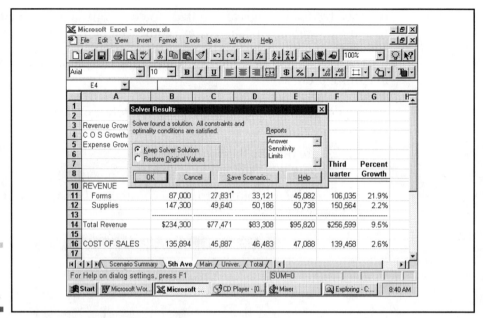

Results with
constraints
Figure 11-10.

Instead of saving the solution in the workbook, try using the Scenario Manager option instead.

10. Click on the Save Scenario button.

11. Type **adv20000** in the Scenario Name box.

12. Click on OK.

13. Back in the Solver Results dialog box, click on the Restore Original Values button, then click on OK.

Saving a Model

When you save a workbook, the latest settings you defined for Solver are saved with the workbook. If you want to set up several problems and save them for later viewing, you can use the Save Model option. You must find a range in your workbook where you can store the settings. Follow these steps to save the current problem.

1. Open the Tools menu and choose Solver.

2. Click on the Options button. The Solver Options dialog box opens, as shown here:

3. Click on the Save Model button. The Save Model dialog box opens, as shown here (your default range of cells may be different):

It is asking for a range of cells as a destination for the save parameters. You want the range away from the data, but close enough to be easily found. The destination range should be empty.

4. Highlight $E$22:$E$26, type **J1:N1**, and click on OK.

5. Click on OK again to close the Solver Options dialog box, and click on Close to close the Solver Parameters dialog box.

The information you need in order to load the solution has been stored in your workbook, as shown in Figure 11-11.

To load the model, follow these steps.

1. Open the Tools menu and choose Solver.

2. Click on the Options button. The Solver Options dialog box opens.

3. Click on the Load Model button. The Load Model dialog box opens:

Solution data
stored in the
workbook
Figure 11-11.

4. Type **J1:N1** in the Select Model Area box and click on OK. Note that you must enter the complete range. Click on OK to "Reset previous Solver cell selections" in the message box that appears and click on OK again to leave the Solver Options dialog box. The Solver Parameters dialog box opens with all the parameters you set for the model loaded.

5. Click on Close to close the Solver.

Solver is a potent tool with many features—only some of which have been covered here. Along with the other tools presented in this chapter, Solver will save you hours of time by helping you organize your work, create meaningful comparative reports, and solve problems.

Using Visual Basic with Excel

12

Visual Basic is a programming language, one of the newest, easiest to use, and most fully featured of programming languages. With it, you can write programs that direct Excel and your computer to carry out tasks that you would have to otherwise do manually. Once a program is written, you can repeat it, time after time, and never vary a step. Alternatively, a program can be made either to ask for instructions or to look at the situation and tailor itself accordingly each time it runs.

You don't even have to do much of the programming. As you saw in Chapter 10, you can have Excel record many steps and produce Visual Basic commands or statements. Like the Excel 4 macro language, then, the Visual Basic programming language is just a way to communicate with a computer and with Excel and to tell them what to do.

This chapter gives you an overview of using the Excel Implementation of the Visual Basic Programming System, Applications Edition (or Visual Basic for Applications). The terms *Visual Basic for Excel* and *Visual Basic* will be used to refer to this programming system.

Date/Time Stamp in Visual Basic

To get a quick look at Visual Basic and compare it to the Excel 4 macro language, rerecord the Date/Time Stamp macro that you recorded in Chapter 10, but in this case record it in Visual Basic. With your computer on, Windows and Excel loaded, and a blank workbook on your screen, follow these instructions.

1. Point on Record Macro from the Tools menu, click on Record New Macro, type **VB_Date_Time_Stamp**, click on Options, click on Shortcut Key, accept "m" (the default key), click on Personal Macro Workbook (if necessary), accept Visual Basic as the language, and click on OK. "Recording" will appear in the Status bar.

2. Type **=now( )** in the currently active cell (it doesn't matter which one) and press ENTER.

3. Widen the column that contains the active cell to 14.

4. Click on the Copy tool, choose Paste Special from the Edit menu, click on Values and on OK, and press ESC to turn off copying.

5. Click on Stop Recorder and, if it is not hidden, click on PERSONAL.XLS in the Window menu. If you don't see PERSONAL.XLS in the Window menu, click on Unhide in the Window menu and double-click on PERSONAL.XLS in the Unhide dialog box. PERSONAL.XLS will appear on your screen.

6. Click on the Module1 tab and the Visual Basic Date/Time Stamp macro will appear as shown in Figure 12-1.

When you record an Excel macro and choose Visual Basic as the Language option, the resulting macro is in the form of Visual Basic statements or *code* stored on a module sheet. You can then inspect and modify this code directly. An excellent (and recommended) way to supplement your reading of this chapter is to record numerous short macros (as you did in Chapter 10) and inspect the resulting Visual Basic code. As you explore various aspects of the Visual Basic programming language, you might want to modify your recorded macros to see the effect of changes made directly to the code. An essential part of learning any programming language is actually writing programs, so you are encouraged to experiment. In Chapter 13, you'll have a chance to fully practice this by creating an order entry system with Visual Basic and Excel.

12

In the remaining sections of this chapter, each element of the Visual Basic language is discussed. As you are reading about them, come back and look at Figure 12-1, and the many items designated there will be more meaningful. Also, as you are looking at Visual Basic statements, think about how different ways of reading them would help them make more sense. For example, the first line within the Sub procedure might be read as follows: "the active cell contains a formula in R1C1 style which has a value of the string =NOW( )."

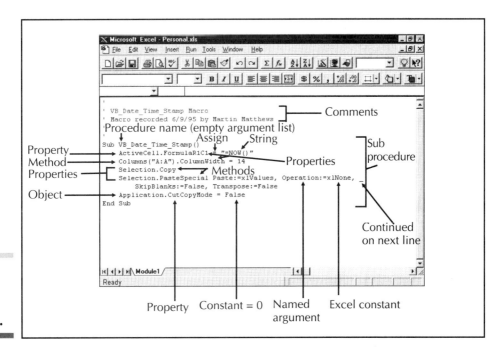

Date/Time
Stamp in
Visual Basic
Figure 12-1.

Sometimes it helps to read the line from right to left. For example, the second line of the Sub procedure could be read as follows: "14 is assigned to the column width of the columns in the current selection." You'll find after you do this a bit that Visual Basic statements are much clearer than they originally seemed. Also, don't be confused by the many element names, like object, method, and property. They are just ways of identifying parts of the language so they can be classified and discussed. How these elements work is much more important than the name.

Excel Help and Examples

Excel 7 offers a vast amount of information on Visual Basic in its online help facility. Choosing MS Excel Help Topics from the Help menu opens the Help Topics dialog box, where there are two Visual Basic topics, "Getting Started with Visual Basic" and "MS Excel Visual Basic Reference." Each topic opens into several subtopics that cover the gamut from how to use Visual Basic to alphabetic listings of each language component. Also, if you press F1 while in a module sheet (where Visual Basic code is stored—see "Visual Basic Module Sheets" later in this chapter) and the insertion point is on a Visual Basic *keyword* (a word recognized by Visual Basic), you get the help topic for that particular keyword, as shown in Figure 12-2. You might find it handy to

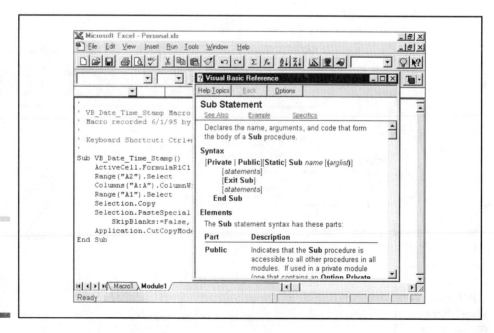

The Visual Basic Reference window

Figure 12-2.

keep the Help Topics dialog box open while reading this chapter and working with your Visual Basic code. This dialog box allows you to quickly find additional information on most Visual Basic topics, as well as code examples that you can copy and use.

Another good source of code that you can study and copy for your own use is the SAMPLES.XLS workbook, included with Excel. This example workbook contains an assortment of short Visual Basic routines (or macros) that perform typical tasks in Excel. When you look at these samples, you will probably agree that the Visual Basic language is easier to understand than the Excel 4 macro language, especially if you have programmed in a procedural language (such as Basic, Pascal, or C) before.

Objects in Visual Basic for Excel   **12**

The understanding of *objects* is fundamental to programming in Visual Basic for Excel. You manipulate objects in your Visual Basic code in order to automate tasks in Excel. There are a large number of objects provided for your use, ranging from the Excel application itself (an Application object) and individual sheets (Worksheet objects), to details like the floor of an Excel chart (a Floor object). Other examples of objects include windows, workbooks, dialog boxes, ranges, charts, and so on. The Visual Basic Reference index for Objects (double-click on the Visual Basic Reference help topic and then double-click on Objects) provides a complete list of every Excel object along with its properties and methods (properties and methods are discussed next). The Object Browser, discussed later in this chapter, is an additional resource for working with objects.

Excel objects can contain other objects. *Container objects* are often themselves contained by yet another object, so nesting of objects is common. For example, a Range object is contained in a Worksheet object, which is contained in a Workbook object, which is contained in an Application object. In writing Visual Basic code, when you need to differentiate between objects in different containers, write the container's name first, followed by a period and the contained object's name. For example, to refer to a chart named "Widget_Sales" in a particular sheet named "October," the expression might look like October.Widget_Sales. This expression would be useful in differentiating between Widget_Sales charts that exist in multiple sheets.

Some Excel objects consist of sets of objects. These objects are *collections*, and the individual members of each collection are *elements*. Common collection objects include charts, sheets, and workbooks. All objects, whether collections or individual objects, have properties, which are discussed next.

The Properties of Objects

The *properties* of an object are characteristics that determine the appearance or behavior of the object. For example, the TextBox object has a Text property, which is the text contained in the text box. You refer to an object's property by following the object name with a period and the property name, as in *object.property*. Some properties have optional object names that can be omitted. For example, the Application object is optional for the ActiveWorkbook and ActiveSheet properties. Commonly used properties include ActiveWorkbook, ActiveSheet, ActiveCell, Column, Row, ColumnWidth, RowHeight, Height, Width, Selection, Value, Bold, and Italic. Most properties apply to more than one object; for instance, the Height property applies to nearly 50 objects.

Properties come in two general classes: Read-only and Read/Write.

♦ **Read-Only** properties allow you to examine a particular aspect of an object by returning the value of the property. You can read the value of any property, but you cannot assign a new value to a read-only property. For example, the ActiveSheet property is a read-only property of Workbook objects, and the expression MyWorkbook.ActiveSheet returns the active sheet (an object) in MyWorkbook.

♦ **Read/Write** properties can have their values changed as well as examined. You can change the condition of the object by changing (or *setting*) the value of a read/write property. For example, the Name property is a read/write property of Worksheet objects. The expression

    MyWorkbook.ActiveSheet.Name

returns the name of the active sheet in MyWorkbook, and the expression

    MyWorkbook.ActiveSheet.Name = "MyWorksheet"

sets the name property of the active sheet in MyWorkbook to "MyWorksheet."

The Methods of Objects

In addition to properties, most objects have one or more *methods* that you can use to cause a specific task or action to be performed on the object. Methods and properties are related because the action of a method sometimes results in a corresponding change to a property. For example, when you remove an item from a Listbox object with the RemoveItem method, the value returned by the List property changes. As with properties, many methods are used by more than one object. Commonly used methods include Activate, Select, Calculate, Offset, Clear, Copy, and Sort.

You refer to an object's method by following the object name with a period and the method name, as in *object.method*. For example, the expression MyWorkbook.Activate makes MyWorkbook the active workbook.

You can pass additional information to some methods in the form of *arguments* (sometimes called *parameters*). When you use a method that takes one or more arguments, you add the arguments after the method name (separated from the method name by a space), as in *object.method arguments*. If there are multiple arguments, separate them from each other by commas (or the list separator for the Language/Country you specify in Tools Options Module General). For example, MyWorksheet.Cells(3,4) returns a range object consisting of the single cell in row 3, column 4 of MyWorksheet. Some methods return a value, as the Cells method just mentioned. If you want to save the return value of a method, enclose the arguments (if any) in parentheses. If the method does not return a value or if the return value is to be discarded, do not use parentheses around the arguments, as in MyWorksheet.PrintOut 1,4,3, which prints three copies of the first four pages of MyWorkbook.

12

Methods can take named arguments instead of the conventional arguments just shown. Named arguments can be passed in any order and are easier to understand. For example, the expression ActiveWorkbook.Close True, "SALES.XLS" (which saves the active workbook as SALES.XLS, then closes it) could be written ActiveWorkbook.Close fileName := "SALES.XLS", saveChanges := True to make it easier to understand.

Visual Basic Module Sheets

As mentioned earlier, when you record a macro the generated Visual Basic code is stored on a *module sheet*, which is similar to a regular sheet but dedicated to storing and displaying Visual Basic code. The location of the module sheet is determined by the settings you choose in the Record New Macro dialog box, as shown in Figure 12-3. If you specify Store in This Workbook, you will find the new module sheet at the bottom of the stack of sheets in the active workbook's window, as shown in Figure 12-4.

If you are unsure of the location of a particular macro, you can view a list of all the currently available macros by choosing Macro from the Tools menu. Highlight the desired macro in the list, then choose the Edit button to bring up the module sheet containing that macro.

You can also manually insert a new module sheet in the current workbook by choosing Macro from the Insert menu and clicking on Module.

Record New
Macro dialog
box expanded
to show
Options
Figure 12-3.

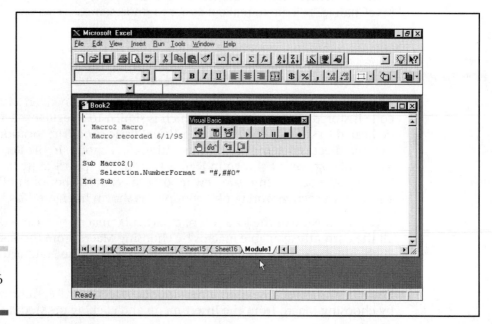

Module sheet
under Sheet16
Figure 12-4.

Visual Basic Procedures

All *executable* code (capable of being run) must be contained in *procedures* (declarations, discussed later in this chapter, are not executable and can be outside procedures). A procedure is a series of instructions or *statements* that is executed as a unit. Each statement accomplishes one kind of action or declaration. Generally, a procedure accomplishes some well-defined and easily understood task, such as formatting a range of cells or calculating and returning a value. Excel 4 macros and user-defined functions are actually two different types of Visual Basic procedures, and both are stored on module sheets.

In Excel 7, macros are Visual Basic *Sub* procedures, and user-defined functions are *Function* procedures (the *Property* procedure is a third, but less commonly used, type of procedure). The following example of a Sub procedure applies the italic font style to a range of cells:

12

```
Sub ItalicFont()
    Range("A2:A10").Font.FontStyle = "Italic"
End Sub
```

The following example of a Function procedure calculates and returns the area of a rectangle from the length and width arguments:

```
Function Area(Length, Width)
    Area = Length * Width
End Function
```

Sub and Function procedures are quite similar, but they do have some important differences. You can create some Sub procedures by recording a macro, but you must create all Function procedures manually by typing code into a module. In addition, Function procedures always return a value while Sub procedures never do. Sub procedures generally accomplish some action by manipulating objects, while Function procedures usually do not perform actions (except calculating and returning a value). A Function procedure can be used exactly like a built-in Excel function (if it does not alter the sheet in any way). Both Sub and Function procedures have the same general structure, which consists of the following parts.

♦ The first line begins with "Sub" or "Function." If the procedure is to return a value (as all functions do, whether built-in or user-defined), then "Function" must be used.

♦ Following "Sub" or "Function" (on the same line) is the procedure's name. Names must begin with a letter, can contain up to 40 letters, numbers, and the underscore (_) character, but cannot contain punctuation or spaces. Function procedure names cannot resemble a cell reference (like A1 or R1C1) and cannot be any Visual Basic reserved words.

♦ After the name (still on the same line) come the arguments, if any, enclosed in parentheses. Arguments are values that the procedure needs in order to accomplish its tasks, and are passed to the procedure each time it is called (run). Both Sub and Function procedures can take arguments. You can specify the data types of arguments and the data type of the value that a Function procedure returns by adding As clauses (see "Declaring Data Types" later in this chapter).

♦ Additional lines of Visual Basic code follow. These are the statements that accomplish the task or tasks of the procedure. In addition to assignment statements (Area = Length * Width), such lines may be used for executing built-in statements and functions (Open "MYFILE" For Input As #1), executing methods (Cells(1,3).Select), setting properties (ActiveSheet.Name = "MyWorksheet"), using control structures (If Score > 50 Then . . .), and so on.

♦ A Function procedure always contains at least one statement that assigns a value to the function name (Count_Function = Count). This is its return value.

♦ The procedure's last line contains either End Sub or End Function.

Calling Procedures

Sub procedures can be called with the Call statement, followed by the Sub procedure name, followed by the arguments enclosed in parentheses. The parentheses are required for the Call statement, even if no arguments are passed. More commonly, the word Call and the parentheses are omitted when calling Sub procedures. For example, to call a Sub procedure named Apply_Bold that takes two arguments (Row_num and Col_num), you could use either of the following statements:

```
Apply_Bold 2,3
```

```
Call Apply_Bold(2,3)
```

Like the arguments for methods (discussed earlier in "The Methods of Objects"), you can use named arguments when calling procedures to make your code easier to write and read. When using named arguments, they can appear in any order. The Apply_Bold procedure could be called using named arguments as follows:

```
Apply_Bold Col_num := 3, Row_num := 2
```

Function procedures can be called in exactly the same way as Sub procedures if you don't want to save the return value. Normally, however, the return value is saved by assigning the Function call to a variable (discussed next). The following are two ways to call the Area Function procedure shown earlier and assign it to a variable named Size:

```
Size = Area(10, 20)
```

```
Size = Area(Width := 20, Length := 10)
```

Using Variables

12

The Area function shown earlier takes two arguments (the length and width of a rectangle). An argument in a procedure represents a value passed to the procedure when it is called, and is itself a type of *variable*. Variables are simply names that represent stored values or objects. You can modify the value assigned to a variable while your program runs. The use of variables is a convenient way to store values and helps make your code more understandable. Here's an example of the use of variables in a Function procedure:

```
Function B&O_Tax(Gross, Deductions)
    Taxable = Gross - Deductions
    If Taxable < 3000 Then
        B&O_Tax = 0
    Else
        B&O_Tax = Taxable * 0.0213
End Function
```

In this example, Taxable is the name of a variable used as a temporary storage location for the amount that is taxable. Gross and Deductions, which are arguments of the B&O_Tax function, are also variables within the function—names of temporary storage locations that are used to hold amounts. In the same sense, B&O_Tax, which is the name of the function, is also a variable that stores the result of the function.

Declaring Variables

You can identify a variable or argument before you use it in your Visual Basic code by *declaring* it. Although it is not necessary to use declarations, there are several advantages to doing so, including the following.

♦ Your code will generally run faster.

♦ Less memory will be used by your code when it runs.

♦ Visual Basic can check for spelling and data type errors in the use of your declared variable or argument.

Variables are typically declared with the Dim statement. The above procedure looks like this when the Taxable variable is declared before being used:

```
Function B&O_Tax(Gross, Deductions)
    Dim Taxable
    Taxable = Gross - Deductions
    If Taxable < 3000 Then
        B&O_Tax = 0
    Else
        B&O_Tax = Taxable * 0.0213
End Function
```

The Dim statement declares Taxable as a variable that is to be used within the B&O_Tax function. Without the Dim statement, if another variable named Taxable already exists when B&O_Tax is called, its value could be changed by the code in the B&O_Tax function. See "Scope of Variables and Constants" later in this chapter for more information on declaring variables.

To enable Visual Basic to check for errors in your spelling of variable names, include the statement Option Explicit at the top of your module. If you include this statement, you must declare all variables before you use them in your procedures. Then, if you misspell a variable name, Visual Basic will display an error message as the code is run (the misspelled name appears as an undeclared variable).

Note that you can have Visual Basic automatically include Option Explicit in all new modules by checking Require Variable Declaration in the Module General Options, as described in "Setting Options for Visual Basic" later in this chapter.

Declaring Data Types

Variables can hold various types of data. The basic data types available in Visual Basic for Excel are Boolean (true or false), Integer (whole numbers), Long (large whole numbers), Single (decimals), Double (large decimals), Currency, Date, Object, and String (characters). In addition, an Array type is a set of sequentially indexed data, a User-defined type is a combination of types that you define, and a Variant type is a general-purpose data type that can accommodate any data (except User-defined types).

In the variable declaration examples shown earlier, the variables are automatically given the Variant data type. You can also specify a specific data type for a variable when you declare it. This can enable Visual Basic to check for errors in assigning values to the variable as well as make your code run more efficiently. For example, to specify the Currency type for the Taxable variable in the earlier example, use the following declaration:

```
Dim Taxable As Currency
```

In addition to variables, you can declare arguments, functions, and constants (discussed next) with specific data types by adding the As clause. For example, the earlier example could have the function's return value and the arguments all declared as the Currency type:

12

```
Function B&O_Tax(Gross, Deductions As Currency) As Currency
```

Using Constants

You can often improve the readability and maintenance of your code by using *constants*. Like a variable, a constant is a name that represents a value. The constant can be used in your code wherever the value is called for. Unlike a variable, however, the value of a constant cannot be changed as your program runs—it *is* constant. Excel and Visual Basic provide many constants, and you can define your own.

To declare a constant, use the Const statement in the same way that you use the Dim statement to declare a variable; for example:

```
Const TAXRATE = 0.0213
```

The names you give your constants must conform to the same naming rules as apply to variable, argument, and procedure names. Traditionally, however, all uppercase letters are used for constant names. In addition, since the built-in Excel and Visual Basic constants begin with "xl" or "vb," you should avoid using these characters to begin the names you give your constants.

You will usually want to declare a constant at the top of the module, outside all procedures. This makes the constant available to all the procedures in the module. The TAXRATE constant could be used in the earlier B&O_Tax example to improve readability and make tax rate changes easier:

```
Const TAXRATE = 0.0213
Function B&O_Tax(Gross, Deductions)
    Dim Taxable
```

```
      Taxable = Gross - Deductions
      If Taxable < 3000 Then
          B&O_Tax = 0
      Else
          B&O_Tax = Taxable * TAXRATE
      End If
End Function
```

Scope of Variables and Constants

The *scope* of a variable or procedure refers to its visibility within all modules and workbooks. Scope determines whether a variable or procedure can be used from a particular procedure in a particular module. In addition, each variable and procedure has a lifetime that determines when it can be used.

Procedures can have Public or Private scope. Public is the default scope of procedures. Public scope makes the procedure available to all procedures in all modules. Private scope makes the procedure available only to other procedures located in the module where it is declared. Procedures can be made to have a Static lifetime, which means that all the variables declared within the procedure retain their values between calls to the procedure. Static lifetime can be combined with either Public or Private scope.

Variables and constants can have Local, Module, or Public scope. Variables declared within a procedure have Local scope, that is, they are available only within that procedure. A variable declared within a procedure can be given Static lifetime, so that it retains its value between calls to the procedure. Variables declared outside all procedures at the top of a module have Module scope; that is, they are available only to the procedures within that module. Module-level variables can be declared with the Private (preferred) or Dim statement. Variables can also be given Public scope, which makes them available to all procedures in all modules. This is accomplished by declaring them at the top of the module, outside all procedures, and using the Public statement.

Entering and Editing Visual Basic Code

As you enter lines of code in a module, they are automatically formatted for you (unless you have this feature turned off). Your code is also checked for the correct syntax as you enter it. Entering and editing code in a module is accomplished using the typical Windows text editing techniques.

Each line is usually a single Visual Basic statement, but you can include multiple statements on a single line or extend a single statement over multiple lines, if needed. To include multiple statements on one line, separate them with a colon (:). Use this feature sparingly, since it can make your code harder to read. More typically, you might want to split a long statement into multiple lines for improved readability. You can accomplish this by adding an underscore (_) to the end of each line that is continued on the next line. The underscore must be preceded by a space when used this way.

Using Comments in Your Code

You should liberally include comments in your code to remind yourself (and others who might later read or modify your code) what it does. A comment is text that is ignored when your procedure runs. Precede your comment text with an apostrophe (') or "rem" (for "remark") and a space. Comments can occupy an entire line or can appear to the right of a statement (if the rem form is used to the right of a statement, it must be preceded by a colon). The apostrophe is most often used for comments and is typically used like this:

12

```
ConstTAXRATE=0.0213    'TAXRATE is the current B&O tax rate.
'This is a full line comment that introduces the following code.
```

You will see numerous comments in the examples that appear in the online Visual Basic Reference and the SAMPLES.XLS workbook.

Using Control Structures (Decision Making)

Visual Basic for Excel contains statements that enable your code to run different statements based on the results of a test. These *control structures* can add important flexibility and power to your procedures because they can change the order in which your statements are run. If you do not use these decision or control structures, your code can run the statements only in the order in which they appear on the module sheet—from top to bottom. Following is a brief discussion of each type of control structure, along with examples.

If. . .Then. . .Else

The If. . .Then. . .Else control structure first tests the expression that follows "If." If it is True, the statements following "Then" are executed. Otherwise, the statements following "Else" are executed. For example:

```
If Taxable < 3000 Then
    B&O_Tax = 0
    Print_Check = False
Else
    B&O_Tax = Taxable * TAXRATE
```

```
        Print_Check = True
End If
```

If you have a single statement to conditionally execute, you can use a
single-line form and omit "End If," as follows:

```
If Print_Check Then MsgBox "Load checks into the printer."
```

On the other hand, if you have multiple conditions to check, you can add
an ElseIf statement for each test, as follows:

```
If Print_Check = False Then
    MsgBox "No Tax is Due."
ElseIf Printer = BUSY Then     'Print_Check is True and Printer is BUSY.
    MsgBox "The printer is busy; can't print B&O tax check now"
Else                           'Print_Check is True and Printer is not BUSY.
    MsgBox "Load checks into the printer."
End If
```

Select Case

If you want to compare the same expression to several different values, use
the Select Case control structure instead of the If. . .Then. . .ElseIf control
structure to make your code more efficient. Select Case evaluates the test
expression once, then compares its value to each case in the structure. If a
match is found, the associated statements are executed. For example:

```
Select Case Print_Job            'Print_Job is evaluated once
    Case "Checks"                'Does Print_Job = "Checks"?
        MsgBox "Load checks into the printer."
    Case "Reports", "Charts"     'Does Print_Job = "Reports" or "Charts"?
        MsgBox "Load Report paper into the printer."
    Case "Letterhead"            'Does Print_Job = "Letterhead"?
        MsgBox "Load Letterhead paper into the printer."
    Case Else            'Print_Job does not match any of the cases.
        MsgBox "Load plain paper into the printer."
End Select
```

As you can see in the above example, a Case expression can be a list of items
separated by commas. The statements associated with the first matching
Case statement are executed. The Case Else statement is optional and
executes if no match is found in the earlier Case statements.

Do. . .Loop

The Do. . .Loop control structure is used to repeatedly execute (or loop through) a series of statements. The loop continues while or until a test condition is True. There are several different forms of the Do. . .Loop, as follows.

♦ **Do While. . .Loop** evaluates the test condition *before* it executes the statements in the loop. This means that if the test condition is initially False, the statements are never run. For example:

```
Loop_Count = 0                          'Initialize Loop_Count.
Do While Amount < 100                   'Exit loop when Amount = 100 or more.
    Amount = Amount + 1                 'Increment Amount.
    Loop_Count = Loop_Count + 1         'Increment Loop_Count.
Loop
MsgBox "Amount =" & Str(Amount) & " after" & Str(Loop_Count) & " loops."
```

The message box displays a value of 0 for Loop_Count if Amount had an initial value of 100 or more.

♦ **Do. . .Loop While** executes the statements in the loop at least once, because the test condition is located at the bottom of the loop:

```
Loop_Count = 0                      'Initialize Loop_Count.
Do
    Amount = Amount + 1             'Increment Amount.
    Loop_Count = Loop_Count + 1     'Increment Loop_Count.
Loop While Amount < 100             'Exit loop when Amount = 100 or more.
MsgBox "Amount =" & Str(Amount) & " after" & Str(Loop_Count) & " loops."
```

This example increments the value of Amount at least once, even if Amount has an initial value of 100 or more.

♦ **Do Until. . .Loop** is identical to the Do While. . .Loop control structure, except that it loops as long as the test condition is False. The following example produces the same results as the Do While. . .Loop example shown earlier, because the test condition is logically reversed:

```
Loop_Count = 0                          'Initialize Loop_Count.
Do Until Amount >= 100                  'Exit loop when Amount >= 100.
    Amount = Amount + 1                 'Increment Amount.
    Loop_Count = Loop_Count + 1         'Increment Loop_Count.
Loop
MsgBox "Amount =" & Str(Amount) & " after" & Str(Loop_Count) & " loops."
```

♦ **Do. . .Loop Until** is identical to the Do. . .Loop While control structure, except that it exits the loop when the test condition is True.

The following example produces the same results as the Do. . .Loop While example shown earlier:

```
Loop_Count = 0                          'Initialize Loop_Count.
Do
    Amount = Amount + 1                 'Increment Amount.
    Loop_Count = Loop_Count + 1        'Increment Loop_Count.
Loop Until Amount Not(< 100)            'Exit loop when Amount = 100 or more.
MsgBox "Amount =" & Str(Amount) & " after" & Str(Loop_Count) & " loops."
```

For. . .Next

The For. . .Next control structure is similar to Do...Loop, but is used when you know the number of times you want the loop statements executed. For. . . Next loops automatically increment or decrement a counter to keep track of the number of loops performed. The following example sets the value in the first ten cells of column 1 to the row number:

```
For Row_Count = 1 To 10
    ActiveSheet.Cells(Row_Count, 1).Value = Row_Count
Next Row_Count
```

You can add the Step clause to specify the value added to the counter variable each time through the loop. If you specify a negative number, the value is decremented, and looping stops when the counter is less than the specified end value. Otherwise, the looping ends when the counter is larger than the specified end value. The following example decrements the counter variable by 2 each time through the loop:

```
For Row_Count = 10 To 2 Step -2   'Decrement counter by 2 each iteration.
    'Copy the formula from the cell in the next column.
    Cells(Row_Count, 1).Formula = Cells(Row_Count, 2).Formula
Next Row_Count
```

For Each. . .Next

The For Each. . .Next loop executes a series of statements for each element in a collection or an array. For example, the following example calculates each sheet in the collection of sheets:

```
For Each Sheet in Worksheets   'Sheet represents each sheet in turn.
    Sheet.Calculate            'Calculates the sheet.
Next Sheet
```

Exit

You might want to exit directly from a Do or a For loop structure, perhaps if you find a value for which you are searching. The Exit Do and Exit For statements end the looping immediately when they are executed, which can speed up your code. The following example illustrates the use of the Exit Do statement:

```
Row_Count = 1                          'Initialize Row_Count variable
Do
    If Cells(Row_Count, 1).Value = 99 Then
        MsgBox "99 was found in row " & Str(Row_Count)
        Exit Do
    End If
    Row_Count = Row_Count + 1
    Continue = MsgBox ("Continue Searching?", vbYesNo)
Loop While Continue = vbYes
```

The following example illustrates the use of the Exit For statement:

```
For Char = 1 To Len(A_String)          'A_String contains a string
    If Mid(A_String, Char, 1) = "*" Then   'Searching for *
        MsgBox "* was found in position " & Str(Char)
        Exit For
    End If
Next Char
```

12

Constructing Expressions

You use *expressions* in your procedures to manipulate characters (strings), perform numerical calculations, and test data of various kinds. Following are a few examples of common types of expressions:

```
Amount < 100

StrComp(String1, String2)

4 + 5

IsNumeric(Cells(2,2).Value)

A Or B

Not C
```

Expressions can contain combinations of Visual Basic and Excel keywords, operators, variables, and constants. Keywords are those words that are recognized by Visual Basic as part of the programming language, and include functions, properties, and methods. The key thing to remember about expressions is that they always *yield a value*, such as a string, number, or object. The next section briefly discusses operators.

Operators

Operators act on data and objects to perform calculations, comparisons, and logical operations and to combine strings. There are four general types of operators, as follows.

- **Logical** operators are used to compare logical (true or false) expressions. The result is itself a logical expression. The logical operators are And, Eqv, Imp, Not, Or, and Xor. The following examples show how these operators are used and the rules for evaluating the resulting expressions.

    ```
    Logical_expr1 And Logical_expr2
    ```

    The And expression is True if both Logical_expr1 and Logical_expr2 are True; otherwise, it is False.

    ```
    Logical_expr1 Or Logical_expr2
    ```

    The Or expression evaluates to False only when Logical_expr1 and Logical_expr2 are both False.

    ```
    Logical_expr1 Eqv Logical_expr2
    ```

    The Eqv (equivalence) expression is True if Logical_expr1 and Logical_expr2 are logically the same; otherwise, it is False.

    ```
    Logical_expr1 Xor Logical_expr2
    ```

    The Xor expression evaluates to False when Logical_expr1 and Logical_expr2 are logically the same; otherwise, it is True.

    ```
    Logical_expr1 Imp Logical_expr2
    ```

    The Imp (implication) expression evaluates to False only when Logical_expr1 is True and Logical_expr2 is False.

    ```
    Not Logical_expr
    ```

    The Not expression evaluates to the opposite (negation) of Logical_expr.

- **Arithmetic** operators are used to perform mathematical operations. They include + (addition), – (subtraction), / (floating-point division), \ (integer division), x (multiplication), ^ (exponentiation), and Mod (remainder).

♦ **Comparison** operators are used to compare two expressions, and evaluate to True or False. They include the following: < (less than), > (greater than), <= (less than or equal), >= (greater than or equal), <> (not equal), and = (equal). In addition, the Is operator tests whether two variables refer to the same object and the Like operator compares two strings.

♦ **Concatenation** operators join two strings (a series of characters). The concatenation operators are & and +. You should use the & operator for concatenation, since the + operator is also an arithmetic operator, so its action depends on the data types of the two expressions used with it.

Debugging Your Code

A *bug* is an error of some sort in your code that causes it to run incorrectly (or not run at all). When your code does not perform as you intend, usually the hardest task is to determine *where* the error is located in your lines of code. Visual Basic detects most errors in syntax (grammatical form and spelling) immediately, unless you turn off this debugging feature (see "Setting Options for Visual Basic" later in this chapter). Other types of errors occur when your code is run and result in *run-time errors* (and an error message from Visual Basic) or simply incorrect results.

Generally, your code will be easier to debug if you include comments that explain what the code is doing, and use meaningful and consistent names for variables. If you can't spot the error in your code by browsing through it (you might want to print out your code), you can use the debugging tools provided by Visual Basic to look inside your code.

Setting Breakpoints

You can suspend execution of your procedure at a particular statement by setting a *breakpoint*. When you run your procedure, execution is suspended at the statement with the breakpoint, but the statement is not executed. You can then examine the values of variables, properties, and statements; observe which procedures have been called; change variable and property values; and step through your code line by line.

To set a breakpoint in your procedure, place the insertion point on the line where you want execution to suspend, then press (or choose Toggle Breakpoint from the Run menu. You can also click on the Toggle Breakpoint button on the Visual Basic toolbar, as shown in Table 12-1.

Tool	Name	Function
	Insert Module	Adds a new Visual Basic module sheet to the current workbook
	Menu Editor	Opens the Menu Editor dialog box
	Object Browser	Opens the Object Browser dialog box, allowing you to see the objects, properties, methods, and procedures in the current workbook
	Run Macro	Opens the Macro dialog box, where you can choose a macro to run
	Step Macro	Opens the Macro dialog box, where you can choose a macro to step through
	Resume Macro	Continues the operation of a macro that has been paused
	Stop Macro	Stops the current macro or stops the recording of a macro
	Record Macro	Opens the Record New Macro dialog box, where you can start the recording of a macro
	Toggle Breakpoint	Adds or removes a breakpoint from a Visual Basic line of code, which causes execution to pause at that point
	Instant Watch	Opens the Instant Watch dialog box, where you can see the value of a selected expression
	Step Into	Executes the next line of Visual Basic code and then pauses; called procedures are also executed one at a time, pausing between each
	Step Over	Executes the next line of Visual Basic code and then pauses; called procedures are fully executed before pausing

Visual Basic
Toolbar Tools
Table 12-1.

Use the same technique to clear the breakpoint from a line: place the insertion point on the line and press F9 or click on the Toggle Breakpoint button. You can clear all breakpoints in the application by choosing Clear All Breakpoints from the Run menu.

Using the Debug Window

When program execution reaches a breakpoint, it switches to Break mode and automatically opens the Debug window, as shown in Figure 12-5.

The Debug window has two halves: the lower part is the *code pane* in which your procedure code is displayed, and the upper part can be either the Immediate pane or the Watch pane. These upper panes are used to observe the values of your variables and expressions, to execute statements, and to display debug messages. The first time you use the Debug window, the Immediate pane appears, as shown in Figure 12-5. In the Immediate pane, you can type statements just as you do in your modules, but these statements are immediately executed when you press ENTER. This enables you to evaluate expressions, assign new values to variables, or test procedures.

If you include Debug.Print statements in your code, they are displayed in the Immediate pane when your procedure runs. You can also type the Print method statements directly into the Immediate pane. For example, Figure 12-6 shows the results of typing Print Amt into the Immediate pane.

Program execution is halted at the breakpoint on the Amt = Amt + 1 line

Figure 12-5.

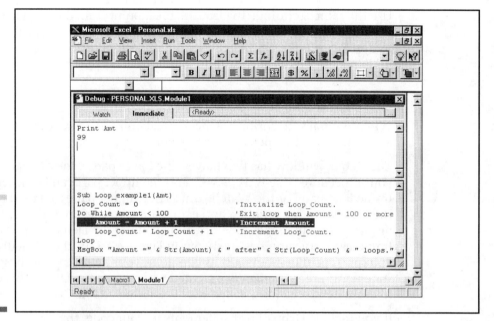

The results of
the Print
statement
appear on the
next line
Figure 12-6.

If you want to monitor the value of a variable or property automatically, you can add a *watch expression* that will be displayed in the Watch pane. To add a watch expression, first select the expression in your code, then choose Add Watch from the Tools menu. The Add Watch dialog box appears, as shown in Figure 12-7. In the Add Watch dialog box, you can also type the expression directly into the Expression text box. Additional options allow you to specify the scope for which the expression will be evaluated (see

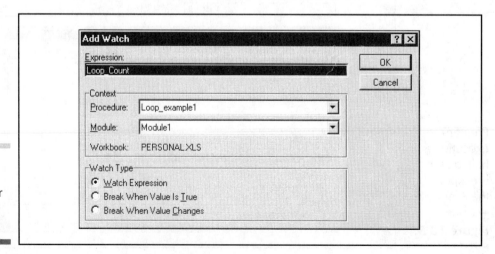

Adding a
Watch
expression for
Loop_Count
Figure 12-7.

"Scope of Variables and Constants" earlier in this chapter) and to specify that execution should halt when the expression's value changes or is True.

To edit or delete a watch expression, double-click on the watch expression or select it, then choose Edit Watch from the Tools menu.

You can also check the value for an expression and add a watch expression for it using Instant Watch. To get the Instant Watch dialog box, first select the expression, then press SHIFT-F9, click on the Instant Watch button, or choose Instant Watch from the Tools menu. The expression and its current value are displayed, as shown here:

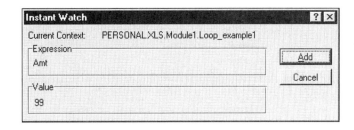

12

Click on the Add button to add a watch for the expression.

Stepping Through Your Code

While execution is halted in Break mode, you can execute one statement at a time by clicking on the Step Into button, or by choosing Step Into from the Run menu. Step Into takes you into the code of any called procedures, so you can follow execution wherever it goes. If you want to go to the next statement rather than stepping into the code of a called procedure, use Step Over instead of Step Into.

Step Over behaves identically to Step Into until it gets to a statement that calls a procedure. At that point, Step Over executes the call but does not take you into the called procedure's code. Instead, you go to the statement after the procedure call. This saves time when you are not interested in stepping through a called procedure.

Setting Options for Visual Basic

You can customize the Visual Basic environment in various ways, including the font and size of the text in modules and the Debug window, the colors used for code elements, whether code is automatically indented to the same level as the previous line, the width (number of spaces) of tabs, whether your code is checked for correct syntax as you enter it, whether Break mode is entered when an error is encountered, and whether variable declarations are

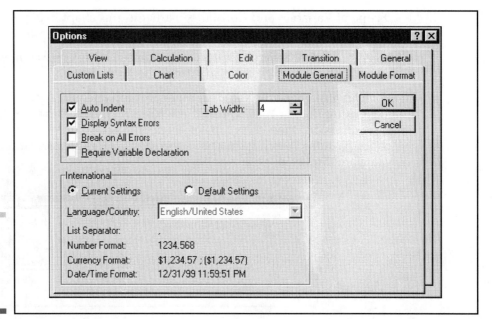

The Module
General tab in
the Options
dialog box
Figure 12-8.

required. To set options for modules, choose Options from the Tools menu.
The Options dialog box appears, as shown in Figure 12-8. Choose the
Module Format tab to customize the font and colors, or the Module General
tab for other options.

Automating a Workbook

13

In this chapter, you will build an automated workbook or application to be used by people who know very little about Excel. This application provides the means of entering, editing, and printing sales orders. All of these functions are as complete as they would be in an actual application. At the same time, there are many enhancements you could add to the application to give it even more features. These enhancements are discussed at the end of the chapter.

Building the application takes several steps. The first is to plan it. You must determine what the application will do and how it will be laid out in the workbook. The second step is to build the working part of the workbook, the title screen, and the database list. Next, you will build a sophisticated dialog box that will be used for data entry. Finally, you will build and test the macros necessary to guide a user through the application. The macros produce a custom menu, accept data from the dialog box, update a database list, and print the list.

Building an application is a detailed process that requires concentration. The reward is to watch the application operate once you finish it. The results in a business environment can be very powerful. With applications like this, you can have people who know very little about Excel doing sophisticated things with it.

Planning an Application

Planning an application entails answering questions in five general areas.

♦ What will the application do and how is the data manipulated? What are the inputs and what are the outputs?

♦ How do these requirements translate into operations performed by Excel?

♦ How will the workbook be laid out? Which parts will go where in the workbook?

♦ What is the logic path for operating the application? How do you logically work through all of its functions and cleanly start and stop it?

♦ How does the logic path translate into Excel capabilities (dialog boxes, menus, and Visual Basic procedures/macros)?

While all five of these steps are important, most applications built with Excel do not go through such a formal process. They generally result from the "build some, try it out, and when it works, build some more" philosophy. This chapter covers only what the application will do, how that translates to Excel, and how it is laid out in the workbook.

What the Application Will Do

Before determining what an application will do, it is important to remind yourself to "keep it simple" and define the minimum set of things that you want to do. It is very easy to describe the Taj Mahal if you ignore what it will take to build it.

Here is the minimum set of things this application should do.

1. Automatically prepare the workbook and display its custom menu
2. Accept sales orders entered with the customer name, salesperson, product description, quantity, unit price, and sales tax rate
3. Build a database list of these items with the tax calculated and the order totaled
4. Provide for editing of the database list items, including changing individual fields and deleting items
5. Print the database list with a heading
6. Save the workbook and leave Excel

This translates well into Excel. You can use a custom dialog box for order entry, a database list to store the orders, and print just the list range in the workbook. Excel's custom dialog box options enable you to create a dialog box specifically designed for this ordering system, and the Data Form option works well for editing and deleting existing records in the database list. The conclusion to be drawn is that Excel can handle all of the specified tasks.

How the Application Will Be Laid Out

You could lay out this application in a number of ways. You must follow only one rule: don't put anything under the database list; it should be able to grow without interference.

The layout adopted for this example is shown in Figure 13-1. The sheet can be broken into three vertical segments. The left segment is used for two screens—one that serves as a Title screen and the other that serves as a backdrop for entering the sales orders and other information. The middle segment contains the database list, with column headings. The right segment contains the list of products. As you can see, the one layout rule was adhered to in forming this layout.

In addition to the order sheet, this application has one dialog sheet for the order entry dialog box and one module sheet for the Visual Basic code for the automation.

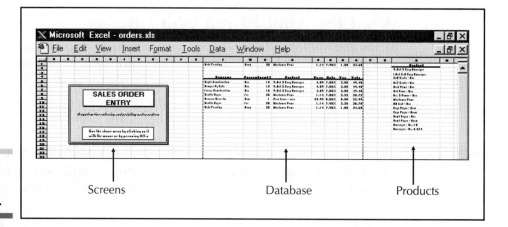

Screens   Database   Products

Building the Order Sheet

There is no right or wrong place to start. Here, you'll start with the screens
and then do the database.

Building Screens

The order entry application you will create utilizes the left part of the sheet
for display purposes. At the top is the Title screen that is used at startup and
whenever the user completes an operation. This screen contains a graphic
object that contains the name of the application and an instruction for
using the menu. The Title screen is shown in Figure 13-2 in its finished form.
The area below the Title screen on the sheet is a blank area that is used as a
backdrop for the Order Entry dialog box. The normal row and column
headings, gridlines, scroll bar, Formula bar, Status bar, Sheet tabs, and
various toolbars usually seen on an Excel screen are turned off when this
application runs, leaving the simple screen shown in Figure 13-2.

Load Excel, open a new workbook and use the following instructions to
build the Title screen:

1. Double-click on Sheet1's tab and rename it OrdSheet. Delete the
    remaining sheets (as many as 15) to simplify things and save a little disk
    space, then save the file as ORDERS.XLS.

    You can now create the Title screen graphic, which consists of three text
    boxes and one rectangle.

2. Maximize both the Excel and the workbook windows by clicking on
    their maximize buttons. Click on the Drawing tool next to the Zoom
    text box in the Standard toolbar to display the Drawing toolbar.

3. Drag the bottom of the Drawing toolbar down until the toolbar becomes a long, narrow two-column window, and then drag the toolbar to the right side of the screen.

4. Click on the Text Box tool, the third tool down in the rightmost column in the Drawing toolbar.

5. Move the crosshair mouse pointer to the upper-left corner of B3 and then drag diagonally to the lower-right corner of H16 to form the outer boundary of the box. Your text box should look like the one shown in Figure 13-3 (after you click once on the border box to select it).

   Notice that the mouse pointer is a single-headed arrow when it is on the border. You can move the box by dragging it with the single-headed arrow. Also notice that the selected box has small "handles" in each of the corners and in the center of each side. When you move the mouse pointer onto one of these handles, it changes to a double-headed arrow. You can resize the box by dragging with the double arrow.

6. Adjust your text box until it is the size you want. It is not necessary that it look precisely as shown in Figure 13-3. You will have to adjust the centering of the title box later when the borders and bars are turned off.

7. Click on the border of the text box to select it if you haven't already, then click the right mouse button and choose Format Object.

13

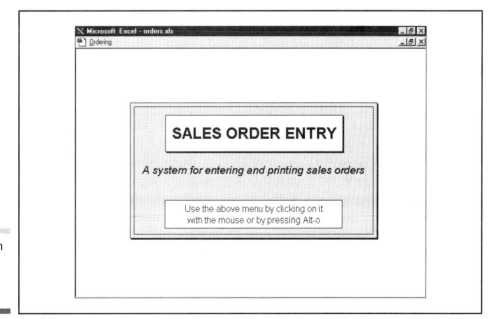

Title screen in its finished form

Figure 13-2.

You can move
the box when
the mouse
pointer looks
like this
Figure 13-3.

8. In the Format Object dialog box, click on the Font tab, then choose Italic for the Arial font style and 14 point for the font size. Click on the Alignment tab and choose Center for both the horizontal and vertical text alignment. Finally, click on the Patterns tab. Notice that the current fill is indicated by a thin border around a colored square (the default color is white), and a sample is shown in the Sample box at the lower-right corner. Click on the gray color (second row, second from the right) or any other color that you want for your title box. Click on OK to close the Format Object dialog box.

9. While the text box is still selected, click on the Drop Shadow tool (second from the bottom in the left column of the Drawing toolbar).

10. Click anywhere inside the text box to place the insertion point in the center, then type **A system for entering and printing sales orders**. Your text box should now look approximately like the one shown in Figure 13-4.

11. Click on the Text Box tool again and create a second text box on top of the first, by dragging *approximately* from the upper-left corner of C4 to the lower-right corner of G7.

12. Double-click on the border of the new text box to open the Format Object dialog box and give the new text box the Bold font style, 20 point font size, centered horizontal and vertical text alignment, and

specify white (or your choice) for the fill. Click OK to close the Format Object dialog box.

13. Give the new text box a drop shadow and then click in it and type **SALES ORDER ENTRY**. If necessary, resize the text box to display the text on a single line as shown here:

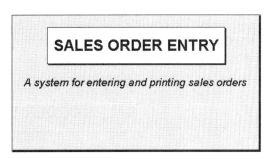

14. Once more, click on the Text Box tool and create a third text box in the lower part of the main text box, extending from approximately the upper-left corner of C12 to the lower-right corner of G15.

15. From the Format Object dialog box, give the new text box the Regular font style, 12 point font size, centered horizontal and vertical text

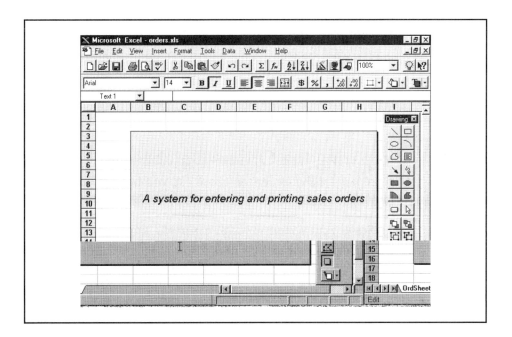

alignment, and specify white (or your choice) for the fill. Close the dialog box and resize the text box, if necessary.

16. Type **Use the above menu by clicking on it**, press ENTER to go to the next line, and then continue typing: **with the mouse or by pressing Alt-o**.

17. Select the open Rectangle tool in the top right of the Drawing toolbar and create a rectangle by dragging the tool from the upper left to the lower right just inside the main text box so that the resulting rectangle looks like this:

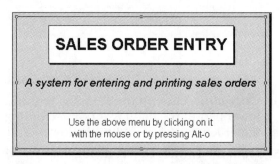

18. Once your text boxes and rectangle look the way you want them, hold down SHIFT while you click on each of the four objects (three text boxes and the rectangle) in turn. Then, while they are all selected, point on Placement from the Format menu and then click on Group.

    This enables you to move the entire graphic as a unit for fine-tuning the centering after the borders and bars are turned off.

19. Click on the Close button of the Drawing toolbar to turn it off and then click on the Save tool to save your work.

That completes the title screen. Next, you will prepare the orders and product lists.

Preparing the Orders Database

To prepare for the Orders database list, you need to enter a set of headings, adjust the column widths, and apply formats to the columns.

1. Scroll your screen so that L1 is in the upper-left corner.

2. Widen columns L and O to 25, and narrow columns P, Q, and R to 7. You can hold down CTRL while selecting the columns with the mouse to do L and O together and then do P, Q, and R together.

3. Enter the headings in row 4 that are shown next, plus headings of **Tax** in R4 and **Total** in S4. Center them, make them bold, and put a bottom

border under them using the three appropriate tools on the Formatting toolbar.

	L	M	N	O	P	Q
1						
2						
3						
4	Company	Person	Quantity	Product	Price	Rate
5						
6						

4. Click on L1, click on its reference in the name box (at the left end of the Formula bar), then type **Company_Name** and press ENTER. This name will be used later to reference cell L1.

5. Repeat step 4 for cells M1 through S1, and assign them the names **Salesperson_Name**, **Quantity_Ordered**, **Product_Descrip**, **Unit_Price**, **Tax_Rate**, **Tax**, and **Total**. Be sure to press ENTER after typing each name.

It is important that these names are correct. If you make a mistake, you can delete the name you typed and replace it in the Define Name dialog box, which is reached from the Name option on the Insert menu and is shown here with the correct names:

13

6. Format the database list columns as follows: hold down CTRL and click on the L, M, and O column headings. Choose Cells from the Format menu, click on the Number tab and the Text Category, and then click OK. Then use the tools on the Formatting toolbar and apply the #,##0 format code to the N column, the #,##0.00 format code to columns P, R, and S, and the 0.00% format code from the Percentage category to column Q.

7. Click on L4 and then click in the Name box of the Formula bar and type **Orders_Database**.

Again, save your work.

Preparing the Products List

Next create a list of the available products, to be entered into orders with these instructions.

1. Scroll your screen so that V1 is visible at the top, make it the active cell, and widen column V to 30.

2. Enter the **Product** heading in row 1, and apply the same formatting that you used for the other list. (Hint: try the Format Painter.) Below the heading, enter the items that are shown in Figure 13-5 (or any other products that you want on the list).

3. Select the range of cells, starting with the first product item below the heading and going down to the last item in the list. Give the selected cells a name by choosing Insert Name Define and typing **Products** in the text box. Click the OK button.

4. Save the workbook again.

Most of the remaining work involves creating macros that are stored on a module sheet. You will come back to the order sheet later.

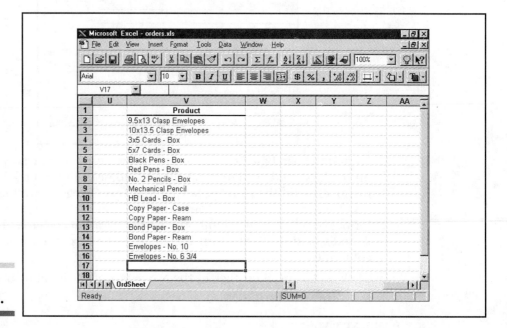

Product list
Figure 13-5.

Building the Macros

The next step is to automate the order sheet. This is done through a combination of recording macros and then modifying them. The macros are divided into five sections. In the first section, you will build a means to prepare and control the sheet and the screen. In the next section, you will build a dialog box to accept entries for the database and then build the macros to update the list with those entries. In the third section, you will record the macros used to print the database list, save the workbook, and quit Excel. In the fourth section, you will build macros for use with Excel's Data Form in editing the database list. In the final section, you will build a custom menu and a macro that provides access to the rest of the macros. These macros provide the means for entering, editing, and printing data and saving and quitting the application. They also represent the five choices in the menu built in the final section.

While this may sound like a major undertaking, you will find it goes faster than you think. It is, however, not a trivial task. Remember that you are building a fully operable, complete application that allows a novice to do some sophisticated things with Excel. By working through this application, you should be able to build almost any application of your own.

13

Think of a series of interconnected macros as a logic path, a set of stepping stones along a main path that leads to other paths branching off from it. You start out on the main path and come to a branch. You make a choice, branch off, do some task, and then return to the original path. In this application you start out with a menu that provides five choices: entering, editing, printing, saving, and quitting. You choose one, do it, and then return to the menu again to make another choice. Figure 13-6 shows a simplified logic path for the order entry application.

There are two ways to build a group of macros that represent an application: using a few large macros or using many small macros. Using a few large macros—for example, one macro for each item on the menu—has the benefit of clearly delineating the program flow. Many small macros, which you would combine to perform the menu functions, have two overpowering benefits. First, it is easier to build and test the small macros because they are small. Second, there are several small tasks that are common subtasks in larger tasks. By building small macros that can be called by the larger tasks, you reduce repetition. Therefore, the instructions that follow have you build many small macros and then combine them to carry out the menu choices.

It is also easier to work with a large number of macros and their associated code when they are all on one module sheet. The examples in the rest of the chapter assume there is only one sheet, Module1, used to store the macros and Visual Basic code. If you wind up creating macros on subsequent sheets, for example: Module2, Module3, and so forth, simply copy the code using

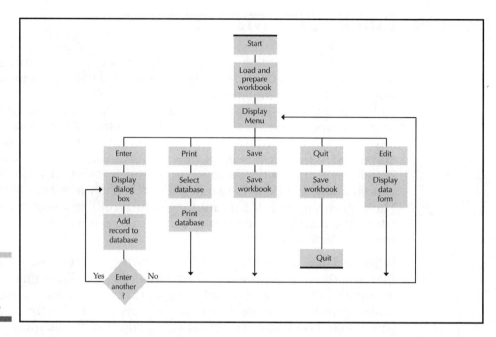

Order entry
logic path
Figure 13-6.

CTRL-C from the new module sheet and paste it (CTRL-V) at the end of the code
in Module1. Then delete the new module sheet, as it is no longer needed.

Preparing and Controlling the Order Sheet

Five separate macros are used to prepare and control the order sheet and the
screen. The first simplifies the Excel display and positions the title graphic.
The second undoes what the first did, so when you are done with the
application you can return to the normal Excel environment. It is important,
as you are building macros, to always have *reversing* macros so that when
you test a macro you can undo its effects. You will see several reversing
macros here.

The third macro maximizes the windows and calls the first macro. Here
you see the first of many instances of one macro calling one or more other
macros. The fourth and fifth macros position the screen on the title graphic
and on a blank area of the sheet, respectively.

Preparing the Order Sheet

The first macro to be created turns off the row and column headings,
gridlines, scroll bar, Formula bar, Status bar, sheet tabs, and all the toolbars.
Finally, it centers the title graphic in the window.

1. Make sure that the active cell is *not* A1 (the upper-left corner of the sheet). You want to explicitly make A1 the active cell while recording the macro.

2. Point on Record Macro from the Tools menu and click on Record New Macro. Type **Prepare_Sheet**, then click on the Options button to expand the Record New Macro dialog box. Make sure that Store in This Workbook and Visual Basic are selected. Click on OK to begin recording the macro.

3. Press CTRL-HOME to position the title graphic in the center of the screen (it will probably not be in the center yet—you can fine-tune its position later).

4. Choose Options from the Tools menu and click on the View tab. Click on Formula Bar, Status Bar, Gridlines, Row & Column Headers, Horizontal Scroll Bar, Vertical Scroll Bar, and Sheet Tabs to remove the check and turn these features off. Click on OK.

5. Choose Toolbars from the View menu and uncheck the Standard and Formatting check boxes to remove those toolbars. If other toolbars are checked in your Toolbars dialog box uncheck them also (but don't uncheck the Stop Recording box). Click on OK.

13

6. Click on Stop Recording to stop the recording, then press CTRL-PGDN (since the sheet tabs are now turned off) until the macro sheet containing your new macro appears.

7. Add the line shown in Figure 13-7, just above the End Sub statement beginning "Range("F13")." This line hides the active cell behind the title graphic. This statement could not be recorded in the macro because clicking on a graphic object selects it instead of the underlying cell.

8. Type the two comments opposite the two Toolbar statements as shown in Figure 13-7. These are the only statements in this macro that are not self-documenting.

   Your macro's Sub procedure might not look exactly the same as the one shown here if you turned off additional toolbars. Look over the statements in your macro and edit it as necessary to make it look like the one shown in Figure 13-7, unless you have additional toolbars.

9. Press CTRL-PGUP to get back to the order sheet (OrdSheet).

Restoring the Order Sheet

Next you need a macro to restore the gridlines, headings, bars, and so forth to reverse the steps you just completed.

```
 Microsoft Excel - orders.xls                                    _|8|X|
  File  Edit  View  Insert  Run  Tools  Window  Help            _|8|X|
'
' Prepare_Sheet Macro
' Macro recorded 6/7/95 by Martin Matthews
'
'
Sub Prepare_Sheet()
    Range("A1").Select
    With ActiveWindow
        .DisplayGridlines = False
        .DisplayHeadings = False
        .DisplayHorizontalScrollBar = False
        .DisplayVerticalScrollBar = False
        .DisplayWorkbookTabs = False
    End With
    With Application
        .DisplayFormulaBar = False
        .DisplayStatusBar = False
    End With
    Toolbars(1).Visible = False            'Standard Toolbar
    Toolbars(2).Visible = False            'Formatting Toolbar
    With Application
        .ShowToolTips = True
        .LargeButtons = False
        .ColorButtons = True
    End With
    Range("F13").Select       'Park the active cell behind the title box
End Sub
```

Prepare_Sheet
macro code
Figure 13-7.

1. Point on Record Macro from the Tools menu and click on Record New Macro. Type **Return_Sheet** and click on OK.

2. Choose Options from the Tools menu and click on the View tab. Click on Formula Bar, Status Bar, Gridlines, Row & Column Headers, Horizontal Scroll Bar, Vertical Scroll Bar, and Sheet Tabs to turn the features back on. Click on OK.

3. Choose Toolbars from the View menu and click on the Standard and Formatting check boxes to turn the toolbars back on. Turn on again any other toolbars that you turned off in the Prepare_Sheet macro. Click on OK.

4. Click on Stop Recording to complete the second macro, and click on the Module1 tab to view your macro code. Compare this macro's code with that of the previous macro to make sure that everything that was turned off got turned back on.

5. Type the toolbar comments shown in Figure 13-8.

6. Switch back to OrdSheet by clicking on its tab.

7. Save your work.

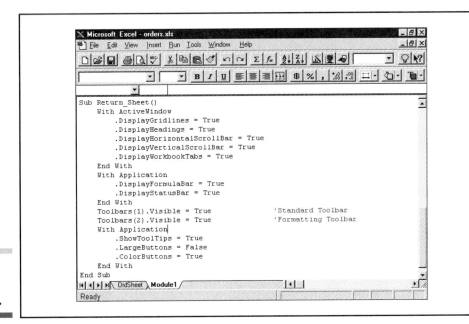

Return_Sheet
macro code
Figure 13-8.

Maximizing Windows and Preparing the Sheet

The third macro maximizes the Excel and workbook windows and calls the Prepare_Sheet macro.

1. If your Excel application window has been maximized, click on the Restore button or choose Restore from the Control menu at the left end of the Title bar to reduce it to normal size (it does not matter what size it is). Do the same with the ORDERS.XLS document window.

2. Choose Record Macro from the Tools menu and click on Record New Macro. Type **Max_Prepare** and click on OK.

3. Click on the Maximize buttons for both the Excel application window and the ORDERS.XLS document window.

4. Choose Macro from the Tools menu and select Prepare_Sheet from the list of macros. Click on Run.

5. Click on Stop Recording to complete the macro, then press CTRL-PGDN until the macro sheet appears. Compare your Max_Prepare macro code with that shown here:

```
' Max_Prepare Macro
' Macro recorded 6/7/95 by Martin Matthews
'

Sub Max_Prepare()
    Application.WindowState = xlMaximized
    ActiveWindow.WindowState = xlMaximized
    Application.Run Macro:="orders.xls!Prepare_Sheet"
End Sub
```

Positioning the Screen

Two macros are used to position the screen. The first positions the screen on the title graphic and the second on the blank sheet area directly below it.

1. Type the code for the first (Return_Home) macro directly into the module sheet, as shown next (it isn't as clean if you record it):

```
'
'Return_Home Macro
'
Sub Return_Home()
    Range("A1").Select       'Center the title graphic in the screen
    Range("F13").Select      'Park the active cell behind the title box
End Sub
```

Now you can record the second macro, as follows.

1. Press CTRL-PGUP to get back to OrdSheet.

2. Choose Record Macro from the Tools menu and click on Record New Macro, type **Next_Page** and click on OK.

3. Press CTRL-HOME, then press PGDN. This scrolls the title graphic up, leaving a blank screen.

4. Click on the Stop Recording tool to complete the macro, then press CTRL-PGDN until the macro sheet appears. Your macro should look like this:

```
'
' Next_Page Macro
' Macro recorded 6/7/95 by Martin Matthews
'
'
Sub Next_Page()
    Range("A1").Select
    ActiveWindow.LargeScroll Down:=1
    Range("A26").Select
End Sub
```

5. Now, remove the next-to-last line and add the two comments so that your macro looks like this:

```
'
' Next_Page Macro
' Macro recorded 6/7/95 by Martin Matthews
'
'
Sub Next_Page()
    Range("A1").Select              'Center the title graphic
    ActiveWindow.LargeScroll Down:=1    'Scroll down to blank area
End Sub
```

Removing the last Range( ).Select statement leaves the active cell out of sight for a cleaner background.

6. Press CTRL-PGUP to get back to OrdSheet, then, choosing Macro from the Tools menu, select and run the Return_Sheet macro to restore the normal Excel screen.

7. Save the workbook.

Testing and Debugging Your Macros

13

You now have five macros: Prepare_Sheet, Return_Sheet, Max_Prepare, Return_Home, and Next_Page. Because of the macros' small size and the use of the recorder to create them, with the illustrations in this book serving as a guide, they are probably error free. You still need to prove this by trying them out. Do so now.

1. Make sure that neither the Excel application nor the ORDERS.XLS windows are maximized. Restore them if necessary.

2. Choose Macro from the Tools menu, select Max_Prepare from the list of macros, and click on Run. This macro calls the Prepare_Sheet macro, so you actually are testing two macros in one.

You should get the title graphic displayed with nothing other than the Title bar and Menu bar at the top of your screen, as shown in Figure 13-9. You might need to center the title graphic in the center of the screen by dragging it (first make sure that you have grouped all its parts).

If you did not get the results shown in Figure 13-9, first study what you did get. Repeat the macro several times to observe what is going on. Look at any error messages. Often with macros you get an error message and are shown the line in the macro that is causing the problem. If you type in macro commands, spelling errors are frequently the cause. After looking at what happens when you execute the macro, go over to the module sheet and look carefully at the offending macro. Look at spelling, parentheses, quotation marks, and Macro function arguments. Compare what you see with the figures and illustrations shown here. These illustrations were produced by operating macros (really!).

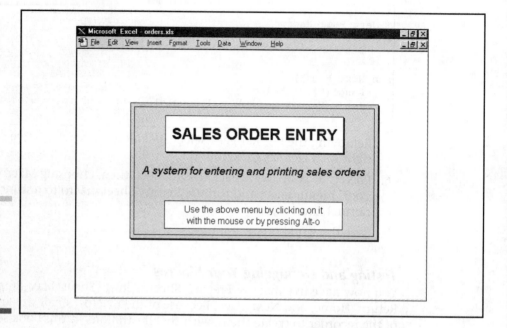

Drag the title
graphic, if
necessary, to
the center of
the screen
Figure 13-9.

3. After the Max_Prepare macro performs as expected, run the Next_Page macro to position the blank page on your screen. Except for the Title and Menu bars (and the mouse pointer), you should have a blank screen.

4. Run the Return_Home macro to position the title graphic and active cell on your screen.

5. Run the Return_Sheet macro to return to normal Excel Display mode.

You should now have five proven macros. If you do not, fix them before going on and then save the workbook.

Building the Data Entry Tools

The data entry tools consist of a data entry dialog box and three macros—one that supports the dialog box controls, one that updates the database list, and one that ties the two others together.

Building a Custom Dialog Box

Building a dialog box usually involves two main tasks. The first is constructing the graphic object, and the second is writing the code necessary to make the dialog box function the way you want it to. The code creation is covered in the next section. To construct the graphic object that the user of

The completed dialog box with the Forms toolbar

Figure 13-10.

this application will see, you start out with a skeletal dialog box on the screen and then add several text boxes, a check box, a drop-down list box, two buttons, and text. You also size and position each control, and specify properties for it. Figure 13-10 shows the completed dialog box used in this application

The Forms toolbar provides the means for you to build a dialog box graphically by positioning and sizing controls (buttons, text boxes, and so forth) on the dialog box. The techniques used to construct the graphic part of a custom dialog box are similar to those you used earlier to construct the title graphic. You choose the tool for the control you want to create, and then place and size it in the dialog box. If there is text involved, you can type the text. After you have placed a *control*, you can specify various format options for it. A control is basically any object you place on the form from the Forms toolbar such as the label, edit, and drop-down list boxes you will use shortly. As you construct the dialog box, you see exactly how the completed box will look, and you can even run it to see how it operates.

Begin the process of creating a dialog box by inserting a dialog sheet into the ORDERS workbook.

1. Point on Macro from the Insert menu and click on Dialog to create a new dialog sheet that looks like the one shown in Figure 13-11. Double-click on its tab and rename it OrderDialog.

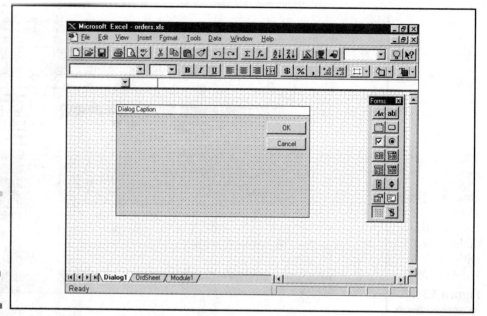

The skeletal
dialog box
contains two
buttons and a
sample caption
Figure 13-11.

2. Select the text in the Title bar, Dialog Caption, and type **Order Entry** to replace it.

3. Enlarge the dialog box a bit, and drag the two buttons to the bottom to get them out of the way, as you can see in Figure 13-12.

4. Click on the Label button in the upper-left corner of the Forms toolbar, then click and hold down your mouse button while dragging to create a small text box in the upper-left corner of the dialog box—don't worry about exact position, you will adjust it later. Refer to Figure 13-10 for approximate positioning.

5. Drag over the existing text inside the new label box and type **Company**.

6. Repeat steps 4 and 5 to create the five other labels (Salesperson, Quantity, Tax Rate, Unit Price, and Product), as shown in Figure 13-10. Don't worry too much about their sizes and positions at this point.

7. Click on the Edit Box tool in the upper right of the Forms toolbar, then drag the mouse to create an edit box control, just as you created the label boxes. Position the edit box to the right of the Company label, using Figure 13-10 as a guide.

8. With the new edit box control selected, click on the Control Properties tool (second from the bottom on the left of the Forms toolbar). Then, on the Control tab, verify Text for the Edit Validation setting is chosen.

Enlarged
dialog box
with the
buttons moved
Figure 13-12.

This setting specifies that only text input will be accepted by the edit box. Click on OK to close the dialog box.

9. Repeat steps 7 and 8 to place edit box controls opposite the Salesperson, Quantity, Tax Rate, and Unit Price labels. Specify Text Validation for the Salesperson edit box, Integer Validation for the Quantity edit box, Number Validation for the Tax Rate edit box, and Number Validation for the Unit Price edit box. When you are done, your screen should look like Figure 13-13.

10. Create the Product list box by clicking on the Combination Drop-Down Edit tool (fifth down on the right in the Forms toolbar). Then drag the control to size in the dialog box.

    A combination drop-down edit control allows you to enter an item not on the list by typing it into the text box.

11. Click on the Control Properties tool while the new control is selected. Click on the Control tab, then type **Products** for the Input Range. This setting identifies the list that will appear in the drop-down list. Recall that you assigned this name to the Products list when you created it. The Input Range could also be specified as V1:V16. Specify the number of Drop Down Lines as 15 and click on OK.

12. Click on the Check Box tool (third down on the left in the Forms toolbar) and drag the check box control into place opposite Tax Rate in

Labels and
edit boxes in
place
Figure 13-13.

the dialog box. Drag across the existing text and replace it with
Taxable?. For the Control Properties of the check box, specify Checked
for the Value (or specify Unchecked, if you want that to be its initial
state). Then click on OK.

13. Select the word "OK" in the OK button and replace it with **Enter**. With
the button still selected, click on the Control Properties tool, select the
Default and Dismiss properties if not already checked, and E (or e) for
the Accelerator Key, if they are not already selected.

14. Change the Cancel button text to **Close**, and select Cancel for its
property and C (or c) for the Accelerator Key.

15. Arrange the controls in the dialog box to your liking. It is not important
to have the dialog box be an exact duplicate of the finished dialog box
shown in Figure 13-14.

This completes the dialog box construction. You might want to point on
Protection from the Tools menu and click on Protect Sheet to prevent
accidental changes to the dialog box on the OrderDialog sheet. You will
have to unprotect it before you can make changes to it.

Finished
dialog box
Figure 13-14.

13

Creating the Event Handler Procedure

Before your dialog box will work, you need to create a procedure that runs
each time the Enter button is chosen. This procedure is called an *event
handler* because it responds to the Enter button's click event. This procedure,
which must be created manually in the module sheet, is named
Button2_Click. Button2 is the button name (which appears in the Formula
bar when the button is selected), and Click is the event that causes this
procedure to run.

Recall that you assigned names to cells L1 through S1 in the workbook that
correspond to the fields in the database list. The Button2_Click procedure
copies the values entered by the user in the Order Entry dialog box to those
named cells. In addition, it performs some simple calculations of the tax and
total.

The procedure is attached to the Enter button in the dialog box by creating a
code stub from the dialog box and then inserting in the stub the code you
want executed. The stub contains the following:

```
'
' Button2_Click Macro
'
'
Sub Button2_Click()
End Sub
```

The stub is created by selecting the Enter button in the dialog box and then clicking on the Edit Code tool in the Forms toolbar. This writes the stub in the module sheet. Do that now (you should still have the dialog box on your screen).

1. Click on the Enter button to select it and then click on the Edit Code tool (second from the bottom on the right) in the Forms toolbar. The module sheet is activated and the stub is written as shown above.

   You may have "OrderDialog_," the dialog box's name, in front of Button2. It works the same either way since you have only one dialog box.

   Next, you need to enter the code to be executed by this procedure. Type it carefully; for it to work, the spelling here must be the same as the range names you entered earlier. About two-thirds of the way through the code you will see the Excel constant "x1On" that is used to determine if a check box is checked. In the middle of the constant are two *letters*, a lowercase "l" and a capital "O"; they are not numbers.

2. Position the insertion point on the E in End Sub, press ENTER, and then on the new line you just created, begin typing the Button2_Click listing shown next. When you are done, the End Sub statement should be on a line by itself at the end.

```
Dim Quant, Unit, Rate, Tx     'Variables for computing tax & total

'Copy company name to the order sheet
Range("Company_Name").Value = _
     DialogSheets("OrderDialog").EditBoxes(1).Text

'Copy salesperson name to the order sheet
Range("Salesperson_Name").Value = _
     DialogSheets("OrderDialog").EditBoxes(2).Text

'Copy quantity to the order sheet
Quant = Val(DialogSheets("OrderDialog").EditBoxes(3).Text)
Range("Quantity_Ordered").Value = Quant

'Copy tax rate to the order sheet
Rate = Val(DialogSheets("OrderDialog").EditBoxes(4).Text)
Range("Tax_Rate").Value = Rate

'Copy unit price to the order sheet
Unit = Val(DialogSheets("OrderDialog").EditBoxes(5).Text)
Range("Unit_Price").Value = Unit

'Check whether the taxable checkbox is checked (xlOn)
```

```
If (DialogSheets("OrderDialog").CheckBoxes(1).Value = xlOn) _
   Then
        Tx = Quant * Unit * Rate
   Else
        Tx = 0
End If

'Copy tax to the order sheet
Range("Tax").Value = Tx

'Calculate total and copy to the order sheet
Range("Total").Value = Quant * Unit + Tx

'Copy product description to the order sheet
Range("Product_Descrip").Value = _
        DialogSheets("OrderDialog").DropDowns(1).Text
```

3. Save your work.

Next, try using the dialog box with the following steps and see what
happens.

13

4. Make the OrderDialog sheet the active sheet, then choose Run Dialog
   from the Tools menu. The dialog box should open as shown here
   (without the data):

5. Enter some sample data. Pressing TAB to move to each box, choose the
   first product from the drop-down list box, and then choose the Enter
   button. If your dialog box is working correctly, it will close (leaving the
   model you built earlier, which was underneath the running dialog box).
   Now switch to the order sheet and check cells L1 through S1. They
   should contain the values that you entered in the dialog box.

If something went wrong, double-check your Button2_Click procedure code for spelling errors and compare it with the listing above. Also, check the properties you gave your dialog box controls, and verify that the names assigned to the cells on the order sheet match those used in the Button2_Click procedure. Keep working on it until all the values you enter in the dialog box (plus the computed tax and total) are transferred to the order sheet cells.

Updating the Database List

The next task is to build a macro that takes the data placed in L1 through S1 of the order sheet and adds it to the bottom of the database list.

1. Make OrdSheet the active sheet by clicking on its tab. Scroll the sheet until L1 is in the upper-left corner of the window.

2. The first row of cells (L1:S1) should contain the data that was copied from the dialog box during testing. If it doesn't, go back and complete that step, then return to step 1. Start the database list by copying this row to the first row under the database list headings. Click on L1, then press CTRL-SHIFT-RIGHT ARROW to select all the named cells.

3. Click on the Copy tool to copy the cells, click on the cell immediately below the Company heading (L5), and press SHIFT-RIGHT ARROW seven times to select the destination cells. Then choose Copied Cells from the Insert menu and verify that Shift Cells Down is specified in the dialog box. Click on OK to copy the values and create the first row of the database list. Now you are ready to record the macro. Press ESC to clear the marquee.

4. Choose Record Macro from the Tools menu and click on Record New Macro. Type **Add_Record** and click on OK.

5. Again click on L1, then press CTRL-SHIFT-RIGHT ARROW to select all the named cells (containing the dialog box values). Press CTRL-C to copy the cells.

6. Click on the Company heading (L4). Press CTRL-DOWN ARROW, then DOWN ARROW again, then SHIFT-RIGHT ARROW seven times. You have now selected the first blank line underneath the last record in the database. By pressing CTRL-DOWN ARROW, you perform an important step because it can get you to the bottom of a database list of any length.

7. Choose Copied Cells from the Insert menu and verify that Shift Cells Down is specified in the dialog box. Click on OK.

8. Press ESC to clear the marquee, run the Return_Home macro, then the Next_Page macro.

9. Click on the Stop Recorder tool to complete the macro, then press CTRL-PGDN until the macro sheet appears. As a reminder, if your macro

appears in a new macro sheet, copy the macro code and paste it to the
end of the code in the Module1 sheet. Delete the new macro sheet. Your
Add_Record macro should look like this:

```
'
' Add_Record Macro
' Macro recorded 6/7/95 by Martin Matthews
'
'
Sub Add_Record()
    Range("L1:S1").Select
    Selection.Copy
    ActiveWindow.SmallScroll ToRight:=-1
    Range("L4").Select
    Selection.End(xlDown).Select
    Range("L6:S6").Select
    Selection.Insert Shift:=xlDown
    Application.CutCopyMode = False
    Application.Run Macro:="orders.xls!Return_Home"
    Application.Run Macro:="orders.xls!Next_Page"
End Sub
```

13

10. The statement **Range("L6:S6").Select** must be changed because it is
    an absolute reference to the sixth row. Since your database list will
    grow, this reference needs to be a relative reference. Change the line to
    Selection.Offset(1, 0).Range("A1:H1").Select. This statement
    specifies a relative offset (down one row) and a relative range (the first 8
    cells to the right) for the selection.

11. Also, If you have a line "ActiveWindow.SmallScroll ToRight :=-1", you
    can delete it. This positioned your screen so you could click on L4 and
    isn't needed in the code. Your revised Add_Record macro should look
    like this:

```
'
' Add_Record Macro
' Macro recorded 6/7/95 by Martin Matthews
'
'
Sub Add_Record()
    Range("L1:S1").Select
    Selection.Copy
    Range("L4").Select
    Selection.End(xlDown).Select
    Selection.Offset(1, 0).Range("A1:H1").Select
    Selection.Insert Shift:=xlDown
    Application.CutCopyMode = False
    Application.Run Macro:="orders.xls!Return_Home"
    Application.Run Macro:="orders.xls!Next_Page"
End Sub
```

Tying Together the Data Entry Tools

Next, create a third procedure that displays the dialog box, runs the
Add_Record macro, and repeats the process until the user is finished. The
Orders_Dialog procedure uses a built-in message box to find out whether the
user wants to enter another order. Type the following code below the
Add_Record procedure in the module sheet.

```
'
'Orders_Dialog Macro
'
Sub Orders_Dialog()
Dim Continue As Integer
ShowDialog:                      'Line label for GoTo
    'Show the custom dialog box: True if user clicks the Enter button
    If DialogSheets("OrderDialog").Show Then
        Application.Run Macro:="orders.xls!Add_Record"
        'Note line-continuation characters in the following statement
        Continue = MsgBox(Prompt:="Enter another order?", _
        Buttons:=vbYesNo + vbInformation, _
        Title:="Order Entry")
        If Continue = vbYes Then
            GoTo ShowDialog
        End If
    End If
End Sub
```

Now test your data entry routines all together, by running the Orders_Dialog
macro from the OrdSheet sheet. Click on the OrdSheet tab or press CTRL-PGUP
to return to the order sheet. Run the Max_Prepare macro first, then run the
Next_Page macro, and then run the Orders_Dialog macro. You should be
able to keep adding orders to the database list as long as you want. After you
finish, check the list to make sure that the records are being added properly.

Using Data Form for Editing

With a database list in place, you now need to be able to edit and delete
records. Excel has a built-in capability for this in the Data Form option. Build
a macro to use this feature next.

1. From the OrdSheet sheet, choose Record Macro from the Tools menu
   and click on Record New Macro. Type **Edit_It** and click on OK.

2. Open the reference area box on the Formula bar and choose
   Orders_Database to go there.

3. Choose Form from the Data menu. Excel's data form is displayed, as
   shown in Figure 13-15.

Excel's data
form
Figure 13-15.

In the data form, you can edit individual fields of a record, add and delete records, and find records based on criteria you enter. (Yes, you could have used this in place of the dialog box you built, but then you would not have had such an excellent opportunity to build a custom dialog box.)

4. Click on the scroll bar to go from record to record, or use the Find buttons.

5. Click on Close to leave the data form, then run the Return_Home macro.

6. Click on the Stop Recorder tool, then switch to the module sheet. The Edit_It macro is shown below, with these three lines added:

```
Selection.CurrentRegion.Select      'Select the database
Selection.Name = "Database"
ActiveWindow.LargeScroll Down:=1     'Scroll down to blank area
```

The database needs to be selected and named "Database" because the macro form of Data Form will only operate on a database so named or one beginning in the range A1:B2. (If you try to execute the code you recorded you will get an error.) The third new line is needed to get an uncluttered backdrop for the data form.

The active cell must remain in the list in order for the data form to recognize where the database list is.

```
'
'  Edit_It Macro
'  Macro recorded 6/7/95 by Martin Matthews
'
'
Sub Edit_It()
    Application.Goto Reference:="Orders_Database"
    Selection.CurrentRegion.Select        'Select the database
    Selection.Name = "Database"
    ActiveWindow.LargeScroll Down:=1      'Scroll down to blank area
    ActiveSheet.ShowDataForm
    Application.Run Macro:="Orders.xls!Return_Home"
End Sub
```

Printing, Saving, and Quitting

You next need to be able to print and save your workbook and leave Excel. Build macros for those purposes now.

Building a Printing Macro

The printing macro is actually two macros: one to select the print area and the other to do the printing. Build both of these next.

1. From the OrdSheet sheet, choose Record Macro from the Tools menu and click on Record New Macro. Type **Select_Database** and click on OK.

2. Click on the down arrow next to the reference area box in the Formula bar and choose Orders_Database. Press CTRL-DOWN ARROW to select the bottom row's first cell, then press END-RIGHT ARROW to select the right-most bottom cell in the list. This procedure does not select the database list, but inserts code that can be manually augmented to accomplish the task.

3. Click on the Stop Recorder tool and inspect your macro code, which should look like this:

```
'
'  Select_Database Macro
'  Macro recorded 6/7/95 by Martin Matthews
'
'
Sub Select_Database()
    Application.Goto Reference:="Orders_Database"
    Selection.End(xlDown).Select
    Selection.End(xlToRight).Select
End Sub
```

The macro as recorded just selects the lower-right corner of the database list. An additional line can be added to select the range between the upper-left corner (Orders_Database) and the active cell (the lower-right corner).

4. Add the new line beginning "Range("Orders" and the comments to your code to make it look like this:

```
'
' Select_Database Macro
' Macro recorded 6/7/95 by Martin Matthews
'
'
Sub Select_Database()
    Application.Goto Reference:="Orders_Database"
    Selection.End(xlDown).Select     'Lower left-hand corner of the list
    Selection.End(xlToRight).Select 'Lower right-hand corner of the list
    Range("Orders_Database", ActiveCell).Select 'The entire database list
End Sub
```

To prepare your workbook for printing, you'll first make the necessary settings in the Page Setup dialog box and then record the macro. This means that if you change your page setup for some reason, you must come back and redo it to print the database.

13

1. Switch back to the order sheet, open the Page Setup dialog box from the File menu, and click on the Margins tab. Set the Top and Bottom margins to 1 if not already set, the Left and Right margins to 0, and click on Horizontally Center on Page.

2. Click on the Header/Footer tab and the Custom Header button. Put the date in the left box using the Calendar button, the word "ORDERS" in the center box, and "Page " and the page number (using the Page Number button) in the right box. Click on OK to return to the Page Setup dialog box. Open the Footer drop-down list box and choose (none). Click on OK to close the Page Setup dialog box.

3. Choose Record Macro from the Tools menu and click on Record New Macro, type **Print_It**, and click on OK.

4. Run the Select_Database macro.

5. Choose Print from the File menu, click on Selection, then click on OK. The result is shown here:

	6/8/95			ORDERS				Page 1

Company	Person	Quantity	Product	Price	Rate	Tax	Total
Ralph's Construction	Alice	10	9.5x13 Clasp Envelopes	4.59	7.80%	3.58	49.48
Hungry Pig Cafe	Alice	10	9.5x13 Clasp Envelopes	4.59	7.80%	3.58	49.48
Jerry's Construction	Alice	10	9.5x13 Clasp Envelopes	4.59	7.80%	3.58	49.48
Scott's Repair	Joe	25	Mechanical Pencil	1.14	7.80%	2.22	30.72
Harvey's Drive-In	Sam	1	Pizza boxes - case	22.99	0.00%	0.00	22.99
Scott's Repair	Joe	25	Mechanical Pencil	1.14	7.90%	2.25	30.75
Bob's Trucking	Alison	20	Mechanical Pencil	1.14	7.90%	1.80	24.60

6. Run the Return_Home macro to return to the title screen.

7. Click on the Stop Recording tool, then switch to the module sheet. Your code should look like that shown here:

```
'
' Print_It Macro
' Macro recorded 6/7/95 by Martin Matthews
'
'
Sub Print_It()
    Application.Run Macro:="orders.xls!Select_Database"
    Selection.PrintOut Copies:=1
    Application.Run Macro:="orders.xls!Return_Home"
End Sub
```

Saving and Quitting

The saving and quitting macros are trivial by comparison to what you have already done. Build them here.

1. First, save the ORDERS workbook. Now if something goes wrong, you do not lose anything.

2. Choose Record Macro from the Tools menu and click on Record New Macro. Type **Save_It** and click on OK.

3. Run the Return_Home macro to ensure you are at the title screen, then choose File Save.

4. Click on the Stop Recording tool.

5. Choose Record Macro from the Tools menu and click on Record New Macro, type **Quit_It**, then click on OK.

6. Run the Return_Sheet macro to return to the normal Excel display, then run the Save_It macro to save the workbook.

7. Click on the Stop Recording tool.

8. Add the **Application.Quit** statement immediately before the End Sub statement in order to actually leave Excel. The revised macro is shown here:

```
'
' Save_It Macro
' Macro recorded 6/7/95 by Martin Matthews
'
'
Sub Save_It()
    Application.Run Macro:="orders.xls!Return_Home"
    ActiveWorkbook.Save
End Sub
'
' Quit_It Macro
' Macro recorded 6/7/95 by Matthews
'
'
Sub Quit_It()
    Application.Run Macro:="orders.xls!Return_Sheet"
    Application.Run Macro:="orders.xls!Save_It"
    Application.Quit
End Sub
```

Building and Using a Menu

13

To tie together all of the macros you have built into a system with a menu, you need one more macro and the custom menu. The menu you create is stored with the ORDERS workbook and automatically appears when the workbook is opened. The macro is used to prepare the display, run the data entry and update tasks, then redisplay the title screen. The first step is to create a macro to "package" the Orders_Dialog macro.

1. From the order sheet, choose Record Macro from the Tools menu and click on Record New Macro, type **Enter_It**, and click on OK.

2. Run the Max_Prepare macro, run the Next_Page macro, run the Orders_Dialog macro, click on Close, and run the Return_Home macro.

3. Click on the Stop Recorder tool. The Enter_It code is shown here:

```
'
' Edit_It Macro
' Macro recorded 6/7/95 by Martin Matthews
'
'
Sub Edit_It()
    Application.Run Macro:="orders.xls!Max_Prepare"
    Application.Run Macro:="orders.xls!Next_Page"
    Application.Run Macro:="orders.xls!Orders_Dialog"
    Application.Run Macro:="orders.xls!Return_Home"
End Sub
```

Next, build the menu.

1. Run the Return_Sheet macro to restore the screen, click on the module tab to make it the active sheet, then choose Menu Editor from the Tools menu. The Menu Editor dialog box is shown in Figure 13-16.

2. Click on the top item in the Menus list, then click on the Delete button repeatedly to delete all the Menus.

3. Click on the Insert button, type **&Ordering** in the Caption box.

4. Click in the Menu Items list, click on the Insert button, and type **&Edit Database** in the Caption box. Assign a macro to this menu item by typing **Edit_It** in the Macro box. Click on Insert again.

5. Repeat the process described in step 4 to add the following menu items and associated macros to the Menu Items list: a hyphen (-) to create a divider bar (no associated macro); "&Quit Ordering" (the Quit_It macro); "&Save Database" (the Save_It macro); "&Print Database" (the Print_It macro); hyphen; "&Order Entry" (the Enter_It macro). The finished Menu Editor looks like this:

6. Click on OK. The new menu system appears whenever the ORDERS workbook is active.

Automatically Setting Up the Workbook

You can create a special macro named Auto_Open that Excel automatically runs when the workbook is opened. The Auto_Open macro makes OrdSheet the active sheet and prepares the display by calling the Max_Prepare macro. Also, since the above menu definition turned off the menus, you need a way to turn them back on again with a shortcut key. Enter both of these short macros next.

1. Type the Auto_Open and Reset_Menu macros shown next:

```
'
'Auto_Open Macro
'
Sub Auto_Open()
    Sheets("OrdSheet").Select
    Application.Run Macro:="orders.xls!Max_Prepare"
End Sub
'
Reset_Menu Macro(Ctrl - r)
'
Sub Reset_Menu()
    Sheets("OrdSheet").Select
    ActiveMenuBar.Reset
    Application.Run Macro:="orders.xls!Return_Sheet"
End Sub
```

2. When you have entered these last two macros, choose Macro from the Tools menu to open the Macro dialog box. Click on Reset_Menu to select it and then click on Options.

3. Click on the Shortcut Key check box to turn it on, click in the key text box and type **r**, click on OK to close the Macro Options dialog box, and click on Close to close the Macro dialog box.

The Auto_Open procedure can be located anywhere in any module of the workbook. Also, if you want ORDERS.XLS to start automatically every time you start Excel, put ORDERS.XLS in the C:\MSOFFICE\EXCEL\XLSTART directory.

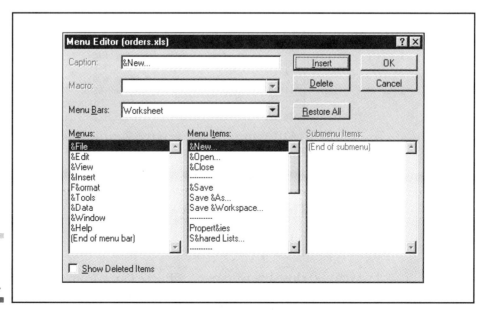

Menu Editor
dialog box
Figure 13-16.

Testing and Correcting the Macros

The normal testing process is primarily one of trying out the macros and seeing what happens. Then, based on what you have seen, you can make the necessary corrections. To speed up that process, print out your macros and compare them to the illustrations in this chapter. Also, print out your reference names and compare them. Sometimes "desk checking" like this can eliminate the majority of errors, which are usually typographical, before you ever run the macros.

Also, if you haven't done it already, it is a good time to restore the normal menus and turn on the Status bar, Formula bar, scroll bars, and toolbars. Use these instructions to restore your screen and print out the macros and the range names:

1. Press CTRL-R to restore the menus and screen and then click on the module sheet and choose Print from the File menu.

2. Click on the OrdSheet sheet and scroll your sheet so Z1:AA14 is visible. Click on Z3, point on Name from the Insert menu, click on Paste, and then click on the Paste List command button.

3. Type and format the headings and adjust the column widths, as shown here:

	Y	Z	AA	AB
1				
2		**Name**	**Reference**	
3		Company_Name	=OrdSheet!$L$1	
4		Orders_Database	=OrdSheet!$L$4	
5		Product_Descrip	=OrdSheet!$O$1	
6		Products	=OrdSheet!$V$2:$V$16	
7		Quantity_Ordered	=OrdSheet!$N$1	
8		Salesperson_Name	=OrdSheet!$M$1	
9		Tax	=OrdSheet!$R$1	
10		Tax_Rate	=OrdSheet!$Q$1	
11		Total	=OrdSheet!$S$1	
12		Unit_Price	=OrdSheet!$P$1	
13				

4. Select Z2:AA13, choose Print from the File menu, click on Selection, and click on OK. The range names are printed.

5. Compare your printouts to the related illustrations and figures above.

Working Through the Application

The next step is to execute each part of the macro and see what happens. Use the following steps for that purpose.

1. Save and close the workbook. Choose Open from the File menu, select ORDERS.XLS, and click on OK. The macro begins by displaying the title screen with the single Ordering menu, as shown in Figure 13-2.

2. Select the menu, and it should open like this:

3. Choose Order Entry and the dialog box opens in which you can enter the database information as shown in Figure 13-17.

4. Enter a record. What you put in the fields does not matter. Use TAB to go from field to field and ENTER to complete the entry.

When you press ENTER (or click on the Enter command button) you should see the database being updated. Then the second dialog box appears, asking if you want to enter another order, like this:

13

Working
Order Entry
dialog box
Figure 13-17.

Click on Yes and enter another item. Follow the same procedure outlined in step 4. When you get to the "Enter another order?" message, type **n**.

5. Choose Edit Database from the menu and try out the various options on Excel's Data Form.

6. Choose Print Database. The output you get should be similar to that shown earlier in the "Building a Printing Macro" section.

7. Choose Save Database. You should see some indication that the workbook is being saved.

8. Finally, choose Quit Ordering. You should be returned to Windows.

If your macros did not execute perfectly the first time, take heart—it happens to almost everybody. Observe what is not working right. Compare your printed list of macros with the ones presented here. Within a few iterations of trying the macros and making changes, you should get them to operate properly.

Future Enhancements

A number of improvements can be made to enhance this application.

One easy enhancement is to sort the orders by Company and prepare statements from the results. Also, by sorting on the product you can look at sales by product.

Another enhancement that would usually have been in the original product is to add a date field to both the database and the data entry dialog box.

You now have an exceptionally powerful tool at your disposal. You can make of it just about whatever you wish.

Integrating Excel with Office 95

14

Can you envision a time when you will be able to create a document on your computer that incorporates detailed formatted text, in-depth spreadsheet analysis, significant relational database data, and presentation-quality graphics, all from one seamless application? Although that convenient and efficient software is still on the drawing board, Microsoft Office 95 provides a good working approximation of what desktop computing might be in the not-too-distant future.

In the old days of personal computer usage (which can be loosely defined as anything from the early eighties through last year), you bought a specific application to accomplish a particular task. A word processing application did a wonderful job producing documentation, a database application stored and retrieved data faster than a speeding bullet, a spreadsheet program crunched numbers effortlessly, and a graphics program made artwork available to non-artists. But what happened when you wanted to combine the talents of these individual applications? The MS-DOS world certainly didn't lend itself toward any integration until Windows 3.x provided a reasonably stable environment for exchanging data within an operating system. The Clipboard provided the means to transfer *objects* (files of text, databases, clip art, and just about anything else you can create on your computer) from one application to another using copy and paste commands. Although this capability was a dramatic improvement over anything previous, it still fell short of many users' expectations and needs.

Office 95 provides the foundation for the optimal use of three pathways that allow a user to feel like they are working in one application while using multiple applications:

♦   OLE (object linking and embedding)

♦   VBA (Visual Basic, Applications)

♦   DDE (dynamic data exchange)

This chapter concentrates on defining OLE and seeing how it's used to integrate Excel with other Office 95 applications. You've already gotten a glimpse of the power and flexibility of what Visual Basic can do in Chapters 12 and 13. In Office 95, you can extend the Visual Basic language to the other applications in the suite, giving you a common framework in which to tie them together. In concert with an advanced feature of OLE, called OLE Automation, you can use the two elements to totally run other OLE-capable applications from a single application. DDE, an alternative and more complex solution to what OLE offers, has been largely relegated to the domain of programmers that need to have non-OLE compatible applications communicate. To expand your knowledge of integrating the Microsoft Office 95 suite of applications beyond the introductory nature of this chapter, read

Osborne/McGraw-Hill's *Making Microsoft Office Work*, by Ralph Soucie for a more in-depth look into this subject.

OLE provides another feature, not as automated as the ability to embed and link objects, but probably used more often: drag and drop between applications. This capability, coupled with the Windows 95 capability to drag *scraps* of data onto the desktop for eventually dragging and dropping into other applications, provides an enormous array of data exchange and sharing.

Defining OLE and the Office 95 Suite

Windows 95 and Office 95 add 32-bit processing power to take full advantage of OLE 2.0, the latest version of Microsoft's linking and embedding facility.

Before you actually begin to put OLE to use with Excel, you need to have a thorough understanding of OLE's two principle elements—linking and embedding—along with other components of an integrated document. This section provides the background material that is essential to effectively use the OLE features.

Linking vs. Embedding

14

The common element between linking and embedding is that work done in another application can be included in your current application, as shown in Figure 14-1 where an Excel chart is opened in a Word document. How this is accomplished is where the two elements of OLE take two separate and distinct paths. The nature of your project and how you plan on distributing it among its anticipated recipients will help you decide which direction is best for you.

Linking

As the name implies, linked files form a bond between the *source* file and the *destination* file. For example, the source file might be an Excel spreadsheet, some or all of which is used in a destination Word file. As long as the link is established between the two files, any change to the spreadsheet in Excel will be reflected in the spreadsheet's *placeholder* within the Word document. The spreadsheet isn't actually a part of the Word document; there's merely a "window" through which you can "see" the spreadsheet residing in Excel. This is a tremendously powerful capability when you think about it. From one source file, such as the Excel spreadsheet in our example, you can update that data in several documents that are linked to it. Another benefit to linking is the size of the destination file. You might have several linked

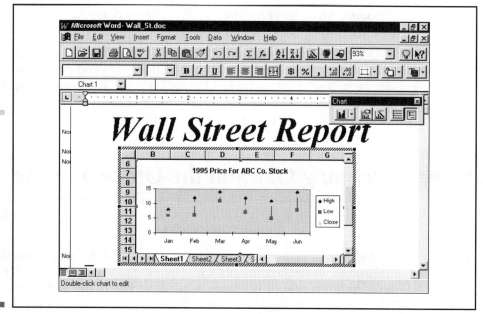

Editing an
Excel chart
embedded
within a Word
file (notice
Excel menu
and Formula
bars replacing
Word's menu
bars)
Figure 14-1.

objects in one destination file, which if pasted in the file could quickly
inflate the size of the file beyond that for efficient handling. By linking the
objects, you generally require fewer resources to establish and maintain the
links than including the data directly in the destination file.

There is, of course, some downside risk in using linked files. The major
source of either missing or erroneous data happens when the links are
broken. This generally occurs when the source files are moved to another
folder or are renamed. You'll see later in this chapter how a link appears in
the destination file and how you can see if the link may have been severed.
Another aspect of linking that you might find undesirable in certain
situations is its inability to be easily given to another person outside a
network environment with the linkages intact. In most corporate setups, the
source file is available on a server to which any number of users can connect
and link the file into their own destination documents. As long as the
destination documents stay within access of the server, all is well. However,
if you have a associate across the country who needs your destination file
you would have to include all linked source files and establish new links
based on a new drive and folder structure. The second element in OLE,
embedding, would make a better choice in this instance, as described next.

Embedding

More closely related to conventional copying and pasting, embedding places a copy of an object from the source application into a file in the destination application. The major advantage of OLE embedding over normal copying and pasting is you can edit or change the object while remaining in the destination application. With normal copying and pasting, you have to switch to the source application, make the change, and then recopy it into the destination file. The destination application basically turns over control to the source application for the purposes of editing the embedded object, as Figure 14-1 shows. After you make any edits, you return control back to the destination application and the only vestige of the source application is the updated object. The major benefit of embedding over linking is its independent and exportable form. You are not bound by the links associated with linked objects. You can embed objects in a file, transfer them to associates across the country, and, assuming they have the destination software, they can open it like any other document. Additionally, if they have the embedded object's source software, they also can edit or modify it, as you will see shortly.

Documents containing embedded objects can become quite large, even larger than the sum of the source files, because along with the data comes a certain amount of overhead associated with the embedding process. Another consideration to keep in mind when using embedded objects is that changes made to the original source file are not updated in the destination files, and visa versa, as they were with linked files.

14

Compound Documents

In 1990s terminology, files that contain embedded or linked objects are referred to as *compound* documents. As more and more organizations (and individuals) realize the benefits of sharing data through conventional networks and groupware products such as Lotus Notes, the greater reliance there will be on compound documents to provide information to a larger number of people, faster and more reliably.

Office 95 Applications

Office 95 is offered in two different configurations. The standard release contains the following suite of Microsoft applications.

♦ **Excel**, which offers comprehensive spreadsheet and database facilities, flexible charting, and detailed analysis tools, as demonstrated in the 13 previous chapters in this book

♦ **Word**, which provides robust, yet easy to use, word processing features

♦ **PowerPoint**, which provides tools to prepare professional-quality presentations, both printed and online

♦ **Schedule+**, which offers a graphical, user-friendly means to schedule meetings, appointments, and maintain data on your contacts over a network

If you have the professional suite, you have the above-listed applications with the addition of Microsoft's VBA-compatible relational database, Access. In either case, Office 95 offers several other features, including Binders, which allows you to create a folder-like container for data files from multiple Office 95 applications. Documents in a binder are treated as one file, which then can be printed with consecutive page numbers and distributed as you would a single file.

In terms of how the main Office 95 applications (Excel, Word, PowerPoint, and Access) are used to create compound documents, each can be categorized as to how well it serves as a container for other objects, or as a creator of objects. This is not to say that any application cannot perform in either role, just that some are more generally suited for one role over the other. The following table shows that Word and PowerPoint are the predominate container applications, which have objects pasted into them. Excel and Access are used primarily to store data, which is then copied and pasted into the container applications.

Office Application	OLE Object Container	OLE Object Creator
Excel		X
Word	X	
PowerPoint	X	
Access		X

Using OLE

Although the discussion on OLE—with source and destination files, linked and embedded objects, and compound documents—might create an uneasy atmosphere for new users to jump right into, the actual mechanics involved in using OLE are quite straightforward. There are several ways in which you transfer data to be shared by embedding or linking. The type of object you are sharing (text, graphic, or entire file) will determine which option(s) is suitable and the ultimate format of the object in the destination application. The options are:

♦ Using Copy in conjunction with the Paste Special dialog box

♦ Inserting an object by locating its file using the Insert menu Object and Picture options

♦ Dragging an object from the source application to the destination application, either directly or by using the desktop as an intermediary

Using the Paste Special Dialog Box

Regardless of whether you link or embed, the first action you take is to copy an object in the source document using the Copy option from the source application's Edit menu, toolbar, popup menu, or by pressing CTRL-C. Sharing data with OLE uses the Clipboard just as in a conventional copy operation. The "business end" of the process occurs while pasting objects into the destination document, using the Paste Special dialog box shown in Figure 14-2.

You've used the Paste Special dialog box in previous chapters and it looked different. The Paste Special dialog box has a somewhat chameleon nature that causes it to change appearance and function depending on the data that's on the Clipboard. As the you can see in Figure 14-2, the source of the data on the Clipboard is from Word and thus a candidate for embedding or linking. You would get the same dialog box if you copied, for example, a chart in Excel, a slide in PowerPoint, and a database in Access, because the type of object you have copied is *registered* in Windows 95 as a type of OLE object. If you copy an Excel range, the more familiar Paste Special dialog box, shown next, opens, allowing you to choose which attributes of the text

14

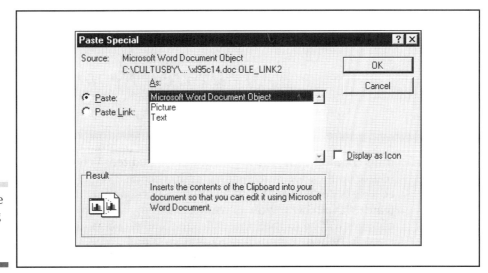

The OLE Paste Special dialog box

Figure 14-2.

or numbers to paste. As you saw in Chapter 9, you can use the Paste Link button to link data between Excel sheets and workbooks.

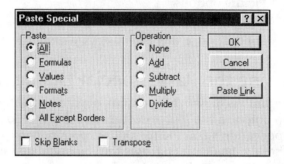

Returning to Figure 14-2, there are three other key areas in the dialog box besides the one which displays the source application and the path to the file where the object is located. The first is the As list box which lets you choose in what format you would like this particular object to be pasted. Secondly, you can either embed the object by choosing the Paste option or link the object by choosing Paste Link. Lastly, you can choose to have the object appear as an icon in the destination document (only available for the Word Document Object format).

In this example, the text that was copied in Word can be pasted (embedded) into Excel as a Word document Object, as a picture (or graphic), or as plain text. Notice the differences, or seeming lack of differences, in the three format types, shown below:

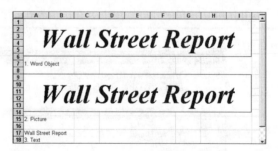

The first two methods look the same as the original did in Word. The difference lies in how the two objects are edited. When you paste using the source application's native format, in this case Word Document Object, editing is done using Word within the Excel application. You have Word's features available to you as you would if you were in Word itself. Your changes will be in the font, style, and size you choose from Word. In contrast, when you edit the paste done as a Picture, you "remain" totally in Excel and have the Format Object dialog box available to you to change appearance and positioning only. Pasting in the Text format strips away any native formatting from the source application and inserts the text in the default size, font, and style of Excel's general text.

If you do not want to display the full pasted object until needed, you can select the Display as Icon check box. This option is only available for objects that are in their native format such as a Word Document Object (you cannot display as an icon either the picture or the text options). When checked, pasted objects are reduced to an icon, as shown here, that can be opened to reveal the complete object by double-clicking on them.

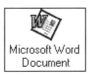

There are obvious reasons why you might choose one format over the other. If you want an exact copy that is fully editable by the source application, choose the native format. If you need the exact appearance, but are not anticipating any changes, the Picture option can potentially save on file storage, especially for larger data transfers. The Text format is best suited when you just want the basic text and intend on formatting after it's pasted in the destination document.

The examples used above assumed the object was pasted by embedding it into Excel. If you chose Paste Link in the Paste Special dialog box, you would have the same three formats to choose from, although the only one that would work properly is the Word Document Object. The other two formats cause a #Value! error value in Excel when paste linked because neither format is native to Word and any changes in the source application (Word) could not be transferred through the link to update the object in Excel.

Try using both embedding and linking from Word into Excel in the next series of steps. In addition to Excel, of which you should have a fair understanding , you are probably more comfortable with Word than the other Office 95 applications. The basic concepts are the same for any application, although each application has its own native objects that might behave slightly differently.

Embedding Using Paste Special
There are a few built-in features in Windows 95, Office 95, and the Office 95 applications that make opening and switching between the applications easy. First, there is a Microsoft toolbar, available from the View Toolbars option as shown here:

14

From here you can switch to other Microsoft applications if they are running or open them if they are not. Secondly, if you chose to display the Office Shortcut Bar, you have access to the Office 95 applications as well as other Office 95 features, as shown next:

Finally, you can use the Windows 95 Start button/Start menu to quickly open an application and the Taskbar to switch between them. Using the method you are most comfortable with, open both Word and Excel, ending with Word as your active application.

1. In Word, type **Wall Street Report** at the top of a new document and format (using the Formatting toolbar) as Times New Roman font, 48-point size, and styled bold and italic. The actual wording and formatting are not important.

2. Switch to Excel using one of the methods previously described, and type in the range of stock prices (A1:G4) shown next:

	A	B	C	D	E	F	G	H
1		Jan	Feb	Mar	Apr	May	Jun	
2	High	8	12	14	12	11	14	
3	Low	6	6	11	7	5	8	
4	Close	7	10	13	9	10	13	
5								

3. Select the range and click on the ChartWizard tool. Drag the ChartWizard pointer from B6:G15 to define the size of the chart. Accept the range if correct, then click on Next.

4. Choose the Line chart, click on Next, and then choose the number 7 type to create a High-Low-Close chart. Click on Next.

5. Accept Excel's default data series assignment by clicking on Next and then in the final ChartWizard type **1995 Price for ABC Co. Stock** in the Chart Title text box. Click on Finish. Your screen should look similar to Figure 14-3.

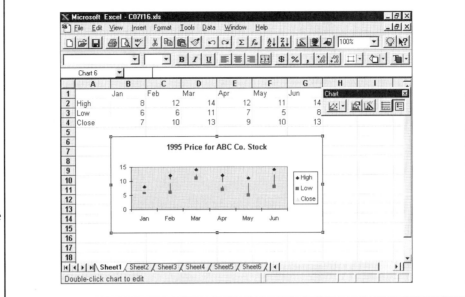

Creating a
High-Low-Close
chart to
embed into
Word
Figure 14-3.

6. With the chart selected (thin border around it with eight sizing handles), press CTRL-C to copy the chart to the Clipboard.

14

7. Switch back to Word and center the insertion point a line or two below the title, Wall Street Report.

8. Choose Paste Special from the Edit menu, accept the format in the As list box, Excel Chart Object, and select Paste to embed the object. Click on OK. The chart is pasted into the Word document as shown in Figure 14-4.

Editing an Embedded Object

At this point, you can continue with the remainder of your Word document, and if the chart and its underlying data don't change, your embedding is complete. However, you could have done that with a conventional copy and paste operation. Let's suppose there was an error in the closing price of the stock for June and the chart needs to be updated. See how convenient it is to edit an embedded object in the following steps.

1. In Word, double-click on the embedded chart. As you saw in Figure 14-1, the Menu bar and toolbars become Excel's although you are still in Word.

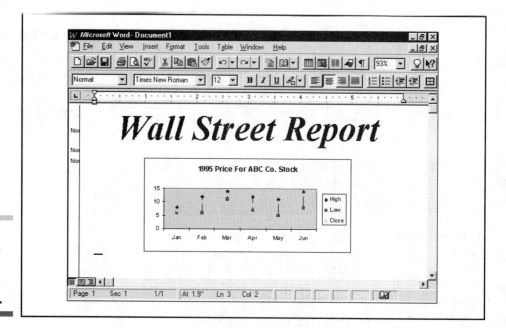

Excel chart
embedded in
a Word
document
Figure 14-4.

2. Use the scroll bars in the chart object to display the range of prices and edit cell G4 to replace the 13 with a 9. Notice the immediate change in the chart.

3. Scroll so the chart is fully visible, then click outside the chart to return control to Word. You can then use the sizing handles to reduce the object size so just the border of the chart is visible.

4. Switch to Excel and the original document. Notice that cell G4 retained the original value, 13.

Embedding does not affect the source data. In this instance you would have to be careful to update the original data to reflect the new value or you would run the risk of later using the Excel data with incorrect information. To circumvent this possible scenario, try this next exercise using linking to see how well it handles information that is apt to change.

Linking Using Paste Special
You should still be in Excel with the High-Low-Close chart on your screen.

1. Highlight the chart so the sizing handles appear on its border and click on Copy in the toolbar. The chart is again copied to the Clipboard.

2. Switch to Word, select the embedded chart (if necessary), and press DEL. Be sure to delete the object and not use Cut, as Cut will replace the original chart from Excel that is currently on the Clipboard.

3. Choose Paste Special from the Edit menu, accept the Excel Chart Object format, choose Paste Link, and click on OK. The chart appears as before minus the border.

4. Switch to Excel and edit G4 so the 13 is replaced by 9. The accompanying chart in Excel changes to reflect the new closing price.

5. Switch to Word, and presto, the chart automatically reflects the changed value.

The same effect would hold true if Word were closed and you updated the Excel data. The next time you opened the document in Word, the chart would display the most recent changes in the Excel range.

The Links Dialog Box

You can glean considerable information about a linked object by choosing the Edit menu Links option, which opens the Links dialog box, shown in Figure 14-5.

The Source File list box displays all links in a document and an abbreviated summary of their source file, unique item name, type, and updating method. The information for a selected link is shown below the list box in its entirety. You can choose to manually update the link instead of accepting the automatic updating that is on by default. The command buttons on the right side of the dialog box allow you to manually update the link, open the

14

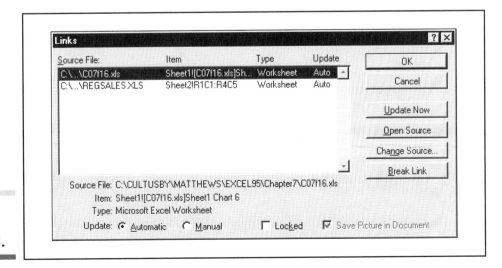

The Links
dialog box

Figure 14-5.

selected object in its source application, change the source application, and break the link between the source application and the object. Breaking the link will leave you with a copy of the object. Links once broken cannot be reestablished without repeating the original process.

Another Edit menu option that becomes available when a linked object is selected is Linked *Type* Object. From its submenu you can edit, open, and convert objects, depending on their type.

Using the Insert Menu

In addition to the Paste Special dialog box, you can add both embedded and linked objects to an Office 95 document by using the various object types that appear as options in an Office 95 application's Insert menu. Each application displays slightly different choices, depending on whether it's a container-oriented or creator-oriented application. The applicable sections of the Insert menus for Word, Excel, and PowerPoint are shown next.

Word's Insert menu objects:

Excel's Insert menu objects:

PowerPoint's Insert menu objects:

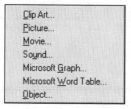

The container applications are very apparent from these object listings.

To compare embedding and linking using the Insert menu instead of the Paste Special dialog box, have Excel running on your computer with either a new workbook or a sheet.

1. In Excel, choose Object from the Insert menu. The Object dialog box opens as shown in Figure 14-6.

   The two tabs allow you choose between inserting new objects or ones that are saved as files. The Object Type list box in the Create New tab lists the available registered Windows 95 objects. The same list appears in all applications (except, an application doesn't list its own objects). New objects are embedded in your destination document (the one you are currently working in) with the object's menus and toolbars available for editing, as we saw previously when using the Paste Special dialog box. Notice that there are quite a few applications available in addition to the Office 95 suite. The Create from File tab, shown in Figure 14-7, lets you browse for a particular file and embed it, or select the Link to File check box to create a link between the inserted file and the destination document.

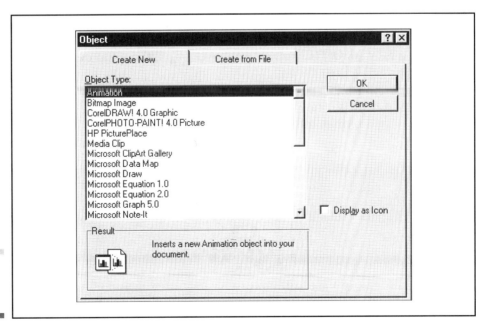

14

The Object
dialog box
Figure 14-6.

The Create
from File tab
of the Object
dialog box
Figure 14-7.

2. Click on the Create from File tab and then the Browse button.
   In the Browse dialog box, locate your Office 95 folder (should be
   MSOFFICE, unless you've changed the setup default), and open the
   Clipart subfolder.

3. Choose AUTO.BMP, click on Insert to place the path in the Object
   dialog box File Name text box, and then click on OK to embed the
   bitmap into your sheet, as shown here:

Picture 1 ▼		=EMBED("Bitmap Image","")			
A	**B**	**C**	**D**	**E**	**F**

Actually, if you are going to embed a graphic object you are better off
using the Insert Picture option. Since clipart is something that all users
of Office 95 probably have in the same folder, it was chosen for its
availability. The Picture dialog box provides a preview window to view

graphics before you insert them in your document. It doesn't, however, provide a way to link the file as does the Object dialog box.

Notice the syntax of the embedded object in the edit area of the Formula bar. In Word, the reference is referred to as a *field,* which is usually hidden text and not visible. You view field codes in a Word document by selecting the Show Field Codes check box in the View tab of the Tools menu Options dialog box.

4. Double-click on the bitmap. The Windows 95 graphics application, Paint, opens within Excel and allows you to edit the bitmap. Click outside the bitmap to return control back to Excel.

Linking files with the Insert menu options is doing nothing more than locating the file and checking the Link to File check box, if available. An Excel range linked to a Word document appears as follows when the field codes are shown:

```
{ LINK·Excel.Sheet.5·"C:\\SHEET\\REGSALES.XLS"·""·\a·\p 🖼}
```

The syntax for a linked object in Word is shown in the document. Although you may never have to do more than initially create a link to have a fully functional compound document, it might come in handy to see how the syntax is organized.

The general syntax for an OLE link is:

```
[Object type][path\filename of object file][object itself][switches]
```

A parameter that doesn't have an entry, as the [object itself] parameter above, is a null and is indicated by double quote marks (""). The available switches are listed in the following table.

14

Switch	Description
\a	Automatically updates the link when changes are made to the source file
\b	Displays the linked object as a bitmap
\d	Saves disk space by not saving the graphic data with the file
\p	Displays the linked object as a Word picture
\r	Displays the linked object as formatted text
\t	Displays the linked object as unformatted text

Dragging and Dropping to Share Data

One of the most convenient features of recent versions of Windows is the ability to drag and drop data within an application. Prior to OLE 2.0, this capability has been confined to singular applications. OLE 2.0 makes it possible to cross the boundaries of Office 95 and other compliant applications.

Windows 95 has increased drag-and-drop functionality by incorporating the ability to copy segments of files such as an Excel range, paragraphs from a Word document, and records from a database to the desktop as icons—icons that later can be dragged and dropped into another application. See how direct drag and drop, as well as using the desktop as a temporary stopping point, can greatly improve your cross-application productivity.

Using Drag and Drop Direct

The first step for easy direct dragging and dropping is to have the participating applications displayed simultaneously on your screen. Figure 14-8 shows Excel and Word set up side by side for data transfer.

In this instance, a vertical, or side-by-side, orientation for the applications is not the most ideal because each application extends toward the right farther than the limited screen width of each application allows. A horizontal orientation would offer the full width, but it does limit the number of lines

Excel and Word in position vertically to drag and drop information

Figure 14-8.

of text or number of rows. You can dramatically improve on the amount of visible document space you have by turning off the toolbars, Status bars, rulers, and any other screen elements that you don't absolutely need, as shown in Figure 14-9. Also, you can reduce the zoom to less than 100%.

The actual mechanics of dragging and dropping are rather anticlimatic once your screen is organized. It's no different than other dragging and dropping you've done within Excel, except the data or objects transferred may become embedded in the destination application, depending on the nature of what is being transferred into what screen element. Try positioning OLE 2.0-compliant applications on your screen and transfer data and objects between them. You will find that some drag and drops transfer the data seamlessly, while others create an embedded object that doesn't quite fit in with its surrounding environment. Trial and error, unfortunately, is your only avenue to see how a certain operation will behave.

There are a few considerations you can keep in mind. Similar to conventional drag and drop, when you press CTRL before you drag, you leave a copy of the selected data in its original place. Otherwise, the dragging operation removes the original selected data. Also, unlike some other actions that prompt you when you might be deleting data, if you overwrite any data with drag and drop across applications, it's deleted without any notification.

14

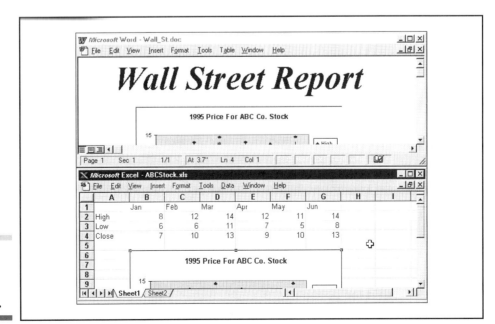

Applications oriented horizontally
Figure 14-9.

Using Scraps to Transfer Data

One of the major limitations of Windows 3.*x* is that anything that is copied or cut to the Clipboard is removed by the next copy or cut. There was no queue that you could cycle through to find previous snippets of data. Additionally, the data placed in the Clipboard was only as permanent as your current Windows session. Any data place on the Clipboard was gone forever once you closed Windows. Your only recourse was to copy the data to a new document, sheet, or other file format and save it as a file.

Windows 95, in partnership with OLE, has provided a very handy workaround to this problem. Although conventional cut and copy operation still behaves the same as in Windows 3.*x*, you now have a way to quickly access small blocks of data that can be retained for as long as you like. These blocks of data, which can be phrases or paragraphs of text, Excel ranges, and just about anything you can highlight and drag, are stored on your desktop as icons, as shown here:

Similar to other objects on the desktop, scraps have attributes that can be modified through the popup menu Properties option that appears when you right-click on them, as shown next:

From the popup menu, you can manipulate a scrap as you would a standard file by copying and cutting, renaming, and transferring it to other devices

Properties
dialog box for
a scrap

Figure 14-10.

both on and physically removed from your computer. If you view the
Properties dialog box, shown in Figure 14-10, it appears a scrap has the look
and feel of a standard file, which is exactly what it is. Scraps are stored in the
\WINDOWS\DESKTOP folder of your hard drive. Using the Explorer or My
Computer, you can move the scrap object from the DESKTOP subfolder and
its icon will be removed from the desktop. You can still move the scrap into
an application by locating its icon in My Computer or the Explorer and
dragging it to its destination application.

This chapter provided a brief glimpse of what OLE can do to improve
your productivity. Whether you are creating complex compound
documents to support corporate-level decision making or are sharing data
between applications using drag and drop, you will find OLE working
behind the scenes.

14

Index

+ operator, 50, 51
+ sign pointer, 155
- operator, 50, 51
/ operator, 50, 51
* formatting symbol, 177
* operator, 50, 51
* wildcard character, 123, 280
=
    entering formulas with, 105, 139
    for entering functions, 358
= operator, 51, 280, 357
< operator, 50, 51, 280, 357
<= operator, 50, 51, 280, 357
<> operator, 50, 51, 280, 357
> operator, 50, 51, 280, 357
>= operator, 50, 51, 280, 357
#, displaying across cells, 104-105
formatting symbol, 174
$, indicating an absolute reference, 147
% formatting symbol, 177
% operator, 50, 51

& operator, 50, 51
    in Visual Basic, 427
:, in Visual Basic code, 420-421
: operator, 47, 51
; formatting symbol, 175
!, in addresses, 46
, (comma) formatting symbol, 175
, (comma) operator, 47, 51
', in Visual Basic code, 421
" " formatting symbol, 176
@ formatting symbol, 176
\ formatting symbol, 176
. (period) formatting symbol, 175
 (space) operator, 47, 51
? formatting symbol, 175
? wildcard character, 123, 280
^ operator, 50, 51
_, in Visual Basic code, 421
_ formatting symbol, 175
0 formatting symbol, 174
2-D charts, 214-216

3-D Area chart, 223, 224
3-D Bar chart, 224, 225, 226
3-D charts, 216-217
3-D Column chart, 227, 228
3-D Line chart, 227, 229
3-D Pie chart, 231
3-D Surface charts, 233-234
100% Stacked Bar chart, 224, 225, 226

A

About Windows 95 option, in the Help
    facility, 41
ABS function, 362
Absolute addresses, 284
Absolute addressing, 143, 145-147
Absolute value, returning, 362
Access, in Office 95, 476
Accessibility Options icon, in Control
    Panel, 31
Accessories, in Windows 95, 2-4
Accessories folder, 18
Accessories submenu, 19
Activated charts, 242
Active border, 215, 216
Active cell, 71, 72
Active sheet, 72
Active window, 19-20, 70, 71
Active workbook, 314
Add Constraint dialog box, 403
ADD indicator, 86
Add New Hardware icon, in Control Panel,
    31
Add Report dialog box, 397-398
Add Scenario dialog box, 393
Add Watch dialog box, 430
Add/Remove Programs icon, in Control
    Panel, 31
Addition (+) operator, 50, 51
Addresses, 46
Advanced Filter, 281-288
Advanced Filter dialog box, 285-286, 287

Alignment
    for text, 98-99
    types of, 99
Alignment formatting option, for charts,
    251
Alignment tab, in the Format Cells dialog
    box, 102
Alignment tool, on the Formatting toolbar,
    81
Allow Cell Drag and Drop check box, 143
ALT, 24, 112
ALT- - (hyphen), 29
ALT-BACKSPACE (Undo), 91, 92, 109, 112
ALT-CTRL-F1, 93
ALT-CTRL-F2, 93
ALT-CTRL-SHIFT-F2, 93
ALT-ENTER, 112
ALT-F1 (New), 93
ALT-F2 (Save), 92, 93
ALT-F4, 30, 93
ALT-H, 40
ALT-PG DN, 88, 90
ALT-PG UP, 88, 90
ALT-SHIFT-F1, 92, 93, 326
ALT-SHIFT-F2, 93
ALT-SPACEBAR, 27, 28, 29
Always Create Backup check box, 165
Analysis, preparing for, 388-390
Analysis tools, 388-406
AND, in the Custom AutoFilter dialog box,
    281
AND function, 363
And logical operator, in Visual Basic, 426
Answer Wizard, 58, 62
Apple Macintosh format, 331
Application object, in Visual Basic, 411
Applications
    building, 434
    laying out, 435-436
    in Office 95, 475-476
    planning, 434-436
    switching to Microsoft, 480
    testing the order entry, 468-470

Arctangent, returning, 362
Area charts, 223, 224
ARGUMENT command, 383-384
Arguments
    specifying for functions, 356-358
    in Visual Basic, 413, 416
Arithmetic operators, 50
    in Visual Basic, 426
Arrange option, in the Window menu, 59
Arrange Windows dialog box, 316
Array data type, in Visual Basic, 418
Arrays, 326, 357
    as arguments in functions, 357
Ascending order, 34, 267
ASCII
    character, returning, 362
    comma delimited format *See* CSV
    delimited file format, 330
    text files, importing, 333-339
    text format, 329
    .TXT file format, 330
Assign Macro dialog box, 371
Assign String, in Visual Basic code, 409
Assumptions, 145
    building a table of, 145
    moving, 190
ATAN function, 362
Auditing toolbar, 82
Auto Arrange option, 10
AutoCalculate, 294
AutoComplete, 107-108
AutoCorrect, 111
AutoFill, 150
AutoFill option, 262-263
AutoFilter, 278-279
AutoFormat, 76, 186-189
    for charts, 249, 250
AutoFormat dialog box, 187
AutoSum tool, 57, 80, 152
AVERAGE function, 288
Axes option, on the Insert menu, 245
Axis, formatting, 251

Axis tab, of the Format Bar Group dialog
    box, 249, 250
Axis Title, formatting, 251

B

BACKSPACE, 109, 110, 112
Backup accessory, in Windows 95, 3
Backups, creating, 165
.BAK extension, 165
Bar charts, 224-226
Binders, in Office 95, 476
Bitmap graphic, embedding, 486
Blinking marquee, 116
Bold tool, on the Formatting toolbar, 81
Books *See* Workbooks
Boolean data type, in Visual Basic, 418
Border dialog box, 134, 135
Borders
    placing in spreadsheets, 133-135
    of windows, 11, 12
Borders palette, 134
Borders tool, on the Formatting toolbar, 82
Breakpoints, setting in Visual Basic, 427,
    429

C

Calculate mode, 85
Calculation, order of, 50-51
Calculator accessory, in Windows 95, 3
Call statement, in Visual Basic, 416
Cancel box, in the Formula bar, 84
CAPS indicator, 86
Cascade view, for overlapping windows,
    316
Cascaded windows, 59, 61
Category axis, 214, 215, 216
Category names, 215
CD Player accessory, in Windows 95, 3
CELL function, 364
Cell Note dialog box, 193

Cells, 46-47, 71
   adding notes to, 192-193
   clearing ranges of, 155-157
   contents of, 47
   copying the contents of, 77
   erasing a group of, 194-195
   highlighting a group of, 55
   moving the contents of, 77
   moving one at a time, 87
   naming, 83
Center Across Columns tool, 81, 133
Center across selection option button, 133
Center tool, 102
CHAR function, 362
Character Map accessory, in Windows 95, 3
Chart Area, formatting, 252
Chart option, on the Insert menu, 212-213, 217-218
Chart sheets, 212
Chart Title, formatting, 251
Chart Title check box, in the Titles dialog box, 244
Chart Title text box, 237-238
Chart titles, 215
   changing, 252-253
Chart toolbar, 82, 218-222
Chart Type dialog box, 240
Chart Type option, from the Format menu, 247
Chart Type palette, 220-221
Chart Type tool, 218, 219-221
Charts, 65-67
   activating, 242-243
   activating compared to selecting, 242
   changing with direct edits, 250-256
   characteristics of, 213-217
   closing, 256-257
   creating, 212
   embedding, 212
   formatting, 250-256
   modifying, 242-250
   producing, 212-257
   selecting types of, 222-234

ChartWizard dialog boxes, 236-238
ChartWizard tool, 58, 212, 218, 221
   creating embedded charts with, 239-241
   editing charts with, 242
   on the Standard toolbar, 81
Check boxes, in dialog boxes, 25, 26
Check marks, in menus, 24
Circles, calculating the area of, 52
Circular mode, 85
Clear option, in the Edit menu, 156-157
Clicking, 7, 8
Clicking on, 7, 8
Clipboard, 2
   copying to, 37
   transferring objects with, 472
Clipboard Viewer accessory, in Windows 95, 3
Close button, in windows, 10, 11, 12
Close option, in Control menu, 28, 29-30
Code, 409
   debugging, 427-431
   entering, 420-421
   stepping through, 431
Code pane, in the Debug window, 429
Code stub, creating, 455-456
Collections, in Visual Basic, 411
colon (:), in Visual Basic code, 420-421
Color tool, on the Formatting toolbar, 82
Colors
   changing in charts, 254
   specifying the display of, 178
Column charts, 66-67, 226-227, 228
Column headings, 70, 71
   centering, 185
Column Width dialog box, 179-180
Column widths
   adjusting, 191-192
   setting overall, 179-180
   versus contents width, 103-104
Columns, 44, 45-46
   deleting, 159-160, 190-191
   and fields, 64
   inserting, 159-160

COLUMNS function, 363

COLUMN.WIDTH macro command, 378-379

Columnwise chart, 214

Combination Drop-Down Edit tool, 453

Comma delimited format *See* CSV

Comma Style tool, on the Formatting toolbar, 81

Command buttons, in dialog boxes, 25, 26

Command macros, 364

distinguishing from function macros, 382

Commands, 52-58

from the keyboard, 58

from menus, 53-54

from the mouse, 55-56

from the popup menu, 54-55

from toolbars, 56-57

Comments, in Visual Basic code, 421, 409

Comparison operators, 50

in Visual Basic, 427

Compound documents, 475

Concatenation, 50

Concatenation (&) operator, 51

Concatenation operators, in Visual Basic, 427

Const statement, in Visual Basic, 419

Constants, 409, 419-420

Constraints, on variables in Solver, 398, 402-404

Container applications, 476

Container objects, in Visual Basic, 411

Contents tab, of the Help facility, 38

Contents width, versus column width, 103-104

Context-sensitive help, 39, 40, 62

Control menu, 27-30

opening in Explorer, 28

options in, 28

Control menu icon, in windows, 10, 11, 12

Control Panel

icons in, 30, 31-32

setting defaults with, 30-34

Control structures, in Visual Basic, 421-425

Controls, placing, 451

Copy option, in the Explorer Files popup menu, 37

Copy range combinations, 152, 153

Copy to range, defining in Advance Filter, 286, 287

Copy tool, on the Standard toolbar, 80

Copying, 151-152

across workbooks, 312-317

cells, 77

files, 36, 37

formulas, 142-144

values, 208-209

Corners, in 3-D charts, 216, 217

COUNT function, 288

Create from File tab, in the Object dialog box, 485-486

Create New tab, in the Object dialog box, 485

Create Shortcut option, in the Explorer Files popup menu, 37

Criteria

rules on specifying for Advanced Filter, 284

for selecting in Autofilter, 280

Criteria range, for Advanced Filter, 282-285

Crosshairs pointer, 22

.CSV extension, 120, 329, 337

CSV file format, 330

CSV (Macintosh) file format, 331

CSV (OS/2 or DOS) file format, 331

CTRL-:, 112

CTRL-;, 112

CTRL-', 112

CTRL-", 112

CTRL-ALT-TAB, 112

CTRL-DELETE, 112

CTRL-DOWN ARROW, 89, 90

CTRL-END, 89, 91, 112

CTRL-F2 (Info), 93

CTRL-F4 (Close), 93

CTRL-F5 (Restore), 94

CTRL-F6 (Window), 94
CTRL-F7 (Move), 94
CTRL-F8 (Size), 94
CTRL-F9 (Minimize), 94
CTRL-F10 (Maximize), 94
CTRL-F11, 94
CTRL-F12 (Open), 94
CTRL-HOME, 90, 89, 112
CTRL-LEFT ARROW, 89, 90, 112
CTRL-PG DN, 90, 91
CTRL-PG UP, 90, 91
CTRL-R, 468
CTRL-RIGHT ARROW, 90, 112
CTRL-SHIFT-END, 187
CTRL-SHIFT-F6, 94
CTRL-SHIFT-F12 (Print), 94
CTRL-SHIFT-LEFT ARROW, 113
CTRL-SHIFT-RIGHT ARROW, 113
CTRL-UP ARROW, 89, 90
CTRL-X, 374
CTRL-Z, 109, 112
Currency data type, in Visual Basic, 418,
    419
Currency formatting, 183-184, 185
Currency Style tool, on the Formatting
    toolbar, 81
Current date functions, 348
Current time functions, 348
Custom AutoFilter dialog box, 279-281
Custom dialog box, building, 450-455
Custom format, creating, 271
Custom Lists tab, of the Options dialog
    box, 353-354
Custom menus, building, 465-466
Customization, of spreadsheets, 160-164
Customize dialog box, for toolbars, 83, 277
CUT macro command, 374
Cut option, in the Explorer Files popup
    menu, 37
Cut tool, on the Standard toolbar, 80

D

Data, guidelines for charting, 213-214
Data commands, 65
Data entry tools, building, 450-460
Data form, editing with, 460-462
Data labels, 215, 216
    changing in charts, 253-254, 255
    formatting, 251
Data Labels dialog box, 244-245
Data Labels formatting option, for charts,
    251
Data marker, 215
Data menu, 65, 77-78
Data points, 213
    formatting, 252
    identifying in charts, 215
Data series, 213
    distinguishing, 215
    formatting, 252
Data Series option, generating dates and
    times with, 350
Data Tables, 295
    creating, 295-298
Data type numbers, 383
Data types
    changing for macro results, 383
    declaring in Visual Basic, 418-419
Database list, updating, 458-459
Database statistical functions, 289
Databases, 63-65, 260
    analyzing information from, 288-298
    building, 260-264
    defining for the Advanced Filter, 282
    filtering, 278-288
    formatting, 263-264
    re-sorting, 268, 269
    selecting information from, 268-288
    and sheets, 260
    sorting, 265-268
Date button, in the Header dialog box, 199
Date category, of format codes, 173
Date data type, in Visual Basic, 418

Date formats, 344-345
DATE function, 346
Date functions, 345-347
Date serial numbers, 342
Date and time, current, 52
Date and time arithmetic, 355-356
Date/Time icon, in Control Panel, 31
Date/Time Stamp macro
    creating, 377-379, 380
    in Visual Basic, 408-410
Dates
    direct entry of, 349
    entering consecutive, 261-262
    entering as a series, 269-271
    and Excel, 342-343
    generating a series of, 350-351
    procedures for entering, 342-343
DATEVALUE function, 346
DAVERAGE function, 289, 291, 293
DAY function, 347
Days
    specifying the display of, 178
    See also Weekdays
.DBF extension, 120
DBF file formats, 331
DCOUNT function, 289, 291, 292
DDE, 472
Debug window, in Visual Basic, 429-431
Debugging
    code in Visual Basic, 427-431
    macros, 374, 381-382
Debug.Print statements, in Visual Basic
    code, 429
Decimal digits, fixing the number of,
    106-107
Declaring
    data types in Visual Basic, 418-419
    variables in Visual Basic, 417-418
Decrease Decimal tool, on the Formatting
    toolbar, 82
Default Chart tool, 212, 218, 219, 220
Default folder, selecting, 122
Define Name dialog box, 290-291, 377, 441

Degrees, converting to radians, 362
DEL, 112
    in Edit mode, 110
    erasing a group of cells with, 194
Delete dialog box, 159
Delete option, in the Explorer Files popup
    menu, 37
Deleting, rows and columns, 159-160
Delimited ASCII files, 334
Delimited text files, opening, 334-335
Delimiters, 334
Depreciation expense, calculating, 361
Descending order, 34, 267
Desk checking macros, 468
Desktop, on the Windows 95 screen, 4, 6
Destination file, 473
Destination range, 151
Details view, in Explorer, 34
Dial-Up Networking accessory, in
    Windows 95, 3
Dialog boxes, 4
    building custom, 450-455
    components of, 26
    in menus, 23, 78-79
    moving around in, 27
    in Windows 95, 24, 25-26
.DIF extension, 120
DIF file format, 331
Dim statement, 418, 420
Dimmed options, 23, 115
Direct Cable Connection accessory, in
    Windows 95, 3
Direct drag and drop, 488-489
Direct mouse commands, 55-56
Direction keys, 58, 87-91
Disk Defragmenter accessory, in Windows
    95, 3
Display characters, specifying in formats,
    176
Display icon, in Control Panel, 31
#DIV/0! error value, 155, 357, 358
Division (/) operator, 50, 51
Do Until...Loop control structure, 423

Do While...Loop control structure, 423
.DOC extension, 333
Document windows, 10
Documentation, for macros, 368-369
Do...Loop control structure, 423-424
Do...Loop Until control structure, 423-424
Do...Loop While control structure, 423
Dots, next to menu options, 24
Double data type, in Visual Basic, 418
Double-clicking, 7, 8
    testing, 33
Double-headed arrow pointer, 7, 13
Double-line borders, adding, 134
Doughnut charts, 231-232
DOWN ARROW, 87, 90, 113
Drag and drop, 77
    for copying columnar formulas, 143-144
    direct, 488-489
Dragging, 7, 8
    windows, 13
Drawing tool, on the Standard toolbar, 81
Drawing toolbar, 82
DriveSpace accessory, in Windows 95, 3
Drop-down list boxes, in dialog boxes, 25,
    26
DSUM function, 289, 291, 293

E

E+- formatting symbol, 177
Edit area, of the Formula bar, 84
Edit Fill Series option, 261-262
Edit keys, summary of, 111-113
Edit menu, 74
Edit mode, 85, 109, 110
Edit tab, in the Options dialog box, 101
Editing
    after entry, 110-111
    with data form, 460-462
    during entry, 109
    embedded objects, 481-482
    formulas, 147-150
    with the mouse, 113-114
Elements, in Visual Basic, 411
Ellipsis (...), in menus, 23, 78
ElseIf statement, in Visual Basic, 422
Embedded charts, 212
    creating with ChartWizard, 239-241
Embedded objects, editing, 481-482
Embedding, 475
    compared to linking, 473-475
    with Paste Special, 479-481, 108
END, 87, 90, 112
END-DOWN ARROW, 90
END-HOME, 90, 91
END-LEFT ARROW, 90
END-RIGHT ARROW, 90
END-UP ARROW, 89
ENTER, 112
Enter mode, 85
Entries
    completing, 107
    making changes to, 108-113
Equal to (=) operator, 51, 280, 357
Eqv logical operator, in Visual Basic, 426
Error values
    in functions, 357-358
    replacing with 0, 363
ESC, 112
    for canceling menu selections, 27
    erasing entire entries with, 109
Event handler procedure, creating, 455-458
EXACT function, 362
Excel 3.0 file format, 330
Excel 4.0 file formats, 330
Excel 4 macros, deleting, 377
Excel
    and dates, 342-343
    help with Visual Basic in, 410-411
    integrating with Office 95, 472-491
    leaving, 123-124
    and times, 343-344
Excel application window, 70, 71, 72-86
Excel Workbook file format, 330
Exclamation point (!), in addresses, 46

Executable code, 415
Exit Do statement, 425
Exit For statement, 425
Exploded pie chart, 229-230, 231
Explorer, 21
    creating folders with, 34-38
    panes in, 34-36
Explorer window, 21
Exponentiation (^) operator, 50, 51
Expressions, constructing in Visual Basic,
    425-427
EXT indicator, 86
Extensions
    for filenames, 119-120
    of registered files, 169
External ranges
    adding, 322-326
    linking, 326-329
External reference formula, 319, 320
External references, importance of names
    in, 321-322

F

F1 (Help), 39, 91, 93
F2 (Edit), 84, 91, 93, 109, 110, 112
F4 (Absolute), 93, 146
    pressing for mixed references, 312
F5 (Goto), 92, 93
F6 (Pane), 94
F7, 94
F8 (Extend), 86, 94
F9 (Calculate), 94
F10 (Menu), 27, 94
F11 (New), 94
F12 (Save), 92, 94
Fax Cover Page Editor accessory, in
    Windows 95, 3
Fax icon, in Control Panel, 32
Fax Properties dialog box, 25
Fax Viewer accessory, in Windows 95, 3
Field names, 64, 261, 260

Fields, 63, 260
    and columns, 64
    copying selected with the Advanced
        Filter, 286-288
    in Word, 487
File button, in the Header dialog box, 200
File formats, for saving files, 329-331
File icon, in windows, 11, 12
File linking, 60-62
File Manager *See* Explorer
File menu, 73, 120-121
File popup menu options, in Explorer, 36,
    37
Filename extensions, 119-120
Filenames, 119
Files, 44, 118-123
    combining, 322-329
    copying, 36, 37
    cutting, 36, 37
    deleting, 36, 37
    linked, 474
    linking, 60-62
    listing the last four used, 73
    moving, 36
    naming, 37, 119-120
    registered, 169
    renaming, 36-37
    retrieving, 122-123
    saving, 120-122
    selecting, 36
    and spreadsheets, 44-45
Fill Down, from the Edit menu, 116, 117
Fill handle, 143
Fill operation, 77
Filter mode, 85
Filtering, 278
Financial functions, 360-361
Find tab, of the Help facility, 39, 40
First level button, in the outline structure,
    276
FIX indicator, 86, 107
Fixed Decimal option, 86, 106

Fixed decimal places, specifying to the
    right, 174
Floor, in 3-D charts, 216, 217
Floor object, in Visual Basic, 411
.FM3 extension, 120
FM3 file format, 330
FMT (ALL) file format, 330
.FMT extension, 120
Folder icon, in windows, 11, 12
Folder windows, 10-11, 12
Folders, 4, 122
    creating with the Explorer, 34-38
Font button, in the Header dialog box, 199
Font Color tool, on the Formatting toolbar,
    82
Font dialog box, 199, 200-201
Font formatting option, for charts, 251
Font tab, in the Format Data Label dialog
    box, 253, 254
Font tool, on the Formatting toolbar, 81
Fonts icon, in Control Panel, 31
Footers, entering for printing, 198
For Each...Next loop, 424
For...Next control structure, 424
Format, separating sections of, 175
Format Bar Group dialog box, 247-250
Format Cells dialog box, Alignment tab in,
    102
Format codes, 173
Format dialog box options, 251
Format menu, 76-77
    modifying charts with, 246-250
Format Painter tool, 184
    on the Standard toolbar, 80
Format symbols, 173-179
Formats, preselected in AutoFormat, 187
Formatted Text file format, 330
Formatting
    charts, 250-256
    databases, 263-264
    dates, 344-345
    times, 344-345
    workbooks, 169-180

Formatting symbols, entering along with
    numbers, 105-106
Formatting toolbar, 71, 79, 82, 185-186
    tools on, 81-82
Forms toolbar, 82
    building dialog boxes with, 451
Formula bar, 71, 83-85
Formulas, 49, 51
    building, 138-142
    building for databases, 291-295
    copying, 142-144
    copying columns of, 150-151
    copying rows of, 155
    editing, 147-150
    entering with =, 105
    moving, 190
    parentheses in, 51
    for summarizing sheets, 162-164
    versus functions, 140-141
Freecell accessory, in Windows 95, 3
Full Screen tool, adding, 276-278
Full Screen toolbar, 82
Function keys, 58, 86, 91-94
    summary of, 93-94
Function macros, 364, 382-386
    entering, 384
Function procedures, 415
    calling in Visual Basic, 417
    creating, 415
    structure of, 415-416
Function Wizard, 58
Function Wizard dialog boxes, 292-293,
    359
Function Wizard tool, 80, 84
Functions, 52, 356-359
    entering, 358-359
    lookup, 305-307
    versus formulas, 140-141
Future value, returning, 360
FV function, 360

G

General alignment, 99
General format, 179, 170
Goal Seek, 388, 390-392
Goal Seek dialog box, 391
Goal Seek Status dialog box, 391
Grabber hand pointer, 63
Graphic objects
  embedding, 486
  inserting in charts, 246
Greater than (>) operator, 50, 51, 280, 357
Greater than or equal to (>=) operator, 50,
  51, 280, 357
Greater-than symbols (>>), in dialog boxes,
  26
Gridlines, 215, 216
  displaying horizontal in charts, 222
  formatting, 252
Gridlines dialog box, 245-246
Gridlines option, on the Insert menu, 245
Group (right arrow) tool, in the Query and
  Pivot toolbar, 304

H

Header dialog box, 199
Header/Footer tab, in the Page Setup dialog
  box, 198-199, 201
Headers, entering for printing, 198
Headings
  centering in columns, 185
  entering rows of, 133, 134
Hearts accessory, in Windows 95, 3
Help, in Windows 95, 38-41
Help menu, 62
Help tool, 62
  on the Standard toolbar, 81
Help Topics dialog box, 92
Help Topics option, in the Help facility,
  40-41
Hide Detail (minus sign) tool, in the Query
  and Pivot toolbar, 304

High-Low-Close chart, 228-229, 230
Highlighting, 8
  a range of cells, 55
HLOOKUP function, 305
HOME, 87, 89, 90, 112
Horizontal Gridlines tool, 218, 222
Horizontal scroll bar, 71
  in windows, 11, 12
Horizontal scroll box, 15-16
Horizontal split-bar, 59
Horizontal table lookup function, 305-306,
  307
HOUR function, 347, 356
Hourglass pointer, 23
Hours, specifying the display of, 178
HyperTerminal accessory, in Windows 95, 3

I

I-beam pointer, 22, 85
Icons, 4
  in Control Panel, 30, 31-32
IF function, 363
If...Then...Else control structure, 421-422
Immediate pane, in the Debug window,
  429
Imp logical operator, in Visual Basic, 426
Increase Decimal tool, on the Formatting
  toolbar, 82
Increment number, 261
Index tab, of the Help facility, 38-39
Informational functions, 363-364
Input cell, 295
INS, 113
Insert dialog box, 158
Insert menus, 75
  embedding and linking with, 485
  modifying charts with, 243-246
  objects displayed in, 484
Insert mode, 110
Insert Module tool, on the Visual Basic
  toolbar, 428

Insertion point, 22, 84-85
Instant Watch dialog box, 431
Instant Watch tool, on the Visual Basic toolbar, 428
Integer data type, in Visual Basic, 418
Integrated data structure, 44
Interest rates, calculating for investments, 361
Internal rate of return, function for, 360
Intersections, 47, 48-49
IRR function, 360
ISBLANK function, 364
ISERROR function, 364
ISTEXT function, 364
Italic tool, on the Formatting toolbar, 81

J

Jump terms, 63

K

Keyboard
    commands from, 58
    Excel's use of, 86-94
    in Windows 95, 24, 27
Keyboard icon, in Control Panel, 31
Keyboard indicators, 86
Keys, identifying, 266-267
Keywords, in Visual Basic, 410, 426

L

Labels
    changing text in, 252
    entering columns of, 129-132
Landscape orientation, 198
Large Icons option, in Explorer, 34
Layouts, changing, 190-195
Left alignment, 98-99
LEFT ARROW, 87, 90, 113

Left mouse button, 6
Left-handed option button, 30
Legend, 215
    formatting, 252
Legend tool, 218, 222
LEN function, 362
Less than (<) operator, 50, 51, 280, 357
Less than or equal to (<=) operator, 50, 51, 280, 357
Line charts, 65-66, 227-229
    creating, 234-238
Linked files, negative aspects of using, 474
Linked sheets, summing, 328
Linked Type Object option, in the Edit menu, 484
Linking, 473-474
    compared to embedding, 473-475
    external ranges, 326-329
    files, 60-62
    with Paste Special, 482-483
    workbooks, 310-322
Linking formulas, creating, 317-320
Links, breaking, 484
Links dialog box, 483-484
List box, in dialog boxes, 25, 26
Lists, subtotaling, 274-278
Literal characters, specifying, 176
Literals, 50
Load Model dialog box, 405-406
Loan, returning the payment required, 360
Local scope, 420
Logic path, for the order entry application, 443, 444
Logical formulas, 50
Logical functions, 363
Logical operators, 357
    specifying in formats, 178
    in Visual Basic, 426
Logical values, 357
Long data type, in Visual Basic, 418
Lookup functions, 305-307
Lotus 1-2-3, help for users of, 62

Lotus .PRN space delimited text file format, 330

M

Macintosh format, 331
Macro commands, 364, 382, 383
Macro dialog box, 369
    Delete button in, 377
Macros, 52, 58-59, 364-365
    attaching to tools on toolbars, 370-371
    building, 443-450
    building for printing, 462-464
    building for saving and quitting, 464-465
    creating, 365, 372-379
    debugging, 374, 381-382
    desk checking, 468
    documenting, 368-369
    entering, 379-382
    entry rules for, 381
    error-handling of, 385
    executing one step at a time, 381-382
    naming, 367
    positioning the screen with, 448-449
    recording, 365-368
    reversing, 444
    running, 365, 369-370
    storing, 366
    testing and correcting, 468-470
    testing and debugging, 449-450
Magnifying glass pointer, 203
Mail and Fax icon, in Control Panel, 32
Map tool, on the Standard toolbar, 81
Margins, setting for printing, 201-202
Margins tab, in the Page Setup dialog box, 201-202
Mark Position for Recording, 376
Marquee, blinking, 116
Mathematical functions, 361-362
MAX function, 288
Maximize button, in windows, 10, 11, 12
Maximize option, in Control menu, 28

Media Player accessory, in Windows 95, 3
Memory, available to Windows 95, 41
Menu bar, 71, 72-79
    activating, 72, 114
Menu Editor dialog box, 466, 467
Menu Editor tool, on the Visual Basic toolbar, 428
Menu options, selecting, 53
Menus, 114-117
    building, 465-466
    canceling selections in, 27
    choosing options in, 22
    commands from, 53-54
    opening, 24, 53, 114
    options in, 22-23
    selecting, 22, 53
    in Windows 95, 22-24
Message area, in the Status bar, 85
Methods
    of objects, 412-413
    in Visual Basic code, 409
Microsoft applications, switching to, 480
Microsoft Exchange mail, setting properties for, 32
Microsoft Network option, in the Help menu, 62
Microsoft toolbar, 82, 479-480
MID function, 362
MIN function, 288
Minesweeper accessory, in Windows 95, 3
Minimize option, in Control menu, 28
Minus button, in the outline structure, 276
MINUTE function, 347
Minutes, specifying the display of, 178
MINVERSE function, 362
Mixed addresses, types of, 147
Mixed addressing, 143
Mixed references, pressing F4 for, 312
Models, saving in Solver, 404-406
Modems icon, in Control Panel, 32
Module General tab, in the Options dialog box, 432
Module scope, 420

Module sheets, in Visual Basic, 413-414
MONTH function, 347
Months
    generating a list of, 352-354
    specifying the display of, 178
Mortgage payment, calculating, 361
Mouse
    editing with, 113-114
    in Windows 95, 6-10
Mouse button, 6
Mouse icon, in Control Panel, 32
Mouse pointer, 6, 7
Mouse Properties dialog box, 30, 33
Move macro, creating, 372-374, 375
Move option, in Control menu, 28
Move_Selection macro, 375
Multimedia icon, in Control Panel, 32
Multiple workbooks
    creating, 310-312
    handling, 313-316
    saving, 321
Multiplication (*) operator, 50, 51
My Computer window, 8, 9

N

#N/A error value, 357, 358, 384-385
Name Define option, on the Insert menu, 379-380
#NAME? error value, 357, 358
Named arguments, 409, 413
Names
    building custom lists of, 354
    versus addresses for ranges, 290
Names and Values formatting option, for charts, 251
Negation (-) operator, 50, 51
Nested parentheses, 50
Net present value, returning, 360
NetWatcher accessory, in Windows 95, 3
Network icon, in Control Panel, 32
New Data dialog box, 246

New Data option, on the Insert menu, 246
New Workbook tool, on the Standard toolbar, 80
Nonadjacent sections, 235
Nondelimited ASCII files, 334, 335
Nondelimited text files, opening, 337-339
Not equal to (<>) operator, 50, 51, 280, 357
Not logical operator, in Visual Basic, 426
NotePad program, 3, 19-20
Notes
    adding to cells, 192-193
    reading, 193
NOW function, 52, 348, 356
NPV function, 360
#NULL! error value, 357, 358
NUM indicator, 86, 106
NUM LOCK, 106
#NUM! error value, 357, 358
Number format, changing, 170
Number formatting option, for charts, 251
Number signs (#), displaying across cells, 104-105
Number tab, in the Format Cells dialog box, 171, 182, 271
Numbers
    in cells, 47
    converting to text, 363
    creating a series with AutoFill, 262-263
    entering, 104-106
    entering columns of, 137-138
    entering consecutive, 261-262
    rounding, 362
Numeric formulas, 50
Numeric keypad, 106

O

Object Browser tool, on the Visual Basic toolbar, 428
Object data type, in Visual Basic, 418
Object dialog box, 485
Object linking and embedding *See* OLE

Object Packager accessory, in Windows 95, 3
Object Type list box, 485
Objects
    methods of, 412-413
    properties of, 412
    Reference index for, 411
    selecting with the mouse, 6
    transferring with the Clipboard, 472
    in Visual Basic, 409, 411-413
Office 95, applications in, 475-476
Office Shortcut Bar, 480
OLE, 472, 476-487
OLE links, syntax for, 487
OLE Paste Special dialog box, 477-478
One-input data table, 295
Open dialog box, 122-123, 168-169
Open File tool, on the Standard toolbar, 80
Open option, in the Explorer Files popup menu, 37
Operators, in Visual Basic, 426-427
Option buttons, in dialog boxes, 25, 26
Option Explicit statement, 418
Optional digits, specifying, 174
Options
    dimmed, 23
    selecting in menus, 114-115
    setting for Visual Basic, 431-432
Options dialog box, 78-79
    in the Tools menu, 100-101
Options Edit dialog box, 106-107
Options tab, of the Format Bar Group dialog box, 249
OR, in the Custom AutoFilter dialog box, 281
Or logical operator, in Visual Basic, 426
Order sheet
    building for the order entry application, 436-442
    preparing and controlling, 444-450
Orders database list, preparing, 440-441
Ordinary annuity, 361
Orientation, for printing, 198

Outline buttons, 276
Outline structure, 276
Overlapping workbooks, displaying, 313
Overtype mode, 110

P

Page button, in the Header dialog box, 199
Page Setup dialog box, 25, 196, 197-202
Page tab, in the Page Setup dialog box, 197-198
Pages, scaling for printing, 198
Pages button, in the Header dialog box, 199
Pages level, in pivot tables, 304
Paint accessory, 4, 19, 20
Panes, 34-36, 59
Parameters
    setting for printing, 195-202
    See also Arguments, in Visual Basic
Parentheses
    in formulas, 51
    with functions, 358
    nested, 50
Passwords icon, in Control Panel, 32
Paste Link, 326
Paste Special dialog box, 208-209, 324, 477-484
Paste Special option, 324, 325-326
    embedding with, 479-481, 482
    from the Edit menu, 322
    linking with, 482-483
Paste tool, on the Standard toolbar, 80
Pasting
    as a picture, 478-479
    as plain text, 479
    in source application formats, 478, 479
Path, 119
Patterns, adding in charts, 254-256
Patterns formatting option, for charts, 251
Patterns tab, in the Format Data Series dialog box, 255
Payment for a loan amount, returning, 360

Pencil pointer, 22
Percent Style tool, on the Formatting toolbar, 81
Percentage (%) operator, 50, 51
Percentage formats, creating, 181-183
Percentage macro, creating, 376-377, 378
Percentages, calculating, 154
Personal Macro Workbook, 366, 368
PG DN, 87, 88, 90
PG UP, 87, 88, 90
Phone Dialer accessory, in Windows 95, 4
PI function, 52
Picture option, on the Insert menu, 246
Pie charts, 66, 229-232
Pivot tables, 298
    creating, 298-305
    reordering, 302-303
    updating, 305
PivotTable Field dialog box, 303-304
PivotTable Wizard, 58, 298-302
Placeholders, 174, 473
Placement formatting option, for charts, 251
Plot Area, formatting, 252
Plus sign pointer, 155
PMT function, 360
Point mode, 86
Pointing, versus typing for building formulas, 139
Pointing on, 7, 8
Popup menus
    displaying, 7
    opening, 54-55
Portrait orientation, 198
PowerPoint, in Office 95, 476
Precedence number, of operators, 50-51
Present value, 52, 361
Preview, of printed output, 203-204, 205
Preview screen, 203-204, 205
Print area, identifying, 196-197
Print dialog box, 203
Print Manager, in Windows 95, 205
Print Preview, 203-204, 205

Print Preview tool, on the Standard toolbar, 80
Print tool, on the Standard toolbar, 80
Printer, preparing, 202
Printers icon, in Control Panel, 32
Printing
    common problems with, 206-207
    performing, 202-205
    setting parameters for, 195-202
    workbooks, 195-207
Printing macros, building, 462-464
Printing message box, 204, 205
Private scope, 420
Private statement, 420
.PRN extension, 120
Procedures, 415-417
    calling, 416-417
    scope of, 420
Products list, preparing, 442
Program folders, 18
Program windows, 10, 18-22
Programs, starting in Windows 95, 16-22
Programs option, in the Start menu, 16-17
Programs submenu, 17-18
PROPER function, 362
Properties
    of objects in Visual Basic, 412
    in Visual Basic code, 409
Properties dialog box, for scraps, 491
Properties option, in the Explorer Files popup menu, 37
Property procedures, in Visual Basic, 415
Public scope, 420
PV function, 52, 361

Q

QuattroPro for DOS WQ1 file format, 331
Query and Pivot toolbar, 82
Question mark pointer, 39, 62
Quick View option, in the Explorer Files popup menu, 37

Quitting macro, building, 464-465

R

Radar charts, 232, 233
Radians, converting to degrees, 362
RAM (random access memory), 44-45
RAND function, 362
Random numbers, returning, 362
Ranges, 47, 48
    adding external, 322-326
    clearing, 155-157
    defining for the Advanced Filter, 282
    filling contiguous, 150
    highlighting, 55
    identifying for summing, 140
    linking external, 326-329
    naming, 290-291
    selecting for plotting on line charts, 235
    types of, 48
Re-sorting databases, 268, 269
Read-only properties, 412
Read/write properties, 412
Ready mode, 85, 86
Record at Mark suboption, 376
Record Macro tool, on the Visual Basic
    toolbar, 428
Record New Macro dialog box, 365-366,
    413, 414
Recording area, setting for macros, 375-376
Recording mode, 86
Records, 63, 260
    copying selected with the Advanced
        Filter, 286-288
    entering, 263-264
    identifying with the Advanced Filter,
        285-286
    and rows, 64
Recycle Bin, removing files to, 37
#REF! error value, 357, 358
Reference area, in the Formula bar, 83-84
Reference names, 49

versus addresses in macros, 381
Refresh Data (exclamation point) tool, in
    the Query and Pivot toolbar, 305
Regional Settings icon, in Control Panel, 32
Registered files, 169
Registered objects, 477
Relational operators, in the Custom
    AutoFilter dialog box, 280
Relative addresses, 284
Relative addressing, 143
Rename option, in the Explorer Files
    popup menu, 37
Repeat tool, on the Standard toolbar, 80
Replace Text as You Type section, of the
    AutoCorrect dialog box, 111
Report Manager, 396-398
Reports, creating with Scenario Manager,
    395-398, 399
Resources, displaying percentage in use, 41
Restore button, in windows, 10, 11
Restore option, in Control menu, 28
RESULT command, 383
Resume Macro tool, on the Visual Basic
    toolbar, 428
RETURN command, for ending function
    macros, 384
RETURN macro command, 374
Reversing macros, 444
Right alignment, 98-99
RIGHT ARROW, 87, 90, 113
RIGHT function, 52
Right mouse button, 7
    opening popup menus with, 54
Right-clicking, 7, 8
ROUND function, 362
ROW function, 364
Row headings, 70, 71
Row labels, entering, 129-132
Rows, 44, 45-46
    deleting, 158-159, 159-160
    inserting, 157-158, 159-160
    and records, 64
Rowwise chart, 214

Run Macro tool, on the Visual Basic
 toolbar, 428
Run-time errors, 427
Running, macros, 365, 369-370

S

SAMPLES.XLS workbook, 411
Save As dialog box, 121, 136
Save Changes dialog box, 124
Save File tool, on the Standard toolbar, 80
Save Model dialog box, 405
Save Options dialog box, 165
Save as Type list box, 329
Save Workspace command, 321
Saving macro, building, 464-465
Scale formatting option, for charts, 251
Scaling pages for printing, 198
ScanDisk accessory, in Windows 95, 4
Scatter charts, 232, 233
Scenario Manager, 388, 392-398
Scenario Manager dialog box, 392-393, 394
Scenario Summary dialog box, 395
Scenario Values dialog box, 393-394
Scenarios, 392
    creating, 392-394
    creating a summary of, 395-396, 397
    modifying, 395
    viewing existing, 394-395
Schedule+, in Office 95, 476
Scientific format, specifying, 177
Scope, of variables and constants, 420
Scraps, 48
    dragging, 473
    transferring data with, 490-491
Screens
    building, 436-440
    moving one at a time, 88
    positioning with macros, 448-449
    for Windows 95, 4-6
Scroll arrows, 14
Scroll bars, 13-16

Scroll boxes, 14
    positions of, 15
Scrolling, through windows, 14
SECOND function, 347
Second level button, in the outline
    structure, 276
Seconds, specifying the display of, 178
Select Case control structure, in Visual
    Basic, 422
SELECT macro command, 374
Selected Object option, in the Format
    menu, 247
Selecting, with the mouse, 8
Selection criteria, for Advanced Filter,
    282-285
Send To option, in the Explorer Files
    popup menu, 37
Serial numbers, for dates, 342
Series, entering dates as, 269-271
Series axis, 216
Series dialog box, 262
    generating a date series with, 350-351
Series Order tab, of the Format Bar Group
    dialog box, 248
Sets, of values, 392
Shared devices, 8
Sheet names, 46, 71
Sheet tab, 72
Sheets, 45-46
    customizing individual, 160-164
    and databases, 260
    formulas for summarizing, 162-164
    grouping, 128-129
    moving around the periphery of active,
        88-90
    moving one at a time, 90
    renaming, 46
    selecting multiple, 128-129
    typing on, 98-108
    See also Spreadsheets
SHIFT-F1, 39, 93
SHIFT-F2 (Note), 93
SHIFT-F5 (Find), 94

SHIFT-F6, 94

SHIFT-F8 (Add), 94, 86

SHIFT-F9, 94

SHIFT-F10, 94, 114

SHIFT-F11, 92, 94, 326

SHIFT-F12, 94

SHIFT-LEFT ARROW, 113

SHIFT-RIGHT ARROW, 113

SHIFT-TAB, 113
   in dialog boxes, 27

Shortcut character, for macros, 367

Show Details (plus sign) tool, in the Query
   and Pivot toolbar, 304

Show option, in the Scenario Manager
   dialog box, 394-395

Shut Down dialog box, 29

Simple mode, 109

SIN function, 362

Sine, returning, 362

Single data type, 418

Single Step dialog box, 382

Single-line borders, adding, 134

Size option, in Control menu, 28

Size tool, on the Formatting toolbar, 81

Sizing handle, in windows, 11, 12

Slider, 26

.SLK extension, 120

SLN function, 361

Small Icons option, in Explorer, 34

Solver, 388, 398-399
   setting up, 399-402

Solver Options dialog box, 404-405

Solver Parameters dialog box, 400, 403

Solver Results dialog box, 401, 403

Sort Ascending tool, on the Standard
   toolbar, 80

Sort Descending tool, on the Standard
   toolbar, 80

Sort dialog box, 265-266

Sort keys, identifying, 266-267

Sort order, specifying, 267

Sort range, selecting, 265-266

Sorting, 265

Sound notes, adding to cells, 193

Sound Recorder accessory, in Windows 95,
   4

Sounds icon, in Control Panel, 32

Source file, 473

Source File list box, in the Links dialog
   box, 483

Source range, 151

SPACEBAR, in dialog boxes, 27

Spaces, specifying in formats, 175

Spelling dialog box, 131

Spelling tool, on the Standard toolbar, 80,
   130-132

Spinners, 25, 26, 79

Split, from the Window menu, 59

Split-bar, dragging, 59

Spreadsheet window, 45

Spreadsheets, 44-63
   creating, 126-166
   and files, 44-45
   planning, 126-128
   See also Sheets

SQRT function, 362

Square root, calculating, 362

Stacked Bar chart, 224-226

Stairstepping, workbooks, 314, 315

Standard toolbar, 71, 79, 82
   restoring, 277-278
   tools on, 80-81

Start button, in Windows 95, 480

Start menu, 16
   opening, 14
   options in, 17

Start number, 261

Statements, in Visual Basic, 415

Static lifetime, 420

Statistical functions, difference from
   database statistical functions, 289

Status bar, 71, 85-86
   in windows, 10, 11, 12

Step clause, 424

Step command, in the Macro dialog box,
   381-382

Step Into, from the Run menu, 431
Step Into tool, on the Visual Basic toolbar, 428
Step Macro tool, on the Visual Basic toolbar, 428
Step number, 261
Step Over tool, on the Visual Basic toolbar, 428
Stop Macro tool, on the Visual Basic toolbar, 428
Stop number, 261, 262
Stop Recording toolbar, 82, 367
String data type, in Visual Basic, 418
Sub procedures, 409, 415
    calling, 416-417
    creating, 415
    structure of, 415-416
Subtotal dialog box, 274
Subtotals, adding to lists, 274-278
Subtraction (-) operator, 50, 51
Subtype tab, of the Format Bar Group dialog box, 248
SUM function, 52, 140, 141, 288, 356
    entering from a toolbar, 57
SUM= indicator, 86
Summarization, of sheets, 162-164
Summary report of scenarios, creating, 395-396
Summing, across networks, 328
SYLK file format, 331
Symbolic Link format, 331
Symbols, entering along with numbers, 105-106
Syntax
    for entering functions, 358
    for OLE links, 487
System icon, in Control Panel, 32
System Monitor accessory, in Windows 95, 4

T

Tab button, in the Header dialog box, 200
TAB key, 113
Table dialog box, 296
Tabs, 25, 26, 79
Taskbar, on the Windows 95 screen, 4-6
Template file format, 330
Templates, 207-210
Text
    in cells, 47
    entering, 98-104
Text box, in dialog boxes, 25, 26
Text file format, 330
Text files
    importing, 333-339
    opening delimited, 334-335
    opening nondelimited, 337-339
    saving workbooks as, 329-333
Text format, 329
    pasting, 479
Text formula, 50
TEXT function, 363
Text functions, 362-363
Text Import Wizard, 58
Text Import Wizard dialog boxes, for nondelimited text files, 337-339
Text (Macintosh) file format, 331
Text operator (&), 50
Text (OS/2 or DOS) file format, 331
Text strings, comparing, 362
Third level button, in the outline structure, 276
Thousands separator, specifying, 175
Tick marks, 215, 216
Tiled view, of windows, 315-316
Tiled windows, 59, 60, 123, 124
Time arithmetic, 355-356
Time button, in the Header dialog box, 199
Time formats, 344-345
TIME function, 347
Time functions, 345-346, 347
Times

direct entry of, 349-350
and Excel, 343-344
generating a series of, 351-352, 353
specifying the display of, 178
TIMEVALUE function, 347
TipWizard, 58, 63
TipWizard tool, on the Standard toolbar, 81
TipWizard toolbar, 82
Title bar, 72, 71
in dialog boxes, 25, 26
in windows, 10, 11, 12
Title screen, building, 436-440
Titles
centering in spreadsheets, 132-133
changing text in, 252
changing in worksheets, 207-208
Titles dialog box, 244
Titles option, of the Insert menu, 243-244
TODAY function, 348, 356
Toggle Breakpoint tool, on the Visual Basic
toolbar, 427, 428
Toolbars, 56, 79-83
attaching macros to tools on, 370-371
commands from, 56-57
creating customized, 83
customizing, 277
customizing with macros, 371
default, 82
in windows, 10, 11, 12
Toolbars popup menu, 186
opening, 79, 83
Tools, pointing to short descriptions on
screen, 56-57
Tools menu, 76-77
running macros from, 369-370
Totals, producing, 152-154
TRUE function, 363
Two-input data tables, 296-298
.TXT extension, 120, 329
.TXT file format, 330

U

Underlined tool, on the Formatting
toolbar, 81
Underscore (_), in Visual Basic code, 421
Underscores, as word separators in macro
names, 367
Undo, 92, 109, 195
Undo Paste option, 116
Undo tool, on the Standard toolbar, 80, 109
Ungroup (left arrow) tool, in the Query
and Pivot toolbar, 304
Unhide dialog box, 367
Unions, 47, 48-49
highlighting, 55-56
UP ARROW, 87, 90, 113
UPPER function, 356
Uppercase, converting the first character
to, 362
User-defined data type, 418

V

Value axis, 214, 215
Value Axis Title text box, 238
#VALUE! error value, 357, 383
Values, copying, 208-209
Variables
constraining in Solver, 398, 402-404
declaring in Visual Basic, 417-419
scope of, 420
Variant data type, 418, 419
VBA, 472
Vertical scroll bar, 71
in windows, 11, 12
Vertical scroll box, 15-16
Vertical split-bar, 59
Vertical table lookup function, 305-306,
307
View Manager add-in program, accessing,
74, 75
View menu, 23, 74-75
VisiCalc file format, 331

Visual Basic, 408
    objects in, 411-413
    online help for, 410-411
    procedures in, 415-417
    setting options for, 431-432
Visual Basic Reference window, 410
Visual Basic routines, assortment of
    sample, 411
Visual Basic toolbar, 82
    tools on, 428
Visual interface, for Windows 95, 2
VLOOKUP function, 305
Volume Control accessory, in Windows 95,
    4

W

Wall, in 3-D charts, 216
Watch expression, adding to Visual Basic
    code, 430
Watch pane, in the Debug window, 429,
    430
WEEKDAY function, 347
Weekdays
    generating a list of, 353-354
    See also Days
What-if situation, 294-295
Wildcard characters, 123, 280
Window border, 11, 12
Window menu, 78, 123, 314-315
Windows, 4
    arranging, 316
    dragging, 13
    scrolling through, 14
    splitting into panes, 59
    in Windows 95, 10-13
Windows 95, 2
    accessories in, 2-4
    displaying information about, 41
    leaving, 41
Windows 95 Explorer *See* Explorer
Windows 95 Help facility, 38-41

Windows 95 Print Manager *See* Print
    Manager
Windows 95 screen, 4-6
Wizards, 58
.WK1 extension, 120
WK1 file format, 330
.WK3 extension, 120
WK3 file format, 330
.WK4 extension, 120
WK4 file format, 330
.WKS extension, 120
WKS file format, 331
Word, in Office 95, 476
WordPad accessory, 4
    displaying files in, 329, 331-332
Workbook document window, 70-72
Workbook objects, in Visual Basic, 411
Workbook windows, 59-60
Workbooks, 44
    automatically formatting, 186-189
    automating, 434
    combining, 322-329
    copying across, 312-317
    creating multiple, 310-312
    customizing, 317, 318
    handling multiple, 313-316
    linking, 310-322
    linking multiple, 61-62
    loading, 168-169
    printing, 195-207
    printing multipage, 197
    saving, 136
    saving multiple, 321
    saving as text files, 329-333
    setting up automatically, 466-467
    stairstepping, 314, 315
Workgroup toolbar, 82
Worksheet objects, in Visual Basic, 411
.WQ1 extension, 120
WQ1 file format, 331

X

X-axis, 214, 215, 216
.XLA extension, 120
.XLB extension, 120
.XLC extension, 120
.XLL extension, 120
.XLM extension, 120
xlOn Excel constant, 456
.XLS extension, 120, 121
.XLS file format, 330
.XLT extension, 120
.XLT template file format, 330
.XLW extension, 120
.XLW file format, 330
Xor logical operator, in Visual Basic, 426
XY charts, 232, 233

Y

Y-axis, 214, 215, 216
Y-Error Bars formatting option, for charts, 251
YEAR function, 347, 355
Years, specifying the display of, 178

Z

Z-axis, 216
Zoom, 117-118, 119
Zoom Control tool, on the Standard toolbar, 81

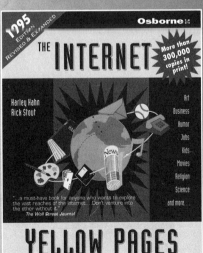

Draw on Our Expertise

Revolutionary Information on the Information REVOLUTION

The Business Week Guide to Global Investments Using Electronic Tools
by Robert Schwabach
Includes Three 3.5-Inch Disks
$39.95 U.S.A. ISBN: 0-07-882055-3

Alluring opportunities abound for the global investor. But avoiding investment land mines can be tricky business. The first release in the Business Week Library of Computing lets you master all the winning strategies. Everything is here—from analyzing and selecting the best companies, to tax planning, using investment software tools, and more. Disks include MetaStock, Windows On WallStreet, and Telescan, the leading investment analysis software.

The Business Week Guide to Multimedia Presentations
Create dynamic presentations that inspire.
by Robert Lindstrom
Includes One CD-ROM
$39.95 U.S.A.
ISBN: 0-07-882057-X

The Internet Yellow Pages Second Edition
by Harley Hahn and Rick Stout
$27.95 U.S.A.
ISBN: 0-07-882098-7

Fundamental Photoshop: A Complete Introduction Second Edition
by Adele Droblas Greenberg and Seth Greenberg
$27.95 U.S.A.
ISBN: 0-07-882093-6

Multimedia: Making It Work, Second Edition
by Tay Vaughan
Includes One CD-ROM
$34.95 U.S.A.
ISBN: 0-07-882035-9

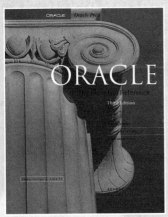

ORACLE: THE COMPLETE REFERENCE

Third Edition

by George Koch
and Kevin Loney

Get true encyclopedic coverage of Oracle with this book. Authoritative and absolutely up-to-the-minute.

Price: $34.95 U.S.A.
Available Now
ISBN: 0-07-882097-9
Pages: 1104, paperback

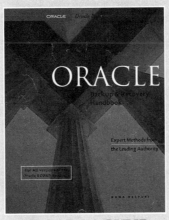

ORACLE BACKUP AND RECOVERY HANDBOOK

by Rama Velpuri

Keep your database running smoothly and prepare for the possibility of system failure with this comprehensive resource and guide.

Price: $29.95 U.S.A.
Available Now
ISBN: 0-07-882106-1
Pages: 400, paperback

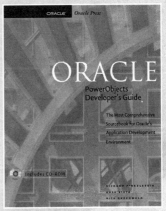

ORACLE POWER OBJECTS DEVELOPER'S GUIDE

by Richard Finkelstein,
Kasu Sista, and Rick Greenwald

Integrate the flexibility and power of Oracle Power Objects into your applications development with this results-oriented handbook.

Price: $39.95 U.S.A.
Includes One CD-ROM
Available September, 1995
ISBN: 0-07-882163-0
Pages: 656, paperback

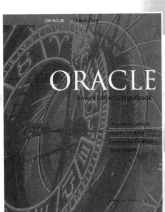

ORACLE POWER OBJECTS HANDBOOK

by Bruce Kolste
and David Petersen

This is the only book available on Oracle's new single/multi-user database product.

Price: $29.95 U.S.A.
Available August, 1995
ISBN: 0-07-882089-8
Pages: 512, paperback

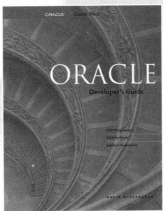

ORACLE DEVELOPER'S GUIDE

by David McClanahan

Learn to develop a database that is fast, powerful, and secure with this comprehensive guide.

Price: $29.95 U.S.A.
Available November, 1995
ISBN: 0-07-882087-1
Pages: 608, paperback

ORDER BOOKS DIRECTLY FROM OSBORNE/McGRAW-HILL

For a complete catalog of Osborne's books, call 510-549-6600 or write to us at 2600 Tenth Street, Berkeley, CA 94710

Call Toll-Free: *1-800-822-8158*
24 hours a day, 7 days a week in U.S. and Canada

Mail this order form to:
McGraw-Hill, Inc.
Customer Service Dept.
P.O. Box 547
Blacklick, OH 43004

Fax this order form to:
1-614-759-3644

EMAIL
7007.1531@COMPUSERVE.COM
COMPUSERVE GO MH

Ship to:

Name _____

Company _____

Address _____

City / State / Zip _____

Daytime Telephone: _____
(We'll contact you if there's a question about your order.)

ISBN #	BOOK TITLE	Quantity	Price	Total
0-07-88				
0-07-88				
0-07-88				
0-07-88				
0-07-88				
0-07088				
0-07-88				
0-07-88				
0-07-88				
0-07-88				
0-07-88				
0-07-88				
0-07-88				
0-07-88				

Shipping & Handling Charge from Chart Below		
Subtotal		
Please Add Applicable State & Local Sales Tax		
TOTAL		

Shipping & Handling Charges

Order Amount	U.S.	Outside U.S.
Less than $15	$3.50	$5.50
$15.00 - $24.99	$4.00	$6.00
$25.00 - $49.99	$5.00	$7.00
$50.00 - $74.99	$6.00	$8.00
$75.00 - and up	$7.00	$9.00

Occasionally we allow other selected companies to use our mailing list. If you would prefer that we not include you in these extra mailings, please check here: ☐

METHOD OF PAYMENT

☐ Check or money order enclosed (payable to Osborne/McGraw-Hill)

☐ AMERICAN EXPRESS   ☐ DISCOVER   ☐ MasterCard   ☐ VISA

Account No. ☐☐☐☐☐☐☐☐☐☐☐☐☐☐☐

Expiration Date _____

Signature _____

In a hurry? Call 1-800-822-8158 anytime, day or night, or visit your local bookstore.

Thank you for your order   Code BC640SL